Butterflies
OF SOUTHERN AFRICA

Butterflies
OF SOUTHERN AFRICA
A FIELD GUIDE

Mark Williams

SOUTHERN
BOOK PUBLISHERS

Copyright © 1994 by the author

All rights reserved. No part of this publication may be
reproduced or transmitted in any form or by any means without
prior written permission from the publisher.

ISBN 1 86812 516 5

First edition, first impression 1994

Published by
Southern Book Publishers (Pty) Ltd
PO Box 3103, Halfway House, 1685

Cover design by Abdul Amien
Illustrations of early stages by Elizabeth Boomker
Colour plates of adults photographed by Heleen Smit

CONTENTS

Preface   vii
Acknowledgements   ix

PART 1
Basic butterfly biology   3
Observing butterflies in nature   10
Identifying butterflies in the field   13
How to use this guide   15
Common southern African butterflies   18

PART 2
List of colour plates   22
Colour plates
The papilionids (family Papilionidae)   23
The pierids (family Pieridae)   33
The nymphalids (family Nymphalidae)   65
   The nymphalines (subfamily Nymphalinae)   65
   The charaxines (subfamily Charaxinae)   98
   The acraeines (subfamily Acraeinae)   112
   The satyrines (subfamily Satyrinae)   128
   The danaines (subfamily Danainae)   148
   The libytheines (subfamily Libytheinae)   153
The lycaenids (family Lycaenidae)   156
   The liptenines (subfamily Lipteninae)   158
   The miletines (subfamily Miletinae)   163
   The theclines (subfamily Theclinae)   169
   The lycaenines (subfamily Lycaeninae)   203
   The polyommatines (subfamily Polyommatinae)   204
The hesperiids (family Hesperiidae)   235

PART 3
Checklists   269
Genera and families of larval foodplants   274
Bibliography   281
Glossary   285

CONTENTS

Index to scientific names 287
Index to Afrikaans common names 294
Index to English common names 298

PREFACE

This book has been written to serve a long felt need for a southern African butterfly field guide that can be used by people who have a general interest in nature. It is intended, also, to stimulate the interest of the young in their fast diminishing natural heritage. It has been assumed that the user has little knowledge of butterflies, so the layout and text have been kept simple. It has also been assumed that the user wishes to identify the butterfly being observed without killing it – consequently the guide has been designed with this requirement in mind.

Most field guides, whether they are about animals or plants, deal with their subject in a systematic way (the various species that are dealt with are grouped together in families and genera) and therefore assume that the user has some knowledge of the subject. While this is the desirable format for a reference work it is of little use to the lay person whose primary concern is the identification of the different species and who knows virtually nothing about their classification.

This book is different!
First, the major aim is to allow the user to assign the butterfly he or she wishes to identify to a particular **common name group** consisting of related species or genera. The rationale for choosing group identification rather than species identification is twofold:
- identification is greatly simplified (there are over 850 different species but only about 85 common name groups in southern Africa); and
- species identification in many genera is sometimes difficult for even the most expert lepidopterist (i.e. someone who studies butterflies and moths).

Second, all the butterflies of similar colouring and size, irrespective of their taxonomic relationships, are grouped together in the colour plates at the beginning of Part 2.

Third, the undersides of the butterflies are illustrated with the wings closed, thus affording some idea of the outline of the wings when the insect is perched in the wild.

Finally the main text, which follows the plates, has been written in such a way as to give the reader further clues that will assist identification without having to kill the insect under observation. This book is thus designed to be of maximum usefulness to the lay person **in the field.**

The 233 species illustrated in the guide were chosen because they are common and widespread and therefore likely to be seen by the casual observer. A few scarcer and more local species were selected because they are typical representatives of the group to which they belong.

Throughout the book English and Afrikaans vernacular names of the various species and groups are used, with the scientific names given in parentheses. Accepted common names are used wherever possible but some have been updated or modified in order to bring them into line with the group names under which they fall. Those butterflies and groups that have no current common name have been given names, which it is hoped are appropriate.

The book consists of three parts, as indicated on the contents page. Although not essential, it would be wise to read Part 1 before trying to use the guide in the field because it deals with basic butterfly biology, observing butterflies in nature, identifying butterflies in the field and how to use this guide.

ACKNOWLEDGEMENTS

Many persons have been directly or indirectly involved in the production of this field guide, for which I thank them. I wish to thank, in particular, the following people:

My parents for encouraging my interest in natural history as a child. Their patience with my, at times, obsessional interest is much appreciated.

Elizabeth Boomker for the wonderful paintings of the early stages of the butterflies. Her unique blend of scientific and artistic approach to the subject is very special. Also for proofreading parts of the manuscript. Finally for her patient encouragement when the going was tough and for always being willing to let me bounce ideas off her – the down-to-earth feedback was often necessary to keep my feet on the ground!

Nolan Owen-Johnstone for the loan of many cabinet specimens, without which the colour plates would not have been possible.

Rolf Oberprieller for a teutonically thorough and professional proofreading of the whole manuscript.

Stephen and Graham Henning for their interest in the progress of the work and for the loan of cabinet specimens.

Herman Staude for the set specimens of day-flying moths depicted in one of the colour plates, together with the common and scientific names and other pertinent information.

Jonathan Ball and Graham Henning for permission to use their list of recently updated English common names of southern African butterflies.

Heleen Smit for the photography for the colour plates.

John Jardine for his input of ideas as a naturalist with a casual interest in butterflies.

Last, but not least, to Louise Grantham, Marina Pearson, Tildie Theron and the rest of the staff at Southern Book Publishers for their enthusiasm and professional approach to the production of this field guide.

PART 1

BASIC BUTTERFLY BIOLOGY

Before one goes into the field and observes butterflies it is useful to know something about their way of life. The emphasis in this section is on those aspects of butterfly biology that may be of assistance in identifying a particular insect and in helping you understand the information that appears in Part 2.

Life cycle
Butterflies have a four-stage life cycle consisting of the adult (imago), egg (ovum), caterpillar (larva) and chrysalis (pupa). Female butterflies that have been mated lay their eggs (oviposit) singly or, less commonly, in batches in a suitable site. For most butterflies the oviposition site is a leaf or twig of the plant on which the caterpillar will feed (the larval foodplant). Some butterfly species have larvae that feed on a variety of different plants (polyphagous species) but most are restricted to a few plants or even to a single plant species (monophagous species). **Larval foodplants** should not be confused with the plants that adults use as a source of nectar. Adults usually feed from the flowers of plants that are unrelated to the larval foodplants.

The egg stage normally lasts a week or two, the caterpillar chewing its way through the top of the egg. The larvae feed mainly on leaf matter but many feed on flower buds and fruits; there are even some carnivorous species. In order to grow butterfly larvae must shed their skin (moult) periodically. This they do four to six times during their development; each stage between two moults is known as an instar and the last moult transforms the final instar larva into a largely immobile pupa. The size of the adult butterfly is determined by the size that the larva attains; in small butterflies the final instar may be only 15 mm long whereas those of large butterflies may reach 60 mm or more. The duration of the larval stage varies greatly between species – and even within certain species – and may last from three weeks to many months. In those instances where the larval stage is prolonged this is accomplished by means of diapause. During diapause (often in winter) the caterpillar stops feeding and becomes inert.

The fully fed caterpillar ready to pupate finds a suitable site and suspends itself by the tail end from a silk pad which it spins for the purpose. In some families (chiefly the pierids and papilionids) the larva also spins a silken girdle in which it hangs. Unlike most moths, which pupate within a silken cocoon, butterfly pupae are naked. Inside the pupa metamorphosis into the adult butterfly takes place. This may take a few weeks but in some species pupal diapause occurs and, exceptionally, may even last several years. Usually pupal diapause is associated with unfavourable climatic conditions such as low winter temperatures or prolonged periods of drought. The adult butterfly emerges (ecloses) from the pupa by splitting it along several suture lines. The small, crumpled wings are expanded by forcing blood into the wing veins by means of abdominal contractions. Within a few hours the wings have hardened sufficiently for the butterfly to take its maiden flight.

During a single year a particular butterfly species may have several generations. In some species there are no diapauses during any of the stages of the life cycle: such species are continuous-brooded. In those species with diapauses, which are usually larval or pupal, there is generally only one or two generations a year; such species are single-brooded or double-brooded.

Size
The largest butterfly in southern Africa is the Emperor Swallowtail (fig. 222) with a wingspan of up to 120 mm. The largest butterfly in the world is the giant Alexander's Birdwing of the Malay Archipelago which may have a wingspan of nearly 300 mm. At the other end of the scale is the minute Dwarf Blue (fig. 154) with a wingspan of only about 12 mm. The Dwarf Blue, which occurs in southern Africa, is reputed to be one of the smallest butterflies in the world.

Variation
Butterflies are extremely variable with respect to the colours and patterns on their wings. The most important kind of variation as far as the scientist is concerned, however, is **specific variation**. This refers to variation between species, also called interspecific variation, and is the basis on which species are distinguished. The species concept is more fully explained in the glossary.

Within a particular species of butterfly there are four main types of variation: sexual, seasonal, individual and geographical. These are collectively known as intraspecific variation. **Sexual variation** refers to differences between the sexes of the same species. Males and females may look very much alike (for example the Guineafowl butterfly, fig. 95), they may be fairly similar (for example the Yellow Pansy, fig. 237) or they may be very dissimilar (such as the Common Diadem, figs 45 & 200). The sexual differences

BASIC BUTTERFLY BIOLOGY 5

are referred to as sexual dimorphism. In southern Africa some species of butterfly show **seasonal variation** (seasonal dimorphism). In seasonal dimorphism there are differences between those individuals that hatch in summer and those that hatch in autumn or winter. The summer form is also known as the wet season form (WSF) and the winter form as the dry season form (DSF). The differences between the WSF and DSF may be slight (e.g. the Marsh Commodore, fig. 249) or there may be extreme seasonal dimorphism (e.g. the Gaudy Commodore, figs 56 & 157). It is also possible, on rare occasions, to find individuals that are intermediate between the WSF and DSF. Note that both sexes are equally affected by seasonal dimorphism. **Individual variation** refers to differences between individuals of the same population and is usually not very pronounced. However, there is a special kind of individual variation known as **polymorphism** (meaning many forms) where there is a marked difference between individuals of the same population. This is well illustrated by females of the Mocker Swallowtail (figs 194 & 225), which show female polymorphism, and by the Variable Diadem (figs 195 & 227), which has two very distinct forms affecting both sexes. Lastly, **geographical variation** may occur between geographically separated populations of the same species. If there are consistent differences between these separate populations (they are usually small) each is given a scientific name and they are known as **subspecies**. Although many species of southern African butterfly have one or more described subspecies these have not been dealt with in this field guide as they are usually very difficult to distinguish in the field.

Habitat and distribution

Scientists have divided southern Africa into a number of habitat types according to the dominant flora and fauna. These habitat types are known as **biomes**. Depending on how broadly or narrowly these plant–animal associations are viewed, a variable number of biomes are recognised. For the purposes of this field guide the following biomes were selected (see map, p. 6):

1) **Forest**, divided into temperate forest and subtropical forest or bush
2) **Savanna**, divided into frost-free savanna (bushveld) and frost-prone savanna (thornveld)
3) **Grassland**
4) **Karoo**, divided into the moister eastern Karoo and the drier western Karoo (including the succulent Karoo)
5) **Fynbos**
6) **Desert**.

6 BASIC BUTTERFLY BIOLOGY

Biome map of southern Africa

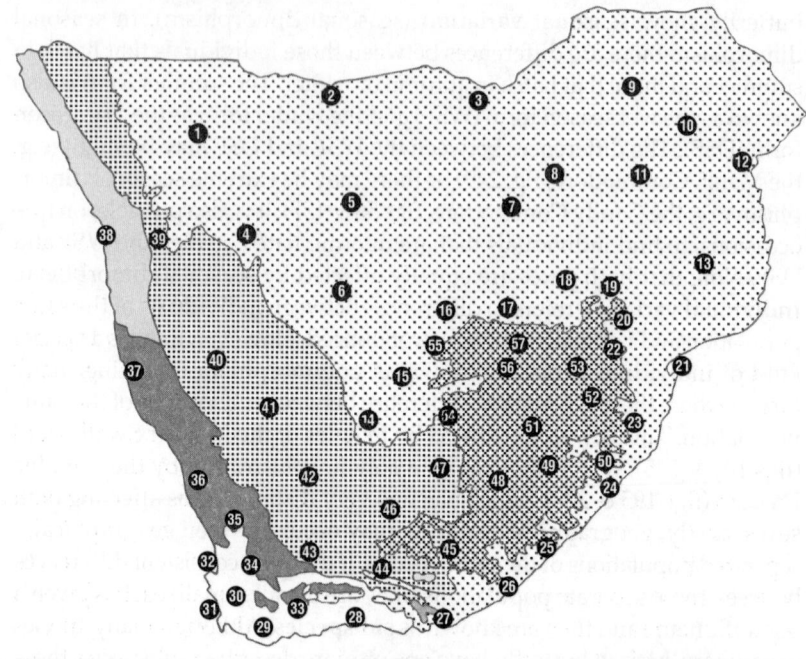

Legend:
- Savanna
- Succulent Karroo
- Grassland
- Fynbos
- Karroo
- Desert

1 – Grootfontein
3 – Kasane
5 – Ghanzi
7 – Francistown
9 – Harare
11 – Masvingo
13 – Chigubo
15 – Vryburg
17 – Thabazimbi
19 – Tzaneen
21 – Maputo
23 – Ubombo
25 – Port St Johns
27 – Port Elizabeth
29 – Bredasdorp
31 – Cape Town
33 – Ladismith
35 – Calvinia
37 – Lüderitz
39 – Windhoek
41 – Upington
43 – Beaufort West
45 – Queenstown
47 – Bloemfontein
49 – Kranskop
51 – Harrismith
53 – Mbabane
55 – Mafikeng
57 – Pretoria

2 – Andara
4 – Gobabis
6 – Tshane
8 – Bulawayo
10 – Mutare
12 – Beira
14 – Postmasburg
16 – Gaborone
18 – Pietersburg
20 – Graskop
22 – Nelspruit
24 – Durban
26 – East London
28 – Knysna
30 – Worcester
32 – Piketberg
34 – Sutherland
36 – Springbok
38 – Swakopmund
40 – Keetmanshoop
42 – Carnarvon
44 – Cradock
46 – Colesberg
48 – Maseru
50 – Eshowe
52 – Piet Retief
54 – Welkom
56 – Johannesburg

The abundance and diversity of butterflies tend to be highest in forest and savanna biomes and decrease sequentially in grassland, fynbos, Karoo and desert. Since most of the commoner butterflies dealt with in this book occur in forest or savanna biomes they tend to have an easterly distribution. Typically these butterflies occur from the Mossel Bay–Knysna area of the southern Cape Province and extend in a widening belt through the eastern Cape Province, Transkei, Natal, Swaziland, Transvaal, Mozambique, Zimbabwe, northern Botswana and northern Namibia. The greater parts of the Cape Province, Lesotho, the Orange Free State, southern Transvaal and southern Namibia consist of grassland, Karoo, fynbos and desert biomes. These are generally poorer in both abundance and diversity of species. They do, however, have a large number of specialised endemic species and genera, especially satyrines (subfamily Satyrinae, p. 128) and lycaenids (family Lycaenidae, p. 156).

Behaviour
The behaviour of adult butterflies is fairly stereotyped. Males search for food or mates while females, in addition, must look for suitable places to lay their eggs (oviposit). Within this simple framework, however, there is a complex array of behavioural patterns that needs to be appreciated when one observes butterflies in nature. Most species show specific behavioural patterns that can be used to identify them. Experienced lepidopterists can identify many butterflies from a distance of 50 metres or more simply by observing characteristic patterns of behaviour.

Many people are under the false impression that butterflies feed solely on nectar (composed mainly of the simple sugar fructose) which they obtain from flowers. Some lycaenids (family Lycaenidae), such as those belonging to the liptenines (subfamily Lipteninae, p. 158), feed on the sugary solution known as "honeydew" that is secreted by sap-sucking bugs belonging to the insect suborder Homoptera (e.g. scale insects and aphids). Some groups, such as the nymphalids (family Nymphalidae), shun sweet liquids, preferring to suck up alcohols from fermenting fruit. Sometimes the culinary habits of butterflies verge on the nauseating. Some, especially charaxines (subfamily Charaxinae), can be found drinking fluids from animal droppings. Both herbivore dung and carnivore scats appear to be attractive. A few species even relish the fluids exuding from rotting animal carcasses.

The males, in particular, of many species of butterfly often congregate on mud and damp patches of sand on the banks of rivers or the shores of dams. This behaviour is known by the rather quaint name of **mud-puddling**. Here they may suck up large quantities of fluid from which they extract salts and other nutrients. If the insect is carefully watched, drops of water can be seen to be excreted from the tip of the abdomen at regular intervals. Places where animals have urinated on the mud or sand are even more attractive, presumably because of the salts contained in the urine.

Until recently it was thought that all adult butterflies feed. A few years ago it was discovered that some lycaenids do not feed at all as adults. These are the Skollies (pp. 165–8), Zulus (pp. 158–9) and Rocksitters (pp. 162–3). The "tongue" (proboscis) of butterflies is normally a long, coiled tube but in the above-mentioned groups it is rudimentary and appears to be non-functional.

Male butterflies locate potential female mates by means of two basic strategies – **searching** and **perching**. Usually a particular species employs either one or the other basic strategy but there are occasions when males will exhibit a searching behaviour and at other times will show a perching behaviour. Searching is non-territorial and the male flies more or less at random, actively seeking virgin females with which to mate. The males of some species appear to be able to sense where there is a pupa containing a female that is about to hatch and may remain in the vicinity, waiting for her to emerge. Perching is a territorial behaviour and occurs when a male selects a perch such as a tree, bush, grass stem or even a rock on which to perch within this territory. Flying intruders, ranging from small wasps to small birds, are vigorously chased out of the territory, after which the male returns to his favoured perch. Should a female of the correct species enter the territory he will immediately court her and, if she is unmated, copulation is likely to ensue. Very often these territories are established on some high point in the landscape, such as a koppie or mountain top. This type of perching behaviour is known as **hilltopping** and is shown by many species of southern African butterfly. Virgin females of species that exhibit this behaviour will ascend the hill and actively search for a potential mate by going to a place where he is likely to be found. In some species searching and perching behaviour may be combined. This **mixed** behaviour is seen, for example, when a male flies to and fro along a particular stretch of ground (**patrolling**).

Mating in butterflies normally takes place soon after the female has emerged from the pupa. Consequently, most females that are observed in the wild are likely to already be mated and will either be searching for food or for places to lay their eggs (oviposition sites). Once you start to observe butterflies more closely you will soon be able to recognise the characteristic behaviour of females looking for oviposition sites. Such a female may be said to be in "laying mode". In most species the eggs are laid singly on the leaves of the caterpillar's foodplant. The female of a particular species will usually only lay eggs on the "correct" foodplant(s), which she recognises by sight, touch and taste. The plant is "tasted" while the female makes a rapid, drumming movement with her front legs on the leaf surface. (Species and groups in which egg-laying behaviour differs from the above pattern are dealt with in the appropriate places in Part 2.)

Finally, this section on behaviour would not be complete without consideration being given to the interesting phenomenon of butterfly migration. Most people are aware of the periodic migrations of very large numbers of white butterflies, usually in a north-easterly direction, during the summer or autumn of some years. Although more than a dozen different species of butterfly have, at one time or another, been recorded as migrants in southern Africa, there are two species in particular that consistently migrate in very large numbers. These are the Brownveined White (fig. 14) and the African Migrant (figs 4 & 29). It is thought that, under favourable conditions, numbers of these butterflies build up so rapidly that the larval foodplants are stripped of their foliage, inducing the adult butterflies to seek "better pastures". The migrations appear to originate in the Karoo and Kalahari, although there is no direct evidence of this being so. What makes them all fly in the same direction, how they navigate and what happens to them, are questions to which there are no satisfactory answers as yet. Studies on the migrations of the famous American Monarch butterfly have shown that small amounts of magnetite, present in the head of the butterfly, may act as a biological compass!

Flight period
The adults of most common species of butterfly are on the wing in most months of the year because they are continuous-brooded. Even so, species that fly throughout the year tend to become more abundant towards late summer and autumn (January to April) because the more favourable summer conditions shorten each of the early stages, allowing numbers to build up to a peak in autumn. Numbers then decline to reach their lowest levels in late winter and spring (August to October) when they gradually begin to increase again. Many lycaenids (family Lycaenidae) and satyrines (subfamily Satyrinae) have only one or two broods a year. In single-brooded species this is either in spring or autumn and in double-brooded ones in spring and autumn. Details of the flight periods of individual species and groups are given in Part 2.

OBSERVING BUTTERFLIES IN NATURE

Having read the section above dealing with basic butterfly biology, you are ready to go out and observe butterflies in their natural habitat. All you require are curiosity, patience, your eyes and this field guide. Although the largest number and variety of butterflies are to be seen in undisturbed natural habitats (there are precious few of these left!) they may, in fact, be found nearly anywhere, even, on occasion, inside one's home (see remarks under the Garden Commodore, p. 71). Most people are rather unobservant when it comes to butterflies and will only notice them at certain times, for example, when they are migrating in huge numbers, as the Brownveined White does nearly every summer (see p. 37). But, like most human skills, being observant comes with practice. The more you look for butterflies, and at them, the more you will wonder why they had escaped your notice before.

There are many places to look for butterflies. If you have a garden, especially a large one, this is a good place to start. On p. 269 is a list of butterflies that are regularly encountered in suburban gardens and parks. Nature rambles and hiking trails provide an excellent opportunity to study butterflies as many of these trails traverse relatively unspoilt tracts of land. Please remember to obtain permission before you enter private property. Landowners are, not surprisingly, often somewhat sceptical when told that you are watching butterflies.

Many species of butterfly can be seen on the wing in virtually any month of the year, but generally they tend to be more abundant in summer. Others fly only at specific times of the year – mainly spring or autumn, or both. In winter only the frost-free areas of the subcontinent (mainly the east and north) have numbers of butterflies on the wing. Butterflies generally fly in warm, sunny weather. Wind appears to have little effect on their activity and most seem to tolerate even quite strong winds. Cold, damp or cloudy weather usually causes most to remain hidden in the vegetation. Many hesperiids and some satyrines are exceptional in that they will fly only at dawn or dusk (crepuscular behaviour), and sometimes on overcast days or even in light drizzle.

Butterflies tend to be concentrated in certain places within a particular area. Wherever there are stands of nectar-producing flowers you are likely to find butterflies enjoying the feast, especially in the morning. In the afternoon the males of many species go in search of mud and damp patches on the banks of streams or the edges of pans and dams. Here they may congregate in their hundreds and, rarely, even thousands, sucking up moisture from the soil. The tops of koppies and mountains are a very good place to observe the males of those species that habitually hilltop. You may even be lucky enough to see a female arrive and be courted by a territorial male! Most hilltopping butterflies can be found on the tops of the koppies between 10h00 and 14h00, although there are some that ascend the hills earlier or later in the day. While they are feeding from flowers, mud-puddling or hilltopping, butterflies are much more easily approached and are therefore easier to identify.

Getting close enough to a butterfly to identify it with certainty can be tricky. While engaged in feeding, mud-puddling or hilltopping butterflies will usually not fly away if approached cautiously. The secret is to move slowly and very deliberately towards them. Butterflies have compound eyes that excel at detecting sudden and rapid movements. In effect the butterfly perceives your movements as a threat but does not regard your physical presence as a danger. Occasionally I have actually managed to "rub noses" with a perched butterfly by stalking it very slowly. Many butterflies will also become accustomed to your presence and allow you to get closer and closer. Similar tactics may be employed when trying to photograph butterflies in nature. One can always resort to making a butterfly net with which to capture the butterfly you wish to identify. The insect should be lightly trapped between the folds and shaded so that it is less active. Once it has been identified, it can be released. This method works well for both wary and small butterflies. Finally, there are those butterflies that habitually perch or feed on the tops of trees, out of reach of a short-handled butterfly net. Most nature lovers own good binoculars and these can be used to good effect in identifying treetop specimens.

In order to understand the biology of a particular species of butterfly one needs to be familiar with its early stages (egg, caterpillar and chrysalis or pupa) as well as the adult stage. For most species of butterfly it is much more difficult to find the early stages than it is to find the more mobile and conspicuous adults. A thorough knowledge of the larval foodplants and considerable experience are required but the rewards are high (see plates 28–32).

In the field one can follow female butterflies around to discover on which plants they lay their eggs. Eggs and larvae can then be collected from the plants and reared to adults at home. This is a fascinating and rewarding pastime but is beyond the scope of this book (see bibliography for source material). Part 2 contains brief summaries of the early stages, usually under the group common name. In the case of those species that have complex and interesting life histories (especially the lycaenids, p. 156) more detail will be found.

IDENTIFYING BUTTERFLIES IN THE FIELD

Using the colour plates in this guide and the clues provided below you will be able to identify most groups of butterflies with a reasonable degree of success.

Clues to identification
There are five very important clues to the identity of a live butterfly in the wild:
1) The dominant colour(s) and patterns on the upperside of the wings.
2) The dominant colour(s) and patterns on the underside of the wings.
3) The size of the butterfly.
4) The habitat in which it is found.
5) The behavioural patterns shown.

Dominant upperside colour(s)
Generally speaking the colours on the upperside of the wings of butterflies are more intense than those on the underside and are therefore more obvious when the insect is in flight. The colour plates therefore concentrate, to a large extent, on the upperside coloration. If one colour predominates on the upperside of the wings the butterfly is placed in the first set of plates depicting unicolorous butterflies (plates 1–15). If two colours predominate it is classified as bicolorous (plates 15–26). In addition to the plates depicting butterflies there is a plate showing some common day-flying moths (plate 27) that are often confused with butterflies. A full list of the plates and the colour coding for each group can be found on p. 22.

Dominant underside colour(s)
When a butterfly is perched it will usually close its wings so that only its underside is visible. As the underside colours and markings are sometimes very different from those on the upperside of the wings this can present a problem in identification. The underside patterns are therefore illustrated with those of the upperside on the same colour plate.

Size
In each colour group the butterflies are illustrated more or less in order of decreasing size. All the species are depicted at about three quarters of life size.

Habitat
Particular species and even common name groups often occur in very specific habitats. Thus there are those that are strictly forest-dwellers while other species occur only in grassland or savanna. Yet others are found only in or close to wetlands, while some are found only at high elevations. Habitat preferences, as you will discover, are largely determined by the availability of the specific foodplant(s) required by the larval (caterpillar) stages of the particular butterfly. The habitat preferences of the different groups and species are given in Part 2 and there are also checklists of the butterflies typical of specific biomes on pp. 269–73.

Behavioural patterns
What a butterfly is doing, where it is flying and how it is flying are all crucially important in making a correct identification. This information is also provided in Part 2.

IDENTIFICATION FORMULA
- Look at the dominant colour or colours when the insect is in flight
- Look at the dominant colour or colours on the upperside of the wings
- Note the size of the butterfly – small, medium-sized or large
- Note the type of habitat
- Look for specific behaviours:
    flight height
    territorial versus random flight
    feeding – flowers, fermenting fruit, mud-puddles

HOW TO USE THIS GUIDE

When observing a butterfly that you wish to identify, form an impression of its general coloration. If it is predominantly one colour it will occur in one of the first 15 plates depicting unicolorous butterflies. If two colours predominate then your insect will be found in the plates of bicolorous butterflies (plates 15–26). Note that the plates are arranged according to the **upperside** coloration. Once you have found what you think is the correct colour plate series, look at the size of your insect and find similar looking species of the same general colour and size. Pick out the butterfly that most closely resembles the one you are watching and turn to the appropriate page in Part 2.

Read the text dealing with identification, habitat and distribution, behaviour and flight period to check whether this fits the particular specimen you are observing. If there is doubt about your identification use the checklists or go back to the relevant plate and read the information provided in Part 2 for similar looking species.

In describing each butterfly under the heading "identification" I have tried to use simple terms for the location of patterns and markings on the wings. These terms are as shown in the following diagrams.

Basic butterfly anatomy

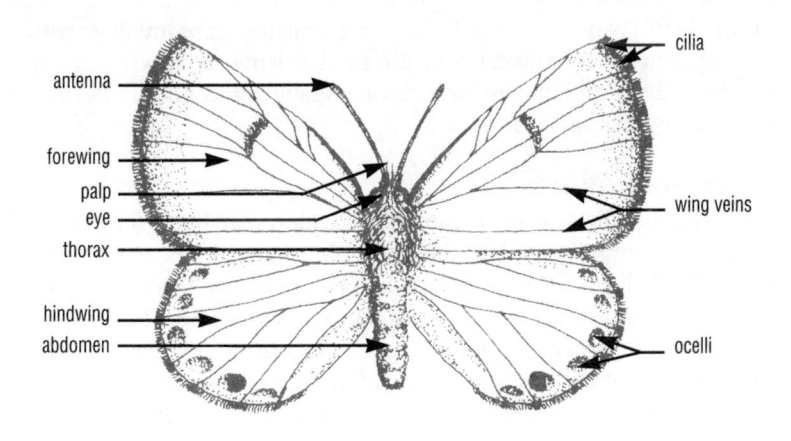

16 HOW TO USE THIS GUIDE

Descriptive terms used in butterfly identification

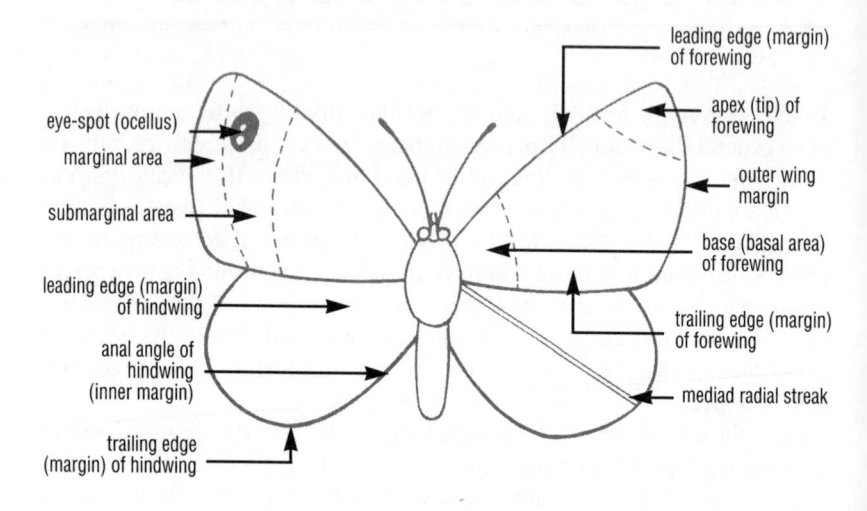

- leading edge (margin) of forewing
- apex (tip) of forewing
- eye-spot (ocellus)
- marginal area
- outer wing margin
- submarginal area
- base (basal area) of forewing
- leading edge (margin) of hindwing
- trailing edge (margin) of forewing
- anal angle of hindwing (inner margin)
- mediad radial streak
- trailing edge (margin) of hindwing

The main text (Part 2)

You will notice that the main text, which begins on p. 23, is organised along taxonomic lines. Once you have identified your insect and read the text concerning it you can page back until you reach the description of the common name group, subfamily or family to which your butterfly belongs. This will provide you with information about the subdivisions in the taxonomic group. In this way you will get a feel for the relationships involved between the different levels or taxa. It will also be instructive to browse through the text from the beginning onwards. Soon you will know your butterflies forwards as well as backwards!

The checklists (Part 3)

There are checklists of very common and widespread butterflies, butterflies found commonly in gardens and butterflies found in the various biomes (pp. 269–73). Browse through these lists before you go to a particular habitat or use them as a reference source. The lists will also enable people who think they have seen a particular species in a forest, for example, to look under the forest butterfly checklist and find that the species is not listed in that checklist. You will know therefore that you have probably made a misidentification.

The genera and families of larval foodplants (Part 3)
All the genera of the larval foodplants that appear in the main text are listed alphabetically, with the plant family to which they belong together with the butterfly species that use them as larval foodplants (pp. 274–80). This has been done for two reasons. First, it makes the main text less cumbersome by placing the plant families elsewhere. Second, it will help the interested person to identify an egg or caterpillar if the genus of plant is known. This list can also be used as a guide by gardeners wanting to plant trees and shrubs that will attract butterflies.

The bibliography (Part 3)
For those who want to know more about southern African butterflies and butterflies in general, an annotated bibliography is provided (pp. 281–4).

The glossary (Part 3)
The meanings of all the important terms used in the text are explained in this section (pp. 285–6).

COMMON SOUTHERN AFRICAN BUTTERFLIES

To identify butterflies one needs some knowledge of their classification. In the middle of the 18th century Carl Linné (latinised later to Carolus Linnaeus), a Swedish naturalist, devised a system for naming living creatures. The system that he invented is still in use today and is known as the binomial system of nomenclature. Every different plant or animal is given an internationally recognised specific name (the species name) as well as a generic name that relates it to similar species. Over the last 250 years a number of higher taxonomic categories have been introduced so that today classifications of plants and animals are in a standard hierarchy.

The most fundamental level of classification is the **species**. A species consists basically of populations of interbreeding individuals. Closely related species are grouped together to form a **genus**. Related genera are grouped in **families** and related families in **orders**. Similar orders constitute a **class**; classes are grouped in a **phylum** and finally, related phyla form a **kingdom**.

Butterflies are animals (kingdom **Animalia**) that, as adults, possess a hard (chitinous) external skeleton (exoskeleton) and jointed legs. These characteristics distinguish them as arthropods (phylum **Arthropoda**). Butterflies have three pairs of legs which make them insects (class **Insecta**). The only insects that have scales covering their bodies and wings are butterflies and moths (order **Lepidoptera**). Someone who studies butterflies or moths is called a lepidopterist.

Between the major categories as given above, subgroupings are often used. For example **superfamily** falls between order and family and **subfamily** between family and genus.

As an example, consider the classification of the **African Monarch** butterfly:

species:	*chrysippus*	(the species name always begins with a small letter and is italicised)
genus:	*Danaus*	(begins with a capital letter and is italicised)
subfamily:	Danainae	(subfamily ends in -inae)
family:	Nymphalidae	(family ends in -idae)
superfamily:	Papilionoidea	(superfamily ends in -oidea)
order:	Lepidoptera	

COMMON SOUTHERN AFRICAN BUTTERFLIES

class: Insecta
phylum: Arthropoda
subkingdom: Invertebrata
kingdom: Animalia

The terms butterfly and moth do not really have any specific meaning for the scientists who classify them. The order Lepidoptera, which includes all the butterflies and moths, is divided into about 20 **superfamilies**. Only three of these superfamilies contain Lepidoptera that we would normally consider to be butterflies. These are:

- The **hedyloids** (superfamily Hedyloidea). These are moth-like butterflies that often fly at night and have thin (filiform), pointed feelers or antennae, unlike true butterflies, which usually have clubbed antennae. In some species the antennae are even feathery (pectinate), a characteristic commonly seen in moths. They are so moth-like that until 1986 lepidopterists classified them together with the geometrid moths. Hedyloids are found only in South and Central America (see bibliography for further information).
- The **hesperioids** (superfamily Hesperiioidea). Often called Skippers because of the typical bouncy, skipping flight of many species. Like the hedyloids they are somewhat moth-like in appearance and behaviour but do not appear to be closely related to the hedyloids. There are about 480 species in Africa of which some 125 species are found in southern Africa. They all fall into a single family, the **hesperiids** (family Hesperiidae). The characteristics of the family are considered in more detail on p. 235.
- The **papilionoids** (superfamily Papilionoidea). This superfamily includes by far the majority of the butterflies, a total of some 3 040 species having been recorded from Africa, 730 of which occur in southern Africa. They are usually brightly coloured and are active in warm, sunny weather but this is by no means always the case. The superfamily is divided into a number of families, four of which occur in southern Africa:

Papilionids (family Papilionidae) – see p. 23
Pierids (family Pieridae) – see p. 33
Nymphalids (family Nymphalidae) – see p. 65
Lycaenids (family Lycaenidae) – see p. 156

More information on each of these families is given on the pages cited above.

Because they are large and diverse families, nymphalids and lycaenids are divided into subfamilies, of which the following occur in southern Africa:

The nymphalid family:

Nymphalines (subfamily Nymphalinae) – see p. 65
Charaxines (subfamily Charaxinae) – see p. 98
Acraeines (subfamily Acraeinae) – see p. 112
Satyrines (subfamily Satyrinae) – see p. 128
Danaines (subfamily Danainae) – see p. 148
Libytheines (subfamily Libytheinae) – see p. 153

The lycaenid family:

Liptenines (subfamily Lipteninae) – see p. 158
Miletines (subfamily Miletinae) – see p. 163
Theclines (subfamily Theclinae) – see p. 169
Lycaenines (subfamily Lycaeninae) – see p. 203
Polyommatines (subfamily Polyommatinae) – see p. 204

More information regarding these subfamilies can be found on the pages cited.

PART 2

LIST OF COLOUR PLATES

Plate 1   White butterflies (figs 1–6)
Plate 2   White butterflies (figs 7–14)
Plate 3   White butterflies (figs 15–26)
Plate 4   White butterflies, yellow butterflies (figs 27–38)
Plate 5   Yellow butterflies, orange/red butterflies (figs 39–46)
Plate 6   Orange/red butterflies (figs 47–55)
Plate 7   Orange/red butterflies (figs 56–67)
Plate 8   Orange/red butterflies (figs 68–88)
Plate 9   Brown/black butterflies (figs 89–95)
Plate 10   Brown/black butterflies (figs 96–108)
Plate 11   Brown/black butterflies (figs 109–25)
Plate 12   Brown/black butterflies (figs 126–54)
Plate 13   Blue butterflies (figs 155–66)
Plate 14   Blue butterflies (figs 167–84)
Plate 15   Blue butterflies, black & white butterflies (figs 185–95)
Plate 16   Black & white butterflies (figs 196–9)
Plate 17   Black & white butterflies (figs 200–207)
Plate 18   Black & white butterflies (figs 208–21)
Plate 19   Black & yellow butterflies (figs 222–4)
Plate 20   Black & yellow butterflies (figs 225–8)
Plate 21   Black & yellow butterflies (figs 229–36)
Plate 22   Black & yellow butterflies, black & orange/red butterflies (figs 237–41)
Plate 23   Black & orange/red butterflies (figs 242–6)
Plate 24   Black & orange/red butterflies (figs 247–60)
Plate 25   Black & blue butterflies (figs 261–3)
Plate 26   Black & blue butterflies (figs 264–8)
Plate 27   Day-flying moths (figs 269–92)
Plate 28   Early stages of papilionids & pierids (figs 293–304)
Plate 29   Early stages of nymphalines (figs 305–16)
Plate 30   Early stages of nymphalines, charaxines, acraeines & satyrines (figs 317–28)
Plate 31   Early stages of danaines, lycaenids, liptenines & miletines (figs 329–38)
Plate 32   Early stages of lycaenids, theclines, polyommatines & hesperiids (figs 339–49)

Figs. 1–6 PLATE 1

1 Common Mother-of-pearl (a – ♂ upp.; b – ♂ uns.) p. 80
2 Large Vagrant (a – ♂ upp.; b – ♂ uns.; c – ♀ uns.) p. 46
3 Cambridge Vagrant (a – ♀ upp.; b – ♀ uns.) p. 47
4 African Migrant (a – ♂ upp.; b – ♂ uns.) p. 62
5 Vine-leaf Vagrant (a – ♂ upp.; b – ♂ uns.) p. 45
6 Queen Purple Tip (a – ♂ upp.; b – ♂ uns.) p. 49

PLATE 2   Figs. 7–14

7 False Dotted Border White (a – ♂ upp.; b – ♂ uns.) p. 35
8 Common Dotted Border (a – ♂ upp.; b – ♂ uns.) p. 58
9 Twin Dotted Border (a – ♂ upp.; b – ♂ uns.) p. 59
10 Trimen's Dotted Border (a – ♂ upp.; b – ♂ uns.) p. 60
11 African Veined White (a – ♂ upp.; b – ♂ WSF uns.; c – ♂ DSF uns.)
p. 38

12 Forest White (a – ♂ upp.; b – ♂ uns.; c – ♀ upp.; d – ♀ uns.) p. 36
13 African Common White (a – ♂ upp.; b – ♂ uns.) p. 37
14 Brownveined White (a – ♂ upp.; b – ♂ uns.; c – ♀ upp.; d – ♀ uns.)
p. 37

Figs. 15–26　　　　　　　　　　　　　　　　　　　　　　PLATE 3

15 Diverse Rainforest White (a – ♂ upp.; b – ♂ uns.) p. 42
16 Ant-heap Small White (a – ♂ upp.; b – ♂ uns.) p. 40
17 African Small White (a – ♂ upp.; b – ♂ uns.) p. 39
18 Banded Gold Tip (a – ♂ upp.; b – ♂ uns.) p. 56
19 Scarlet Tip (a – ♂ upp.; b – ♂ uns.; c – ♀ upp.; d – ♀ uns.) p. 50
20 Red Tip (a – ♂ upp.; b – ♂ uns.; c – ♀ upp.; d – ♀ uns.) p. 52
21 Common Orange Tip (a – ♂ upp.; b – ♂ WSF uns.; c – ♂ DSF uns.; d – ♀ upp.; e – ♀ uns., DSF) p. 53
22 Smoky Orange Tip (a – ♂ upp.; b – ♂ uns.) p. 54
23 Small Orange Tip (a – ♂ upp.; b – ♂ uns.) p. 55
24 Speckled Sulphur Tip (a – ♂ upp.; b – ♂ uns.) p. 53
25 Common Meadow White (a – ♂ upp.; b – ♂ uns.) p. 43
26 African Wood White (a – ♂ upp.; b – ♂ uns.) p. 43

PLATE 4

Figs. 27 – 38

27 Whitecloaked Skipper (a – ♂ upp.; b – ♂ uns.) p. 244
28 Barkly's Copper (a – ♂ upp.; b – ♂ uns.) p. 180
29 African Migrant (a – ♀ upp.; b – ♀ uns.) p. 62
30 Autumn-leaf Vagrant (a – ♂ upp.; b – ♂ uns.; c – ♀ uns., DSF) p. 45
31 Common Dotted Border (a – ♀ upp.; b – ♀ uns.) p. 58
32 False Dotted Border White (a – ♀ upp.; b – ♀ uns.) p. 35
33 Ant-heap Small White (a – ♀ upp.; b – ♀ uns.) p. 40
34 Lemon Traveller Tip (a – ♂ upp.; b – ♂ uns.) p. 56
35 Battling Glider (a – ♂ upp.; b – ♂ uns.) p. 95
36 Sulphur Orange Tip (a – ♂ upp.; b – ♂ uns., WSF; c – ♂ uns., DSF) p. 51
37 Spiller's Sulphur Small White (a – ♂ upp.; b – ♂ uns.) p. 41
38 Broadbordered Grass Yellow (a – ♂ upp.; b – ♂ uns.) p. 63

Figs. 39 – 46   PLATE 5

39 Saffron Sapphire (a – ♂ upp.; b – ♂ uns.) p. 192
40 Spotted Pentila (a – ♂ upp.; b – ♂ uns.) p. 160
41 Common Buff (a – ♂ upp.; b – ♂ uns.) p. 161
42 Yellow Zulu (a – ♂ upp.; b – ♂ uns.) p. 159
43 Pearl Charaxes (a – ♂ upp.; b – ♂ uns.) p. 99
44 Bush Beauty (a – ♂ upp.; b – ♂ uns.) p. 140
45 Common Diadem (a – ♀ upp.; b – ♀ uns.) p. 82
46 African Monarch (a – ♂ upp.; b – ♂ uns.) p. 149

PLATE 6   Figs. 47 – 55

47 Boisduval's False Acraea (a – ♂ upp.; b – ♂ uns.) p. 92
48 Large Spotted Acraea (a – ♂ upp.; b – ♂ uns.) p. 124
49 Natal Acraea (a – ♂ upp.; b – ♂ uns.) p. 120
50 Window Acraea (a – ♂ upp.; b – ♂ uns.) p. 123
51 Dusky Acraea (a – ♂ upp.; b – ♂ uns.) p. 119
52 Broadbordered Acraea (a – ♂ upp.; b – ♂ uns.) p. 125
53 Clubtailed Charaxes, DSF (a – ♂ upp.; b – ♂ uns.) p. 104
54 Pearlspotted Charaxes (a – ♂ upp.; b – ♂ uns.) p. 105
55 Painted Lady (a – ♂ upp.; b – ♂ uns.) p. 69

Figs. 56 – 67   PLATE 7

56 Gaudy Commodore, WSF (a – ♂ upp.; b – ♂ uns.) p. 74
57 Pirate (a – ♂ upp.; b – ♂ uns.) p. 79
58 African Leopard (a – ♂ upp.; b – ♂ uns.) p. 66
59 Blotched Leopard (a – ♂ upp.; b – ♀ uns.) p. 67
60 Spotted Joker (a – ♂ upp.; b – ♂ uns., WSF; c – ♂ uns., DSF) p. 86
61 African Joker (a – ♂ upp.; b – ♂ uns., WSF; c – ♂ uns., DSF) p. 87
62 Rooibok Acraea (a – ♂ upp.; b – ♂ uns.) p. 122
63 Blacktipped Acraea (a – ♂ upp.; b – ♂ uns.) p. 121
64 Garden Acraea (a – ♂ upp.; b – ♂ uns.; c – ♀ upp.; d – ♀ uns.) p. 141
65 Wandering Donkey Acraea (a – ♂ upp.; b – ♂ uns.) p. 115
66 Blood-red Acraea (a – ♂ upp.; b – ♂ uns.) p. 126
67 Orange Acraea (a – ♂ upp.; b – ♂ uns.) p. 117

PLATE 8 Figs. 68 – 88

68 Common Mimic Acraea (a – ♂ upp.; b – ♂ uns.) p. 120
69 Duskyveined Acraea (a – ♂ upp.; b – ♂ uns.) p. 115
70 Light-red Acraea (a – ♂ upp.; b – ♂ uns.) p. 125
71 Little Acraea (a – ♂ upp.; b – ♂ uns.) p. 122
72 Dancing Acraea (a – ♂ upp.; b – ♂ uns.) p. 117
73 Marsh Acraea (a – ♂ upp.; b – ♂ uns.) p. 116
74 Polka Dot (a – ♂ upp.; b – ♂ uns.) p. 127
75 African Clouded Yellow (a – ♂ upp.; b – ♂ uns.; c – ♀ upp.; d – ♀ uns.) p. 61
76 Warrior Silverspotted Copper (a – ♂ upp.; b – ♂ uns.) p. 178
77 Common Scarlet (a – ♂ upp.; b – ♂ uns.; c – ♀ upp.; d – ♀ uns.) p. 175
78 Apricot Playboy (a – ♂ upp.; b – ♂ uns.) p. 198
79 Boland Skolly (a – ♂ upp.; b – ♂ uns.) p. 166
80 Roodepoort Copper (a – ♂ upp.; b – ♂ uns.) p. 179
81 Aranda Copper (a – ♂ upp.; b – ♂ uns.) p. 182
82 Damara Copper (a – ♂ upp.; b – ♂ uns.) p. 182
83 Eastern Sorrel Copper (a – ♂ upp.; b – ♂ uns.) p. 203
84 Karoo Daisy Copper (a – ♂ upp.; b – ♂ uns.) p. 183
85 Lydenburg Opal (a – ♂ upp.; b – ♂ uns.) p. 185
86 Water Opal (a – ♂ upp.; b – ♂ uns.) p. 185
87 Common Opal (a – ♂ upp.; b – ♂ uns.; c – ♀ upp.; d – ♀ uns.) p. 186
88 Dark Opal (a – ♂ upp.; b – ♀ uns.) p. 187

Figs. 89 – 95   PLATE 9

89 Common Evening Brown (a – ♂ upp., DSF; b – ♂ uns., DSF; c – ♂ upp., WSF; d – ♂ uns., DSF) p. 129
90 Bluespangled Charaxes (a – ♂ upp.; b – ♂ uns.) p. 110
91 Satyr Charaxes (a – ♂ upp.; b – ♂ uns.) p. 107
92 Van Son's Charaxes (a – ♂ upp.; b – ♂ uns.) p. 109
93 Dusky Charaxes (a – ♂ upp.; b – ♂ uns.) p. 108
94 Brown Pansy (a – ♂ upp.; b – ♂ uns.) p. 78
95 Guineafowl (a – ♂ upp.; b – ♂ uns.) p. 97

PLATE 10　　　　　　　　　　　　　　　　　　　　　　　　　Figs. 96 – 108

96 Cape Autumn Widow (a – ♂ upp.; b – ♂ uns.) p. 141
97 Dingaan's Widow (a – ♂ upp.; b – ♂ uns.) p. 142
98 Orange Widow (a – ♂ upp.; b – ♂ uns.) p. 143
99 Cape Spring Widow (a – ♂ upp.; b – ♂ uns.) p. 144
100 Natal Tree Nymph (a – ♂ upp.; b – ♂ uns.; c – ♀ upp.; d – ♀ uns.) p. 89
101 Boisduval's Tree Nymph (a – ♂ upp.; b – ♂ uns.) p. 88
102 African Snout (a – ♂ upp.; b – ♂ uns.) p. 154
103 Striped Policeman (a – ♂ upp.; b – ♂ uns.) p. 236
104 Strelitzia Nightfighter (a – ♂ upp.; b – ♂ uns.) p. 260
105 Clouded Flat (a – ♂ upp.; b – ♂ uns.) p. 239
106 Kroon's Flat (a – ♂ upp.; b – ♂ uns.) p. 240
107 Common Bush Brown (a – ♂ upp.; b – ♂ uns.) p. 131
108 Eyed Bush Brown (a – ♂ upp.; b – ♂ uns.) p. 132

Figs. 109 – 125 PLATE 11

109 Savanna Brown (a – ♂ upp.; b – ♂ uns.) p. 134
110 Western Hillside Brown (a – ♂ upp.; b – ♂ uns.) p. 138
111 Greybottom Brown (a – ♂ upp.; b – ♂ uns.) p. 136
112 Drakensberg Brown (a – ♂ upp.; b – ♂ uns.) p. 135
113 Rainforest Brown (a – ♂ upp.; b – ♂ uns.) p. 133
114 Natal Brown (a – ♂ upp.; b – ♂ uns.) p. 135
115 Spotted-eye Brown (a – ♂ upp.; b – ♂ uns.) p. 137
116 Pondo Shadefly (a – ♂ upp.; b – ♂ uns.) p. 145
117 Impure Ringlet (a – ♂ upp.; b – ♂ uns.) p. 147
118 Dark Webbed Ringlet (a – ♂ upp.; b – ♂ uns.) p. 147
119 Eriksson's Highflier (a – ♂ upp.; b – ♂ uns.) p. 171
120 Basutu Skolly (a – ♀ upp.; b – ♀ uns.; c – ♂ upp.; d – ♂ uns.) p. 168
121 Knysna Skolly (a – ♂ upp.; b – ♂ uns.) p. 167
122 Woolly Legs (a – ♂ upp.; b – ♂ uns.) p. 164
123 Twinspot Blue (a – ♂ upp.; b – ♂ uns.) p. 226
124 Free State Blue (a – ♂ upp.; b – ♂ uns.) p. 223
125 Common Smoky Blue (a – ♂ upp.; b – ♂ uns.) p. 229

PLATE 12 Figs. 126 – 154

126 Variable Blue (a – ♂ upp.; b – ♂ uns.) p. 222
127 Dusky Copper (a – ♂ upp.; b – ♂ uns.) p. 181
128 Apricot Playboy (a – ♀ upp.; b – ♀ uns.) p. 198
129 Brown Playboy (a – ♂ upp.; b – ♂ uns.) p. 200
130 Purple-brown Hairstreak (a – ♀ upp.; b – ♀ uns.) p. 194
131 Henning's Black Eye, (a – ♂ upp.; b – ♀ uns.) p. 197
132 Blackstriped Hairtail (a – ♂ upp.; b – ♂ uns.) p. 206
133 Silverspotted Grey (a – ♂ upp.; b – ♂ uns.) p. 188
134 Tailed Black Eye (a – ♂ upp.; b – ♂ uns.) p. 196
135 Black Heart (a – ♂ upp.; b – ♂ uns.) p. 209
136 Whitebranded Swift (a – ♂ upp.; b – ♂ uns.) p. 264
137 Olivehaired Swift (a – ♂ upp.; b – ♂ uns.) p. 265
138 Small Elfin (a – ♂ upp.; b – ♂ uns.) p. 242
139 Dismal Sylph (a – ♂ upp.; b – ♂ uns.) p. 252
140 Small Marbled Elf (a – ♂ upp.; b – uns.) p. 241
141 Macken's Dart (a – ♂ upp.; b – ♂ uns.) p. 259
142 Common Hottentot (a – ♂ upp.; b – ♂ uns.) p. 266
143 Greenmarbled Sandman (a – ♂ upp.; b – ♂ uns.) p. 248
144 Netted Sylph (a – ♂ upp.; b – ♂ uns.) p. 251
145 Fulvous Ranger (a – ♂ upp.; b – ♂ uns.) p. 253
146 Barber's Ranger (a – ♂ upp.; b – ♂ uns.) p. 254
147 Wallengren's Ranger (a – ♀ upp.; b – ♀ uns.) p. 255
148 Pale Ranger (a – ♂ upp.; b – ♂ uns.) p. 257
149 Peppered Hopper (a – ♂ upp.; b – ♂ uns.) p. 262
150 Karoo Dancer (a – ♂ upp.; b – ♂ uns.) p. 249
151 Geranium Bronze (a – ♂ upp.; b – ♂ uns.) p. 211
152 Cupreous Small Blue (a – ♀ upp.; b – ♂ uns.) p. 232
153 Grass Jewel Blue (a – ♂ upp.; b – ♂ uns.) p. 221
154 Dwarf Blue (a – ♂ upp.; b – ♂ uns.) p. 221

Figs. 155 – 166   PLATE 13

155 Cambridge Vagrant (a – ♂ upp.; b – ♂ uns.) p. 47
156 Goldbanded Forester (a – ♂ upp.; b – ♂ uns.) p. 96
157 Gaudy Commodore, DSF (a – ♂ upp.; b – ♂ uns.) p. 74
158 Trimen's Sapphire (a – ♂ upp.; b – ♀ upp.; c – ♀ uns.) p. 191
159 Southern Sapphire (a – ♂ upp.; b – ♀ upp.; c – ♀ uns.) p. 190
160 Common Figtree Butterfly (a – ♂ upp.; b – ♂ uns.) p. 170
161 Hutchinson's Highflier (a – ♂ upp.; b – ♂ uns.) p. 172
162 Mimosa Sapphire (a – ♂ upp.; b – ♂ uns.) p. 193
163 Azure Hairstreak (a – ♂ upp.; b – ♂ uns.) p. 194
164 Bowker's Sapphire (a – ♂ upp.; b – ♂ uns.) p. 190
165 Natal Bar (a – ♂ upp.; b – ♂ uns.) p. 173
166 Silvery Bar (a – ♂ upp.; b – ♂ uns.) p. 174

PLATE 14　　　　　　　　　　　　　　　　　　　　　　　Figs. 167 – 184

167 Patricia Blue (a – ♂ upp.; b – ♀ upp.; c – ♂ uns.) p. 227
168 Twinspot Blue (a – ♀ upp.; b – ♀ uns.) p. 226
169 Koppie Blue (a – ♂ upp.; b – ♀ upp.; c – ♂ uns.) p. 225
170 Mashuna Blue (a – ♂ upp.; b – ♂ uns.) p. 228
171 Potchefstroom Blue (a – ♂ upp.; b – ♂ uns.) p. 224
172 Restless Indigo Blue (a – ♂ upp.; b – ♂ uns.) p. 228
173 Common Meadow Blue (a – ♂ upp.; b – ♂ uns.) p. 231
174 Longtailed Pea Blue (a – ♂ upp.; b – ♂ uns.; c – ♀ upp.) p. 217
175 Brown Playboy (a – ♀ upp.; b – ♀ uns.) p. 200
176 Purple-brown Hairstreak (a – ♂ upp.; b – ♂ uns.) p. 194
177 Common Hairtail (a – ♂ upp.; b – ♀ upp.; c – ♂ uns.) p. 205
178 Pale Hairtail (a – ♂ upp.; b – ♂ uns.) p. 207
179 Common Pea Blue (a – ♂ upp.; b – ♂ upp.; c – ♂ uns.) p. 216
180 Sabie Smoky Blue (a – ♂ upp.; b – ♂ uns.) p. 230
181 Dusky Blue (a – ♂ upp.; b – ♂ uns.) p. 218
182 Bush Bronze (a – ♂ upp.; b – ♀ upp.; c – ♂ uns.) p. 210
183 Common Dotted Blue (a – ♂ upp.; b – ♂ uns.; c – ♀ upp.) p. 214
184 Cape Dotted Blue (a – ♂ upp.; b – ♀ upp.; c – ♂ uns.) p. 215

Figs. 185 – 195   PLATE 15

185 Hintza Pie (a – ♂ upp.; b – ♀ upp.; c – ♂ uns.) p. 212
186 Topaz Spotted Blue (a – ♂ upp.; b – ♀ upp.; c – ♂ uns.) p. 233
187 Velvet Spotted Blue (a – ♂ upp.; b – ♂ uns.) p. 233
188 Cupreous Small Blue (a – ♂ upp.; b – ♂ uns.) p. 232
189 Sooty Blue (a – ♂ upp.; b – ♀ upp.; c – ♂ uns.) p. 218
190 Gaika Blue (a – ♂ upp.; b – ♂ uns.) p. 219
191 Rayed Blue (a – ♂ upp.; b – ♂ uns.) p. 220
192 Otacilia Hairtail (a – ♂ upp.; b – ♀ upp.; c – ♂ uns.) p. 208
193 Common Friar (a – ♂ upp.; b – ♂ uns.) p. 151
194 Mocker Swallowtail, ♀ form *hippocoonides* (a – upp.; b – uns.) p. 25
195 Variable Diadem, form *wahlbergi* (a – ♂ upp.; b – ♂ uns.) p. 83

PLATE 16 Figs. 196 – 199

196 Novice Friar (a – ♂ upp.; b – ♂ uns.) p. 151
197 Whitebanded Swallowtail (a – ♂ upp.; b – ♂ uns.) p. 26
198 Whitebarred Charaxes (a – ♂ upp.; b – ♂ uns.) p. 102
199 Forest-king Charaxes (a – ♀ upp.; b – ♀ uns.) p. 103

Figs. 200 – 207   PLATE 17

200 Common Diadem (a – ♂ upp.; b – ♂ uns.) p. 82
201 Veined Swordtail (a – ♂ upp.; b – ♂ uns.) p. 31
202 Angola White-lady Swordtail (a – ♂ upp.; b – ♂ uns.) p. 30
203 Southern Wanderer (a – ♀ upp.; b – ♀ uns.) p. 113
204 Dusky Acraea (a – ♂ upp.; b – ♂ uns.) p. 119
205 Bushveld Charaxes (a – ♂ upp.; b – ♂ uns.) p. 106
206 Satyr Charaxes (a – ♀ upp.; b – ♀ uns.) p. 107
207 Van Son's Charaxes (a – ♀ upp.; b – ♀ uns.) p. 109

PLATE 18 Figs. 208 – 221

208 Clubtailed Charaxes, WSF (a – ♂ upp.; b – ♂ uns.) p. 104
209 Battling Glider (a – ♀ upp.; b – ♀ uns.) p. 95
210 Pied Piper (a – ♂ upp.; b – ♂ uns.) p. 84
211 Common Sailer (a – ♂ upp.; b – ♂ uns.) p. 91
212 Spotted Sailer (a – ♂ upp.; b – ♂ uns.) p. 90
213 Diverse Rainforest White (a – ♀ upp., WSF; b – ♀ uns., WSF; c – ♀ upp., DSF; d – ♀ uns., DSF) p. 42
214 African Clouded Yellow, ♀ form *aurivillius* (a – upp.; b – uns.) p. 61
215 Orangebarred Playboy (a – ♀ upp.; b – ♀ uns.) p. 199
216 Bufftipped Skipper (a – ♂ upp.; b – ♂ uns.) p. 244
217 Spotted Velvet Skipper (a – ♂ upp.; b – ♂ uns.) p. 245
218 Asterodia Sandman (a – ♂ upp.; b – ♂ uns.) p. 246
219 Common Sandman (a – ♂ upp.; b – ♂ uns.) p. 247
220 Woolly Legs (a – ♀ upp.; b – ♀ uns.) p. 164
221 Black Pie (a – ♂ upp.; b – ♂ uns.) p. 213

Figs. 222 – 224 PLATE 19

222 Emperor Swallowtail (a – ♂ upp.; b – ♂ uns.) p. 28
223 Citrus Swallowtail (a – ♂ upp.; b – ♂ uns.) p. 27
224 Mocker Swallowtail (a – ♂ upp.; b – ♂ uns.) p. 25

PLATE 20 Figs. 225 – 228

225 Mocker Swallowtail, ♀ form *cenea* (a – upp.; b – uns.) p. 25
226 Whitebanded Swallowtail (a – ♀ upp.; b – ♀ uns.) p. 26
227 Variable Diadem, form *mima* (a – ♂ upp.; b – ♂ uns.) p. 83
228 Chief Friar (a – ♂ upp.; b – ♂ uns.) p. 152

Figs. 229 – 236　　　　　　　　　　　　　　　　　　　　PLATE 21

229 Forest-king Charaxes (a – ♀ upp.; b – ♀ uns.) p. 103
230 Chief False Acraea (a – ♂ upp.; b – ♂ uns.) p. 93
231 Southern Wanderer (a – ♂ upp.; b – ♂ uns.) p. 113
232 Dusky Acraea (a – ♂ upp.; b – ♂ uns.) p. 119
233 African Veined White (a – ♀ upp.; b – ♀ uns., WSF; c – ♀ uns., DSF) p. 38
234 Zebra White (a – ♂ upp.; b – ♂ uns.) p. 34
235 African Common White (a – ♀ upp.; b – ♀ uns.) p. 37
236 Veined Tip (a – ♂ upp.; b – ♂ uns.) p. 49

PLATE 22 Figs. 237 – 241

237 Yellow Pansy (a – ♂ upp.; b – ♂ uns.) p. 75
238 Yellowbanded Acraea (a – ♂ upp.; b – ♂ uns.) p. 118
239 Table Mountain Beauty (a – ♂ upp.; b – ♂ uns.) p. 139
240 Greenveined Charaxes (a – ♂ upp.; b – ♂ uns.) p. 100
241 Flamebordered Charaxes (a – ♂ upp.; b – ♂ uns.) p. 100

Figs. 242 – 246   PLATE 23

242 Foxy Charaxes (a – ♂ upp.; b – ♂ uns.) p. 101
243 Bushveld Charaxes (a – ♀ upp.; b – ♀ uns.) p. 106
244 Bluespangled Charaxes (a – ♀ upp.; b – ♀ uns.) p. 110
245 Dry-leaf Commodore (a – ♂ upp.; b – ♂ uns.) p. 72
246 Soldier Pansy (a – ♂ upp.; b – ♂ uns.) p. 77

PLATE 24 Figs. 247 – 260

247 Garden Commodore (a – ♂ upp., WSF; b – ♂ uns., WSF; c – ♂ upp., DSF; d – ♂ uns., DSF) p. 71
248 Longtailed Admiral (a – ♂ upp.; b – ♂ uns.) p. 68
249 Marsh Commodore (a – ♂ upp., WSF; b – ♂ uns., WSF; c – ♂ upp., DSF; d – ♂ uns., DSF) p. 73
250 Golden Piper (a – ♂ upp.; b – ♂ uns.) p. 85
251 Bush Nightfighter (a – ♂ upp.; b – ♂ uns.) p. 261
252 Large Sprite (a – ♂ upp.; b – ♂ uns.) p. 237
253 Orangebanded Protea (a – ♂ upp.; b – ♂ uns.) p. 202
254 Orangebarred Playboy (a – ♂ upp.; b – ♂ uns.) p. 199
255 Common Arrowhead (a – ♂ upp.; b – ♂ uns.) p. 176
256 Amakosa Rocksitter (a – ♂ upp.; b – ♂ uns.) p. 162
257 Goldspotted Sylph (a – ♂ upp.; b – ♂ uns.) p. 250
258 Orangespotted Hopper (a – ♂ upp.; b – ♂ uns.) p. 263
259 Morant's Orange (a – ♂ upp.; b – ♂ uns.) p. 258
260 Chequered Ranger (a – ♂ upp.; b – ♂ uns.) p. 256

Figs. 261 – 263   PLATE 25

261 Greenbanded Swallowtail (a – ♂ upp.; b – ♂ uns.) p. 28
262 Large Striped Swordtail (a – ♂ upp.; b – ♂ uns.) p. 31
263 Forest Queen (a – ♂ upp.; b – ♂ uns.) p. 111

PLATE 26　　　　　　　　　　　　　　　　　　　　　　Figs. 264 – 268

264 Forest-king Charaxes (a – ♂ upp.; b – ♂ uns.) p. 103
265 Dusky Charaxes (a – ♀ upp.; b – ♀ uns.) p. 108
266 Blue Pansy (a – ♂ upp.; b – ♂ uns.) p. 76
267 Eyed Pansy (a – ♂ upp.; b – ♂ uns.) p. 77
268 Dark Opal (a – ♂ upp.; b – ♂ uns.) p. 187

Figs. 269 – 292   PLATE 27

269 Apollo Emperor (*Pseudaphelia apollinaris*): Saturniidae – forest and savanna
270 Superb False Tiger (*Heraclia superba*): Agaristidae – savanna
271 Beautiful Tiger (*Amphicallia bellatrix*): Arctiidae – montane forest
272 Bright Tiger (*Callioratis abraxas*): Geometridae – near cycads
273 Peach Moth (*Egybolis vaillantina*): Noctuidae – coastal forest
274 Oriental Bee Hawk (*Cephonodes hylas*): Sphingidae – widespread
275 Monarch Looper (*Cartaletis libyssa*): Geometridae – forest
276 Monarch Looper (*Cartaletis libyssa*): Geometridae – forest
277 Butler's False Tiger (*Heraclia butleri*): Agaristidae – forest
278 White Bear (*Nyctemera leuconoe*): Arctiidae – coastal forest
279 Cheetah (*Argina amanda*): Arctiidae – forest and woodland
280 Cheetah (*Argina amanda*): Arctiidae – forest and savanna
281 Leopard Magpie (*Zerenopsis leopardina*): Geometridae – near cycads
282 Crimson Speckled Footman (*Utetheisa pulchella*): Arctiidae – widespread
283 Festive Red Tiger (*Brephos festiva*): Agaristidae – grassland
284 Clouded Orange (*Petovia dichroaria*): Geometridae – savanna
285 Pondo Tigerlet (*Veniloides pantheraria*): Geometridae – east coast
286 Banded Vapourer (*Aroa discalis*): Lymantriidae – forest and savanna
287 Orange Tiger (*Secusio strigata*): Arctiidae – savanna
288 Wisp Wing (*Coenina poecilaria*): Geometridae – grassland and savanna
289 Cool Maiden (*Syntomis kuhlweinii*): Arctiidae – montane forest
290 Satin (*Marblepsis* sp.): Lymantriidae – forest
291 Threaded Looper (*Nassunia caffraria*): Geometridae – savanna
292 Vestal (*Rhodometra sacraria*): Geometridae – widespread

PLATE 28   Figs. 293 – 304

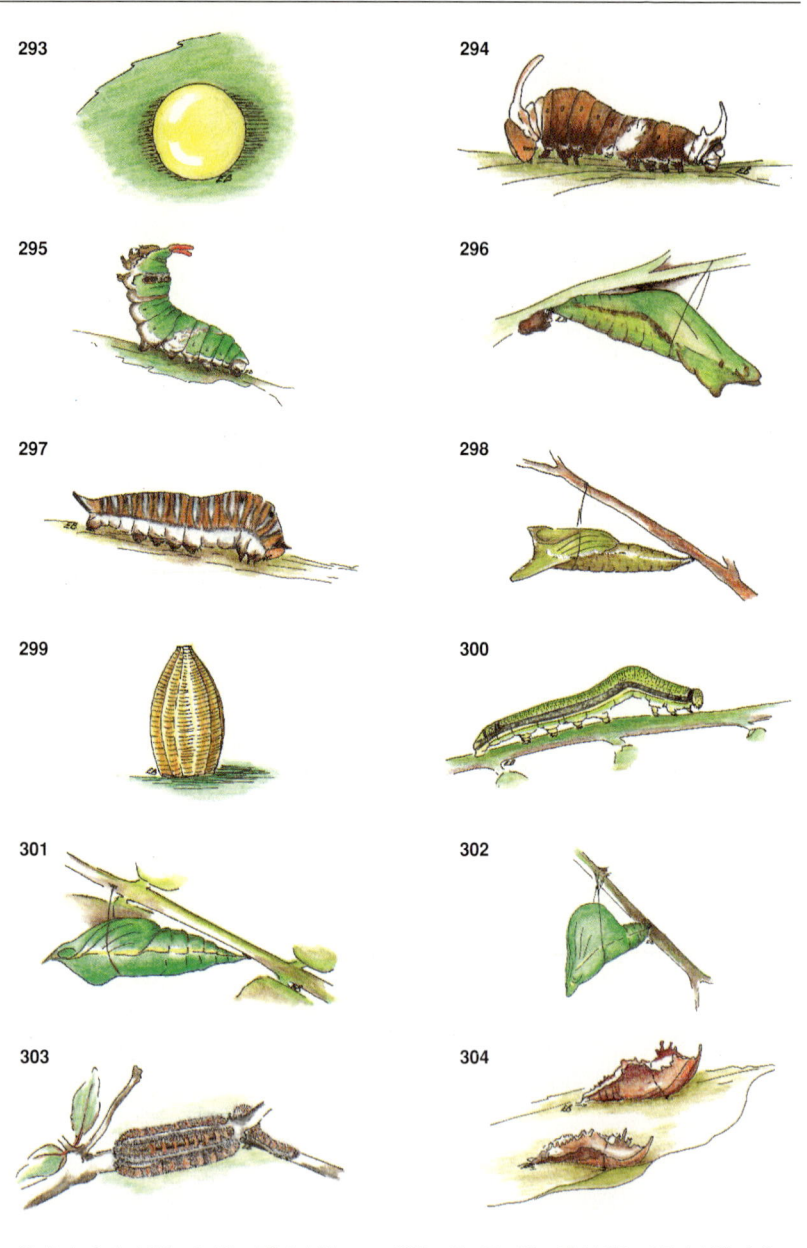

293 Egg of the Mocker Swallowtail (diameter 1,2 mm). Typical of the papilionid family.
294 Third instar larva of the Mocker Swallowtail (length 10 mm). Typical of the papilionid family. From above the larva resembles a bird dropping.
295 Mature larva of the Citrus Swallowtail (length 40 mm). Typical of the Swallowtails. The larva has assumed a defensive pose by rearing up and extruding the osmeterium.
296 Pupa of the Citrus Swallowtail (length 35 mm). Typical of the papilionid family. Note the silken girdle and discarded larval skin (left).
297 Mature larva of the Small Striped Swordtail (length 32 mm). Typical of the Swordtails.
298 Pupa of the Small Striped Swordtail (length 28 mm). Typical of the Swordtails.
299 Egg of the African Migrant (height 1,6 mm). Typical of the pierid family. Note the elongated barrel shape.
300 Mature larva of the African Migrant (length 47 mm). Typical of the pierid family.
301 Pupa of the African Migrant (length 32 mm). Typical of the pierid family. Note the girdle, as in the papilionids.
302 Pupa of the Bushveld Purple Tip (length 27 mm). An example of a pierid pupa with produced or keeled wing cases.
303 Mature larvae of the Common Dotted Border (length 32 mm). Pierid larvae that are very hairy and also highly gregarious.
304 Pupae of the Common Dotted Border (length 22 mm). Pierid pupae with numerous surface projections.

Figs. 305 – 316   PLATE 29

305 Egg of the African Leopard (height 0,8 mm). A nymphaline egg typical of the tribe Argynnini.
306 Mature larva of the African Leopard (length 26 mm). A nymphaline larva typical of the tribe Argynnini.
307 Pupa of the African Leopard (length 16 mm). A nymphaline pupa typical of the tribe Argynnini.
308 Egg of the Gaudy Commodore (height 0,7 mm). A nymphaline egg typical of the tribe Nymphalini.
309 Mature larva of the Gaudy Commodore (length 45 mm). A nymphaline larva typical of the tribe Nymphalini.
310 Pupa of the Gaudy Commodore (length 25 mm). A nymphaline pupa typical of the tribe Nymphalini.
311 Egg of the African Joker (height 0,7 mm). A nymphaline egg typical of the tribe Byblini.
312 Mature larva of the African Joker (length 28 mm). A nymphaline larva typical of the tribe Byblini.
313 Pupa of the African Joker (length 19 mm). A nymphaline pupa typical of the tribe Byblini.
314 Egg of the Spotted Sailer (height 0,8 mm). A nymphaline egg typical of the tribe Neptini.
315 Mature larva of the Spotted Sailer (length 21 mm). A nymphaline larva typical of the tribe Neptini. Note the absence of the branched spines.
316 Pupa of the Spotted Sailer (length 14 mm). A nymphaline pupa typical of the tribe Neptini.

PLATE 30   Figs. 317 – 328

317 Mature larva of the Chief False Acraea (length 32 mm). A nymphaline larva typical of the tribe Limenitidini.
318 Pupa of the Chief False Acraea (length 27 mm). A nymphaline pupa typical of the tribe Limenitidini.
319 Mature larva of the Guineafowl (length 30 mm). A nymphaline larva of the tribe Limenitidini with long lateral setae that act as shadow-breakers.
320 Egg of the Foxy Charaxes (height 1,5 mm). Typical egg of the charaxine subfamily. The brown ring develops after the egg has been laid.
321 Mature larva of the Foxy Charaxes (length 55 mm). Typical of the charaxine subfamily. Note the characteristic horns on the headshield.
322 Pupa of the Foxy Charaxes (length 27 mm). Typical of the charaxine subfamily.
323 Egg of the Garden Acraea (height 0,7 mm). Typical of the acraeine subfamily.
324 Mature larva of the Marsh Acraea (length 33 mm). Typical of the acraeine subfamily. The branched spines are as in many nymphalines.
325 Pupa of the Garden Acraea (length 19 mm). Typical elongated pupa of the acraeine subfamily.
326 Egg of Swanepoel's Widow (height 1,1 mm). Typical of the satyrine subfamily.
327 Mature larva of Swanepoel's Widow (length 35 mm). Typical of the satyrine subfamily. Note the large head.
328 Pupa of Swanepoel's Widow (length 23 mm). Typical of the satyrine subfamily.

Figs. 329 – 338　　　　　　　　　　　　　　　　　　　　　　　　　　　　　　PLATE 31

329 Egg of the African Monarch (height 1,2 mm). Typical of the danaine subfamily.
330 Mature larva of the African Monarch (length 50 mm). Typical of the danaine subfamily. Note the long processes.
331 Pupa of the African Monarch (length 20 mm). Typical of the danaine subfamily.
332 Egg of the Common Black Eye (height 0,45 mm). Typical of the lycaenid family.
333 Pupa of the Common Black Eye (length 11 mm). Typical of the lycaenid family.
334 Egg of the Amakosa Rocksitter (height 0,45 mm). Typical of the liptenine subfamily.
335 Mature larva of the Amakosa Rocksitter (length 17 mm). Typical of the liptenine subfamily. The larva is densely covered with hairs.
336 Pupa of the Amakosa Rocksitter (length 10 mm). Typical of the liptenine subfamily. Note the unusual hairiness.
337 Egg of the Basutu Skolly (height 0,5 mm). Typical of the Skollys. Note the unique lipped edge.
338 Fourth instar larva of the Basutu Skolly (length 18 mm). Typical of the Skollys. Note the deep pits on the surface.

PLATE 32 Figs. 339 – 349

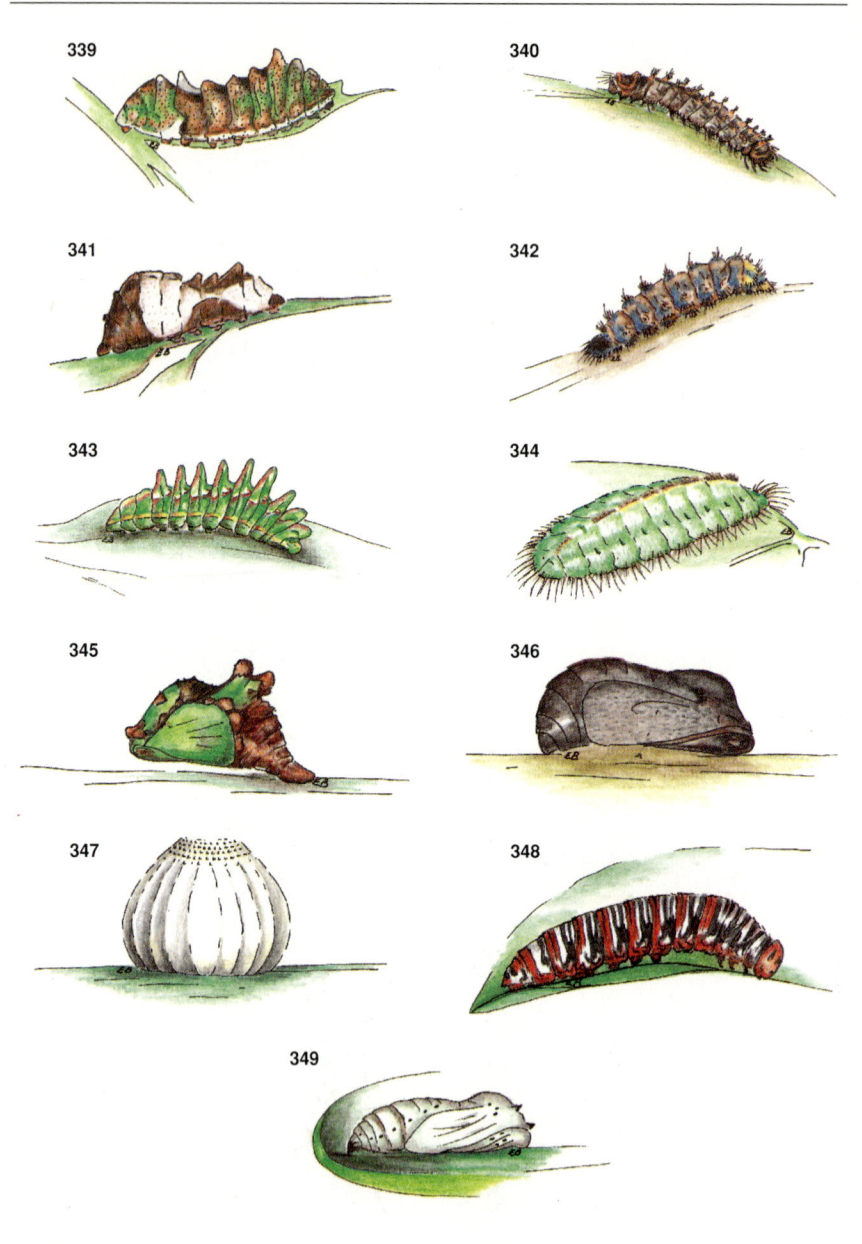

339 Mature larva of the Common Figtree Butterfly (length 20 mm). Typical of the lycaenid family.
340 Mature larva of the Natal Bar (length 25 mm). Typical of many larvae of the thecline subfamily.
341 Mature larva of Trimen's Sapphire (length 22 mm). Typical of the Sapphires. The larva closely resembles a bird dropping.
342 Mature larva of the Brown Playboy (length 19 mm). Typical of the Playboys. The larva burrows into seeds and fruit.
343 Mature larva of the Common Hairtail (length 14 mm). Typical of the Hairtails.
344 Mature larva of the Black Pie (length 12 mm). A rather atypical example of a larva of the lycaenid family.
345 Pupa of Bowker's Sapphire (length 13 mm). Typical of the Sapphires.
346 Pupa of the Short-toothed Pea Blue (length 7 mm). Typical of the lycaenid family.
347 Egg of the Red-tab Policeman (height 0,75 mm). Typical of the hesperiid family.
348 Mature larva of the Red-tab Policeman (length 46 mm). Typical of the hesperiid family.
349 Pupa of the Red-tab Policeman (length 24 mm). Typical of the hesperiid family. The pupa is contained within a rolled-up leaf and covered by white powder.

THE PAPILIONIDS
(Family Papilionidae)

Papilionids are a family of large to very large butterflies that are generally showy, conspicuous insects. Included in the family are the largest butterflies in the world, the Birdwings of the Malay Archipelago, some of which have wingspans of nearly 300 mm. There are about 85 species of papilionid in Africa but only 17 of these occur in southern Africa, one of which is endemic. The paucity of species in the subcontinent is due to papilionids being primarily forest butterflies, with a lesser number in frost-free savanna. The southern African species are divided into two groups: the Swallowtails (genus *Papilio*) and the Swordtails (genus *Graphium*), both of which are dealt with below. Female papilionids lay their eggs singly on the leaves or young leaf shoots of the larval foodplants. For Swallowtails these are trees belonging to the citrus family (Rutaceae) and for Swordtails shrubs or trees of the custard-apple family (Annonaceae). The eggs are spherical, smooth, pale yellow and about 1 mm in diameter (fig. 293). The larva hatches within a week and consumes the empty egg shell as its first meal. It feeds on the edges of young leaves and rests in the middle of the upper surface of the leaf. There are five larval stages (instars), which take three to four weeks to develop to maturity. In Swallowtails the first four larval instars resemble bird droppings (fig. 294) and in certain species this resemblance is enhanced by the larva's kinking its body in the middle; in the final (fifth) instar the larvae are green with some brown or white markings, rather slug-like and well camouflaged (fig. 295). In Swordtails the larvae tend to be marked with variously coloured transverse bands (fig. 297). All papilionid larvae have a remarkable eversible forked organ just behind the head, known as an osmeterium. When the larva is alarmed this brightly coloured organ is everted and releases a pungent citrus-like odour. Papilionid pupae are long and cylindrical, resembling a twig, or leaf-shaped, and are suspended by a silken girdle (fig. 296 & 298). In some species the pupa may be green or brown, depending on the surroundings in which the larva pupates. Such dimorphic pupae are seen in the Citrus and Greenbanded Swallowtails. The adult butterflies may eclose from the pupa after a few weeks or the pupae may undergo diapause ("hibernate") in autumn and butterflies eclose only the following spring, some four to six months later. Because of this pupal diapause adult papilionids are mostly seen on the wing from about September, reach a peak in numbers in February and March and become scarce by May. Few are seen during the winter months of June to August, except in the warmer coastal areas of Natal and Mozambique. Some species of Swordtail that occur in more arid savanna habitats can diapause as pupae for several years, should drought conditions persist.

SWALLOWTAILS
SWAELSTERTE
(Genus *Papilio*)

Seven species of Swallowtail are found in southern Africa, five of which are illustrated in this guide. Swallowtails are large to very large insects and include the largest butterfly in the subregion – the spectacular Emperor Swallowtail (fig. 222), with a wingspan of up to 120 mm. Although the common name of the group would lead one to expect that all Swallowtails have tails on their hindwings, tails are in fact absent in the Whitebanded (figs 197 & 226), Citrus (fig. 223) and Greenbanded (fig. 261) Swallowtails and in females of the Mocker Swallowtail (figs 194 & 225). All Swallowtails are showy butterflies with predominantly black and yellow patterns on their wings. Generally the male and female of a particular species are similar in appearance, with the striking exception of the mimetic females of the Mocker Swallowtail and the Whitebanded Swallowtail.

The Swallowtails are closely related to the Swordtails (p. 29), both groups belonging to the papilionid family (see above). Most species of Swallowtail are found in subtropical and temperate forests but the familiar Citrus Swallowtail and, to a lesser extent, the Greenbanded Swallowtail are more widespread, particularly the former, which is found even in the Karoo. All Swallowtails are active and fairly strong fliers, prefer sunny warm weather, and spend a lot of time in search of flowers from which to feed. They appear to be especially fond of red and blue flowers. While feeding at flowers they characteristically flutter their wings as if in constant readiness to fly off at the first sign of danger. Also noticeable are their long spindly legs, which create the impression that they are hovering in mid-air above the flower from which they are sipping nectar.

The males of some species, particularly those of the Citrus and Greenbanded Swallowtails, often congregate in small groups on damp sand or on mud, where they sit motionless for many minutes, sucking up the fluids (mud-puddling). Male Swallowtails are very inquisitive and will momentarily interrupt their random flight to inspect a realistic decoy, or dead specimen of the same species, placed on the ground. Swallowtails generally locate mates by a searching behaviour; the exception is the male Citrus Swallowtail, which shows a strong territorial behaviour. Female Swallowtails are slower fliers and less conspicuous than the males. They tend to keep to the forest understorey, where they fly about in search of flowers, or plants on which to lay their eggs. Trees and shrubs belonging to the citrus family (Rutaceae) are the usual larval foodplants for Swallowtails. The early stages are described under papilionids, above.

Mocker Swallowtail
Na-aper-swaelstert
(Papilio dardanus) **figs 194, 224 & 225**

Identification: Large (75–90 mm); sexes very different; males seasonally variable; females extremely genetically variable. Male upperside cream-yellow with wide black margin on forewing; uneven, often broken, black band down middle of hindwing and scalloped black wing margin; well developed club-shaped tail on hindwing. Underside forewing yellow with outer third light to dark brown; hindwing and tails marked in light and dark brown. Female extremely variable with at least 12 described forms; tails absent; only the two commonest forms are illustrated: form *cenea* (fig. 225) – black with white spots on forewing and on hindwing margin; large, deep-yellow patch at base of hindwing; form *hippocoonides* (fig. 194) – black with large white areas and white marginal dots on both wings.

Distinguishing characters and similar species: The male is distinctive. Female form *cenea* is a mimic of the unpalatable Chief Friar (fig. 228) and female form *hippocoonides* is a mimic of the Common Friar (fig. 193). Compare also with the female of the Whitebanded Swallowtail (fig. 226), which closely resembles form *cenea* and the two forms of the Variable Diadem (figs 227 & 195), one of which resembles form *cenea* and the other form *hippocoonides*.

Habitat and distribution: The Mocker Swallowtail is a common species of temperate and subtropical forests from the Mossel Bay district in the southern Cape Province north-eastwards through the eastern Cape Province, Transkei, Natal, Swaziland, eastern and northern Transvaal, Mozambique and the eastern border of Zimbabwe.

Behaviour: The males are active, fairly strong fliers and keep from two to four metres above the ground. They are conspicuous on forest margins and fly at random. When a cloud obscures the sun they settle on low vegetation, with closed wings. The males often mud-puddle. Females are less frequently seen, keep to the semi-shaded forest undergrowth and fly more slowly. Both sexes are fond of flowers.

Flight period: October to April in the cooler forests but all year in those on the Natal and Mozambique coasts.

Early stages: Typical of papilionids (see p. 23). Breeds mainly on white ironwood (*Vepris undulata*), twinberry tree (*Oricia bachmanni*), Natal teclea (*Teclea natalensis*) and occasionally on cultivated citrus (*Citrus* species).

Whitebanded Swallowtail
Witlint-swaelstert
(*Papilio echerioides*) figs 197 & 226

Identification: Large (75–80 mm); tailless; sexes very different. Male upperside velvety-black with distinct creamy bands across wings, broken into regular patches on forewing; cream dots on hindwing margin. Underside variegated brown with bands of upperside mirrored, but narrower. Female closely resembling female form *cenea* of Mocker Swallowtail on upperside (fig. 225) but undersides different.

Distinguishing characters and similar species: The male is distinctive. The female Whitebanded Swallowtail mimics the Chief Friar (fig. 228) and also resembles form *cenea* of the Mocker Swallowtail (fig. 225).

Habitat and distribution: The Whitebanded Swallowtail is a common but strict inhabitant of temperate forests from the Amatola Mountains in the eastern Cape Province north-eastwards to Natal, eastern and northern Transvaal and the eastern border of Zimbabwe.

Behaviour: The males are often seen on forest edges, flying weakly about a metre above the ground. They keep to the semi-shade and fly at random. The females are also slow fliers and keep to the forest undergrowth. Both sexes are often seen feeding from flowers, especially those of impatiens and plectranthus.

Flight period: September to April.

Early stages: Typical of papilionids (see p. 23). The larvae feed mainly on horsewood (*Clausena anisata*).

Citrus Swallowtail
Lemoen-swaelstert
(Papilio demodocus) **fig. 223**

Identification: Large (70–90 mm); tailless; sexes similar. Male upperside black with broken, yellow band on both fore- and hindwing and extensive yellow spotting; eye-spots at leading and inner margins of hindwing. Underside similar to upperside. Female larger.

Distinguishing characters and similar species: Similar in markings to the Emperor Swallowtail (fig. 222), which has tails and is much larger. Two other, similar Swallowtails (neither illustrated in this guide) occur in southern Africa: 1) Constantine's Swallowtail (*Papilio constantinus*) – similar in size to the Citrus Swallowtail but has tails, more regular yellow markings, and lacks eye-spots. Occurs in localised populations in frost-free savanna in northern Natal, eastern and northern Transvaal, Mozambique, Zimbabwe and eastern Botswana; 2) Bush-kite Swallowtail (*P. euphranor*) – very like Constantine's Swallowtail but is a strict inhabitant of temperate forests in Transkei, Natal and eastern Transvaal. Males establish aerial territories in forest clearings and float like kites, many metres above the ground.

Habitat and distribution: The Citrus Swallowtail is very common and widespread. It is absent only from the desert areas in the northwest of the subregion.

Behaviour: Flies briskly, one to three metres above the ground, usually at random. The males often establish territories on hilltops or in groves of trees. The males are very fond of mud-puddles and both sexes feed from flowers.

Flight period: Summer, but also in winter in warm areas such as the eastern seaboard.

Early stages: Typical of papilionids (see p. 23). The larvae feed on the leaves of many plants, including cultivated citrus (*Citrus* species), wild Rutaceae such as Cape chestnut (*Calodendrum capense*) and small knobwood (*Zanthoxylum capense*), fennel (*Foeniculum vulgare*) and sneezewood (*Ptaeroxylon obliquum*).

Greenbanded Swallowtail
Groenlint-swaelstert
(*Papilio nireus*) fig. 261

Identification: Large (80–90 mm); tailless; sexes similar. Male upperside velvety-black with metallic blue-green bands through fore- and hindwing; blue-green spots in tip of forewing and along hindwing margin. Underside blackish-brown with thin, cream, submarginal band on hindwing. Female similar but bands dull metallic-green and underside variegated brown to pinkish-brown without cream band of male.

Habitat and distribution: The Greenbanded Swallowtail is common and widespread in forest and savanna habitats in the eastern and northern parts of southern Africa.

Behaviour: Has a fast, undulating flight, one to four metres above the ground. The direction of flight is random. Males often congregate to suck at muddy places. Both sexes feed readily from flowers. Females are most often seen in the undergrowth of forests or in dense bush.

Flight period: Summer; also in winter in warmer areas.

Early stages: Typical of papilionids (see p. 23). Breeds mainly on white ironwood (*Vepris undulata*), horsewood (*Clausena anisata*), Cape chestnut (*Calodendrum capense*), Natal teclea (*Teclea natalensis*) and cultivated citrus (*Citrus* species).

Emperor Swallowtail
Koning-swaelstert
(*Papilio ophidicephalus*) fig. 222

Identification: Very large (90–120 mm); has tails; sexes similar. Male upperside blackish-brown with yellow bands and spots on both fore- and hindwing; two blue and orange eye-spots on each hindwing; large, clubbed tail resembling snake's head on each hindwing. Underside similar to upperside but yellow markings more extensive. Female very similar but larger.

Distinguishing characters and similar species: Superficially resembles the Citrus Swallowtail (fig. 223) but the latter is smaller and lacks a tail on the hindwing.

Habitat and distribution: The Emperor Swallowtail is a fairly common but strict inhabitant of temperate coastal forests from Transkei to southern Natal and the temperate montane forests of the Natal Midlands, eastern and northern Transvaal and the eastern border of Zimbabwe.

Behaviour: A brisk, random flier, often along streambeds or roads through the forest. Usually keeps from two to five metres above the ground. Males mud-puddle, especially in the afternoon. Both sexes are fond of flowers. Females keep to the semi-shaded forest understorey.

Flight period: October to April.

Early stages: Typical of papilionids (see p. 23). The main larval foodplants are horsewood (*Clausena anisata*) and knobwood (*Zanthoxylum davyi*).

SWORDTAILS
SWAARDSTERTE
(Genus *Graphium*)

Swordtails are large butterflies closely related to the Swallowtails (p. 24). Characteristically they possess a long, sword-like tail on each hindwing, for example the Large Striped Swordtail (fig. 262). Some species, such as the Angola Whitelady Swordtail (fig. 202) and the Veined Swordtail (fig. 201), are however tailless. Swordtail species are variable in both colour and patterning but the sexes of a particular species are very similar. They are strong and rapid fliers, usually keeping from one to three metres above the ground. The 10 species found in southern Africa occur mostly in coastal bush and in frost-free savanna further inland. They are therefore confined to the easterly and northerly portions of the subregion. They fly during the summer months and there is often a big hatch of adults in spring. They are not often seen feeding from flowers but the males of some species occasionally congregate in large numbers on damp sand or mud. They rarely engage in hilltopping behaviour. Whereas the Swallowtails use plants belonging mainly to the citrus family (Rutaceae) as larval foodplants, the Swordtails appear to breed exclusively on members of the custard-apple family (Annonaceae). The early stages are considered under papilionids (see p. 23).

Angola White-lady Swordtail
Angola-witnooientjie
(Graphium angolanus) **fig. 202**

Identification: Large (65–75 mm); tailless; sexes similar. Male upperside black with large white patch on trailing edge of forewing and on basal portion of hindwing; numerous white spots elsewhere, especially on forewing. Underside with white markings corresponding to those on upperside but black replaced on base of wings by maroon and on wing margins by light brown. Female similar but larger.

Distinguishing characters and similar species: Easily confused with two related species, not illustrated, that also occur in southern Africa: 1) Small White-lady Swordtail (*Graphium morania*) – smaller and occurs in the same areas as the Angola White-lady Swordtail but spreads further south in Natal and further to the west in Transvaal; 2) Schaffgotsch's White-lady Swordtail (*G. schaffgotschi*) – also smaller and is found in Ovamboland in Namibia. These three Swordtails somewhat resemble pierids (p. 33) in flight but fly much more rapidly.

Habitat and distribution: The Angola White-lady Swordtail is common in frost-free savanna in the eastern half of the subregion from northern Natal to the lowveld of Swaziland and Transvaal, Mozambique, Zimbabwe, Botswana and northern Namibia.

Behaviour: A fast, direct flier, two to three metres above the ground. Both sexes feed from flowers and the males congregate at mud patches.

Flight period: October to April.

Early stages: Typical of papilionids (see p. 23). The larvae feed on wild custard-apple (*Annona senegalensis*) and *Sphedamnocarpus pruriens*, a scrambling creeper that grows in rocky habitats.

Veined Swordtail
Bont-swaardstert
(Graphium leonidas) **fig. 201**

Identification: Large (75–85 mm); tailless; sexes similar; somewhat variable. Male upperside black with numerous, scattered, pale bluish-white to greenish-white spots; large, white basal area on hindwing tinged with orange, especially towards inner margin. Underside brown with pale spots corresponding to upperside. Female larger than male. Another form (form *brasidas*) has fewer pale spots, especially on underside.

Habitat and distribution: The Veined Swordtail is common in frost-free savanna and on forest margins from the East London district in the eastern Cape Province north-eastwards to the Natal coast, Swaziland, eastern Transvaal, Mozambique and Zimbabwe.

Behaviour: Flies rapidly, irregularly and at random, two to four metres above the ground. Males sometimes hilltop and show perching behaviour, and sometimes mud-puddle. They are often seen on the edge of thick bush and open forest. They roost on twigs, with the wings folded and hanging down, when they look remarkably like some of the unpalatable danaines.

Flight period: September to April.

Early stages: Typical of papilionids (see p. 23). Breeds mainly on dwaba-berry (*Monanthotaxis caffra*) and small cluster-pear (*Uvaria caffra*).

Large Striped Swordtail
Jag-swaardstert
(Graphium antheus) **fig. 262**

Identification: Large (70–75 mm); sexes similar. Male upperside black with numerous, scattered, pale turquoise patches and stripes of varying size; long, slender, white-tipped black tail on hindwing and small, blood-red spot at inner margin on hindwing. Underside light brown, with turquoise markings corresponding to those on upperside and two red spots on hindwing. Female larger with paler blue markings.

Distinguishing characters and similar species: Five other, similar species of Swordtail occur in southern Africa (none illustrated in this guide): 1) Small Striped Swordtail (*Graphium policenes*) – smaller, with straight, turquoise bars on the leading edge of the forewing (the bars are wavy in the Large Striped Swordtail). Common along the Transkei and Natal coasts and in Mozambique; 2) Mamba Swordtail (*G. colonna*) – smaller and darker with the stripes and spots fewer and deep greeny-blue. Relatively common in subtropical coastal forests of northern Natal and Mozambique. Flies lower down and more slowly than the other similar Swordtails; 3) Dark Swordtail (*G. porthaon*) – smaller, with the stripes and spots pale yellow-green. A relatively scarce butterfly of frost-free savanna in northern Natal, Mozambique, Transvaal north of the Soutpansberg, Zimbabwe and northern Botswana; 4) Dancing Swordtail (*G. polistratus*) – small and dark like the Mamba Swordtail, but the stripes and spots are very pale green. A scarce species occurring along the Mozambique coast as far south as Maputo; 5) Junod's Swordtail (*G. junodi*) – small, with wide, pale-green bands and stripes. A rare species found in Mozambique, especially along the coast.

Habitat and distribution: The Large Striped Swordtail is common in frost-free savanna and subtropical coastal bush in the eastern half of the subcontinent from Port St Johns in Transkei north-eastwards.

Behaviour: Flies rapidly and erratically along the edges of bush, one to five metres above the ground. Both sexes feed readily from flowers and males mud-puddle. It flies at random.

Flight period: Summer.

Early stages: Typical of papilionids (see p. 23). Breeds on small clusterpear (*Uvaria caffra*), wild custard-apple (*Annona senegalensis*), shakama plum (*Hexalobus monopetalus*) and red hookberry (*Artabotrys monteiroae*).

THE PIERIDS
(Family Pieridae)

The pierid family has some 180 species in the Afrotropical Region and is represented by 54 species in southern Africa. Pierids are generally medium-sized butterflies with white, yellow or orange wings usually with some black markings. They are most numerous in the savanna biome but are also common in forests. They are most active in warm, sunny weather, fly at random and are very fond of flowers. Unlike some members of other butterfly families they are not territorial and do not hilltop. I have divided the pierids into seven common name groups. The **Whites**, **Vagrants** and **Tips**, which constitute the majority of species (40), breed mainly on plants belonging to the caper family (Capparaceae). The **Dotted Borders** (seven species) breed mainly on "mistletoes" (family Loranthaceae). The larvae of the **Clouded Yellows**, **Migrant** and **Grass Yellows** (seven species) use leguminous plants (family Fabaceae). Pierid eggs are usually laid singly on the leaves of the foodplant (fig. 299) but in some Whites and in the Dotted Borders they are laid in neat clusters. Typically the larvae are long and cylindrical and have a finely granulated surface with fine hairs (figs 300 & 303). The pupae are cylindrical and tapered at both ends (fig. 301). They are suspended at the rear end and by means of a silken girdle around the middle (like papilionids). In some species the pupa is markedly keeled (fig. 302). Usually the surface of pierid pupae is fairly smooth but in the Dotted Borders and some Whites there are projections on the pupal surface (fig. 304).

WHITES
WITJIES
(Genera *Pinacopteryx*, *Belenois*, *Dixeia*, *Appias*, *Pontia* and *Leptosia*)

There are 16 species of White in southern Africa, 12 of which are illustrated in this guide. They are mostly of medium size and are predominantly white or yellow, with black markings. The sexes are similar except in the genera *Belenois* and *Appias*. Whites are found mainly in the moist eastern half of the subcontinent, in and around forests and in moist to dry, frost-free savanna. Exceptions are the very widespread Brown-veined White (fig. 14) and Common Meadow White (fig. 25), which occur in most biomes in southern Africa. Whites are most active on hot, sunny days, keeping to open areas of full sunshine. Most are medium-fast fliers, from one to four metres above the ground. Exceptional in this regard is the African Wood White (fig. 26) which flies feebly, near the ground, in shady forest undergrowth. The males of a number of species are avid mud-puddlers and both sexes are very fond of flowers. Males appear to fly at random in search of mates, or of flowers on which to feed. They do not establish territories or hilltop. Females fly at random in search of flowers, or plants on which to lay their eggs. The eggs are usually laid singly on leaves or shoots of the larval foodplant, but are laid in batches in the Brownveined White and African Common White. For nearly all Whites the foodplants are members of the caper family (Capparaceae) but the Common Meadow White uses certain plants belonging to the cabbage family (Brassicaceae). The eggs, larvae and pupae are typical of pierids (see above).

Zebra White
Kwagga
(Pinacopteryx eriphia) **fig. 234**

Identification: Medium-sized (50–60 mm); sexes similar; wet and dry season forms. Male upperside with alternating, roughly horizontal black and yellow bands across wings. Underside a mosaic of pale-yellow and cinnamon-coloured areas. Female similar but with yellow bands paler. Dry season form similar to wet season form but underside more heavily marked with brown scaling.

Habitat and distribution: The Zebra White is a common to very common inhabitant of savanna from the south-western to the eastern Cape Province, Transkei, Natal, Swaziland, Transvaal, Mozambique, Zimbabwe, Botswana and northern Namibia.

Behaviour: Flies relatively slowly, near the ground (usually under a metre high) and has a random, wandering flight pattern. Both sexes are fond of flowers.

Flight period: All year.

Early stages: Typical of pierids (see p. 33). The larvae feed on shepherd's tree (*Boscia albitrunca*), bastard shepherd's tree (*Boscia oleoides*) and bush-cherry (*Maerua cafra*).

False Dotted Border White
Valsvoëlent-witjie
(Belenois thysa) **figs 7 & 32**

Identification: Medium-sized (55–65 mm); sexes dissimilar; wet and dry season forms. Male upperside pure white with black markings on wing margins. Underside forewing orange at the base, then white, then yellow at the tip; underside hindwing yellow with double row of black dots. Female more heavily marked with black scaling and with orange-yellow scaling on hindwing. Underside yellow with broad orange suffusion at base of forewing. Dry season form male like wet season form but dry season form female deep orange-yellow on upperside.

Distinguishing characters and similar species: Easily misidentified as the Common Dotted Border (figs 8 & 31), but the latter flies more slowly and has a single row of black dots on the underside of the hindwing. May also be confused with females of the Large Vagrant (fig. 2c).

Habitat and distribution: The False Dotted Border White is a fairly common butterfly in coastal bush on the eastern side of the subcontinent from Transkei to Natal, Mozambique and the eastern border of Zimbabwe.

Behaviour: Flies fairly rapidly (much faster than the similar Common Dotted Border) but often feeds from flowers. Flies at random on the margins of bush, from one to three metres above the ground.

Flight period: All year.

Early stages: Typical of pierids (see p. 33). Breeds on forest bush-cherry (*Maerua racemulosa*) and wild capers (*Capparis* species).

Forest White
Boswitjie
(Belenois zochalia) **fig. 12**

Identification: Medium-sized (50–55 mm); sexes dissimilar; female variable. Male upperside white with black markings on forewing tip and wing margins; black bar on leading edge of forewing. Underside of forewing tip and hindwing pale-yellow, with network of black markings. Three female forms: 1) as in male but with heavier black markings; 2) with white forewing and deep yellow hindwing; 3) rare form with pale-yellow forewing and deep-yellow hindwing. Also a geographical form of the Forest White (form *immaculata*), in which underside largely lacks the black markings of the usual form. Form *immaculata* occurs in some mountains of central Transvaal, especially the Magaliesberg.

Distinguishing characters and similar species: The Forest White can be confused with other Whites belonging to the same genus, particularly the Brownveined White (fig. 14), male African Common White (fig. 13) and male African Veined White (fig. 11). The female form with yellow hindwings can be mistaken for Trimen's Dotted Border (fig. 10).

Habitat and distribution: The Forest White is found mainly in temperate and subtropical forest but also occurs in wooded kloofs in drier areas, such as the Suikerbosrand and Magaliesberg in Transvaal. Distributed from the Mossel Bay district in the southern Cape Province northwards and eastwards to Mozambique and Zimbabwe.

Behaviour: Flies randomly and fairly fast, from one to four metres above the ground. Both sexes visit flowers.

Flight period: All year but commoner in summer.

Early stages: Typical of pierids (see p. 33). The larvae feed on forest bush-cherry (*Maerua racemulosa*) and bush-cherry (*Maerua cafra*).

Brownveined White
Grasveldwitjie
(Belenois aurota) **fig. 14**

Identification: Medium-sized (45–50 mm); sexes similar. Male upperside white with black markings on tip of forewing and margin of hindwing. Underside has veins of forewing apex and hindwing heavily outlined in brown. Female pale cream-white with extensive dark brown scaling of wing margins. Underside as in male but with much of ground colour pale orange-yellow.

Distinguishing characters and similar species: Easily confused with related species such as the Forest White (fig. 12), male African Common White (fig. 13) and male African Veined White (fig. 11).

Habitat and distribution: The Brownveined White is extremely common and widespread throughout the subcontinent.

Behaviour: Well known to most people as a migrant in summer and autumn, when countless millions of these white butterflies can be seen flying in a north-easterly direction over much of the interior (see also remarks on migration on p. 9). When not migrating it flies at random, one to three metres above the ground, fairly rapidly. It often feeds from flowers and the males mud-puddle.

Flight period: Flies all year but is commoner in summer.

Early stages: The eggs are laid in batches of up to 20 and the larvae are gregarious in their early stages, otherwise the life history is similar to that of other pierids (see p. 33). The larvae feed on shepherd's tree (*Boscia albitrunca*), bastard shepherd's tree (*Boscia oleoides*) and bush-cherry (*Maerua cafra*).

African Common White
Afrikaanse Gewone Witjie
(Belenois creona) **figs 13 & 235**

Identification: Medium-sized (45–50 mm); sexes very dissimilar. Male upperside white with black markings on forewing tip and hindwing margin. Underside forewing white with tip black, spotted with yellow; underside hindwing pale yellow with greenish tinge. Female distinctive: yellowish-green with very wide, almost solid, black wing margins. Underside yellow with extensive dark brown wing margins, and veins of hindwing outlined in brown.

Distinguishing characters and similar species: The male can be confused with the superficially similar Forest White (fig. 12), Brownveined White (fig. 14) and male African Veined White (fig. 11).

Habitat and distribution: The African Common White is a very common species in frost-free savanna on the eastern side of the subcontinent, from Mossel Bay in the southern Cape Province northwards.

Behaviour: Flies relatively slowly (especially the female), one to three metres above the ground, in a random fashion. Regularly visits flowers and the males are avid mud-puddlers. Occasionally migrates, usually together with the Brown-veined White, but in lesser numbers.

Flight period: All year.

Early stages: Similar to those of other pierids (see p. 33). Breeds on bastard shepherd's tree (*Boscia oleoides*), "wag-'n-bietjie" (*Capparis fascicularis*) and bush-cherry (*Maerua cafra*).

African Veined White
Laeveldwitjie
(Belenois gidica) **figs 11 & 233**

Identification: Medium-sized (50–55 mm); sexes dissimilar; wet and dry season forms. Male upperside white with black markings on tip of forewing and on hindwing margin. Underside off-white with reticulate pattern of black markings on tip of forewing and on hindwing. Two female forms: usual form deep-yellow with wide, dark brown margins on fore- and hindwing; underside yellow with reticulate pattern of brown markings as in male; scarcer female form with ground colour of wings greyish-white. Distinct dry season form with reduced black (male) and brown (female) markings on upperside; ground colour in female dry season form pale yellow. In both sexes underside of forewing tip and whole of hindwing almost uniform cinnamon, with prominent white streak running through middle of hindwing from base to margin of wing.

Distinguishing characters and similar species: The male African Veined White can be mistaken for males of the Forest White (fig. 12), Brownveined White (fig. 14) and African Common White (fig. 13). The female can only be confused with the Brownveined White female (fig. 14).

Habitat and distribution: The African Veined White is a common species in frost-free savanna and of the coastal zone, from the Mossel Bay district in the southern Cape Province north-eastwards through Natal, Swaziland, eastern and northern Transvaal, Mozambique, Zimbabwe, northern Botswana and northern Namibia.

Behaviour: Flies fast, one to three metres above the ground, at random. Both sexes feed from flowers and the males often congregate on damp patches.

Flight period: All year.

Early stages: Similar to those of other pierids (see p. 33). The main larval foodplants are wild caper-bush (*Capparis sepiaria*) and woolly caper-bush (*Capparis tomentosa*).

African Small White
Kusstreek-witjie
(Dixeia charina) **fig. 17**

Identification: Medium-sized (40–45 mm); sexes similar. Male upperside pure white with small black markings and dots on wing margins. Underside forewing tip and whole of hindwing usually finely speckled with brownish to blackish scales. Female has more extensive black markings on upperside but underside is similar to that of male.

Distinguishing characters and similar species: The African Small White may be mistaken for the male Ant-heap Small White (fig. 16) and the larger male Diverse Rainforest White (fig. 15). Two other related species of Small White, not illustrated in this guide, occur in southern Africa: 1) Blackveined Small White (*Dixeia doxo*); 2) Spotless Small White (*D. leucophanes*). Both are similar in size to the African Small White. They are white with a black forewing tip and have the wingveins clearly outlined in black, especially the males. The Blackveined Small White is found in northern Natal, far north-eastern Transvaal, Mozambique and Zimbabwe while the Spotless Small White occurs in north-eastern Zimbabwe and parts of Mozambique.

Habitat and distribution: The African Small White is common along the eastern coastal zone, from Mossel Bay in the southern Cape Province to Natal and Mozambique. Also found in the mountains above Barberton, Transvaal.

Behaviour: Flies medium-fast, one to two metres above the ground, at random. Feeds from flowers. On the southern Cape coast the foodplant grows on the seashore and the butterflies can therefore be seen flying on the beach.

Flight period: All year but commonest from October to April.

Early stages: As for other pierids (see p. 33). The main larval foodplant is wild caper-bush (*Capparis sepiaria*).

Ant-heap Small White
Miershoopwitjie
(Dixeia pigea) **figs 16 & 33**

Identification: Medium-sized (45–50 mm); sexes dissimilar; several female forms; some seasonal variation. Male upperside pure white with narrow, black forewing tip and small black dots on hindwing margin. Underside white with two rows of black dots on hindwing. Female pale yellowish-white with heavier black markings on wings. Underside similar to that of male but yellowish. A rare female form occurs with orange-yellow upperside; underside resembles underside of False Dotted Border White male (fig. 7). An even rarer female form (*rubrobasalis*) resembles normal female but has orange suffusion at base of forewing underside. Dry season form of both sexes similar to wet season form, but black markings reduced.

Distinguishing characters and similar species: Easily confused with other smallish white butterflies, especially the African Small White (fig. 17) and the male Diverse Rainforest White (fig. 15).

Habitat and distribution: The Ant-heap Small White is common in coastal bush and frost-free savanna, from the Port St Johns district in Transkei north-eastwards through Natal, the Transvaal lowveld, Mozambique and the eastern border of Zimbabwe.

Behaviour: A medium-fast, random flier. Keeps to open places and the edges of bush. Both sexes feed from flowers.

Flight period: All year.

Early stages: Typical of pierids (see p. 33). The usual larval foodplants are wild caper-bush (*Capparis sepiaria*) and woolly caper-bush (*Capparis tomentosa*).

Spiller's Sulphur Small White
Spiller-geletjie
(Dixeia spilleri) **fig. 37**

Identification: Small (35–40 mm); sexes similar; slight seasonal variation. Male upper- and underside bright canary yellow; narrow black margin at tip of forewing on upperside. Female similar but butter-yellow to orange-yellow. Dry season form male with orange coloration on hindwing underside and along leading margin of forewing. Dry season form female similar to wet season form female.

Distinguishing characters and similar species: Spiller's Sulphur Small White may be confused with other smallish yellow butterflies, particularly the Grass Yellows (fig. 38). The latter generally have more black on the tips and margins of the wings on the upperside and are very weak fliers by comparison.

Habitat and distribution: Spiller's Sulphur Small White is usually fairly scarce but in some years may swarm in coastal bush. Found along the coastal zones of Natal and Mozambique and also sparingly in far north-eastern Transvaal and eastern parts of Zimbabwe.

Behaviour: A medium-fast and restless butterfly, flying one to two metres above the ground. Very conspicuous against the dark green background of bush. Flies at random and regularly feeds from flowers.

Flight period: All year.

Early stages: Similar to those of other pierids (see p. 33). The larvae feed on wild caper-bush (*Capparis sepiaria*).

Diverse Rainforest White
Willawitjie
(Appias epaphia) **figs 15 & 213**

Identification: Medium-sized (50–55 mm); sexes dissimilar; seasonally variable. Male upperside white with fairly extensive black scaling on tip and leading edge of forewing and black dots on hindwing margin. Underside white with yellow-orange basal flush on forewing. Female distinctive: white with very wide blackish-brown margins on both fore- and hindwing and dark brown at base of forewing. Underside similar but with less extensive brown markings; basal yellow flush in forewing as in male. Dry season form male lacks marginal spots on hindwing. Dry season form female has less extensive black markings; ground colour pale yellowish-white; orange basal suffusion on underside of forewing.

Distinguishing characters and similar species: The male can easily be mistaken for other common Whites such as the male of the smaller Antheap Small White (fig. 16) and the African Small White (fig. 17). In the north-eastern portion of the subregion there is another member of the same genus, the Albatross Rainforest White (*Appias sabina*), not illustrated, of which the male is very similar to the Diverse Rainforest White. The Albatross Rainforest White is scarce and localised, occurring in a few forests in north-eastern Transvaal, on the eastern border of Zimbabwe and in parts of Mozambique.

Habitat and distribution: The Diverse Rainforest White is common to very common in the eastern coastal zone, from Transkei through Natal and the eastern Transvaal lowveld into Mozambique and Zimbabwe.

Behaviour: A relatively slow, random flier, one to two metres above the ground. Often seen on flowers. Males mud-puddle.

Flight period: All year.

Early stages: As for other pierids (see p. 33). The larvae feed on forest bush-cherry (*Maerua racemulosa*) and wild caper-bush (*Capparis sepiaria*).

Common Meadow White
Bontrokkie
(Pontia helice) **fig. 25**

Identification: Smallish (40–45 mm); sexes similar. Male upperside white with black markings on forewing tip and black bar in middle of leading edge of forewing. Underside of forewing tip and hindwing have mosaic pattern of brown, yellow and white. Female similar but has more extensive dark brown markings on forewing and on hindwing margin. No distinct seasonal forms.

Distinguishing characters and similar species: The distinctive underside makes identification of this small white butterfly easy.

Habitat and distribution: The Common Meadow White is a very common butterfly, widespread in open habitats throughout southern Africa.

Behaviour: A slow-flying species that keeps close to the ground (less than a metre) and flies at random. Very fond of flowers. Usually found in meadows: open country with short grass. Large numbers can sometimes be seen feeding from the flowers in lucerne fields.

Flight period: All year.

Early stages: Much like those of other pierids (see p. 33). Breeds on a number of small herbaceous plants, such as *Heliophila linearis*, alyssum (*Alyssum minutum*), Cape pepper cress (*Lepidium capense*), wild mustard (*Sisymbrium* sp.), *Rapistrum rugosum* (an introduced weed) and "katstertbossie" (*Reseda lutea*).

African Wood White
Fladderpapiertjie
(Leptosia alcesta) **fig. 26**

Identification: Small (35–40 mm); sexes very similar. Male upperside pure white with very rounded forewings; discrete, small, black forewing tip and black patch in outer third of forewing. Underside white with black patch corresponding to one on upperside; fine dusting of black scales on tip and base of forewing and on hindwing. Female almost identical but larger.

Habitat and distribution: A common forest species, also occurring in dense bush, along the Natal coast to Swaziland, Mozambique, the eastern Transvaal lowveld and eastern border of Zimbabwe.

Behaviour: Flies slowly and feebly, less than a metre above the ground, in the shady undergrowth of forests and thick bush. Resembles a floating piece of tissue paper. The flight is random. Both sexes feed from small flowers near the ground.

Flight period: All year.

Early stages: Like those of other pierids (see p. 33) but the larva and pupa are very small. Known to breed on "wag-'n-bietjie" (*Capparis fascicularis*).

VAGRANTS
SWERWERS
(Genera *Eronia* and *Nepheronia*)

Five species of Vagrant are found in the subregion, four of which are illustrated in this guide. The fifth species, Buquet's Vagrant (*Nepheronia buquetii*), not illustrated, closely resembles the African Migrant (fig. 4), but the former has green eyes while the latter has greyish-brown eyes. Vagrants are medium-sized to large butterflies and show moderate sexual and seasonal variation. All the species are found on the warmer, frost-free eastern side of the subcontinent, in forest, on forest margins and in lowveld savanna. The males are swift to very swift random fliers, often on the edges of forest or bush, and constantly search for flowers or females. The females are slower, also fly at random, and search for flowers or for plants on which to lay their eggs. The larval foodplants are creepers or scrambling shrubs belonging to the caper family (Capparaceae), Rhizophoraceae and Hippocrataceae. The early stages are similar to those of other pierids (see p. 33) but the wing cases of the pupa are markedly produced, giving the pupa a keeled appearance (fig. 302).

Vine-leaf Vagrant
Druiweblaarswerwer
(Eronia cleodora) **fig. 5**

Identification: Medium-sized (55–60 mm); sexes similar; wet and dry season forms. Male upperside white with wide, uneven, black margins on both fore- and hindwing. Underside highly characteristic (fig. 5b) and resembling dead leaf. Female similar but with slight yellowish tinge to upperside white area. Dry season form with black margins on upperside much reduced but distinctive underside markings as in wet season form.

Habitat and distribution: Fairly common in coastal bush and frost-free savanna on the eastern side of the subregion, from the eastern Cape Province (Port Elizabeth district) to Transkei, Natal coast, Swaziland and the Transvaal lowveld and Mozambique.

Behaviour: Flies fast and erratically, on the edges of forest and bush and along watercourses, about one to four metres above the ground. Frequently visits flowers.

Flight period: All year.

Early stages: As for other pierids (see p. 33). The larva feeds on "wag-'n-bietjie" (*Capparis fascicularis*).

Autumn-leaf Vagrant
Herfsblaarswerwer
(Eronia leda) **fig. 30**

Identification: Medium-sized (55–60 mm); sexes dissimilar; distinct seasonal forms in female. Male upperside bright yellow with large orange tip on forewing; extreme tip of forewing sparingly dusted with brown scales. Underside yellow with flecks of brown on forewing tip and, more prominently, on hindwing. Wet season form female similar but with narrow, brown forewing tip and row of dark brown dots in tip. Underside with more diffuse brown scaling and several brown-ringed white dots in forewing tip and on hindwing. Dry season form female with orange forewing tip, like male, but typical underside pattern of wet season form female.

Distinguishing characters and similar species: Can only possibly be confused with the much smaller, similarly marked Sulphur Orange Tip male (fig. 36).

Habitat and distribution: The Autumn-leaf Vagrant is a fairly common inhabitant of the eastern coastal zone, from Transkei (Port St Johns district) north-eastwards along the Natal coast, to the Swaziland and Transvaal lowveld, Mozambique, Zimbabwe and northern Botswana.

Behaviour: A swift and powerful flier, keeping one to three metres above the ground. Very conspicuous against a backdrop of green bush. Flies at random and often visits flowers, but remains on a particular flower for a short time only.

Flight period: All year.

Early stages: As for other pierids (see p. 33). Breeds on woolly caperbush (*Capparis tomentosa*).

Large Vagrant
Grootswerwer
(Nepheronia argia) fig. 2

Identification: Largest pierid in Africa (65–75 mm); sexes dissimilar; some seasonal variation; several different female forms. Male upperside white with black tip and black spots on outer margin of forewing. Underside forewing white with smudges of brown on leading edge, near tip; hindwing underside pale yellow with smaller brown smudges. Usual female has black markings along wing margins; forewing white with broad, pink-orange basal flush; hindwing butter-yellow. Underside similar to upperside but black marginal markings replaced by brown smudges. Other female forms: 1) white above with heavier black marginal markings; 2) white with orange flush at base of forewing; 3) forewing white; hindwing orange-yellow (orange basal flush absent).

Distinguishing characters and similar species: Superficially the female resembles males of the False Dotted Border White (fig. 7) and the Common Dotted Border (fig. 8), especially on the underside. The female form with yellow hindwings resembles Trimen's Dotted Border (fig. 10).

Habitat and distribution: The Large Vagrant is a not uncommon inhabitant of thick bush and forest margins. Occurs in the eastern coastal zone, from Transkei to Natal, Mozambique and the eastern border of Zimbabwe. Also in northern Botswana and Namibia and in riverine forest along major rivers in the eastern Transvaal lowveld (such as the Olifants River).

Behaviour: Has a fast, erratic flight, one to four metres above the ground, usually in a fairly straight line. Like other Vagrants it is fond of flowers.

Flight period: All year but often commoner in autumn.

Early stages: As for other pierids (see p. 33). The larval foodplant in east Africa is *Cassipourea ruwenzoriensis*.

Cambridge Vagrant
Blouswerwer
(Nepheronia thalassina) **figs 3 & 155**

Identification: Medium-sized (60–65 mm); sexes dissimilar; two distinct female forms. Male upperside pale turquoise-blue (Cambridge blue) with fairly extensive, black forewing tip and outer wing margin. Underside almost pure white with characteristic pearly sheen. Usual female creamy-white with bases of wings pale golden-brown; wing margin unevenly brown in forewing; hindwing margin with large brown spots. Underside as in male but with three brown smudges near margin of forewing and pale orange basal flush, especially in forewing. Other female form similar but with hindwing upperside golden-yellow.

Distinguishing characters and similar species: The female form that has the forewings white and the hindwings yellow may be mistaken for Trimen's Dotted Border (fig. 10) and other pierids with this coloration.

Habitat and distribution: The Cambridge Vagrant is a common species in forest and dense bush on the eastern side of the subregion, from northern Natal to the Swaziland lowveld, escarpment forests of the Transvaal Drakensberg and the Soutpansberg, Mozambique, the eastern border of Zimbabwe, northern Zimbabwe, Botswana and Namibia.

Behaviour: The pale blue males are striking against a backdrop of green vegetation. They are fast, random fliers, keeping from two to five metres above the ground. Females are less active and tend to occur inside forest or bush. The pearly-white underside in both sexes is conspicuous when they are feeding from flowers.

Flight period: All year but commoner in summer.

Early stages: As for other pierids (see p. 33). In east Africa they breed on *Hippocratea africana*.

TIPS
PUNTJIES
(Genus *Colotis*)

The Tips consist of a single large genus (*Colotis*) with 19 species in southern Africa, 11 of which are illustrated in this guide. They are small to medium-sized white butterflies with a variable amount of black markings on the wings. Characteristically the tips of the forewings are brightly coloured (usually orange, red or purple) but a few species lack coloured tips, for example the Veined Tip (fig. 236). The sexes are rather dissimilar, the females tending to have more extensive black markings on the wings and restricted coloured tips. There are also quite marked differences between the summer (wet season) forms and the winter (dry season) forms, the winter forms generally being smaller and having reduced black markings on the wings in both sexes. Because of the strong seasonal and sexual dimorphism identification of a particular species can sometimes be difficult. The typical habitat of Tips is savanna, particularly semi-arid to arid frost-free savanna, in which they are often conspicuous butterflies. The adults are on the wing in all months of the year, being most numerous in summer and autumn (December to April). Most Tips are rapid fliers, especially the males. The Purple Tips (fig. 6) and the Lemon Traveller Tip (fig. 34) are exceptionally fast on the wing. The females, particularly those of the smaller species such as the Small Orange Tip (fig. 23), fly more slowly, often close to the ground. All Tips are active only in warm, sunny weather and constantly search for flowers from which to feed. They are particularly attracted to purple flowers. If a cloud obscures the sun they tend to stop flying and rest on the ground or on vegetation, with closed wings. Females usually lay their eggs singly on shrubs and trees belonging to the caper family (Capparaceae). The early stages are typical of the pierid family (see p. 33). The pupae, like those of the Vagrants (p. 44), are often somewhat keeled (fig. 302).

Veined Tip
Bontpuntjie
(Colotis vesta) **fig. 236**

Identification: Small (35–40 mm); sexes similar; seasonally variable. Male upperside yellow-orange with cream at base of wings; fairly heavily marked with black. Female similar but whole of wing yellow. Black markings much heavier in wet season form.

Distinguishing characters and similar species: Two related species, not illustrated, are found in southern Africa: 1) Topaz Tip *(Colotis amata)* – smaller; the male more orange; the female with orange at the base of the wings and yellowish towards the margins. More local and scarcer than the Veined Tip but often flies together with the latter; 2) Doubleday's Tip *(C. doubledayi)* – similar in size to the Veined Tip but is evenly yellow and has black markings on the upperside hindwing streaked along the veins.

Found only in the north-western Cape Province (Vioolsdrift) and southern parts of Namibia.

Habitat and distribution: The Veined Tip is common in hot, dry, frost-free savanna (bushveld). Occurs from the northern half of Natal through Swaziland, the northern parts of Transvaal and the savanna regions of Zimbabwe, Botswana and Namibia.

Behaviour: Has a slowish to medium-fast, random flight, usually not more than a metre above the ground. Often settles on the ground. Both sexes are fond of flowers.

Flight period: All year.

Early stages: As for other pierids (see p. 33). Known to breed on beadbean tree *(Maerua angolensis)*.

Queen Purple Tip
Koningin-perspuntjie
(Colotis regina) **fig. 6**

Identification: Medium-sized (50–60 mm); sexes dissimilar; seasonally variable. Largest Tip in southern Africa. Male upperside white with black wing-veins; large purple tip on forewing. Female upperside with heavier black markings; tip of forewing with distal row of white dots and proximal row of purple dots. Dry season form female has purple tips, as does male.

Distinguishing characters and similar species: There are several other species, not illustrated, in southern Africa with purple or purple-red tips: 1) Bushveld Purple Tip (*Colotis ione*) – smaller and with the purple of the tips in the male more restricted. Female with numerous forms having orange, colourless or brown tips. Widespread in frost-free, arid savanna. Often occurs together with the Queen Purple Tip. Fairly common; 2) Coast Purple Tip (*C. erone*) – very similar to the Bushveld Purple Tip and also has various female forms. Occurs in the coastal bush of Transkei and Natal. Fairly common; 3) Lilac Tip (*C. celimene*) – medium-sized with an extensive, lilac forewing tip in the male and black or lilac tip in the female. Found in dry savanna in northern Natal, northern Transvaal, Zimbabwe, Botswana and Namibia; 4) Dune Purple Tip (*C. eunoma*) – slightly smaller than the Queen Purple Tip. Creamy, with a small crimson tip. Rare and confined to coastal scrub in northern Mozambique.

Habitat and distribution: The Queen Purple Tip is common in savanna, especially semi-arid to arid, frost-free savanna. Occurs from northern Natal to eastern Swaziland, Transvaal, Mozambique, Zimbabwe, Botswana and Namibia.

Behaviour: Flies fast, usually one to two metres above the ground, and appears almost to float (because of its shallow wing beats). Often seen feeding at flowers, especially purple ones. Flies at random but usually in a more or less straight line. Males often fly to the top of koppies but are only cursory visitors and do not establish territories. Rarely seen at damp patches.

Flight period: All year but commoner in summer.

Early stages: Typical of pierids (see p. 33). Breeds on shepherd's tree (*Boscia albitrunca*) and wild capers (*Capparis* species).

Scarlet Tip
Skarlakenpuntjie
(*Colotis danae*) **fig. 19**

Identification: Medium-sized (40–50 mm); sexes dissimilar; seasonally variable. Male upperside white with very large, bright scarlet forewing tip, bordered on inner aspect with black; hindwing border black. Dry season form male smaller with marked reduction of black scaling. Female much more heavily marked with black and with variably coloured tip on forewing (usually orange-red). Some females have the coloured tip reduced to a row of orange markings.

Distinguishing characters and similar species: Males of the Scarlet Tip may be confused with some other Tips, especially the Red Tip (fig. 20a). The Red Tip has smaller, reddish-orange tips and a horizontal black stripe across the wings. The female Scarlet Tip may be mistaken for females of the Red Tip (fig. 20c) and Common Orange Tip (fig. 21c). The distinctive underside of the Scarlet Tip (fig. 19b) helps to separate it from other Tips.

Habitat and distribution: The Scarlet Tip is common in frost-free savanna from Transkei to Natal, Swaziland, Transvaal, Mozambique, Zimbabwe, Botswana and Namibia.

Behaviour: Flies medium-fast (female slower), usually less than a metre above the ground. Has a random, zig-zagging flight. Like other Tips it is fond of flowers. It often flies together with the Sulphur Orange Tip in the same localities.

Flight period: All year.

Early stages: As for other pierids (see p. 33). The larvae feed on the leaves of bead-bean tree (*Maerua angolensis*), mauve cadaba (*Cadaba natalensis*) and pink cadaba (*Cadaba termitaria*).

Sulphur Orange Tip
Swael-oranjepuntjie
(Colotis auxo) **fig. 36**

Identification: Small (30–40 mm); sexes dissimilar; seasonally variable. Male upperside bright yellow with large orange tip on forewing. Female more heavily marked with black. Dry season form male smaller, with black markings absent; female with black markings reduced.

Distinguishing characters and similar species: Similar, in markings and coloration, to the much larger and fast-flying Autumn-leaf Vagrant (fig. 30).

Habitat and distribution: The Sulphur Orange Tip is a common inhabitant of frost-free savanna, occurring from the eastern Cape Province (Grahamstown district) to Transkei, Natal, Swaziland, eastern and northern Transvaal, Mozambique, Zimbabwe and eastern Botswana.

Behaviour: A medium-fast flier, keeping about a metre above the ground and flying at random. Visits flowers frequently. Often flies in the same localities as the Scarlet Tip.

Flight period: All year but commoner in summer.

Early stages: As for other pierids (see p. 33). The larval foodplants include mauve cadaba (*Cadaba natalensis*) and pink cadaba (*Cadaba termitaria*).

Red Tip
Rooipuntjie
(Colotis antevippe) **fig. 20**

Identification: Small to medium-sized (35–45 mm); sexes dissimilar; seasonally variable. Male upperside white with orange-red tip on forewing and black markings. Underside of hindwing has veins streaked with black. Female has orange tip on forewing broken into discrete spots; wings heavily marked with black. Dry season form has reduced black markings and underside of wings speckled with brown scales.

Distinguishing characters and similar species: The males are easily confused with other Tips such as the Scarlet Tip (fig. 19a) and, especially, the Smoky Orange Tip (fig. 22). The female may be mistaken for females of the Scarlet Tip (fig. 19b) and Common Orange Tip (fig. 21b).

Habitat and distribution: The Red Tip is common to very common in savanna and the coastal zone from the George district in the southern Cape Province, through the southeastern Cape Province, Transkei, Natal, Swaziland, Transvaal, Mozambique, Zimbabwe, Botswana and Namibia.

Behaviour: Has a medium-fast, zig-zagging flight, often changing direction. Flies up to a metre and a half above the ground. Both the males and the slower females fly at random and frequently visit flowers. Males occasionally mud-puddle.

Flight period: All year.

Early stages: As for other pierids (see p. 33). The larvae feed on bush-cherry (*Maerua cafra*), wild caper-bush (*Capparis sepiaria*) and bastard shepherd's tree (*Boscia oleoides*).

Common Orange Tip
Gewone Oranjepuntjie
(Colotis evenina) **fig. 21**

Identification: Small to medium-sized (35–45 mm); sexes dissimilar; seasonally variable. Male upperside white with orange tip in forewing and black markings. Female with much heavier black scaling on wings; forewing tip broken up into discrete orange markings. Dry season form has reduced black markings on wings.

Distinguishing characters and similar species: Female rather similar to the Red Tip female (fig. 20b) but the latter has a small black spot in the middle of the forewing. May also be confused with the Scarlet Tip female (fig. 19b). The Kalahari Orange Tip (*Colotis lais*), not illustrated, is similar to the Common Orange Tip but is smaller and is restricted to Griqualand West, southern Namibia and southern Botswana.

Habitat and distribution: The Common Orange Tip is a very common savanna species which also penetrates the grassland and Karoo biomes sparingly. It is found in northern Natal, Swaziland, Transvaal, Mozambique, Zimbabwe, Botswana, Namibia, Little Namaqualand, Griqualand West and the south-western Orange Free State.

Behaviour: The males are medium-fast on the wing while the females fly rather slowly, near the ground. Both sexes usually keep below one metre above the ground, fly at random, and are fond of flowers.

Flight period: All year; September to April in colder areas.

Early stages: As for other pierids (see p. 33). They breed on wild capers (*Capparis* species).

Speckled Sulphur Tip
Grasveld-geelpuntjie
(Colotis agoye) **fig. 24**

Identification: Small (35–40 mm); sexes dissimilar; geographically variable. Male upperside white with small, old-gold tip on forewing; wing-veins black and wings finely speckled with black scales. Female lacks black speckling and black wing-veins of male; forewing tip brown with two elongated orange spots embedded in it.

**Distinguishing characters and similar species: There is a distinct, smaller subspecies of the Speckled Sulphur Tip (subspecies *bowkeri*), not illustrated, which lacks the black speckling in both sexes.

Habitat and distribution: The Speckled Sulphur Tip is widespread in savanna habitats but more localised than other Tips. Found in the northern half of Transvaal, in Zimbabwe, northern Botswana and Namibia. Subspecies *bowkeri* occurs in the western Orange Free State, Griqualand West, Little Namaqualand, southern Botswana and southern Namibia.

Behaviour: The males are medium-fast, random fliers while the females are slower. Subspecies *bowkeri* is a relatively slow-flying insect. Both sexes can often be seen visiting flowers.

Flight period: All year; September to April for *bowkeri*.

Early stages: As for other pierids (see p. 33). The larvae use shepherd's tree (*Boscia albitrunca*) and cadabas (*Cadaba* species) as foodplants.

Smoky Orange Tip
Donker-oranjepuntjie
(Colotis evippe) **fig. 22**

Identification: Small (35–40 mm); sexes similar; seasonally variable. Male white with reddish-orange tip on forewing; wings have horizontal black bands. Female similar but more heavily marked with black. Dry season form, in both sexes, much less heavily marked with black scales.

Distinguishing characters and similar species: The dry season form Smoky Orange Tip male resembles the wet season form Red Tip male (fig. 20a), and the male is superficially similar to the male Small Orange Tip (fig. 23). The Bushveld Orange Tip (*Colotis pallene*), not illustrated, is smaller than the Smoky Orange Tip and less heavily marked with black. The Bushveld Orange Tip has many forms, some of which look like miniature Red Tips. The Bushveld Orange Tip is found in northern Natal, Swaziland, Transvaal, Mozambique, Zimbabwe, Botswana and northern Namibia.

Habitat and distribution: The Smoky Orange Tip is common in savanna and the eastern coastal belt, sparingly penetrating the Karoo. It is absent from the extreme south-western Cape Province (fynbos) and from open grassland. It is probably the most widespread Tip.

Behaviour: Has a medium-fast flight, close to the ground (about half a metre). Often seen flying, with an irregular flight path, along the edges of forest and thick bush. Both sexes are fond of flowers and males occasionally mud-puddle.

Flight period: All year; September to April in colder areas.

Early stages: As for other pierids (see p. 33). Larval foodplants are bush-cherry (*Maerua cafra*), leafless cadaba (*Cadaba aphylla*), wild caper-bush (*Capparis sepiaria*) and bastard shepherd's tree (*Boscia oleoides*).

Small Orange Tip
Klein-oranjepuntjie
(*Colotis evagore*) **fig. 23**

Identification: Small (35–40 mm); sexes similar; seasonally variable. Male upperside white, heavily marked with black; deep orange forewing tip. Lower, inner part of orange tip characteristically has a small spot of black scales. Female similar but more heavily marked with black and with less extensive orange in forewing tip. Dry season form has black scaling much reduced in both sexes.

Distinguishing characters and similar species: Superficially similar to other small Orange Tips, such as the Smoky Orange Tip (fig. 22).

Habitat and distribution: The Small Orange Tip is a common savanna species occurring from the George district in the southern Cape Province to the eastern Cape Province, Transkei, Natal, Swaziland, Transvaal, Mozambique, Zimbabwe, Botswana and Namibia.

Behaviour: A slow, weak flier, keeping close to the ground (usually under half a metre). It has a random, wandering flight and often feeds from flowers.

Flight period: All year.

Early stages: As for other pierids (see p. 33). Breeds on wild caper-bush (*Capparis sepiaria*), leafless cadaba (*Cadaba aphylla*) and bush-cherry (*Maerua cafra*).

Banded Gold Tip
Goudpuntjie
(Colotis eris) **fig. 18**

Identification: Medium-sized (40–45 mm); sexes dissimilar; seasonally variable. Male upperside white with broad, black band across wings; forewing tip with elongate, gold spots, often with purplish sheen over tip in certain lights. Female has narrower black band and broad black forewing tip enclosing white spots. Also a rare female form with ground colour of upperside pale yellow. Dry season form has black wing markings slightly reduced.

Habitat and distribution: A common savanna species from the eastern Cape Province to Natal, Transvaal, Griqualand West, Mozambique, Zimbabwe, Botswana and Namibia.

Behaviour: A very rapid flier, keeping from one and a half to two metres above the ground. It flies at random but in a more or less straight line. The horizontal black band across the wings is fairly conspicuous in males when they are flying. Both sexes are strongly attracted to flowers. Males often fly over the top of koppies and ridges but do not establish territories on them.

Flight period: All year; September to April in colder areas.

Early stages: Similar to those of other pierids (see p. 33). Breeds on shepherd's tree (*Boscia albitrunca*) and bastard shepherd's tree (*Boscia oleoides*).

Lemon Traveller Tip
Suurlemoensmous
(Colotis subfasciatus) **fig. 34**

Identification: Medium-sized (45–50 mm); sexes dissimilar; seasonally variable. Male upperside bright lemon yellow with black forewing tip containing elongate, yellow markings. Female yellow with brown forewing tip containing orange patch. Characteristic straight line and fine brown irroration on hindwing underside. Dry season form has black markings somewhat reduced.

Habitat and distribution: Common in frost-free savanna in the northern parts of the subregion. Occurs from Swaziland to Transvaal, Zimbabwe, Botswana and Namibia. Occasionally observed in the western Orange Free State and Griqualand West.

Behaviour: An extremely rapid flier, from one and a half to two metres above the ground. Often flies in a more or less straight line, but at random. Both sexes are fond of flowers. Like males of the Queen Purple Tip and Banded Gold Tip, the male Lemon Traveller Tip often appears briefly on the summit of koppies.

Flight period: All year but scarcer in winter.

Early stages: As for other pierids (see p. 33). The larvae feed on shepherd's tree (*Boscia albitrunca*).

DOTTED BORDERS
SPIKKELRANDJIES
(Genus *Mylothris*)

The Dotted Borders comprise a single genus (*Mylothris*) with seven species in southern Africa, three of which are illustrated in this guide. They are medium-sized and predominantly patterned in white, yellow and orange. Characteristically they have a row of black dots along the outer margins of both the fore- and hindwing, hence their common name. The sexes are generally very similar, except for the Common Dotted Border, which is sexually dimorphic (figs 8 & 31). Dotted Borders occur mostly in forests and wooded savanna. They fly in a leisurely manner, floating among the branches and foliage of large trees, often many metres above the ground. Both sexes exhibit this behaviour, which is linked to the fact that the parasitic plants on which the larvae feed usually grow on the higher branches of large trees. Both sexes will often descend from the treetops to feed from flowers growing low down or will feed from those of certain trees. Female Dotted Borders lay their eggs in batches, usually on the leaves of various parasitic mistletoes (also known as lighted candles or "voëlent") belonging to the family Loranthaceae. The larvae are highly gregarious and remain in a group until just before pupation. The larvae have the typical cylindrical form characteristic of the pierid family but are densely covered with short, whitish hairs, especially in the later larval stages (fig. 303). The pupae have a number of surface projections (fig. 304), a feature that is not typical of the pierid family but is also found in two genera of Whites (*Belenois* and *Dixeia*). Dotted Borders are continuous-brooded but adults are commonest in summer and autumn.

Common Dotted Border
Gewone Spikkelrandjie
(Mylothris agathina) **figs 8 & 31**

Identification: Medium-sized (55–65 mm); sexes dissimilar. Male upperside white with clear black dots on wing margins. Underside forewing with orange base, white in middle and yellow on tip; hindwing underside yellow. Female yellow-orange on upper- and underside; base of forewing underside orange, as in male.

Distinguishing characters and similar species: Easily confused with the False Dotted Border White (figs 7 & 32), which is apparently a mimic of the Common Dotted Border. Can also be confused with females of the Large Vagrant, especially on the underside (fig. 2c). Compare also with the similar Twin Dotted Border (fig. 9).

Habitat and distribution: The Common Dotted Border is widespread and very common in wooded savanna in the eastern half of the subcontinent. During the 1980s the Common Dotted Border spread westwards from the Port Elizabeth district along the southern Cape coast, right into the Cape Peninsula, where it is now a breeding resident. Occurs from the Cape Peninsula to the southern Cape coast, eastern Cape Province, Transkei, Natal, Swaziland, Transvaal, Mozambique, Zimbabwe and Botswana.

Behaviour: Has a leisurely, floating flight, usually in and around tall trees. It is very conspicuous as it flaps slowly among the branches, many metres above the ground, in search of parasitic plants on which the female lays its eggs. Flowers attract both sexes strongly. Small, sporadic migrations are sometimes observed and this may partially explain the species' extension into the south-western Cape Province.

Flight period: All year in most areas.

Early stages: Typical of Dotted Borders (see above). The eggs are laid in clusters on the leaves of various parasitic mistletoes (Loranthaceae), such as *Erianthemum dregei*, *Tieghemia quinquenervia* and *Tapinanthus oleifolius*. The Transvaal sumach (*Osyris lanceolata*) and Cape sumach (*Colpoon compressum*) are also used as larval foodplants, particularly the latter in the southern and south-western Cape Province.

Twin Dotted Border
Oranjevlerk-spikkelrandjie
(Mylothris rueppellii) **fig. 9**

Identification: Medium-sized (55–60 mm); sexes similar. Male upperside white with black-dotted wing margins; base of forewing flushed with orange and hindwing with yellow. Underside white with strong orange basal flush on forewing underside. Female similar to male but orange flush on upper- and underside more extensive and fading to yellow and then yellowish-white towards outer margins of wings.

Distinguishing characters and similar species: The Twin Dotted border is superficially similar to the Common Dotted Border (figs 8 & 31). Two other, similar species, not illustrated, occur in southern Africa: 1) Yule's Dotted Border (*Mylothris yulei*) – smaller (50 mm) with a yellow flush at the base of the wings on the upperside. Restricted to forests on the eastern border of Zimbabwe and to parts of Mozambique; 2) Streaked Dotted Border (*M. rubricosta*) – a very small (40 mm) Dotted Border that is white, with the leading edge of the forewing rimmed with an orange-red stripe. Found only in papyrus swamps on certain islands in the Zambezi River, near the Victoria Falls, and in the Okavango swamps in Botswana.

Habitat and distribution: The Twin Dotted Border is widespread in the eastern wooded savanna of the subregion and in drier forests but is scarcer and more localised than the Common Dotted Border. It is found in the eastern Cape Province, Natal, Swaziland, Transvaal, Mozambique and Zimbabwe.

Behaviour: Similar to that of the Common Dotted Border (see above) but it prefers wooded kloofs, especially along the banks of streams and rivers.

Flight period: All year but commoner in summer.

Early stages: Typical of Dotted Borders (see p. 57). Known to breed on *Tapinanthus rubromarginatus* but almost certainly uses other members of the family Loranthaceae.

Trimen's Dotted Border
Trimen-spikkelrandjie
(Mylothris trimenia) **fig. 10**

Identification: Medium-sized (50–55 mm); sexes similar. Male upperside has forewing white and hindwing lemon yellow; black dots on outer wing margins. Underside similar. Female like male but with hindwing colour butter-yellow.

Distinguishing characters and similar species: The white forewing plus yellow hindwing pattern of Trimen's Dotted Border appears to be mimicked by several other unrelated members of the pierid family. These include some female forms of the Large Vagrant (fig. 2), a female form of the Cambridge Vagrant (fig. 3) and a female form of the Forest White (fig. 12). There are also two other Dotted Border species, not illustrated, in southern Africa which resemble Trimen's Dotted Border: 1) Lemon Dotted Border (*Mylothris sagala*) – smaller (45 mm) than Trimen's Dotted Border with slightly heavier black markings. Found only in forests in the Vumba Mountains in north-eastern Zimbabwe; 2) Carcasson's Dotted Border (*M. carcassoni*) – smaller (45 mm) with the whole of the upperside yellow. So far it has been found only in the Banti Forest Reserve in north-eastern Zimbabwe.

Habitat and distribution: Trimen's Dotted Border is a fairly common but strict inhabitant of temperate forests. It occurs in coastal and montane forests in the eastern Cape Province and Transkei and in montane (inland) forests in Natal and Transvaal, as far north as the Woodbush Forest Reserve in the Tzaneen district.

Behaviour: Usually flies high up, among the foliage of forest trees. Its flight pattern is similar to that of the Common Dotted Border but slightly more rapid. It flies at random and is quite often seen feeding from flowers.

Flight period: All year but commoner in summer.

Early stages: Typical of Dotted Borders (see p. 57). The larvae feed on *Tieghemia quinquenervia* and *Tapinanthus kraussianus*.

CLOUDED YELLOWS
LUSERNVLINDERS
(Genus *Colias*)

A single abundant, ubiquitous species occurs in southern Africa. The genus is well represented in the northern hemisphere and there are about 50 described species of Clouded Yellow in Europe and North America.

African Clouded Yellow
Lusernvlinder
(*Colias electo*) **figs 75 & 214**

Identification: Medium-sized (40–45 mm); sexes dissimilar. Male upperside bright orange with broad black outer margins on both fore- and hindwing. Underside greenish-yellow. Female has more extensive blackish scaling and pale green spots in black outer margin on forewing. Underside similar to that of male, but deeper green colour. Also a less common female form in which orange ground colour is replaced by greyish-white (form *aurivillius*).

Habitat and distribution: Widespread and abundant throughout the subcontinent, occurring in virtually every biome.

Behaviour: Has a medium-fast to fast, irregular flight, close to the ground (about half a metre). It flies at random and regularly feeds from flowers. Large numbers are often seen in and around fields of cultivated lucerne.

Flight period: All year.

Early stages: Typical of pierids (see p. 33). The eggs are laid singly on various species of legume, especially clovers (*Trifolium* species), lucerne (*Medicago sativa*) and vetches (*Vicia* species). The exotic locust-tree (*Robinia pseudoacacia*) is also used by the larvae. The larvae are green and cylindrical (typical of the pierid family) and sometimes a minor pest on cultivated lucerne and clovers.

MIGRANTS
MIGREERDERS
(Genus *Catopsilia*)

A single, very common, widespread species is found in the subregion.

African Migrant
Afrikaanse Migreerder
(Catopsilia florella) **figs 4 & 29**

Identification: Medium-sized (60–65 mm); female with three forms. Male upperside white with slight greenish tinge; small black dot in middle of forewing. Underside greenish-white with fine brown irrorations. Female very similar, with sparse brown scaling along leading edge of forewing and on upper, outer forewing margin. Also a deep yellow female form with brown markings on upperside wing margins and brown speckling on underside. A third, rare, female form is pale yellow on upperside.

Distinguishing characters and similar species: The African Migrant is easily confused with Buquet's Vagrant (*Nepheronia buquetii*), not illustrated. The latter is smaller and has a large brown spot in the middle of the hindwing underside and green eyes, whereas the African Migrant has greyish-brown eyes. Buquet's Vagrant is found in frost-free savanna from the eastern Cape coast northwards.

Habitat and distribution: The African Migrant is a very common and widespread species in southern Africa, occurring in all biomes except desert. It is rare or absent in the very arid portions of the Karoo.

Behaviour: Has a fast, direct flight from one to three metres or slightly more above the ground. In some years there are huge migrations in summer or autumn. These migrations appear to originate in the north-western Cape Province and Kalahari and the butterflies move in a north-easterly direction (see p. 9). During autumn migrations there are usually many yellow females among the white males and females. When not migrating the African Migrant flies at random, often feeding from flowers; the males also mud-puddle.

Flight period: All year but commoner in summer and autumn.

Early stages: Typical of pierids (see

p. 33). The eggs are laid singly on many indigenous and exotic species of the genus *Cassia*, such as *C. occidentalis*, *C. floribunda*, monkey pod (*C. petersiana*), wild senna (*C. italica*) and peanut cassia (*C. didymobotrya*). The peanut cassia was introduced to gardens in southern Africa from central Africa.

GRASS YELLOWS
GRASVELDGELETJIES
(Genus *Eurema*)

Five species of Grass Yellow, one of which is illustrated in this guide, occur in southern Africa. They are all small, yellow butterflies with black wing borders of varying width. They are difficult to distinguish from one another in the field. There are slight sexual and seasonal differences within the different species. The Broadbordered Grass Yellow (below) is a common inhabitant of the grassland biome whereas the other four species are found in forests and dense bush. Grass Yellows have a weak, fluttering flight and remain close to the ground. The males are fond of sucking at damp patches where they may congregate in small groups. Females lay their eggs singly on low-growing forbs, especially "Boesmanstee" (*Cassia mimosoides*). The early stages are typical of the pierid family (see p. 33). Grass Yellows are continuous-brooded but development of the early stages is slower in the colder months so that adults are most abundant in late summer and autumn (February to April).

Broadbordered Grass Yellow
Gewone Grasveldgeletjie
(Eurema brigitta) **fig. 38**

Identification: Small (35–40 mm); sexes similar; seasonally variable. Male upperside bright yellow with wide, even, black wing margins. Underside yellow, finely speckled with black scales. Dry season form with black on upperside wing margins narrower and underside orange-brown.

Distinguishing characters and similar species: Superficially similar to Spiller's Sulphur Small White (fig. 37), but flies much more slowly.

Four other species of Grass Yellow, not illustrated, occur in southern Africa: 1) Common Grass Yellow (*Eurema hecabe*) – the black border on the forewing margin is very uneven. Common in frost-free savanna from Transkei to Natal, Transvaal, Mozambique and Zimbabwe; 2) Angled Grass Yellow (*E. desjardinsii*) – similar to the Broadbordered Grass Yellow but the outer hindwing margin is distinctly angled, not smoothly curved. Common on the edges of forest and coastal bush in the eastern Cape Province, Transkei, Natal, Transvaal, Mozambique and Zimbabwe; 3) Pale Grass Yellow (*E. hapale*) – very pale yellow. Found in or near forests on the eastern border of Zimbabwe and in Mozambique; 4) Evenbordered Grass Yellow (*E. regularis*) – similar to the Angled Grass Yellow but with the black border on the hindwing with the inner margin even. Distribution as for the Pale Grass Yellow.

Habitat and distribution: The Broadbordered Grass Yellow is very common in both grassland and savanna but also occurs in other biomes. It is absent from the drier portions of the western Karoo and from the south-western Cape Province.

Behaviour: Has a weak, fluttering to zig-zagging flight pattern among grass. Both sexes frequently visit flowers and the males often congregate on mud-patches in small groups on hot, sunny days.

Flight period: All year.

Early stages: Typical of pierids (see p. 33). The eggs are laid singly on the low-growing forbs "Boesmanstee" (*Cassia mimosoides*) and St John's wort (*Hypericum aethiopicum*).

THE NYMPHALIDS
(Family Nymphalidae)

A large and very diverse family of butterflies with some 1 300 species in Africa, of which only about 250 are found in southern Africa. Six subfamilies are considered in this guide: nymphalines (below), charaxines (p. 98), acraeines (p. 112), satyrines (p. 128), danaines (p. 148) and libytheines (p. 153). In a number of works some of these subfamilies are accorded full family status, for example in *Pennington's Butterflies of Southern Africa* (see bibliography). Despite their diversity all nymphalids have rudimentary forelegs. They therefore walk on four legs which accounts for a strutting type of locomotion, typified by charaxines. Nymphalids are medium-sized to large insects and often brightly coloured. They occur mainly in forest and savanna habitats but some are purely grassland insects. The early stages are varied and considered under the subfamily headings.

The nymphalines
(Subfamily Nymphalinae)

Nymphalines are poorly represented in southern Africa, only 71 of the 560 African species being found in the subregion. Nevertheless many of the species are conspicuous, common and widespread. The subfamily itself is diverse and members of seven tribes are illustrated in this guide. It is particularly with respect to the early stages that these tribes differ. The typical egg, larva and pupa of five of the tribes have been illustrated in the colour plates as follows: tribe Argynnini (figs 305–307), tribe Nymphalini (figs 308–310), tribe Byblini (figs 311–313), tribe Neptini (figs 314–316) and tribe Limenitidini (figs 317–319).

LEOPARDS
LUIPERDS
(Genera *Phalanta* and *Lachnoptera*)

Three species of this small group, which belongs to the tribe Argynnini, are found in the subregion, two of which are dealt with below. Leopards are medium-sized and predominantly orange in colour. There is little variation within species, either sexually or seasonally. The African Leopard (below) is widespread but the other two species are strictly forest butterflies. They are active and very restless insects and strongly attracted to flowers. The early stages are typical of the tribe Argynnini (see under nymphalines, above).

African Leopard
Afrikaanse Luiperd
(Phalanta phalantha) **fig. 58**

Identification: Medium-sized (50–55 mm); sexes similar. Male upperside bright orange with scalloped black markings on wing margins and black dots and bars on rest of wing surfaces. Underside pale orange-brown with fine, wavy, brown markings. Female slightly larger.

Distinguishing characters and similar species: Easily mistaken for the much scarcer Forest Leopard (*Phalanta eurytis*), not illustrated, which is very similar but has bolder markings on the underside. The Forest Leopard occurs in coastal and subtropical forests on the Natal coast, in the eastern Transvaal lowveld and in Zimbabwe. The African Leopard may also be confused with the Blotched Leopard (below), the male of which has a greyish patch on the leading edge of the hindwing upperside. In the Blotched Leopard there is also a row of white markings on the hindwing underside. This is absent in the African Leopard.

Habitat and distribution: The African Leopard is common and widespread in most of the eastern and northern portion of the subcontinent. It is absent from the Karoo and south-western Cape Province.

Behaviour: A fast and restless flier, but it often pauses to feed at flowers, when the wings are moved rhythmically up and down. It spends very little time at a particular flower before moving to another one. It flies from one to five metres above the ground, at random. Males occasionally mud-puddle.

Flight period: Summer; also seen in winter in frost-free areas.

Early stages: Typical of the tribe Argynnini (see under nymphalines, p. 65). A number of larval food-plants have been recorded, including dune sour-berry (*Dovyalis rotundifolia*), oval Kei-apple (*Dovyalis zeyheri*), wild mulberry (*Trimeria grandifolia*), spike thorns (*Maytenus* species), willows (*Salix* species) and the alien white poplar (*Populus alba*).

Blotched Leopard
Vaalkol-luiperd
(Lachnoptera ayresii) **fig. 59**

Identification: Medium-sized (50–55 mm); sexes similar. Male upperside bright orange with fine black scalloping of wing margins and a few scattered black spots on rest of wing; patch of grey scales at leading edge of hindwing. Underside flat orange-brown with black patches on trailing margin of forewing and a row of white markings on hindwing. Female similar; upperside dull orange-brown with black dot on leading edge of hindwing, where male has grey patch.

Distinguishing characters and similar species: Easily mistaken for the African Leopard (see above for comparison).

Habitat and distribution: The Blotched Leopard is a common inhabitant of temperate forests from the Port St Johns district in Transkei through the Natal midlands to eastern Transvaal, Mozambique and the eastern border of Zimbabwe.

Behaviour: An active, fast flier, two to 10 metres above the ground. Spends much of its time flying around tall trees on the edges of forest and is then very conspicuous. Large numbers of specimens are sometimes seen feeding together from the flowers of forest trees. The males are territorial, establishing perches on the outer leaves of trees. The females fly more slowly and tend to keep to the semi-shade of the forest.

Flight period: Mainly in summer; occasional specimens in winter.

Early stages: Typical of the tribe Argynnini (see under nymphalines, p. 65). The only known larval food-plant is the forest peach tree (*Rawsonia lucida*).

ADMIRALS
BOSNOOIENTJIES
(Genus *Antanartia*)

Medium-sized, dark brown butterflies with orange markings, and tails on the hindwing. Admirals are found in forests, where they breed on plants belonging to the nettle family (Urticaceae). The flight is rapid but they settle often. The males are territorial and both sexes are frequently seen on flowers. The early stages are typical of the tribe Nymphalini (see under nymphalines, p. 65).

Longtailed Admiral
Langstert-bosnooientjie
(*Antanartia schaeneia*) fig. 248

Identification: Medium-sized (45–50 mm); sexes very similar. Male upperside ground colour dark brown; forewing has large black tip with semicircle of small, white spots, and transverse orange band; hindwing has three distinct tails, upper one much longer; distinct orange marginal band above tails. Underside variegated, complex pattern of browns; pale orange transverse band in forewing corresponding to that on upperside.

Distinguishing characters and similar species: Two other Admirals, not illustrated, occur in the subregion: 1) Northern Short-tailed Admiral (*Antanartia dimorphica*); 2) Southern Short-tailed Admiral (*A. hippomene*). Both are smaller than the Longtailed Admiral and have very short tails on the hindwing. The first species is found in temperate forests from the Pilgrim's Rest district of eastern Transvaal to the eastern border of Zimbabwe while the Southern Short-tailed Admiral occurs in temperate forests from Pilgrim's Rest as far south as the Knysna district in the southern Cape Province.

Habitat and distribution: The Longtailed Admiral is a relatively uncommon insect of temperate forests from the eastern Cape Province to Natal, Transvaal and the eastern border of Zimbabwe. It is often found together with the Short-tailed Admirals (see previous paragraph).

Behaviour: Flies very rapidly but settles often, especially on flowers, in the semi-shade of forest undergrowth. The males usually establish territories along the sides of forest roads and are shy and wary. The males occasionally mud-puddle. It seldom flies more than two metres above the ground.

Flight period: All year but most numerous from February to May.

Early stages: Typical of the tribe Nymphalini (see under nymphalines, p. 65). The larvae feed on various members of the nettle family, including *Laportea peduncularis* and *Pouzolzia parasitica*.

PAINTED LADY
SONDAGSROKKIE
(Genus *Vanessa*)

The Painted Lady is the only representative of this predominantly northern hemisphere genus in southern Africa. It has a virtually worldwide distribution, being absent only from South America and Australasia. The staggering variety of larval foodplants, the tendency of the adults to migrate and their ability to tolerate low temperatures explain its almost cosmopolitan distribution.

Painted Lady
Sondagsrokkie
(Vanessa cardui) **fig. 55**

Identification: Medium-sized (45–50 mm); sexes similar. Male upperside orange with extensive black and brown markings; tip of forewing dark brown with variably sized white spots. Underside forewing similar to upperside but tip light brown, not dark brown; hindwing underside variegated in shades of brown; several submarginal eyespots. Female virtually indistinguishable in flight, but larger.

Habitat and distribution: Abundant and widespread in the whole subcontinent, including the Karoo, south-western Cape Province and Namaqualand. Absent only from sandy deserts and dense forests.

Behaviour: Has a rapid to very rapid flight, usually about one metre above the ground. Males often establish territories on bare patches of ground where they perch with outspread wings, sunning themselves. Both sexes are very fond of flowers. Migrations are occasionally recorded in the Cape Province and Natal. This species is capable of withstanding low temperatures and it may be one of the few butterflies about on cold winter days. Males are often seen flying around bare patches of ground in the rays of the setting sun.

Flight period: All year.

Early stages: As for other members of the tribe Nymphalini (see under nymphalines, p. 65) except that the larvae spin curious silken tents among the foliage on which they are feeding, and live in these. This is a common phenomenon in moth caterpillars but is rare in butterflies in southern Africa. The Painted Lady breeds on an amazing variety of plants belonging to various families, including the daisy family (Asteraceae), nettle family (Urticaceae), legume family (Fabaceae), Boraginaceae and the mallow family (Malvaceae). Particular genera and species used as foodplants include thistles (*Carduus* species), "botterblomme" (*Arctotis* species), *Gnaphalium* species, *Berkheya* species, *Gazania* species and "kiesieblaar" (*Malva parviflora*).

COMMODORES
BLAARVLERKE
(Genus *Precis*)

Seven species of Commodore occur in the subcontinent, four of which are illustrated in this guide. Commodores are medium-sized butterflies that show distinct seasonal dimorphism. This is so marked in the Gaudy Commodore that the wet and dry season forms were, at one time, thought to be different species! (Compare fig. 56 with fig. 157.) The dry season forms tend to have an underside that resembles a dead leaf (fig. 245b). Because the larval foodplants often frost in winter the dry season forms hibernate communally during winter and only lay their eggs on the new foliage that appears in the following spring. To the best of our knowledge Commodores are the only butterflies that hibernate as adults in southern Africa. Together with some related groups, such as the Pansies, they have a characteristic flight pattern. The wings are beaten a few times and then maintained in a horizontal position for a time, allowing the butterfly to glide forward. This can best be described as a flap-flap-glide motion. The early stages are typical of the tribe Nymphalini (see under nymphalines, p. 65).

Garden Commodore
Rots-blaarvlerk
(Precis archesia) **fig. 247**

Identification: Medium-sized (50–60 mm); sexes similar; distinct seasonal forms. Male wet season form upperside dark brown with broad orange bands submarginally on both wings; row of small black dots within bands. Underside like upperside but bands much paler. Female larger. Dry season form dark brown with deep reddish-brown bands; upper forewing has pinky-blue band with row of pinkish-white submarginal spots. Underside shaded in brown, resembling a dried leaf.

Distinguishing characters and similar species: The wet season form of the Garden Commodore is superficially similar to some other Commodores, especially the Dry-leaf Commodore (below), and to the Soldier Pansy (fig. 246). It also resembles the wet season form of the Air Commodore (*Precis actia*), not illustrated. The Air Commodore occurs in wooded savanna in Zimbabwe and Mozambique and has a pale mauve colour on the inner aspects of the orange bands. The dry season form of the Air Commodore has more extensive pinky-blue scaling on the upperside of the wings and hooked forewing tips. There is a blunt tail on each hindwing.

Habitat and distribution: The Garden Commodore is common and widespread in the eastern half of the subcontinent in most types of habitat but has a decided preference for rock-strewn, grassy areas. It is found from the Knysna district eastwards and northwards.

Behaviour: Has the typical flap-flap-glide flight of the Commodores, usually one to two metres above the ground, and is not particularly fast on the wing. As its common name implies it is often found in suburban gardens. Males, especially those of the wet season form, are avid hilltoppers, establishing territories that they vigorously defend against intruders. Within their territories they normally perch on rocks or on the ground. The dry season form hibernates during cold spells in winter, usually in small assemblages under overhanging rocks. It may even enter dark outbuildings or houses for this purpose, roosting in the top corner of a room, sometimes for many weeks if not disturbed.

Flight period: All year; wet season form from October to March and dry season form from March to September. Both forms are sometimes found flying at the same time.

Early stages: As for other members

of the tribe Nymphalini (see under nymphalines, p. 65). The larvae feed on a number of *Plectranthus* species.

Dry-leaf Commodore
Tugela-blaarvlerk
(Precis tugela) fig. 245

Identification: Medium-sized (55–60 mm); sexes similar; seasonally variable but not markedly so. Male upperside blackish-brown with broad, deep-orange submarginal bands, containing a row of small black dots; single white spot in tip of forewing; short, blunt tail on hindwing. Underside remarkably variable but always resembling a dead leaf. Female larger with broader, paler orange bands. Dry season form differs chiefly in markedly hooked forewing apex.

Distinguishing characters and similar species: The Dry-leaf Commodore is similar to the wet season form of the Garden Commodore (above) but the latter has no tails and does not resemble a dead leaf on the underside. Compare also with the Soldier Pansy (fig. 246), which occurs in the same habitat as the Dry-leaf Commodore (see the Soldier Pansy for the differences, p. 77).

Habitat and distribution: The Dry-leaf Commodore is fairly plentiful in temperate montane forests, from the Natal midlands to the Transvaal Drakensberg escarpment and the eastern border forests of Zimbabwe.

Behaviour: Has a slowish to medium-fast flight which is deliberate, but usually at random. It keeps to the semi-shade of the undergrowth and edges of forests, near the ground. The dry season form often roosts or hibernates communally, in groups of up to 60 individuals, in cold weather. When roosting in this manner on a dead shrub they cover it with "dead leaves". At other times they prefer dark holes in embankments in which to hibernate. They are not often seen feeding at flowers.

Flight period: All year but most plentiful from May to July (dry season form) and again from December to March (wet season form).

Early stages: As for other members of the tribe Nymphalini (see under nymphalines, p. 65). Breeds on several *Plectranthus* species.

Marsh Commodore
Moeras-blaarvlerk
(Precis ceryne) **fig. 249**

Identification: Medium-sized (45 mm); sexes similar; moderately different seasonal forms. Male upperside brown with broad orange bands (forked near forewing tip); inner part of orange band paler; row of black dots down middle of orange band; some orange markings in basal area of forewing. Underside orange-brown with scalloped, thin black line bisecting each wing lengthwise. Female larger. Dry season form resembling dead leaf on underside but otherwise similar to wet season form.

Distinguishing characters and similar species: Two other Commodores, not illustrated, that occur in southern Africa and somewhat resemble the Marsh Commodore are: 1) Darker Commodore (*Precis antilope*) – essentially orange (i.e. the orange bands are maximally expanded) with darker markings on the rest of the wings. Common in wooded savanna in Zimbabwe and Mozambique. More rarely seen in parts of Swaziland, Transvaal, northern Botswana and northern Namibia; 2) Paler Commodore (*P. cuama*) – very similar to the Darker Commodore and occurs in the wooded savanna of Zimbabwe and Mozambique.

Habitat and distribution: The Marsh Commodore is locally common in swampy areas and along the edges of streams in grassland habitats, from the Transkei hinterland to the Natal midlands, Transvaal middleveld (Magaliesberg and Waterberg ranges) and in suitable localities in Mozambique and Zimbabwe.

Behaviour: A relatively slow-flying but active and alert insect that seldom strays from its marshy habitat. It settles frequently and both sexes are fond of flowers. Flies at random, one to two metres above the ground.

Flight period: All year but scarce in winter and spring.

Early stages: Typical of the tribe Nymphalini (see under nymphalines, p. 65). Breeds on *Pycnostachys reticulata*, a moisture-loving shrub belonging to the salvia family (Lamiaceae).

Gaudy Commodore
Rooi-en-blou-blaarvlerk
(Precis octavia) **figs 56 & 157**

Identification: Medium-sized (50–60 mm); sexes similar; very different seasonal forms. Male wet season form upperside bright orange-red with black wing margins, submarginal dots and basal areas. Underside similarly marked, but paler. Female larger. Dry season form male upperside deep violaceous-blue with a row of bright red, block-shaped markings submarginally in both wings. Underside charcoal-black to bronzy-black. Female dry season form very similar but larger.

Habitat and distribution: A common species in the escarpment grasslands, from the eastern Cape Province to Natal, Swaziland, Transvaal, Mozambique, Zimbabwe and northern Botswana.

Behaviour: The wet season form males are avid and conspicuous hilltoppers and show both territorial and perching behaviour. They have a medium-fast flight with a typical flap-flap-glide motion, one to two metres above the ground. The dry season form flies at random and, although it sometimes hilltops, is more usually seen at lower elevations, often in close proximity to forests. On warm days from March to September it may be observed flying about but during cold spells individuals tend to congregate in dark places, such as holes in embankments and under overhanging rocks. Here they hibernate, remaining motionless for weeks on end. The Gaudy Commodore may visit gardens in which its larval foodplant is growing but is not often seen feeding from flowers.

Flight period: All year; wet season form from October to March and dry season form from March to September.

Early stages: As for other members of the tribe Nymphalini (see under nymphalines, p. 65). The larvae feed on a number of members of the salvia family (Lamiaceae) including *Plectranthus esculentus*, "vlieëbos" (*Plectranthus fruticosus*), *Rabdosiella calycina*, *Pycnostachys reticulata* and *Pycnostachys urticifolia*.

PANSIES
GESIGGIES
(Genus *Junonia*)

The Pansies are represented in the subregion by seven species. They are closely related to the Commodores (see p. 70) but do not hibernate in winter, show only moderate seasonal dimorphism and possess more or less well developed eye-spots on the wings. Additionally, most Pansies breed on plants belonging to the family Acanthaceae whereas Commodores appear to use only plants of the salvia family (Lamiaceae). Like the Commodores the Pansies typically have a flap-flap-glide type of flight. Male Pansies are territorial but only the Blue Pansy consistently hilltops. The early stages are like those of other members of the tribe Nymphalini (see under nymphalines, p. 65).

Yellow Pansy
Geelgesiggie
(*Junonia hierta*) fig. 237

Identification: Medium-sized (45–50 mm); sexes slightly dissimilar. Male upperside black with large yellow patches, rimmed with orange, on fore- and hindwing; prominent metallic blue spot on hindwing. Underside greyish-brown with large orange area on forewing. Female with less extensive orange markings; blue hindwing spot smaller and dull purple-blue.

Habitat and distribution: A very common and familiar species in both savanna and grassland habitats. Widespread in southern Africa but absent from most of the Karoo and the western Cape Province.

Behaviour: A medium-fast, active insect, usually flying fairly close to the ground (less than a metre). It has a flap-flap-glide flight, like that of members of the closely related Commodores. Males often establish territories on flat, bare ground (more rarely on hilltops) and perch on the ground with open wings. When disturbed while perched the butterfly immediately closes its wings and the cryptic underside coloration then makes it much less conspicuous. Specimens of the Yellow Pansy are often observed in gardens. Both sexes are fond of flowers. Males mud-puddle and are also strongly attracted to fresh herbivore dung. I once saw numbers of Yellow Pansies, together with Spotted Jokers (fig. 60) and Citrus Swallowtails (fig. 223), feeding from piles of fresh elephant dung in the Kruger National Park.

Flight period: All year in warmer areas; August to May in cooler parts.

Early stages: Typical of the tribe Nymphalini (see under nymphalines, p. 65). Numerous plants, all of which are forbs, are used by the larvae, including *Adhatoda densiflora, Asystasia gangetica, Barleria pungens, Chaetacanthus setiger* and *Ruellia cordata*.

Blue Pansy
Blougesiggie
(Junonia oenone) **fig. 266**

Identification: Medium-sized (45–50 mm); sexes somewhat dissimilar. Male upperside black with white markings on forewing and on edges of hindwing; characteristic large, metallic blue spot on hindwing. Underside brown with white markings of forewing upperside repeated on underside. Female with blue spot on hindwing smaller and dull purple.

Habitat and distribution: A common butterfly in savanna and grassland biomes and on the edges of forest. Widespread in the subcontinent, from the eastern parts of the eastern Cape Province eastwards and northwards. The Blue Pansy is absent from the drier portions of the Karoo and from the western Cape Province.

Behaviour: Very similar to the Yellow Pansy (above), but males are much more likely to be seen on the tops of koppies during the warmer hours of the day. When hilltopping the male is highly territorial, perches on a rock or on the ground, and chases any intruder entering its domain. The female tends to fly at random.

Flight period: All year; September to May in colder areas.

Early stages: Typical of the tribe Nymphalini (see under nymphalines, p. 65). The larvae feed on *Asystasia gangetica* and *Adhatoda densiflora*.

Eyed Pansy
Padwagtertjie
(Junonia orithya) **fig. 267**

Identification: Small to medium-sized (35–45 mm); sexes somewhat dissimilar. Male upperside black with extensive royal blue markings on hindwing; submarginal eye-spots, ringed in pinkish-red; some white markings in forewing apex. Underside light brown with orange and cream bands at base of forewing. Female larger with paler, less extensive greyish-blue coloration; large, submarginal eye-spots on both wings.

Habitat and distribution: Fairly common in savanna and grassland habitats from the Natal midlands northwards through Transvaal, the north-western Orange Free State, Mozambique, Zimbabwe, Botswana and Namibia.

Behaviour: The habits of the Eyed Pansy are similar to those of the Yellow Pansy (see p. 75) but the Eyed Pansy does not hilltop and rarely mud-puddles. Males often establish territories on flat, open ground and perch on bare patches on the ground or on low vegetation. The female flies at random, usually in search of plants on which to lay its eggs.

Flight period: Mainly summer but all year in warm areas.

Early stages: Typical of the tribe Nymphalini (see under nymphalines, p. 65). The larvae feed on wild penstemon (*Graderia subintegra*), ink flower (*Cycnium adonense*), *Hygrophila* species and *Plectranthus* species.

Soldier Pansy
Bosgesiggie
(Junonia terea) **fig. 246**

Identification: Medium-sized (45–55 mm); sexes alike. Male upperside brown with transverse orange bands on wings; row of reddish eye-spots along outer margin of orange band on hindwing. Underside has dead-leaf appearance. Female slightly larger.

Distinguishing characters and similar species: The Soldier Pansy may be confused with the wet season form of the Garden Commodore (fig. 247a) and especially with the Dry-leaf Commodore (fig. 245). The latter has a longer tail on the hindwing and the bands on the wings are a deeper orange colour. There is also a row of small, black dots within the orange bands.

Habitat and distribution: The Soldier Pansy is a common species occurring in both coastal and montane forests. It is found from the Port St Johns area in Transkei to Natal, Swaziland, the eastern Transvaal lowveld, Mozambique and Zimbabwe.

Behaviour: Flies fairly slowly, up to two metres above the ground, in the dappled sunshine of forest undergrowth. It perches frequently, often with open wings, on low vegetation or on the ground. Both sexes are often seen feeding from flowers. It flies at random but males may establish loosely defended territories in small, sunlit clearings. When disturbed it seldom flies far before perching again. Males occasionally mud-puddle.

Flight period: All year but much commoner in summer and autumn.

Early stages: Typical of the tribe Nymphalini (see under nymphalines, p. 65). The larval foodplants are low-growing forbs and include *Asystasia gangetica*, *Phaulopsis imbricata* and *Ruellia patula*.

Brown Pansy
Bruingesiggie
(*Junonia natalica*) **fig. 94**

Identification: Medium-sized (45–55 mm); sexes similar. Male upperside dark brown with two reddish-brown bars near base of forewing; row of submarginal reddish-brown eye-spots down both wings; several white spots on forewing. Underside brown, resembling dead leaf. Female larger, otherwise very similar.

Habitat and distribution: A fairly common inhabitant of warmer forests and thick bush, especially on the east coast, from about Port St Johns in Transkei north-eastwards to Natal, the lowveld of Swaziland and Transvaal, Mozambique, Zimbabwe and northern Botswana.

Behaviour: The Brown Pansy has a fairly leisurely flight if not disturbed and keeps from one to two metres above the ground. It prefers to frequent the edges of forest and thick bush and settles often, on low vegetation or on the ground. Both sexes are fond of flowers.

Flight period: All year.

Early stages: Typical of the tribe

Nymphalini (see under nymphalines, p. 65). The larval foodplants are the same as those recorded for the Soldier Pansy (above). In addition the larvae also feed on *Ruellia cordata*.

PIRATE SEEROWER
(Genus *Catacroptera*)

The single species in this group is related to the Commodores and Pansies (above). The early stages are typical of the tribe Nymphalini (see under nymphalines, p. 65). The larvae feed on the same family of plants used by the Pansies – the Acanthaceae.

Pirate
Seerower
(Catacroptera cloanthe) **fig. 57**

Identification: Medium-sized (50–60 mm); sexes very similar; slightly different seasonal forms. Male upperside orange with black-ringed, blue spots submarginally, especially on hindwing; black bars and other markings, particularly on forewing; in certain lights upperside has purplish sheen. Underside of wet season form orange-brown with fine black irrorations; underside of dry season form rust-brown.

Habitat and distribution: A common grassland species, also found in grassy savanna. It is often seen near marshy areas. Found from the Mossel Bay district northeastwards to the eastern Cape Province, Transkei, Natal, Swaziland, Transvaal, Mozambique and Zimbabwe.

Behaviour: The Pirate has a medium-fast, flap-flap-glide flight, much like that of the Commodores and Pansies. It normally flies about a metre above the ground. Males establish territories, which they defend, in open grassland. Both sexes may also fly at random. They are seldom seen feeding from flowers and settle on low vegetation or on bare ground. They may perch with the wings open or closed. When the wings are closed the butterfly is well camouflaged. Usually specimens are encountered singly in the veld.

Flight period: All year but much commoner from September to April.

Early stages: Typical of the tribe Nymphalini (see under nymphalines, p. 65). They breed on *Justicia protracta* and *Ruellia cordata*.

MOTHER-OF-PEARLS
PERLEMOENSKOENLAPPERS
(Genera *Protogoniomorpha* and *Salamis*)

These are large butterflies, three species of which occur in the subregion. Mother-of-pearls are found in the warmer forests and in thick bush and are therefore distributed on the eastern side of the subcontinent. They show slight sexual and moderate seasonal variation. Although continuous-brooded, the adults are commonest in autumn. The larvae feed on forbs belonging to the family Acanthaceae and the early stages are typical of the tribe Nymphalini (see under nymphalines, p. 65).

Common Mother-of-pearl
Gewone Perlemoenskoenlapper
(Protogoniomorpha parhassus) **fig. 1**

Identification: Large (75–95 mm); sexes similar; seasonal forms slightly different. Male upperside pale greenish-white with violet sheen (wet season form) or pearly-white (dry season form); forewing with hooked, black-tipped apex; a few black-ringed, red eye-spots and black spots on fore- and hindwing. Underside greenish-white.

Distinguishing characters and similar species: The Common Mother-of-Pearl may be confused with 1) the much scarcer Clouded Mother-of-pearl (*Protogoniomorpha anacardii*), not illustrated, which is smaller and has heavier black markings, especially at the tip of the forewing. The Clouded Mother-of-pearl occurs in frost-free, wooded savanna in northern Natal, Swaziland, the eastern Transvaal lowveld, Mozambique, Zimbabwe and Botswana (Okavango swamps). 2) The exquisite Lilac Mother-of-pearl (*Salamis cacta*), not illustrated, flies in forests on the eastern border of Zimbabwe. It is brown on the upperside with a strong, violet-purple sheen, black forewing tip and wing margins, and a brown underside resembling a dead leaf.

Habitat and distribution: The Common Mother-of-pearl is a conspicuous and frequently encountered forest butterfly found in coastal and montane forests, as well as in thick bush. It is distributed from Transkei through Natal, Swaziland, eastern Transvaal, Mozambique and Zimbabwe.

Behaviour: Has a ponderous, flapping flight which can be quite fast, from close to the ground to many metres above it. Males may perch 10 or more metres up, on the leaves of forest trees. Often they are seen in and about the understorey. The females usually keep near ground level, in proximity to their low-growing larval foodplants. The species has the habit of sometimes settling on the underside of large leaves and also roosts under leaves at night. The males sometimes mud-puddle.

Flight period: All year but particularly common in autumn.

Early stages: Typical of the tribe Nymphalini (see under nymphalines, p. 65). The larvae feed on buckweed (*Isoglossa woodii*) and *Asystasia gangetica*.

DIADEMS
NA-APERS
(Genus *Hypolimnas*)

Three species, two of which are illustrated in this guide, are found in southern Africa. Diadems are large, showy insects and, excepting the male Common Diadem, are superb mimics of various species of unpalatable danaines (p. 148). The Common Diadem is a widespread species, while the other two are strict inhabitants of forests. Diadems are capable of powerful flight but often the flight is lazy and slow, much like that of their danaine models. The adults are commonest in summer and autumn. Diadems breed on forbs belonging to several plant families and the early stages are typical of the tribe Nymphalini (see under nymphalines, p. 65).

Common Diadem
Gewone Na-aper
(Hypolimnas misippus) **figs 45 & 200**

Identification: Large (70–85 mm); sexes very different; female with different forms. Male upperside black with two white spots in forewing and single, large white spot in middle of hindwing; white spots rimmed with iridescent purplish-blue overlying black ground colour. Underside pinkish-brown, shading to brown and black on forewing; variably sized whitish markings; wing margin with scalloped white and black markings, especially on hindwing. Usual female form orange-brown with broad, white-spotted black tip on forewing and black hindwing margin; single black spot on leading edge of hindwing. Underside patterned as in male but with ground colour orange-brown. There are other female forms, the two most common ones being: 1) with white patch on hindwing upperside; 2) with black and white of forewing tip replaced by orange-brown ground colour.

Distinguishing characters and similar species: The male Common Diadem is distinctive. The female is a remarkable mimic of the unpalatable African Monarch (fig. 46), but has a single black spot on the hindwing upperside whereas the African Monarch has either three (female) or four (male) spots.

Habitat and distribution: The Common Diadem is a common to very common butterfly, widespread in most of the subcontinent but rare or absent in much of the Karoo and western Cape Province.

Behaviour: An alert, active and medium-fast insect which usually keeps fairly close to the ground (under a metre). Both sexes are fond of flowers and are frequently seen in gardens. The males hilltop but may also select territories on the flats. They show a perching behaviour in these territories, resting on the ground, on low vegetation or on rocks. The females fly at random.

Flight period: Summer; particularly common in late summer and autumn (February to May).

Early stages: Typical of the tribe Nymphalini (see under nymphalines, p. 65). They breed on purslane (*Portulaca oleracea*), *Portulaca foliosa*, *Asystasia gangetica* and *Talinum* species.

Variable Diadem
Verneukertjie
(Hypolimnas anthedon) **figs 195 & 227**

Identification: Large (75–90 mm); sexes very similar but with two strikingly different forms. Upperside of form *wahlbergi* black and white; white in two large patches on forewing and covers most of hindwing. Underside corresponds to upperside but white of hindwing is more extensive. Form *mima* is black with small white spots and streaks on both wings; large, golden-yellow patch in basal half of hindwing. Underside similar but ground colour in forewing tip and on hindwing is brown, not black.

Distinguishing characters and similar species: The Variable Diadem is an extraordinary double mimic. Form *wahlbergi* is a mimic of the unpalatable Common Friar (fig. 193), while form *mima* has the unpalatable Chief (fig. 228) and Layman Friars as models. There is another Diadem in southern Africa, the Deceptive Diadem (*Hypolimnas deceptor*), not illustrated. It is similar to form *wahlbergi* of the Variable Diadem. The Deceptive Diadem is very rare on the east coast from East London to Natal but is common in some places along the Mozambique coast. It is also encountered rarely in the Vumba Mountains in northeastern Zimbabwe.

Habitat and distribution: The Variable Diadem is a common butterfly in forests and thick bush, where its models also fly. It is found from the eastern Cape Province (East London) to Natal, the eastern Transvaal escarpment, Mozambique and the eastern border of Zimbabwe.

Behaviour: Usually an active, medium-fast to fast flier that keeps low in the undergrowth or on the edges of forest. At times males perch high in trees, presumably defending aerial territories. Both sexes are alert and wary but sometimes fly around in a leisurely fashion, like their unpalatable models. On the Natal coast they have been observed roosting communally for the night in the lower branches of umdoni trees (*Syzygium cordatum*).

Flight period: Mainly summer but also in winter in warmer coastal forests and bush.

Early stages: Typical of the tribe Nymphalini (see under nymphalines, p. 65). The larvae are known to feed on a stinging nettle, *Laportea peduncularis*.

PIPERS
BOSVLIEËRS
(Genus *Eurytela*)

Both species of Piper occurring in the subcontinent are illustrated in this guide. They are found in heavily wooded, frost-free savanna and on forest margins. They have a gliding flight, one to three metres above the ground, and males patrol territories. Both sexes are attracted to fermenting fruit. Pipers breed on plants belonging to the family Euphorbiaceae. The early stages are typical of the tribe Byblini (see under nymphalines, p. 65).

Pied Piper
Witlint-bosvlieër
(*Eurytela hiarbas*) fig. 210

Identification: Medium-sized (50 mm); sexes similar. Male upperside black with white submarginal band in lower half of forewing and across hindwing. Underside delicately variegated in pinkish-brown, with white bands corresponding to those on upperside. Female has ground colour blackish-brown.

Habitat and distribution: Common on forest margins and in heavily wooded savanna in the eastern half of the subregion. Its distribution extends from the southern Cape Province (Wilderness district) north-eastwards to Natal, Transvaal, Mozambique and the eastern border of Zimbabwe.

Behaviour: Has a leisurely, gliding flight one to three metres above the ground. Males are territorial, select a bush or low tree on which to perch, and patrol to and fro in their territory. They settle frequently, usually with open wings, but are easily alarmed if approached too rapidly. Females fly at random. Both sexes suck the fluids exuding from fermenting fruit and from sucking-holes in trees.

Flight period: All year but scarcer in winter.

Early stages: Typical of the tribe Byblini (see under nymphalines, p. 65). The larvae use *Tragia durbanensis*, *Dalechampia capensis* and castor-oil bush (*Ricinus communis*) as food.

Golden Piper
Oranjelint-bosvlieër
(Eurytela dryope) **fig. 250**

Identification: Medium-sized (50–55 mm); sexes very similar. Male upperside dark brown with wide, yellow-orange bands in lower two-thirds of forewing margin and outer half of hindwing. Underside delicately variegated in shades of brown, giving overall orange-brown appearance.

Habitat and distribution: Fairly common but not as common as the Pied Piper (above), in forests and wooded, frost-free savanna on the eastern side of the subcontinent as far south as Port St Johns in Transkei. The Golden Piper tolerates drier bush than the Pied Piper and has even been found, albeit sparingly, in kloofs on the northern slopes of the Magaliesberg in Transvaal.

Behaviour: Virtually the same as for the Pied Piper (above).

Flight period: All year but scarcer in winter.

Early stages: Typical of the tribe Byblini (see under nymphalines, p. 65). Recorded larval foodplants include *Tragia durbanensis* and castor-oil bush (*Ricinus communis*).

JOKERS
GRASVEGTERS
(Genus *Byblia*)

The two species of Joker found in the subregion are both illustrated in this guide. They are medium-sized and show moderate sexual and seasonal dimorphism. Both Jokers are savanna species that fly fairly slowly, close to the ground. Both sexes are attracted to fermenting fruit. Jokers are closely related to Pipers (both belong to the tribe Byblini) and, like them, breed on Euphorbiaceae. The early stages are typical of the tribe Byblini (see under nymphalines, p. 65).

Spotted Joker
Lelie-grasvegter
(Byblia ilithyia) **fig. 60**

Identification: Medium-sized (45–50 mm); sexes differ slightly; distinct seasonal forms. Male upperside bright orange with scattered black markings; row of black dots down middle of hindwing; black marginal bands joined to thin submarginal black bands by thin black lines, forming reticulate pattern along wing borders. Underside orange-brown with black and cream markings; hindwing has three distinct, parallel cream bands (outer one spotted). Female similar but ground colour more orange-yellow and black markings greyish-black.

Distinguishing characters and similar species: The Spotted Joker is easily confused with the African Joker (below). The row of black spots down the middle of the hindwing upperside in the Spotted Joker is absent in the African Joker. The undersides of the wet season forms of the Spotted Joker and African Joker are distinctive. The dry season forms of both species have three cream bands on the hindwing underside. However, while only the outer band is broken into spots in the Spotted Joker, all three bands are comprised of discrete cream spots in the African Joker.

Habitat and distribution: The Spotted Joker is very common and widespread in the eastern half of southern Africa, occurring mainly in savanna. It penetrates adjacent grasslands sparingly. It is found as far south as the Port Elizabeth district in the eastern Cape Province.

Behaviour: Has a relatively unhurried flight, usually close to the ground (under half a metre). It frequents open, grassy areas or grassy patches between trees and is attracted to fermenting fruit and animal dung; it mud-puddles. Both sexes have a random, wandering flight pattern.

Flight period: All year in warmer areas but commoner in late summer. In colder areas they fly from October to April.

Early stages: Typical of the tribe Byblini (see under nymphalines, p. 65). The larvae feed on *Tragia durbanensis* and *Dalechampia capensis*.

African Joker
Tollie-grasvegter
(Byblia anvatara) **fig. 61**

Identification: Medium-sized (45–50 mm); sexes differ slightly; seasonally variable. Wet season form male upperside bright orange with scattered black markings; black submarginal bands joined to thin marginal black band by black lines, forming a reticulate pattern. Underside orange with black markings; heavily spotted with black at base of hindwing. Female wet season form paler (orange-yellow) with heavier black markings. Male and female dry season form upperside like wet season form but underside hindwing chocolate-brown with three transverse rows of cream spots.

Distinguishing characters and similar species: The African Joker is very similar to the Spotted Joker (above). The differences between the two species are given in the account of the Spotted Joker.

Habitat and distribution: The African Joker is fairly common in moist, frost-free savanna along the east coast from East London in the eastern Cape Province to Natal and thence to the lowveld of Swaziland, Transvaal, Mozambique, Zimbabwe and northern Botswana and Namibia.

Behaviour: As for the Spotted Joker (above).

Flight period: All year.

Early stages: Typical of the tribe Byblini (see under nymphalines, p. 65). The larval foodplants are the same as those used by the Spotted Joker: *Tragia durbanensis* and *Dalechampia capensis*.

TREE NYMPHS
BOOMBRUINTJIES
(Genus *Sallya*)

Six species of Tree Nymph occur in southern Africa. The two commonest species are illustrated in this guide. They are medium-sized and usually brown on the upperside but two species in the north of the subcontinent are violet-blue on the upperside and orange on the underside. Tree Nymphs are forest butterflies and breed on trees belonging to the family Euphorbiaceae. They have the peculiar habit, shared with the African Snout (fig. 102), of perching on the trunks and branches of trees. They are fond of feeding from fermenting fruit. The early stages are similar to those of the tribe Nymphalini (see under nymphalines, p. 65).

Boisduval's Tree Nymph
Boisduval-boombruintjie
(Sallya boisduvali) **fig. 101**

Identification: Small to medium-sized (40–45 mm); sexes similar. Male upperside uniform dark brown. Underside forewing orange-brown with a row of four black spots near tip; hindwing variegated, greyish-brown, with a row of ringed, submarginal black spots. Female like male but with a few orange markings on upper forewing of upperside.

Distinguishing characters and similar species: Boisduval's Tree Nymph may be confused with the Natal Tree Nymph (below) which is larger, more orange-brown and has only minute black spots on the forewing underside. In habits and, to a certain extent, also in coloration, the Tree Nymphs resemble the African Snout butterfly (fig. 102). Close inspection, though, reveals the long palps (located in front of the head) of the African Snout.

Habitat and distribution: Boisduval's Tree Nymph is common in coastal forests but also occurs, less commonly, in temperate forests. It is found in Transkei, Natal, the Transvaal lowveld, Mozambique and the eastern border regions of Zimbabwe.

Behaviour: Has a fluttering, elusive flight a few metres above the ground, usually keeping to the semi-shade of trees. It has the habit of alighting, head downwards, on the trunks and thicker branches of trees. The wings are usually closed but occasionally they are held open. It is an alert and rather wary insect, except when feeding from fermenting fruit or from sap oozing from a wound in a tree. Sometimes there are massive hatches of this butterfly, when it swarms in its habitat. Damp patches of ground in the shade in forests may be visited by males that suck up moisture and nutrients.

Flight period: All year but commoner in summer.

Early stages: Similar to those of the tribe Nymphalini (see under nymphalines, p. 65). Batches of eggs are laid on the leaves of the duiker-berry tree (*Sapium integerri-*

mum) and the gregarious larvae sometimes defoliate individual trees.

Natal Tree Nymph
Natal-boombruintjie
(Sallya natalensis) **fig. 100**

Identification: Medium-sized (45–50 mm); sexes similar. Male upperside orange-brown with darker brown markings towards tip of forewing. Underside forewing orange with grey on tip and dark brown smudge just below grey of tip; underside hindwing variegated, grey-brown. Female larger; colouring like that of male, but with scattered orange markings in upper half of forewing.

Distinguishing characters and similar species: The Natal Tree Nymph may be mistaken for the commoner Boisduval's Tree Nymph (above). See above for the differentiating features. Four other species of Tree Nymph, not illustrated, are found in southern Africa: 1) Trimen's Tree Nymph (*Sallya trimeni*) – very similar to the Natal Tree Nymph but it is yellowish-orange on the upperside. It occurs only in northern Namibia; 2) Morant's Tree Nymph (*S. morantii*) – looks like a large Boisduval's Tree Nymph on the upperside but is almost uniform dark brown on the underside. Rare in southern Africa; it occurs in forests in Natal, Transvaal, Mozambique and the eastern border of Zimbabwe; 3) Rose's Tree Nymph (*S. rosa*) and 4) Lilac Tree Nymph (*S. amulia*) – large, spectacular Tree Nymphs with violet uppersides and mainly orange undersides. Rare in southern Africa, occurring in certain forests in Mozambique and on the eastern border of Zimbabwe.

Habitat and distribution: The Natal Tree Nymph is common in coastal bush and forests from Transkei (Port St Johns) to Natal, the Transvaal lowveld, Mozambique and the eastern border of Zimbabwe.

Behaviour: As for Boisduval's Tree Nymph (above).

Flight period: Mainly summer but odd specimens may be seen in winter.

Early stages: Similar to those of the tribe Nymphalini (see under nymphalines, p. 65). The larvae feed on the leaves of the duikerberry tree (*Sapium integerrimum*) and, like those of Boisduval's Tree Nymph, the gregarious larvae may defoliate individual trees.

SAILERS
SWEWERS
(Genus *Neptis*)

Aside from the two species of Sailer illustrated in this guide there are nine species of Sailer in southern Africa. They are all confusingly similar and can only be separated by experts working with set, dead specimens. All Sailers have the same basic black and white pattern and range in size from the small (30–35 mm) Streaked Sailer (*Neptis goochi*), not illustrated, to the large (50–55 mm) Old Sailer (*Neptis alta*), not illustrated. Most species of Sailer are rare compared to the two common species dealt with below. Sailers are forest insects and have a floating flight with occasional flaps of the wings. The larvae feed on plants belonging to the families Euphorbiaceae and Fabaceae. The early stages are typical of the tribe Neptini (see under nymphalines, p. 65).

Spotted Sailer
Spikkelswewer
(*Neptis saclava*) **fig. 212**

Identification: Medium-sized (40–45 mm); sexes very similar. Male upperside dark brown with white markings on forewing and white band across hindwing. Underside light reddish-brown with white markings corresponding to, but more extensive than, those of upperside. Female larger, otherwise similar to male.

Habitat and distribution: A common species of forest and thick bush, from the Port Elizabeth district in the eastern Cape Province to Natal, Transvaal, Mozambique and Zimbabwe.

Behaviour: Has a characteristic floating flight, with occasional flaps of the wings, two to four metres above the ground, in the semi-shade of the undergrowth. Males are territorial and perch several metres above the ground, on vegetation, with open or partially open wings. Colonies of these butterflies are often found in kloofs and along the banks of streams and dry watercourses. They are occasionally found at sucking-trees and the males sometimes mud-puddle.

Flight period: Mainly summer but all year in warmer areas.

Early stages: Typical of the tribe Neptini (see under nymphalines, p. 65). The main larval foodplant appears to be a small understorey tree, the forest false-nettle (*Acalypha glabrata*), but the larvae also feed on several introduced Asian plants, including hiccup nut (*Combretum bracteosum*), Rangoon creeper (*Quisqualis indica*) and castor-oil bush (*Ricinus communis*).

Common Sailer
Reënwoudswewer
(Neptis laeta) **fig. 211**

Identification: Medium-sized (45–50 mm); sexes very similar. Male upperside blackish-brown with broad, white bars across fore- and hindwing. Underside brown with white markings corresponding to those of upperside but more extensive. Female larger.

Habitat and distribution: A common forest species, also found in thick bush, from Transkei northeastwards along the Natal coast to Swaziland, Transvaal, Mozambique, Zimbabwe and northern Botswana.

Behaviour: Has a slow, leisurely, floating flight with occasional flaps of the wings. Often flies around in circles in forest undergrowth or in clearings, usually remaining two to four metres above the ground. The males are territorial and select perches on vegetation a few metres from the ground, settling on these perches with open wings.

Flight period: All year but most abundant from February to May.

Early stages: Typical of the tribe Neptini (see under nymphalines, p. 65). The larvae feed on the leaves of the viciously spined thorny rope (*Dalbergia armata*) and the related climbing flat-bean (*Dalbergia obovata*). Also known to breed on false-nettles (*Acalypha* species).

FALSE ACRAEAS
VALSROOITJIES
(Genus *Pseudacraea*)

As the group common name implies these butterflies are nymphalines that mimic certain species of the unpalatable acraeines (see p. 112). Four species of False Acraea occur in the subregion, two of which are illustrated in this guide. They are medium-sized to large forest butterflies that often fly slowly, like their unpalatable models, but can fly very fast if alarmed. The territorial males select perches high up on trees. They breed on milkwoods (family Sapotaceae) and the early stages are typical of the tribe Limenitidini (see nymphalines, p. 65).

Boisduval's False Acraea
Boisduval-valsrooitjie
(*Pseudacraea boisduvalii*) **fig. 47**

Identification: Large (75–85 mm); sexes similar. Male upperside bright red with prominent black spotting at base of fore- and hindwing; tip of forewing black, followed by broad orange bar (also a form with transparent forewing tip); hindwing has black margin. Underside similar but ground colour less intense pinkish-red. Female larger with rounder wings and pinkish-red ground colour, muted by dusky scaling, especially in forewing.

Distinguishing characters and similar species: As the common name implies this butterfly mimics the larger red Acraeas, particularly the Large Spotted Acraea (fig. 48). The differences are discussed under the latter (see p. 124).

Habitat and distribution: Boisduval's False Acraea is relatively common in coastal and temperate forests and in frost-free savanna, from the eastern Cape Province (East London district) to Transkei, Natal, Swaziland, the Transvaal lowveld, Mozambique and Zimbabwe.

Behaviour: Has a leisurely, floating flight, usually four or more metres above the ground. In the afternoon it flies lower down, in the forest undergrowth, where it presumably roosts for the night. Males perch high up on the leaves of forest trees and chase intruders entering their aerial territory. They will also hilltop in savanna habitats with suitable koppies. The males sometimes mud-puddle and both sexes sometimes visit flowers, especially those of poinsettia (*Euphorbia pulcherrima*).

Flight period: Mainly summer (September to May); the odd specimen is encountered in winter.

Early stages: Fairly typical of the tribe Limenitidini (see under nymphalines, p. 65). The larva is extraordinary: it is grotesquely shaped, has branched processes on the body, and closely resembles a bit of lichen-encrusted twig. The larval foodplants belong to the milkwood family (Sapotaceae) and include red milkwood (*Mimusops obovata*), forest milk-berry (*Manilkara discolor*), Transvaal milk-plum (*Bequaertiodendron magalismontanum*) and fluted milkwoods (*Chrysophyllum* species).

Chief False Acraea
Bont-valsrooitjie
(Pseudacraea lucretia) **fig. 230**

Identification: Medium-sized (60–70 mm); sexes very similar; three distinct forms. Male upperside in usual form blackish-brown with white spots in forewing and yellow patch on hindwing. Underside lighter brown with white and yellow markings corresponding to those of upperside; group of black dots, in orange-brown patch, at base of hindwing. In the other two forms (both scarcer) the normally white and yellow markings are either all white or all orange.

Distinguishing characters and similar species: The Chief False Acraea is a mimic of the unpalatable Chief Friar (fig. 228). The mimicry complex is discussed under the latter (p. 152). There are, in addition, two much rarer False Acraeas in southern Africa (neither illustrated): 1) Wanderer False Acraea (*Pseudacraea eurytus*) – closely resembles the unpalatable Southern Wanderer (fig. 203). The Southern Wanderer has black spotting only at the base of the hindwing (on the upper- and underside), whereas the Wanderer False Acraea has black spotting at the base of both the fore- and hindwing (on the upper- and underside). Relatively large populations of the Wanderer False Acraea are found at Port St Johns and Embotyi (Transkei), Umdoni Park (Natal south coast) and Eshowe (northern Natal); 2) Monarch False Acraea (*P. poggei*) – an excellent mimic of the unpalatable African Monarch (fig. 46). It is found in the subregion only in the Caprivi Strip in north-eastern Namibia.

Habitat and distribution: The Chief False Acraea is a common inhabitant of warmer forests in Transkei, Natal, Transvaal, Mozambique, Zimbabwe and northern Botswana. It is the commonest of the False Acraeas.

Behaviour: Flies relatively slowly unless alarmed, when it can move with considerable speed. Commonly observed on forest edges or in forest clearings, usually flying one to three metres above the ground. Males are territorial and perch on the leaves of trees, often at great heights. The males are also regularly seen mud-puddling.

Flight period: All year but commoner in summer.

Early stages: Typical of the tribe Limenitidini (see under nymphalines, p. 65). As with other False Acraeas the larval foodplants belong to the milkwood family. They include fluted milkwood (*Chrysophyllum viridifolium*), Natal milk-plum (*Bequaertiodendron natalense*), Transvaal milk-plum (*B. magalismontanum*) and red milkwood (*Mimusops obovata*).

GLIDERS
WITKOPPIES
(Genus *Cymothoe*)

A large number of species of Glider are found in the forests of central Africa but only three species occur in southern Africa, of which one is illustrated in this guide. They are medium-sized and strongly sexually dimorphic. Males establish territories and perch high up on the leaves of forest trees. The larvae feed on the leaves of trees belonging to the family Flacourtiaceae. The early stages are fairly typical of the tribe Limenitidini (see nymphalines, p. 65).

Battling Glider
Alsie-witkoppie
(Cymothoe alcimeda) **figs 35 & 209**

Identification: Medium-sized (45–50 mm); sexes very different; geographically variable. Male upperside cream-yellow with uneven brownish wing margins; small orange spots on wing margins; basal brownish flush on both wings. Underside variable: usually finely variegated, yellowish-brown. Female blackish-brown with white bands in fore- and hindwing and, as in male, small orange spots on wing margins. Underside pinkish-brown with white markings corresponding to those of upperside. In a few females white markings on upperside are replaced by pale yellow or orange-yellow.

Distinguishing characters and similar species: Two other species of Glider, not illustrated, are found in the subregion: 1) Blonde Glider *(Cymothoe coranus)* – very similar in colour and markings, in both sexes, to the Battling Glider but much larger (60–70 mm). The Blonde Glider is restricted to a few forests in Transkei, Natal and the eastern border of Zimbabwe; 2) Vumba Glider (*C. vumbui*) – the male has a mosaic of black, white and grey markings on the upperside. The underside is similar to that of the Battling Glider. The female closely resembles a large Battling Glider female. Confined to the forests of the eastern Zimbabwean border and a few forests in Mozambique.

Habitat and distribution: The Battling Glider is a fairly common species of temperate, wet forests, from the Caledon district of the southern Cape Province, along the eastern escarpment to the Vumba Mountains in north-eastern Zimbabwe.

Behaviour: Males usually fly high up (more than three metres) and select perches on leaves of forest trees, where they sit with open wings; they chase any intruders from their territory. Females generally keep to the semi-shaded undergrowth. Both sexes are often observed mud-puddling; this behaviour is unusual for female butterflies.

Flight period: All year but much commoner in summer.

Early stages: Fairly typical of the tribe Limenitidini (see under nymphalines, p. 65). The eggs are laid in large batches on the underside of leaves of the wild peach tree (*Kiggelaria africana*). The larvae are gregarious and, in their early instars, cluster together on the undersurface of a leaf.

FORESTERS
SKADUWEEDANSERTJIES
(Genus *Euphaedra*)

Like the Gliders (above), there are numerous species of Forester in equatorial Africa. Only a few species occur in the subcontinent, one of which is dealt with below.

Goldbanded Forester
Skaduweedansertjie
(Euphaedra neophron) **fig. 156**

Identification: Large (65–75 mm); sexes very similar but female larger. Male upperside has most of hindwing and basal third of forewing metallic to electric blue; forewing tip has small orange spot, followed by broad black band, broad orange band and final, narrower, black band. Underside is mottled with pinkish-brown and yellowish-brown.

Habitat and distribution: A fairly common species in hot subtropical forests, from the Dukuduku forest near Mtubatuba in northern Natal northwards to Mozambique and parts of the eastern border of Zimbabwe.

Behaviour: Flies with a fast, gliding flight, skimming the surface of the ground. Keeps to the semi-shade of forest but often comes to sunny, open patches and dirt roads. It is an unforgettable sight as it perches on the ground with fully opened wings, sunning itself. At the first sign of danger it will rapidly disappear into the dense undergrowth. Both sexes are attracted to fermenting fruit.

Flight period: All year.

Early stages: Fairly typical of the tribe Limenitidini (see under nymphalines, p. 65). The larva, like that of the Guineafowl (below), has long, feathery structures that project horizontally from the body. These projections probably serve to camouflage the caterpillar by acting as shadow-breakers when it is resting on a leaf. The larval foodplant is a forest understorey shrub, the dune soap-berry (*Deinbollia oblongifolia*).

GUINEAFOWL
TARENTAALTJIE
(Genus *Hamanumida*)

Although closely related to the Foresters, this genus contains only a single, widespread, savanna species.

Guineafowl
Tarentaaltjie
(*Hamanumida daedalus*) fig. 95

Identification: Medium-sized (55–65 mm); sexes alike but female larger with rounder wings; slightly seasonally variable. Male upperside grey with rows of numerous, small white spots ringed with black. Underside brown with white spots in wet season form but plain brown in dry season form.

Habitat and distribution: A very common savanna species, especially where bush-willows (*Combretum* species) are numerous. Found from the Natal bushveld areas northwards to Swaziland, Transvaal, Mozambique, Zimbabwe, Botswana and northern Namibia.

Behaviour: They are conspicuous butterflies and have a medium-fast, gliding flight as they skim over the ground. They rarely fly higher than a metre from the ground and settle often, with open wings, on bare ground, either in the sun or in the shade of trees. When approached they fly for a few metres and alight on the ground again. Both sexes are attracted to fermenting fruit, sucking-trees and even wet cowpats. The males sometimes mud-puddle.

Flight period: All year, with peaks of abundance in midsummer and in midwinter.

Early stages: Fairly typical of the tribe Limenitidini (see under nymphalines, p. 65). The larva, like that of the Goldbanded Forester (above), possesses long lateral fringes (fig. 319). The larvae feed on the leaves of velvet bush-willow (*Combretum molle*), large-fruited bush-willow (*Combretum zeyheri*) and silver terminalia (*Terminalia sericea*).

The charaxines
(Subfamily Charaxinae)

A homogeneous subfamily with about 185 species in Africa, 38 of which occur in the subregion. They are showy, medium-sized to large butterflies usually possessing two pointed tails on each hindwing. They are robust insects with great powers of flight. The eggs are laid singly on the leaves of dicotyledonous trees and shrubs but sometimes on monocots such as bamboo. The eggs are spherical, flat-topped and almost smooth (fig. 320). Most are yellow and develop a brown ring or markings near the top if fertile. The larvae are unmistakable, having four or more long horns, resembling deer antlers, on the head-shield (fig. 321). The larvae are cylindrical, generally green with brown spots or thin yellow bands and a forked tail. The larvae spin silken pads on the leaves on which they rest and to which they return after feeding on foliage some distance away. The pupae are suspended from the tail end, are globose and mainly green (fig. 322).

CHARAXES
DUBBELSTERTE
(Genus *Charaxes*)

The genus *Charaxes* is a large and diverse one represented by some 35 species in southern Africa, 13 of which are illustrated in this guide. Many butterfly enthusiasts regard them as the aristocrats of the butterfly world on account of their generally large size, vivid coloration and bold flight. The males, especially, have robust bodies and powerful wing muscles, making it possible for them to fly very swiftly. Most Charaxes are easily recognised by the paired, pointed tails on each hindwing. Most are forest or savanna species, males in the former habitat establishing territories on the tops of forest trees and males in savanna on hilltops. The flight pattern is of a powerful flap-glide-flap type, somewhat resembling many of the nymphalines. The adults very rarely feed from flowers, preferring such delicacies as fermenting fruit, fermenting sap that oozes from wounds in trees (so-called sucking-trees), carnivore and herbivore scats and droppings, and even the juices from putrefying carcasses. Numbers of Charaxes and other insects may be found at a particular sucking-tree, all competing for the exudations. Charaxes have serrations on the leading edges of their forewings and use these to batter other would-be diners. Charaxes are continuous-brooded, reaching peak population numbers in late summer and autumn, and becoming scarcer in winter and spring.

The larvae feed on the leaves of a great variety of trees, especially those belonging to the legume family (Fabaceae). The early stages are dealt with under the subfamily heading (charaxines, above).

Pearl Charaxes
Pêreldubbelstert
(Charaxes varanes) **fig. 43**

Identification: Large (75–100 mm); sexes similar but female larger. Male upperside orange-brown with large, pearly-white basal flush on both wings; single blunt tail on hindwing. Underside variable, light to dark brown, resembling a dead leaf.

Distinguishing characters and similar species: A closely related species, the Pointed Pearl Charaxes (*Charaxes acuminatus*), not illustrated, occurs in high-lying forests in north-eastern Zimbabwe. It differs from the Pearl Charaxes in having more extensive pearly-white on the upperside and almost black borders on the very pointed forewing.

Habitat and distribution: The Pearl Charaxes is a common species of forest and thick bush in the eastern half of the subcontinent, from the southern Cape Province coast (Knysna district) to Natal, Swaziland, Transvaal, Mozambique, Zimbabwe and northern Botswana and Namibia.

Behaviour: A fairly fast and irregular flier, one to many metres above the ground. It is conspicuous on the wing, flies mostly at random and is usually seen on the edges of bush, in open glades and along roads. Males select trees on which to perch and from which they defend aerial territories. Males are also reputed to hilltop. Both fermenting fruit and sucking-holes in trees strongly attract both sexes and males will come to rotting meat and animal dung.

Flight period: All year but commoner in summer.

Early stages: Typical of charaxines (see p. 98). The larvae feed on the leaves of various forest trees, including dune allophylus (*Allophylus natalensis*), *Allophylus melanocarpus* and balloon-vine (*Cardiospermum grandiflorum*).

Greenveined Charaxes
Skelmdubbelstert
(Charaxes candiope) **fig. 240**

Identification: Large (85–105 mm); sexes similar. Male upperside has base of fore- and hindwing yellowish with green veins; rest of wings orange-brown, overlaid with extensive areas of black on outer margins of wings; two tails on each wing – upper tail short and pointed and lower tail long and blunt. Underside variegated yellowish-brown to brown with prominent green veins at base of wings. Female larger with long, blunt upper tail on hindwing.

Habitat and distribution: A common Charaxes of forest and frost-free savanna, from Transkei (Port St Johns district) to Natal, Swaziland, Transvaal, Mozambique, Zimbabwe, northern Botswana and northern Namibia.

Behaviour: Flies at random from one to many metres above the ground and has a powerful and rapid flight. Males are territorial and perch with half-opened wings high up on the leaves of trees, from which they defend their territories. Both sexes are strongly attracted to fermenting fruit, sucking-trees and animal droppings. Occasionally males mud-puddle.

Flight period: All year but commonest in late summer.

Early stages: Typical of charaxines (see p. 98). The larvae use the leaves of trees such as forest croton (*Croton sylvaticus*) and lavender croton (*Croton gratissimus*).

Flamebordered Charaxes
Vlamdubbelstert
(Charaxes protoclea) **fig. 241**

Identification: Large (80–100 mm); sexes dissimilar. Male upperside black with wide, scarlet marginal bands on fore- and hindwing. Female upperside has reddish-brown wing margins overlaid with black markings, and large, white patches on trailing half of forewing and middle of hindwing.

Habitat and distribution: Fairly common in forest and rarer in frost-free savanna, in Mozambique and along the eastern border of Zimbabwe. Specimens of this Charaxes have also, on occasion, been caught in traps baited with fermenting fruit at Kosi Bay in northern Natal.

Behaviour: Both sexes are attracted to fermenting fruit, sucking-holes in trees, animal droppings and rotting carcasses. Males occasionally mud-puddle. They have a powerful and rapid flight and are very wary.

Flight period: All year.

Early stages: Typical of charaxines (see p. 98). The larvae feed on the leaves of trees such as pod mahogany (*Afzelia quanzensis*), msasa (*Brachystegia spiciformis*), and umdoni (*Syzygium cordatum*).

Foxy Charaxes
Koppiedubbelstert
(Charaxes jasius) **fig. 242**

Identification: Large (75–100 mm); sexes similar. Male upperside orange-brown with broad, blackish outer wing margins; two slender, pointed tails on hindwing (upper one shorter); block-like orange markings on extreme wing margins, becoming white in vicinity of tails with olive-green marking at end of hindwing; a few blue spots in margin near tails. Underside has a complex, variegated pattern of maroon, grey and orange with prominent silvery-white bands running down middle of fore- and hindwing. Female larger, with longer tails.

Distinguishing characters and similar species: The Foxy Charaxes can be confused with females of the Bushveld Charaxes (fig. 243) and Bluespangled Charaxes (fig. 244). There is another very similar species of Charaxes in the Cape Province, the Protea Charaxes (*Charaxes pelias*), not illustrated. The Protea Charaxes is smaller than the Foxy Charaxes; the basal areas of the wings are dark brown, not orange-brown as in the Foxy Charaxes. The Protea Charaxes occurs in the fold mountains of the south-western Cape Province, from Van Rhynsdorp in the west to Grahamstown in the east.

Habitat and distribution: The Foxy Charaxes is a common savanna species, occurring in Natal, the Swaziland lowveld, Transvaal, Mozambique, Zimbabwe, Botswana and northern Namibia.

Behaviour: A powerful, rapid flier, usually one to three metres above the ground, often in a fairly straight line. Males readily establish territories on hilltops and exhibit a perching behaviour by selecting a twig on a low bush. Both sexes are fond of fermenting fruit and the other food sources used by Charaxes butterflies, including animal dung and rotting meat. The males sometimes mud-puddle.

Flight period: All year but commoner in summer and autumn.

Early stages: Typical of charaxines (see p. 98). Many trees are used as larval foodplants, including wild seringa (*Burkea africana*), weeping boer-bean (*Schotia brachypetela*), *Brachystegia* species, pod mahogany (*Afzelia quanzensis*) and pride-of-De Kaap (*Bauhinia galpinii*).

Whitebarred Charaxes
Witstreepdubbelstert
(*Charaxes brutus*) fig. 198

Identification: Large (70–100 mm); sexes very similar. Male upperside black with wide, white bars running down middle of fore- and hindwing (in forewing, upper part of band becomes thinner and breaks up into discrete spots); two distinct, pointed tails of equal length on hindwing. Underside has a complex, variegated pattern; broad white bands corresponding to those of upperside.

Distinguishing characters and similar species: Besides the Foxy Charaxes (fig. 242), Protea Charaxes (not illustrated) and Whitebarred Charaxes (fig. 198), all of which have a similar underside pattern, there are three other species in southern Africa with similar underside markings (none illustrated): 1) Giant Charaxes (*Charaxes castor*) – the largest Charaxes in the subregion (female up to 110 mm). It has a dark brown ground colour and yellow-orange bands on the wings. Found in frost-free savanna and thick bush in northern Natal, Swaziland, the Transvaal lowveld, Mozambique and the eastern border of Zimbabwe; 2) Silverbarred Charaxes (*C. druceanus*) – reddish-brown at the wing bases with orange bands (male) or yellow-orange bands (female) and black wing margins with orange marginal spots. The underside is heavily marked with silvery-white bands and stripes. A species of temperate forests in Natal, Transvaal and north-eastern Zimbabwe; 3) Black-bordered Charaxes (*C. pollux*) – orange-brown with broad, black wing margins. Occurs in forests in Mozambique and on the eastern border of Zimbabwe.

Habitat and distribution: The Whitebarred Charaxes is a common inhabitant of subtropical and temperate forest and thick bush, from the eastern Cape Province (East

London) to Transkei, Natal, Swaziland, eastern and northern Transvaal, Mozambique, Zimbabwe and northern Botswana.

Behaviour: A typical Charaxes, with fast and very powerful flight, several metres above the ground. Both sexes feed from fermenting fruit, at sucking-holes in trees and from animal droppings. The males occasionally mud-puddle. Males are territorial and select perches on the leaves of forest trees at the edges of clearings. They are also known to hilltop.

Flight period: All year but commoner in summer and autumn.

Early stages: Typical of charaxines (see p. 98). Larval foodplants include Natal mahogany (*Trichilia emetica*), forest mahogany (*Trichilia dregeana*), Cape ash (*Ekebergia capensis*) and wild honeysuckle tree (*Turraea floribunda*).

Forest-king Charaxes
Boskoning-dubbelstert
(*Charaxes xiphares*) **figs 199, 229 & 264**

Identification: Large (70–90 mm); sexes dissimilar; geographically variable. Male upperside black with scattered, dark blue spots on forewing and large, dark blue patch in middle of hindwing; row of submarginal blue spots on hindwing; pair of short tails on lower margin of hindwing. Underside variegated in shades of brown with olive tinge in some areas; a few black markings, edged with orange on their inner aspect, towards trailing margin of forewing. Female variable; usually black with band of white spots diagonally across forewing and large, yellow hindwing patch; other females with hindwing patch pinkish-white; some females from forests of the Soutpansberg Mountains with forewing spots yellow, not white.

Distinguishing characters and similar species: There are three other species in the subregion with a similar underside pattern (none illustrated): 1) Bluespotted Charaxes (*Charaxes cithaeron*) – very similar to the Forest-king Charaxes but the hindwing patches in the male are blue-white and the tails are longer. The female has broad white bands on the forewing upperside. Common in subtropical (coastal) forests from the East London district in the eastern Cape Province northwards to Mozambique, spreading inland to the eastern border of Zimbabwe; 2) Violetspotted Charaxes (*C. violet-*

ta) – closely resembles the Bluespotted Charaxes but there is a more or less straight white line (male) or band (female) running down the length of the underside of the hindwing. Found only in forests in Mozambique and on the eastern border of Zimbabwe; 3) Large Blue Charaxes (*C. bohemani*) – upperside with solid areas of powdery blue at the base of the forewing and covering the whole of the hindwing. The underside is, however, typical of this group. Unlike the other three species in this group, which all occur in forest, the Large Blue Charaxes inhabits frost-free savanna, especially *Brachystegia* woodland, from the north-eastern Transvaal lowveld to Mozambique, Zimbabwe, northern Botswana and north-eastern Namibia.

Habitat and distribution: The Forest-king Charaxes is a fairly common inhabitant of temperate forests from the Grootvadersbosch near Swellendam in the south-western Cape Province to the Vumba Mountains in north-eastern Zimbabwe.

Behaviour: A swift and powerful flier, seldom venturing close to the ground. Males select territorial perches high up in the forest canopy. Females fly at random in the forest in search of trees on which to oviposit. The species is strongly attracted to fermenting fruit and to sucking-holes in trees, especially the females. Very occasionally males will mud-puddle.

Flight period: Summer, but most abundant in autumn (March and April).

Early stages: Typical of charaxines (see p. 98). The larvae feed on the leaves of several species of forest tree, including Cape laurel (*Cryptocarya woodii*), cat-thorn (*Scutia myrtina*), thorny elm (*Chaetacme aristata*), hairy drypetes (*Drypetes gerrardii*) and dogwood (*Rhamnus prinoides*).

Clubtailed Charaxes
Wit-en-bruin-dubbelstert
(Charaxes zoolina) **figs 53 & 208**

Identification: Medium-sized (45–55 mm); sexes differ; markedly different seasonal forms (only charaxine to show this). Male wet season form upperside pale greenish-white with blackish-brown wing margins variably spotted with greenish-white; single, clubbed tail at end of hindwing; underside silvery-green with brown bands and markings. Wet season form female larger, with double tails and with less extensive dark markings. Dry season form orange-brown with variable amounts of darker brown markings on margins of wings; underside has a dead-leaf appearance.

Habitat and distribution: Common in hot, frost-free savanna, from the Transkei and Natal coasts to Transvaal, Mozambique, Zimbabwe and northern Botswana.

Behaviour: A medium-fast flier, from two to four metres above the ground, usually in the vicinity of the larval foodplants which are thorny, scrambling acacias. The males select perches on the leaves of trees but both sexes also frequently settle within the canopies of trees. Both sexes are fond of fermenting fruit and sucking-holes in trees. Males sometimes mud-puddle. Both seasonal forms may fly at the same time in a particular locality.

Flight period: All year.

Early stages: Typical of charaxines (see p. 98). The larvae feed on river climbing acacia (*Acacia schweinfurthii*), coast climbing acacia (*A. kraussiana*) and spiny splinter bean (*Entada spicata*).

Pearlspotted Charaxes
Silverkol-dubbelstert
(*Charaxes jahlusa*) **fig. 54**

Identification: Medium-sized (45–60 mm); sexes similar. Male upperside deep orange with black markings; two tails on hindwing. Underside pinkish-brown with silver spotting on hindwing. Female larger, with slightly paler orange ground colour.

Habitat and distribution: A common savanna species that extends into the Little Karoo. Found from the Ladismith district in the southwestern Cape Province to the eastern Cape Province, Transkei, Natal, Transvaal, Mozambique, Zimbabwe and Botswana.

Behaviour: Has a rapid and direct flight, from two to four metres above the ground. Males are frequently found hilltopping, where they select perches on the leaves or twigs of trees or shrubs. Both sexes feed from fermenting fruit and at sucking-trees.

Flight period: All year but commoner in summer.

Early stages: Typical of charaxines (see p. 98). The main larval foodplant is "doppruim" (*Pappea capensis*).

Bushveld Charaxes
Bosveld-dubbelstert
(*Charaxes achaemenes*) figs 205 & 243

Identification: Large (60–80 mm); sexes dissimilar. Male upperside black (brownish towards wing bases) with white bands on both wings, broken into spots towards leading edge of forewing; white spots on wing margins; two long tails on hindwing; in vicinity of tails are green and blue marginal spots. Underside variegated greyish-brown with numerous brown markings towards wing bases. Female larger and black, with reddish-brown wing bases and orange bands and spots; otherwise like male.

Distinguishing characters and similar species: The female Bushveld Charaxes is superficially similar to the Foxy Charaxes (fig. 242) and female Bluespangled Charaxes (fig. 244) with respect to the upperside coloration and markings but the undersides are different. There are two other species of Charaxes, not illustrated, in the subregion with similar underside patterning to the Bushveld Charaxes: 1) Bluemarked Charaxes (*Charaxes etesipe*) – male black with white and blue spots in the forewing and a blue submarginal band in the lower half of the hindwing; underside as in the Bushveld Charaxes but the markings are much more pronounced. The female is black with ochre bands on the wings, broken into spots towards the leading edge of the forewing. Occurs in forest in Mozambique and north-eastern Zimbabwe and more sparingly in Venda (north-eastern Transvaal) and the Lebombo Mountains (northern Natal); 2) Scarce Savanna Charaxes (*C. penricei*) – both sexes are black with white bands broken into spots in the upper forewing. Underside as in the Bluemarked Charaxes. A rare Charaxes, found only in the savanna of central and north-eastern Zimbabwe.

Habitat and distribution: The Bushveld Charaxes is a common savanna species, occurring from the northern parts of Natal through the lowveld of Swaziland to Transvaal, Mozambique, Zimbabwe, Botswana and northern Namibia.

Behaviour: Has a rapid, gliding flight typical of Charaxes and keeps from two to four metres above the ground. Males hilltop and mud-puddle and both sexes are attracted to fermenting fruit and sucking-holes in trees.

Flight period: All year but commoner in summer.

Early stages: Typical of charaxines (see p. 98). Breeds on a number of leguminous trees, including nyala tree (*Xanthocercis zambesiaca*), kiaat (*Pterocarpus angolensis*), round-leaved kiaat (*P. rotundifolius*), large-leaved dalbergia (*Dalbergia boehmii*), *Bauhinia* species and *Brachystegia* species.

Satyr Charaxes
Kusdubbelstert
(Charaxes ethalion) **figs 91 & 206**

Identification: Medium-sized (55–70 mm); sexes dissimilar; female with four distinct forms. Male upperside velvety black; two tails on hindwing. Underside dark brown with linear black markings. Usual female form blackish-brown with white bands broken into spots in upper forewing; red marginal markings, turning to olive green, on hindwing. Female form *rosae* has broad, curved white bands in forewing; female form *aurantimacula* has orange spotting on upper forewing; female form *swynnertoni* has the white bands and spots largely replaced by blue.

Distinguishing characters and similar species: The Satyr Charaxes is just one of 12 species of southern African Charaxes belonging to the so-called "black Charaxes complex". The males of all these species have velvety-black uppersides and are difficult to differentiate from dead, set specimens, let alone from live individuals in nature. For the purposes of this guide the group is divided into those inhabiting forests (five species, including the Satyr Charaxes) and those that occur in savanna (seven species, including the Dusky Charaxes and Van Sons's Charaxes which are dealt with below). The Satyr Charaxes inhabits subtropical, coastal forests but the other four black Charaxes (none illustrated in this guide) that are found in forest are restricted to temperate and montane forests. They are: 1) Karkloof Charaxes (*Charaxes karkloof*) – found in the cooler forests of the southern Cape Province and Natal, from about George in the south to Karkloof in the north; 2) Pondo Charaxes (*C. pondoensis*) – occurs in the temperate coastal forests of Transkei; 3) Marieps Charaxes (*C. marieps*) – a relatively large species that inhabits some of the montane forests of the Transvaal eastern escarpment, from about Sabie in the south to Mariepskop in the north; 4) Montane Charaxes (*C. alpinus*) – a rare black Charaxes found in the forests of the Vumba Mountains in north-eastern Zimbabwe. The males of these four forest Charaxes closely resemble the male Satyr Charaxes. The females resemble those of female form *aurantimacula* of the Satyr Charaxes.

Habitat and distribution: The Satyr Charaxes is found in coastal and subtropical forests in Natal, north-eastern Transvaal, Mozambique and Zimbabwe.

Behaviour: Both sexes fly rapidly and usually at treetop level. Both sexes are attracted to fermenting fruit. Males sometimes mud-puddle.

Flight period: All year but commoner in summer.

Early stages: Typical of charaxines (see p. 98). The larvae feed on various leguminous trees, including flat-crown (*Albizia adianthifolia*), flame acacia (*Acacia ataxacantha*) and tamarind (*Tamarindus indica*).

Dusky Charaxes
Dowwe-dubbelstert
(Charaxes phaeus) **figs 93 & 265**

Identification: Medium-sized (50–65 mm); sexes very different. Male upperside velvety-black. Underside brown with linear black markings. Female larger; black, with extensive, metallic powder blue basal flush on both wings; a few white spots on forewing tip.

Distinguishing characters and similar species: The male Dusky Charaxes is easily confused with other males belonging to the so-called "black Charaxes complex". There are six other, similar species in savanna habitats in southern Africa. Van Son's Charaxes is dealt with below, and Braine's Charaxes (not illustrated) is mentioned in that account. The remaining four species, *C. manica, C. pseudophaeus,* *C. fulgurata* and *C. chittyi* (not illustrated), occur in the north-east of the subregion (Zimbabwe and the northern parts of Mozambique). In respect of both sexes these four species closely resemble the commoner and more widespread Dusky Charaxes.

Habitat and distribution: The Dusky Charaxes is an inhabitant of hot, frost-free savanna, from northern Natal to eastern Swaziland, eastern and northern Transvaal, southern Mozambique, Zimbabwe and eastern Botswana.

Behaviour: Very fond of sucking-holes in trees but also comes to fermenting fruit and wet cowpats. The males are known to hilltop.

Flight period: All year but scarce in winter.

Early stages: Typical of charaxines (see p. 98). The larval foodplants include leguminous trees such as knob thorn (*Acacia nigrescens*), purple-pod acacia (*A. goetzei*) and tamarind (*Tamarindus indica*).

Van Son's Charaxes
Van Son-dubbelstert
(Charaxes vansoni) **figs 92 & 207**

Identification: Medium-sized (50–60 mm); sexes dissimilar. Male upperside velvety black. Female blackish-brown with white bands broken up into spots in upper half of forewing.

Distinguishing characters and similar species: The male is typical of the "black Charaxes complex" and is easily confused with others of the group (see remarks under Satyr Charaxes above). Braine's Charaxes (*Charaxes brainei*), not illustrated, is very similar to Van Son's Charaxes but occurs in northern Namibia and north-western Botswana.

Habitat and distribution: Van Son's Charaxes occurs in frost-free savanna in northern Natal, Swaziland, Transvaal, Zimbabwe and eastern Botswana.

Behaviour: Males are most often seen while hilltopping on koppies in bushveld. Both sexes are attracted to fermenting fruit and sucking-holes in trees.

Flight period: All year but commonest in autumn (March to May).

Early stages: Typical of charaxines (see p. 98). The only known larval foodplant is the weeping wattle (*Peltophorum africanum*).

Bluespangled Charaxes
Blougevlekte-dubbelstert
(Charaxes guderiana) **figs 90 & 244**

Identification: Medium-sized (55–65 mm); sexes very different. Male upperside black with white spots on forewing and along margin of hindwing; blue submarginal band in lower half of hindwing; two tails on hindwing. Underside variegated, rich brown. Female larger with extensive orange bands and orange spotting in forewing and tan-coloured basal flush on both wings.

Distinguishing characters and similar species: The female Bluespangled Charaxes resembles the female Bushveld Charaxes (fig. 243) and Foxy Charaxes (fig. 242) on the upperside but the undersides in these three species are different. The male can be confused with Gallagher's Charaxes (*Charaxes gallagheri*), not illustrated, whose males differ from those of the Bluespangled Charaxes in having a thinner, dull green submarginal band on the hindwing and a greyish-brown underside. The female Gallagher's Charaxes is black, with whitish bands and spots on the wings and a pale underside, similar to that of the male. Gallagher's Charaxes is a rare inhabitant of central and north-eastern Zimbabwe.

Habitat and distribution: The Bluespangled Charaxes is a common insect of *Brachystegia* woodland in Mozambique, Zimbabwe and north-eastern Botswana.

Behaviour: Males have the habit of perching on tree trunks and apparently do not hilltop, both unusual behaviours for a Charaxes. Both sexes are, however, attracted to fermenting fruit and males mud-puddle and come to animal droppings.

Flight period: All year.

Early stages: Typical of charaxines (see p. 98). The larvae feed on leguminous trees such as msasa (*Brachystegia spiciformis*) and several other *Brachystegia* species as well as munondo (*Julbernardia globiflora*) and Scotsman's rattle (*Amblygonocarpus andongensis*).

QUEENS
KONINGINNE
(Genus *Euxanthe*)

The Queens are closely related to the Charaxes (p. 98) but have much rounder wings and lack tails. A single species of this small genus is found in the subregion. The early stages are typical of charaxines (see p. 98)

Forest Queen
Woudkoningin
(*Euxanthe wakefieldi*) fig. 263

Identification: Large (65–80 mm); sexes similar. Male with very rounded wings; upperside black with greenish-white markings and spots. Underside brown with markings and spots corresponding to those of upperside. Female larger, with markings and spots pure white, not greenish as in male.

Distinguishing characters and similar species: The female Forest Queen may be mistaken for the common, unpalatable Novice Friar (fig. 196) but the wings are distinctly rounded in the Forest Queen.

Habitat and distribution: The Forest Queen is an inhabitant of subtropical coastal forest in northern Natal and Mozambique but is also found, more rarely, in south-eastern Swaziland, north-eastern Transvaal and on the eastern border of Zimbabwe.

Behaviour: Both sexes of the Forest Queen, like the Charaxes, are fond of fermenting fruit. Males establish territories in clearings in forests where they perch on low vegetation. Should another male enter this territory a dispute ensues during which both males tumble around in the air until the intruder has been driven off. Males are also known to hilltop. Although their flight is normally slow and floating they will disappear into the undergrowth in a flash if disturbed.

Flight period: All year but commoner in summer.

Early stages: Similar to charaxines (see p. 98) but the larvae have very well developed projections on the head-shield as well as a lateral "skirt" running along the length of the body. The larvae feed on the dune soap-berry (*Deinbollia oblongifolia*), a large-leaved shrub or small tree of the forest understorey.

The acraeines
(Subfamily Acraeinae)

About 55 of the 200 or so African acraeines are found in southern Africa. The subfamily is fairly homogeneous and the members are characterised by their very long wings, slow flight and warning coloration (combinations of red, yellow, black and white). A number of species have part or most of the wings transparent. Three groups are found in the subregion, the bulk of the species falling under the Acraeas (genera *Acraea* and *Hyalites*). Mated female acraeines have an appendage below the tip of the abdomen. This structure is known as a sphragis and is secreted by the male during mating. It is presumed to prevent mating by other males. Acraeine eggs are barrel-shaped and usually laid in clusters (fig. 323). Species that lay large numbers of eggs in a cluster (up to 300) normally lay them in an untidy heap whereas the eggs are more evenly spaced in species that lay smaller batches. The larvae are cylindrical with branched spines (fig. 324) and similar to the spined larvae of the tribe Nymphalini (p. 65) of the subfamily Nymphalinae. The long, cylindrical pupae are characteristic (fig. 325) and are suspended from the tail end.

WANDERERS
RONDDWALERS
(Genus *Bematistes*)

A single species of Wanderer occurs in southern Africa. The comments under Acraeas (below) apply equally to Wanderers.

Southern Wanderer
Swartbont-ronddwaler
(Bematistes aganice) **figs 203 & 231**

Identification: Male medium-sized, female large (55–75 mm); sexes dissimilar. Male upperside blackish-brown with yellow-spotted forewing band and broad, yellow hindwing band. Underside brown with yellow markings corresponding to those of upperside; black-spotted rufous area at base of hindwing. Female much larger and has white, not yellow, markings on wings.

Distinguishing characters and similar species: The unpalatable Southern Wanderer serves as a model for the Wanderer False Acraea (see under Chief False Acraea, p. 93). The Southern Wanderer can also be confused with the very similar Dusky Acraea (figs 204 & 232).

Habitat and distribution: The Southern Wanderer is a common butterfly in subtropical and warmer temperate forests, from Transkei north-eastwards to Zimbabwe and northern Botswana.

Behaviour: Has a slow and leisurely flight, especially the female, from one to three metres above the ground. It perches with closed wings, often high up on the leaves of trees. Males show territorial behaviour and often float around the treetops on the edges of forests. Both sexes visit flowers.

Flight period: All year but commoner in summer.

Early stages: Similar to those of other acraeines (see p. 112) except that the pupa has a number of long projections. The larvae have been recorded on "slangklimop" (*Adenia gummifera*) and exotic passion-flowers (*Passiflora* species), including blue passion-flower (*P. coerulea*) and grenadilla (*P. edulis*).

ACRAEAS
ROOITJIES
(Genera *Acraea* and *Hyalites*)

Of the 50 or so southern African species of this large group of medium-sized butterflies, 19 are illustrated in this guide. Perhaps their most characteristic features are the very elongated forewings, long bodies and slow, leisurely flight. The predominant wing colours are red, black, white and yellow. A number of species also have transparent (hyaline) wing patches. Both the adults and early stages are said to be toxic. The adults, when injured, exude droplets of clear, yellow fluid that contains hydrocyanic acid. Unlike the danaines, which are toxic by virtue of the poisonous plants on which their larvae feed, acraeines are apparently able to synthesise hydrocyanic acid. Some of the unpalatable acraeines are mimicked by palatable species such as the False Acraeas (p. 92). Acraeas are found flying all year but are commoner in summer. The early stages are discussed under the subfamily (p. 112).

Garden Acraea
Tuinrooitjie
(Acraea horta) **fig. 64**

Identification: Medium-sized (45–55 mm); sexes fairly similar. Male upperside reddish-orange with transparent forewing tips and numerous black spots on hindwing. Underside similar but ground colour is lighter. Female larger and dull orange-brown.

Distinguishing characters and similar species: There are six other Acraeas that are similar, of which only the first two are illustrated in this field guide as the others are scarce to rare butterflies: Wandering Donkey Acraea (fig. 65), Dusky-veined Acraea (fig. 69), Machequena Acraea (*Acraea machequena*), Rainforest Acraea (*A. boopis*), Treetop Acraea (*Hyalites cerasa*) and Pale-yellow Acraea (*H. obeira*).

Habitat and distribution: The Garden Acraea occurs in both forest and moist savanna, penetrating other biomes, such as fynbos, sparingly. It occurs from the Cape Peninsula along the southern Cape coast, spreading out in the eastern Cape Province to Natal, the eastern Orange Free State and Transvaal.

Behaviour: It is slow-flying, usually one to four metres above the ground. It is often seen in gardens and is common in the Kirstenbosch Gardens in Cape Town. Sometimes there is a mass emergence, when large numbers may be seen in a particular locality.

Flight period: All year but only in summer in cooler areas.

Early stages: Similar to those of other acraeines (see p. 112). The eggs are laid in batches and the larvae are gregarious in the earlier instars. Larval foodplants include wild peach (*Kiggelaria africana*) and passion-flowers (*Passiflora* species).

Wandering Donkey Acraea
Dwaalesel-rooitjie
(Acraea neobule) **fig. 65**

Identification: Medium-sized (45–55 mm); sexes similar. Male upperside dull orange-red with most of forewing apex transparent; scattered black dots on both wings; hindwing margin black, enclosing a row of orange spots. Underside like upperside but ground colour suffused with white. Female pale orange-brown, otherwise like male.

Distinguishing characters and similar species: The Wandering Donkey Acraea can be confused with the same species as the Garden Acraea (above).

Habitat and distribution: The Wandering Donkey Acraea is common in the eastern Karoo and in savanna in the Cape Province, Orange Free State, Transvaal, Mozambique, Zimbabwe, Botswana and Namibia.

Behaviour: Usually the Wandering Donkey Acraea is observed singly, in open veld, flying in a leisurely manner, one to two metres above the ground. Males are frequently seen hilltopping where they select a tree on which to perch and take quite an active part in the general chasing around of other butterflies. Flowers attract both sexes and the males are occasionally found mud-puddling. In some years the species migrates and specimens will then often visit gardens to feed from flowers.

Flight period: All year but scarcer in winter.

Early stages: Typical of acraeines (see p. 112). The larvae feed on grenadilla (*Passiflora edulis*) and "slangklimop" (*Adenia gummifera*).

Duskyveined Acraea
Vuilvenster-rooitjie
(Hyalites igola) **fig. 69**

Identification: Medium-sized (40–50 mm); sexes similar. Male upperside orange-red with outer half of forewing transparent; even, dusky border around forewing and on outer margin of hindwing; numerous black spots on hindwing. Underside pinkish-orange with black spotting on hindwing as on upperside. Female has ground colour either red, like male, or yellowy-beige.

Distinguishing characters and similar species: The species with which the Duskyveined Acraea may be confused are listed under the Garden Acraea (see p. 114).

Habitat and distribution: The Duskyveined Acraea is fairly common in coastal subtropical forest from Transkei (Port St Johns district) to northern Natal (Ubombo district). Also found in Mozambique and in the eastern border forests of Zimbabwe.

Behaviour: May fly high up in the forest canopy but often ventures to within one to four metres from the ground. It is inclined to settle on trees on the edges of forest or in clearings. May also be seen feeding from the flowers of creepers lower down. For an Acraea it has quite a brisk flight.

Flight period: All year but scarcer in winter.

Early stages: Typical of acraeines (see p. 112). The larval foodplant is climbing nettle (*Urera cameroonensis*).

Marsh Acraea
Moerasrooitjie
(Hyalites rahira) **fig. 73**

Identification: Small (35–40 mm); sexes similar. Male upperside yellow-orange with scattered black spots; wing margins blackish, with veins outlined submarginally in black. Underside similar but with more yellow in ground colour of forewing apex and hindwing. Female ground colour dusky, pale brown.

Habitat and distribution: Found only in marshy areas and along stream banks. Occurs from the south-western to the eastern Cape Province, Natal, Transvaal, Mozambique, Zimbabwe, Botswana and Namibia.

Behaviour: Flies slowly and low down among the vegetation in marshes and along stream banks. It often dwells in large colonies but these are always very localised. Both sexes readily visit flowers growing in the marshy areas that the butterfly frequents.

Flight period: Mainly summer (October to April).

Early stages: Typical of acraeines (see p. 112). Breeds on the water-loving plants *Polygonum pulchrum* and "peperbossie" (*Conyza canadensis*).

Orange Acraea
Oranjerooitjie
(Hyalites anacreon) **fig. 67**

Identification: Medium-sized (40–55 mm); sexes dissimilar; geographically variable. Male upperside bright orange-red with veins of forewing apex black; black hindwing margin enclosing regular, orange dots. Underside yellowish, with base of forewing orange; scattered black spotting, especially on hindwing. Female has ground colour dull, pale orange-brown.

Distinguishing characters and similar species: A very similar species occurring in the Soutpansberg Mountains and eastern Zimbabwe has the tip of the forewing black (*Hyalites induna*), not illustrated.

Habitat and distribution: Common in montane grassland, especially in the vicinity of marshes and streams.

Occurs in the eastern half of the subcontinent. Found from the eastern Cape Province to Natal, eastern Transvaal and eastern Zimbabwe.

Behaviour: Although, like most Acraeas, the Orange Acraea flies close to the ground, it is noticeably swifter on the wing than other Acraeas. It occurs in localised colonies, in grassy spots, usually where rainfall is high. Both sexes are frequently observed feeding from flowers.

Flight period: Summer (October to May).

Early stages: Typical of acraeines (see p. 112). The larval foodplants include *Cliffortia linearifolia*, *Aeschynomene* species and *Adenia* species.

Dancing Acraea
Klein-oranjerooitjie
(Hyalites eponina) **fig. 72**

Identification: Small to medium-sized (35–45 mm); sexes dissimilar. Male upperside orange with fairly broad, blackish wing margins enclosing small orange spots on both wings. Underside forewing orange at base; rest of wings yellow-orange; black spots at base of hindwing, with complex marginal pattern. Female variable; usually dusky-grey with traces of orange on bases of wings; underside similar to that of male.

Habitat and distribution: A very common grassland species in the eastern half of the subcontinent. It also penetrates grassy areas adjoining savanna and forest. Occurs from the eastern Cape Province to Natal, Swaziland, Transvaal, Mozambique, Zimbabwe, Botswana and Namibia.

Behaviour: Flies weakly and very close to the ground (under a metre). Large numbers are sometimes found in a single colony, provided the larval foodplants are abundant.

Both sexes are frequently seen feeding from flowers.

Flight period: All year in warmer areas; summer in cooler ones. Most abundant from March to May.

Early stages: Typical of acraeines (see p. 112). The larvae feed on various species of *Triumfetta* ("klitsbossie") such as *T. rhomboidea*, *T. annua* and *T. pilosa*, and on *Hermannia* species.

Yellowbanded Acraea
Geelstreeprooitjie
(Hyalites cabira) **fig. 238**

Identification: Medium-sized (40–50 mm); sexes very similar. Male upperside blackish-brown with large, yellow-orange patches on fore- and hindwing. Underside with yellowish patches corresponding to those of upperside; base of wings orange-brown; pattern of triplets of black lines on orange-brown background on wing margins. Female larger.

Distinguishing characters and similar species: A related species, the Small Yellowbanded Acraea (*Hyalites acerata*), not illustrated, is smaller and has more extensive patches of yellow-orange on the upperside of the wings. The Small Yellowbanded Acraea occurs in the north of the subregion (northern areas of Mozambique, Zimbabwe and Botswana).

Habitat and distribution: The Yellowbanded Acraea is common in subtropical forest, from Transkei to Natal, Swaziland, the eastern Transvaal escarpment, the Soutpansberg Mountains and the eastern border of Zimbabwe.

Behaviour: Has a slow, weak flight, generally less than a metre above the ground. Specimens are most often seen in sunny spots, such as clearings and roads in forests, or on the edges of forests. Both sexes feed from flowers.

Flight period: All year but scarcer in winter.

Early stages: Typical of acraeines (see p. 112). The larvae feed on *Triumfetta tomentosa* and *Hermannia* species.

Dusky Acraea
Dowwerooitjie
(Hyalites esebria) **figs 51, 204 & 232**

Identification: Medium-sized (50–65 mm); sexes similar; very variable. Male upperside black with white band across forewing and white patch at base of forewing and on hindwing. Other forms have the patches yellow or orange, or forewing band white and other patches red, or forewing band yellow and other patches orange. Female larger and shows same variety of colours as male.

Distinguishing characters and similar species: The Dusky Acraea is easily mistaken for the slightly larger Southern Wanderer (figs 203 & 231), with which it flies in forest habitats.

Habitat and distribution: The Dusky Acraea is a common species of temperate and subtropical forest, especially the warmer subtropical forests, from the eastern Cape Province to Mozambique and Zimbabwe.

Behaviour: Flies slowly in and around forests, from a few to many metres above the ground. Both sexes feed from flowers, low down or high up in trees.

Flight period: Nearly all year; commonest from December to April.

Early stages: Typical of acraeines (see p. 112). The larval foodplants belong to the nettle family (Urticaceae) and include *Laportea peduncularis*, *Pouzolzia parasitica* and tree nettle (*Obetia tenax*).

Common Mimic Acraea
Witstreeprooitjie
(*Hyalites encedon*) **fig. 68**

Identification: Medium-sized (40–50 mm); sexes similar; variable. Male upperside orange-brown with blackish forewing apex crossed by white bar; scattered black spots on fore- and hindwing. Underside similar to upperside but ground colour paler. Several other varieties have ground colour paler (greyish to yellowish). Female larger than male.

Habitat and distribution: A common savanna species also found on the outskirts of forests. It is especially common on the Natal coast. It is absent only from the Karoo and south-western Cape Province.

Behaviour: The Common Mimic Acraea is a slow flier that perches on low-growing vegetation. It somewhat resembles a dwarf African Monarch (fig. 46), a species with which it is confused by beginners. The males are said to hilltop.

Flight period: All year but commonest from March to May.

Early stages: Typical of acraeines (see p. 112). The larvae use the low-growing, creeping forb *Commelina diffusa*, which occurs commonly on the banks of streams and shores of dams.

Natal Acraea
Natal-rooitjie
(*Acraea natalica*) **fig. 49**

Identification: Medium-sized (55–60 mm); sexes similar. Male upperside bright orange-red with orange towards tip of forewing; tip of forewing black; broad, even black marginal band on hindwing; bases of wings black; scattered black spots on both wings. Underside yellow-brown, tinged with pink on hindwing; numerous black spots, especially on hindwing; hindwing margin black with enclosed, hemispherical yellow-brown spots. Female duller, with black markings more extensive.

Distinguishing characters and similar species: Resembles the Large Spotted Acraea (fig. 48) and the Window Acraea (fig. 50).

Habitat and distribution: The Natal Acraea is a very common species of savanna habitats, as well as forest edges, in the eastern half of the subcontinent.

Behaviour: This fairly large and brightly coloured Acraea usually flies at random, some one to two metres above the ground, in a fairly leisurely manner. Males occasionally establish territories in bush and use low vegetation on which to perch. These territories appear to be only loosely defended. Both sexes are strongly attracted to flowering forbs and trees.

Flight period: All year.

Early stages: Typical of acraeines (see p. 112). The larval foodplants include "slangklimop" (*Adenia gummifera*), passion-flowers (*Passiflora* species) and "rooihaarbossie" (*Tricliceras longepedunculatum*).

Blacktipped Acraea
Swartpuntrooitjie
(*Acraea caldarena*) **fig. 63**

Identification: Medium-sized (40–50 mm); sexes similar; wet and dry season forms occur. Male upperside pale yellow-orange to pink-orange with broad, black forewing tip; narrow ocellated dusky border on hindwing; scattered black spots on hindwing. Underside ground colour paler than upperside; base of wings pinkish-red; strongly ocellated hindwing margin; scattered black spots on both wings. Dry season form with ground colour delicate pale pink, and black spotting reduced.

Habitat and distribution: Common in savanna in the eastern and northern Transvaal lowveld, Mozambique, Zimbabwe and northern Namibia.

Behaviour: Has a slow and leisurely, random flight, usually less than a metre above the ground. Both sexes feed readily from flowers. In northern Transvaal, in April and May, large numbers of the dry season form, with its delicate pinkish-orange colour and jet-black forewing tips, may be observed feeding on the purple flowers of certain roadside bushes.

Flight period: All year.

Early stages: Typical of acraeines (see p. 112). The only known larval foodplant is "rooihaarbossie" (*Tricliceras longepedunculatum*).

Rooibok Acraea
Rooibokkie
(*Acraea oncaea*) **fig. 62**

Identification: Medium-sized (45–50 mm); sexes dissimilar. Male upperside pale orange with small, black forewing tip and narrow, black hindwing margin; scattered black spots on both wings. Underside ground colour paler; ocellated hindwing margin; scattered black spots. Female variable but usually orange-brown to greyish with broad, black forewing tip and black hindwing margin; characteristic white bar below forewing apex.

Distinguishing characters and similar species: The female Rooibok Acraea resembles the Common Mimic Acraea (fig. 68), while the male can be confused with the smaller Little (fig. 71) and Light-red Acraeas (fig. 70).

Habitat and distribution: The Rooibok Acraea is common in grassy areas within savanna habitats. Found from the coastal areas of Natal to Transvaal and Mozambique.

Behaviour: Has a very slow and weak flight, just above the level of the grass. Its relatively small size and dull coloration do not readily attract attention. Both sexes are fond of feeding from flowers growing among grass, when they can easily be closely approached.

Flight period: All year.

Early stages: Typical of acraeines (see p. 112). The larvae use African dog-rose (*Xylotheca kraussiana*), "rooihaarbossie" (*Tricliceras longepedunculatum*) and *Adenia* species as food.

Little Acraea
Kuikenrooitjie
(*Acraea axina*) **fig. 71**

Identification: Medium-sized (40–45 mm); sexes similar. Male upperside orange-red with scattered black spots and black hindwing margin. Underside much paler with pinkish tinge on hindwing; ocellated hindwing margin; scattered black spots as on upperside. Female more dusky with broader black hindwing margin.

Distinguishing characters and sim-

ilar species: The Little Acraea may be mistaken for the larger Rooibok Acraea (fig. 62) and the Light-red Acraea (fig. 70).

Habitat and distribution: The Little Acraea is a common butterfly of savanna in northern Natal, Swaziland, Transvaal, Mozambique, Zimbabwe, Botswana and Namibia.

Behaviour: Normally flies weakly near ground level. Males sometimes hilltop and choose trees on the summit on which to perch.

Flight period: Most of the year.

Early stages: The early stages and larval foodplant are not known.

Window Acraea
Vensterrooitjie
(Acraea aglaonice) **fig. 50**

Identification: Medium-sized (45–50 mm); sexes similar. Male upperside orange-red with small, black forewing tip and broad, black hindwing margin; scattered black spots on wings. Underside paler with ocellated hindwing margin and scattered black spots; clear spot near apex of forewing. Female more heavily marked with black, especially at base of wings.

Distinguishing characters and similar species: The Window Acraea is superficially similar to the Natal Acraea (fig. 49).

Habitat and distribution: The Window Acraea is a fairly common butterfly of savanna, from northern Natal to Swaziland, Transvaal, Mozambique, Zimbabwe and Botswana.

Behaviour: Males of this species sometimes hilltop, where they perch on low shrubs or on grass stems on the summit. Normally they are encountered singly, flying at random about a metre above the ground. Both sexes feed readily from flowers.

Flight period: All year.

Early stages: The early stages and larval foodplant are unknown.

Large Spotted Acraea
Ridderrooitjie
(*Acraea acara*) fig. 48

Identification: Large (60–75 mm); sexes similar. Male upperside bright red with extensive black markings on both wings. Underside ground colour lighter with pinkish-white markings near forewing apex and in middle of hindwing; hindwing margin black, enclosing small white spots; black patch with white spots at base of hindwing. Female similar but upperside ground colour orange-red.

Distinguishing characters and similar species: The Large Spotted Acraea is mimicked by Boisduval's False Acraea (fig. 47). The latter is larger and flies more swiftly; the black tip on the forewing is larger and there are black spots on the forewing (these markings are block-like in the Large Spotted Acraea). Finally the black spots on the hindwing are larger in Boisduval's False Acraea.

Three closely related species, not illustrated, occur in southern Africa: 1) Zetes Acraea (*Acraea zetes*) – has the forewing much more heavily suffused with black scales. Enters northern Namibia sparingly from Angola; 2) Barber's Acraea (*Acraea barberi*) – male has black markings on wing margins not as heavy but black spots on hindwing larger. Female has the forewing largely transparent. Found mainly in the western and north-western Transvaal bushveld; 3) Trimen's Acraea (*Acraea trimeni*) – a small species (45–55 mm) with the black markings very reduced. Occurs in the north-western Cape Province, southern Botswana and the south-western Orange Free State.

Habitat and distribution: The Large Spotted Acraea is quite common in savanna, from Transkei to Natal, Swaziland, Transvaal, Mozambique, Zimbabwe and northern Botswana and Namibia.

Behaviour: Flies at random through the bush, in a slow and deliberate manner, from one to two metres above the ground. The large size and bright red colour make this a very conspicuous insect in bushveld. Specimens are usually found singly but on occasion a number may be seen feeding on the tops of flowering trees. The males are reputed to sometimes mud-puddle.

Flight period: All year.

Early stages: Typical of acraeines (see p. 112). The larval foodplants are "bobbejaangif" (*Adenia glauca*) and passion-flowers (*Passiflora* species).

Broadbordered Acraea
Kersboomrooitjie
(Acraea anemosa) **fig. 52**

Identification: Medium-sized (55–60 mm); sexes similar. Male upperside forewing bright orange; hindwing red; extensive black markings on forewing tip, hindwing margin and wing bases. Underside similar but with white spots in hindwing margin and at base of hindwing. Female with forewing dull orange and hindwing fuscous-red.

Habitat and distribution: A common species in savanna habitats, from northern Natal extending to Swaziland, Transvaal, Mozambique, Zimbabwe and northern Botswana and Namibia.

Behaviour: Because of its bright coloration, the Broadbordered Acraea readily draws attention to itself. Specimens are encountered singly in the veld and have the typical, lazy flight of Acraeas, usually about a metre above the ground. Both sexes feed from flowers, near the ground or in trees. Females may spend considerable periods of time on the wing, fluttering around shrubs in search of sites in which to lay their eggs. They are very particular about this because the eggs are laid in batches, making it important to find optimal sites.

Flight period: All year in warmer areas and September to May in cooler ones.

Early stages: Undescribed. The larvae feed on the leaves of "bobbejaangif" (*Adenia glauca*).

Light-red Acraea
Bergrooitjie
(Acraea nohara) **fig. 70**

Identification: Medium-sized (40–45 mm); sexes similar. Male upperside orange-red with narrow, black wing margins and scattered black spots on both wings. Underside paler with ocellated hindwing margin. Female with black markings slightly more pronounced and ground colour duller.

Distinguishing characters and similar species: The Light-red Acraea should be compared with the larger Rooibok Acraea (fig. 62) and Little Acraea (fig. 71), with which it can be confused.

Habitat and distribution: The Light-red Acraea is quite often encountered in certain spots in grassland, usually at medium to fairly high altitudes. Distributed from Transkei (Port St Johns) to Natal, Transvaal, Mozambique and Zimbabwe.

Behaviour: The Light-red Acraea prefers open, grassy habitats that are subject to high rainfall and frequent mist, such as are found on the eastern escarpment of the subcontinent. It is usually found singly although a number may be observed within a restricted area. The flight is slow, rarely more than a metre above the ground. The orange-red coloration of the wings, against the green of the grass, makes it very conspicuous. Both sexes feed from flowering forbs growing among the grass.

Flight period: All year but much scarcer in winter, especially at high altitudes.

Early stages: Typical of acraeines (see p. 112). Larval foodplants include the low-growing forbs "rooihaarbossie" (*Tricliceras longepedunculatum*) and *Basananthe sandersonii*.

Blood-red Acraea
Bloedrooitjie
(*Acraea petraea*) **fig. 66**

Identification: Medium-sized (50–55 mm); sexes dissimilar. Male upperside blood-red with extensive black markings on both wings and with veins outlined in black towards wing margins. Underside similar to upperside but pinkish-red. Female red-orange with white patch near tip of forewing.

Habitat and distribution: A fairly common inhabitant of subtropical forest and coastal bush in Natal and Mozambique.

Behaviour: The species tends to fly on the edges of and in dense bush and on the edges of forest, where the blood-red colour of its wings is shown off to good effect against the verdant green of the vegetation. The flight is slow, from one to four metres above the ground, and the wings are flapped lazily as the butterfly circles about bushes and trees.

Flight period: All year but commoner in summer.

Early stages: Typical of acraeines (see p. 112). The larvae can be found on African dog-rose (*Xylotheca kraussiana*), an attractive shrub with large, yellow-centred white flowers.

POLKA DOT
POLKASTIPPEL
(Genus *Pardopsis*)

This genus consists of a single species, which is closely related to the Acraeas.

Polka Dot
Polkastippel
(Pardopsis punctatissima) **fig. 74**

Identification: Small (30–35 mm); sexes very similar. Male upperside orange with black forewing tip and with both wings uniformly covered in black spots. Underside similar but without black forewing tip. Female slightly larger.

Habitat and distribution: Locally common in medium-altitude grassland, from the eastern Cape Province (Port Elizabeth district) through Natal, eastern Transvaal, Mozambique and Zimbabwe.

Behaviour: Flies very weakly and at random, just above the level of the grass. Usually found in localised colonies often consisting of many individuals. The butterflies tend to occur year after year in the same locality. The colonies are invariably found on the slopes of mountains and high hills that receive abundant rainfall and that are frequently shrouded in mist. Not surprisingly the grassy localities in which the colonies are found are often in close proximity to mist-belt forests.

Flight period: October to April.

Early stages: Similar to those of other acraeines (see p. 112). The larvae feed on the low-growing forb *Hybanthus capensis*.

The satyrines
(Subfamily Satyrinae)

A homogeneous subfamily with some 300 species in the Afrotropical Region, 82 of which are found in southern Africa. Most have a dull brown coloration and rounded wings, and possess a variable number of characteristic eye-spots which are usually better developed on the underside of the wings. In those species that have wet and dry season forms the eye-spots are more prominent in the wet season form. Several groups are endemic to the subregion, including the Beauties, Widows and Shadeflies. Many species shun direct sunlight and are either shade-loving or crepuscular. All satyrines breed on monocotyledons, mainly grasses and bamboos (Poaceae) but also occasionally on related families such as restios (Restionaceae). The eggs are laid singly onto a blade of grass but in some species the females scatter eggs among clumps of grass. The eggs are barrel-shaped to spherical and the surface is smooth or finely sculptured (fig. 326). The larvae are cylindrical with large heads and powerful mouthparts (fig. 327). The well-developed mandibles are necessary in order to chew grass blades which are tough by virtue of their high silicate content. Satyrine larvae are sometimes slow-growing, often taking many months to reach maturity, probably because of the low nutritional value of grasses. During the day larvae hide at the base of grass clumps and emerge at night to feed from the tips of the blades. They are sluggish and if disturbed readily drop off the blade on which they are feeding. Mostly their colours are shades of green or brown with darker stripes down the body. As in the charaxines the tail end of the larva is usually forked. The pupae are short and stout, usually brown in colour, and suspended from the tail end (fig. 328). In some species the pupae lie free among the roots at the base of grass clumps.

EVENING BROWNS
SKEMERBRUINTJIES
(Genera *Melanitis* and *Gnophodes*)

The Evening Browns are a small group of three species in two genera. Only one common, widespread species is illustrated in this field guide. Evening Browns are large butterflies, generally with dark brown coloration. They closely resemble dead leaves on the underside and this effect is enhanced by their wing shape. They are found in forest or dense bush and tend to spend most of the day resting in deep shade among dead leaves. They fly about at dawn and dusk, this being referred to as crepuscular behaviour. The larvae feed on various soft grasses. The early stages are similar to those of other satyrines which are dealt with under this heading, above. The adults are on the wing throughout the year, the Common Evening Brown having distinct wet and dry season forms.

Common Evening Brown
Gewone Skemerbruintjie
(*Melanitis leda*) **fig. 89**

Identification: Large (60–70 mm); sexes similar; distinct seasonal forms. Male wet season form upperside brown with orange-brown flush and eye-spot near tip of forewing; single eye-spot at lower edge of hindwing and short, blunt tail. Underside finely irrorated in grey and brown, with variably sized eye-spots submarginally, in both wings. Female paler brown with eye-spots much more prominent. Dry season form in both sexes larger with hooked forewing apex and better developed blunt tail on hindwing; extensive orange-brown flush, especially around well developed forewing eye-spot. Underside exceedingly variable, resembling a dead leaf; eye-spots virtually absent on underside.

Distinguishing characters and similar species: The Common Evening Brown is similar to the scarcer and more localised Violeteyed Evening Brown (*Melanitis libya*), not illustrated, which is found in forests on the eastern border of Zimbabwe and adjoining areas of Mozambique.

Habitat and distribution: The Common Evening Brown is widespread in the eastern half of the subcontinent in frost-free savanna, but also penetrates the forest and grassland biomes sparingly. The species extends as far south as Wilderness in the southern Cape Province.

Behaviour: During the day this butterfly rests on the ground among leaf litter in deep shade, and is virtually impossible to detect. If accidentally roused it flies ponderously for a few metres and again alights among leaves on the ground, seemingly disappearing in the process. At dawn and dusk, however, it emerges from hiding and flaps around in the gloom, when it is usually mistaken for a large brown moth. On warm, overcast days a few specimens may also take to the wing. Both sexes are attracted to fermenting fruit.

Flight period: All year, the dry season (winter) form being the more plentiful.

Early stages: Typical of satyrines (see p. 128). The larvae are grass feeders and have been recorded on *Cynodon* species and bristle-grass (*Setaria sulcata*). I have also bred them on Kikuyu-grass (*Pennisetum clandestinum*).

BUSH BROWNS
BOSBRUINTJIES
(Genera *Bicyclus* and *Henotesia*)

In southern Africa this group consists of nine similar species in two genera. One species of each genus is illustrated in this field guide. Bush Browns are medium-sized, brown butterflies with rounded wings marked with eye-spots. All the species fly close to the ground, keeping to shady spots in forest or densely wooded savanna habitats. They usually settle with closed wings among dry leaves on the ground, when their coloration affords them good camouflage. Most are fond of feeding from fallen fruit, rarely being seen on flowers. Like the Evening Browns, Bush Browns are often active during overcast weather. They are on the wing all year. The larvae feed on grasses and the early stages are dealt with under the subfamily (p. 128).

Common Bush Brown
Swart-bosbruintjie
(*Bicyclus safitza*) **fig. 107**

Identification: Medium-sized (45–50 mm); sexes similar; seasonally dimorphic. Male wet season form upperside dark, dull brown with paler brown area and two small eye-spots near forewing tip. Underside dark brown, with yellow-brown mediad line down fore- and hindwing; two well developed eye-spots on forewing and row of submarginal eye-spots on hindwing. Female wet season form similar above but underside much paler brown. Dry season form differs chiefly on underside, which has only the larger forewing eye-spot well developed.

Distinguishing characters and similar species: Six other species belonging to the genus *Bicyclus* are found in the subcontinent. They are all quite similar to the Common Bush Brown, but are comparatively scarce.

Habitat and distribution: The Common Bush Brown is a very common inhabitant of coastal and temperate forests, from the Knysna district of the southern Cape Province north-eastwards to the eastern border forests of Zimbabwe.

Behaviour: Has a leisurely, bouncing flight, rarely more than a metre above the ground. It settles frequently, on the ground, usually among leaf litter on the forest floor. Males are territorial and choose sunny patches along forest paths or in clearings in the forest. Should another male enter this territory a dispute invariably follows, with the males circling around each other in tight spirals until one retires from the fray. This species flies on cloudy days and has been seen flying during light drizzle. Both sexes are highly attracted to fermenting fruit.

Flight period: All year but commoner in summer.

Early stages: Typical of satyrines (see p. 112). The larvae feed on various grasses on the forest floor and have been bred on *Ehrharta erecta* in captivity.

Eyed Bush Brown
Moeras-bosbruintjie
(Henotesia perspicua) **fig. 108**

Identification: Small to medium-sized (35–45 mm); sexes very similar; seasonally dimorphic. Male wet season form upperside brown with orange-ringed submarginal eye-spots in fore- and hindwing. Underside light brown with mediad yellow stripe in both wings and well developed submarginal eye-spots. Wet season form female slightly larger. Dry season form upperside as for wet season form but on underside eye-spots are almost invisible, except for a large eye-spot in lower forewing.

Distinguishing characters and similar species: The Pale Bush Brown (*Henotesia simonsii*), not illustrated, has a wet season form very similar to the Eyed Bush Brown but the dry season form is yellow-orange on the upperside, with an orange-brown forewing tip. The Pale Bush Brown is a savanna butterfly of Zimbabwe and northern Botswana.

Habitat and distribution: The Eyed Bush Brown is a fairly common savanna butterfly, from the Transkei and Natal coasts northwards to Swaziland, Transvaal, Mozambique and Zimbabwe. Central Transvaal, especially the Waterberg and Magaliesberg, is a very good area for it.

Behaviour: Very fond of flying near the shady banks of streams and marshes. It keeps just above the grass and even flies between the grass blades, with a bouncy, side to side flight pattern. Its flight is leisurely and in a more or less straight line. It tends to shun direct sunlight, preferring the semi-shade of riverine vegetation, and settles fairly frequently.

Flight period: All year but scarcer in June and July in cooler areas.

Early stages: Typical of satyrines (see p. 128). The larval foodplants are various species of soft grasses. In captivity it has been bred on *Ehrharta erecta* and on Kikuyu-grass (*Pennisetum clandestinum*).

BROWNS
BRUINTJIES
(Genera *Cassionympha, Neita, Coenyropsis, Pseudonympha, Stygionympha* and *Melampius*)

In southern Africa the 34 species in this group include a large number of endemic species and genera. Most are grassland butterflies but a few species occur in savanna and one is a forest butterfly. Browns are characterised by their small to medium size, brown coloration and reddish-orange patches on the upperside of the wings. Like those of other satyrines their wings are ornamented with eye-spots. They have a typical, bouncy flight, just above the tops of the grass, and are often seen feeding from flowers. They are summer butterflies and may have one to a few generations a year. The early stages are discussed under the subfamily (p. 128).

Rainforest Brown
Reënwoudbruintjie
(*Cassionympha cassius*) **fig. 113**

Identification: Small (30–40 mm); sexes very similar. Male upperside brown with single, large eye-spot near forewing tip and usually two small ones on lower edge of hindwing; area of suffused reddish-orange in middle of forewing. Underside like upperside but hindwing is irrorated with pinkish-grey and has two small, widely separated eye-spots. Female slightly larger.

Distinguishing characters and similar species: The Rainforest Brown is confusingly similar to the many other species of satyrines with reddish-brown patches on their wings (about 40 species in all). However, besides the rather different Pondo Shadefly (fig. 116), it is the only species that occurs in true forest habitats.

Habitat and distribution: The Rainforest Brown is a very common inhabitant of temperate forests, from the south-western Cape Province to the Soutpansberg in northern Transvaal.

Behaviour: Flies slowly and weakly, close to the ground, in grassy patches in the forest undergrowth or along the edges of forest and along forest roads. It has the typical bouncing to skipping flight characteristic of satyrines. It tends to alight on the ground and is quite often seen feeding from flowers.

Flight period: All year but commoner in summer.

Early stages: Typical of satyrines (see p. 128). The known larval foodplants are the monocotyledons *Pentaschistis capensis* and *Juncus capensis*.

Savanna Brown
Bosveldbruintjie
(Neita extensa) **fig. 109**

Identification: Medium-sized (40–45 mm); sexes very similar. Male upperside brown with single orange-ringed eye-spot in forewing and two smaller ones on hindwing. Usually an orange-brown area surrounds eye-spots on upperside. Underside similar but with four eye-spots on hindwing. Female larger.

Distinguishing characters and similar species: There are three other, very similar, species in southern Africa. All of them, including the Savanna Brown, can easily be confused with other Browns. The general distribution of the other *Neita* species covers the eastern Cape Province, Transkei, Natal and Lesotho.

Habitat and distribution: The Savanna Brown is widespread in the savanna of Transvaal and Zimbabwe but is found only in rather localised colonies. Occurs especially in the drier central and western areas of Transvaal and in western Zimbabwe.

Behaviour: Has quite a rapid, bouncing flight, usually close to the ground. Found singly in flat thornveld or on the slopes of grassy, dry hills. Both sexes are occasionally seen feeding from flowers.

Flight period: December to April.

Early stages: Typical of satyrines (see p. 128). The larvae feed on grasses.

Natal Brown
Natal-bruintjie
(Coenyropsis natalii) **fig. 114**

Identification: Small (30–35 mm); sexes almost identical. Male upperside brown with single orange-ringed eye-spot in apex of forewing and two smaller eye-spots on hindwing; eye-spots on both wings surrounded by orange-brown patch. Underside forewing as for upperside; hindwing with row of four or five submarginal eye-spots. Female slightly larger.

Distinguishing characters and similar species: Easily confused, when flying, with other Browns. A similar species, the Bera Brown (*Coenyropsis bera*), not illustrated, occurs in north-eastern Zimbabwe. The Bera Brown lacks orange-brown patches around the eye-spots on the upperside of the wings.

Habitat and distribution: The Natal Brown is widespread but found in localised colonies, in savanna (mainly thornveld), in northern Natal, Transvaal north of the Magaliesberg, western Zimbabwe and northern Botswana and Namibia.

Behaviour: Found on flats and on rocky slopes, often in the shade of thorn trees. The flight is slow and leisurely, typically bouncy, and at random. Males sometimes mud-puddle, which is unusual for a satyrine.

Flight period: October to May with peak abundance from January to March.

Early stages: The early stages of this species have not been recorded.

Drakensberg Brown
Drakensberg-bruintjie
(Pseudonympha poetula) **fig. 112**

Identification: Small (35–40 mm); sexes very similar. Male upperside brown with large eye-spot in forewing apex and three or four small eye-spots on hindwing; orange-brown patches on fore- and hindwing. Underside forewing similar to upperside; hindwing irrorated with grey-brown and brown scales; veins of hindwing prominently outlined with greyish-white scales. Female larger.

Distinguishing characters and similar species: There are four other *Pseudonympha* species, not illustrated, which have a very similar hindwing underside pattern: 1) Trimen's Brown (*P. trimenii*) – from the mountains of the Cape Province, including Little Namaqualand; 2) Gaika Brown (*P. gaika*) – from the eastern Cape Province and Lesotho; 3) Golden Gate Brown (*P. paragaika*) – from the north-eastern Orange Free State; 4) Machacha Brown (*P. machacha*) – flies at altitudes greater than 2 750 metres in and around Lesotho.

Habitat and distribution: The Drakensberg Brown is common in high-altitude (montane) grassland along the Drakensberg escarpment from Kokstad in the eastern Cape Province northwards to the Wolkberg (Houtbosdorp) in northern Transvaal.

Behaviour: Has a fairly fast, skipping flight about a metre above the ground. Prefers rocky areas with a grassy cover and rests mainly on stony ground. Both sexes are fond of flowers, in particular a small blue mountain daisy. Because they hatch in early spring they fly about in drab brown grassveld, unlike other browns which are on the wing when the grass is green and lush.

Flight period: Mid-September to mid-October.

Early stages: Not known.

Greybottom Brown
Bergbruintjie
(Pseudonympha magoides) **fig. 111**

Identification: Medium-sized (40–45 mm); sexes very similar. Male upperside brown with single eye-spot in forewing apex and two small eye-spots on hindwing; orange-brown patches on forewing. Underside forewing has eye-spot and large orange-brown patch; hindwing is brown with silvery-brown irroration and a row of eye-spots. Female has rounder wings and stouter abdomen.

Distinguishing characters and similar species: Eight species of *Pseudonympha* have similar underside markings to the Greybottom Brown and are difficult to separate in the field. As a whole their distribution covers most grassy habitats from the south-western Cape Province north-eastwards to the eastern highlands of Zimbabwe.

Habitat and distribution: The

Greybottom Brown is a very common species of high-altitude (montane) grassland where rainfall is high and mists are prevalent. Distributed from the eastern Cape Province to Haenertsburg in north-eastern Transvaal.

Behaviour: Has a slow, skipping flight, less than a metre above the ground. Flies at random on the grassy slopes of hills or mountainsides. Both sexes are occasionally seen feeding from flowers. The flight may be sustained but when resting the insect does so on the ground, between clumps of grass, or sometimes on rocks. They will fly about, apparently unperturbed, on overcast warm days.

Flight period: September to May with peak emergence from November to March.

Early stages: Typical of satyrines (see p. 128). The larvae use various species of grass as foodplants.

Spotted-eye Brown
Koloogbruintjie
(Pseudonympha narycia) **fig. 115**

Identification: Small (35–40 mm); sexes very similar. Male upperside brown, with single eye-spot in forewing surrounded by large orange-brown patch. Underside forewing like upperside forewing; hindwing brown with a row of five or six submarginal eye-spots. Female larger.

Distinguishing characters and similar species: The Savanna Brown (fig. 109) and the Natal Brown (fig. 114), like the Spotted-eye Brown, have a row of four to six submarginal eye-spots on the hindwing underside. However, the Savanna Brown is a larger species and the Natal Brown has an orange patch on the upperside of the hindwing. Furthermore the Spotted-eye Brown is a grassland species whereas the other two species occur in savanna habitats.

Habitat and distribution: The Spotted-eye Brown is a common and widespread species of the grasslands of the eastern Cape Province, eastern Orange Free State and Transvaal. It also occurs sparingly in Lesotho and north-eastern Zimbabwe. It is especially common in south-western Transvaal.

Behaviour: Has a slow, weak, skipping flight about half a metre to a metre above the ground. Flies at random on grassy slopes and often remains on the wing for long periods. When resting it usually perches on the ground or on stones, with closed wings. Both sexes are occasionally seen on flowers. Colonies are mostly encountered in rocky areas on grassy slopes.

Flight period: November to April with peak abundance in December and January.

Early stages: Unknown.

Western Hillside Brown
Rantbruintjie
(Stygionympha vigilans) **fig. 110**

Identification: Medium-sized (40–45 mm); sexes very similar. Male upperside brown with single, large eye-spot in forewing apex; reddish-brown patches in middle of fore- and hindwing. Underside forewing like upperside but reddish-brown patch more extensive; hindwing brown and finely irrorated with yellowish-brown scales. Female slightly larger.

Distinguishing characters and similar species: The Western Hillside Brown is easily mistaken for 1) the Eastern Hillside Brown (*Stygionympha scotina*), not illustrated, and 2) Wichgraf's Brown (*S. wichgrafi*), not illustrated, which are distributed in the north-eastern part of the subregion. There are five other species belonging to this genus in southern Africa. They are generally smaller than the three previously mentioned species and their distribution, as a whole, covers much of South Africa.

Habitat and distribution: The Western Hillside Brown is a very common species in grassy spots and grassland habitats in the mountainous regions of the southern and eastern Cape Province, Lesotho and Natal.

Behaviour: Has a relatively fast, bouncy flight and keeps about a metre above the ground. Prefers rocky areas on hills or mountain slopes and rests frequently on rocks, and sometimes on the ground, with the wings held partially open or closed. It is quite wary, except when feeding from flowers.

Flight period: September to April, with peak emergence in December and January.

Early stages: Typical of satyrines (see p. 128). The larvae are known to feed on the grass-like plant *Restio cincinnatus*, and probably also feed on other grasses.

BEAUTIES
PRAGS
(Genera *Aeropetes* and *Paralethe*)

Both species of Beauty are large, spectacular insects and are illustrated in this guide. Although both are beautiful satyrines, they occur in very different habitats, one being a forest butterfly and the other an insect of montane grasslands. The early stages are covered under the subfamily (p. 128).

Table Mountain Beauty
Bergprag
(*Aeropetes tulbaghia*) **fig. 239**

Identification: Large (75–90 mm); sexes similar. Male upperside dark reddish-brown with two broken, orange bands on forewing and single, continuous orange band on hindwing; four purplish-blue eye-spots submarginally on hindwing. Underside like upperside but with orange markings paler and five brown eye-spots on hindwing. Female larger, with additional orange band at base of forewing.

Distinguishing characters and similar species: A distinctive and large species – the largest satyrine in southern Africa.

Habitat and distribution: The Table Mountain Beauty is fairly common and widespread in mountainous grassy habitats, from the Cape Peninsula to the eastern highland mountains (Inyanga) in Zimbabwe.

Behaviour: Has a rapid and powerful flight, more like that of a large nymphaline than a satyrine. Prefers to fly around open, rocky areas with short grass, high up on mountains. During the hottest hours of the day it seeks out shady embankments and will occasionally also enter buildings. Flies at random and occasionally perches on rocks. This is a very wary insect except when feeding from flowers. Both sexes are inordinately fond of red flowers and in the Cape Peninsula are an important pollinator of the red disa (*Disa uniflora*). They have also been seen feeding on red-hot pokers (*Kniphofia* species), *Nerine*, *Haemanthus*, *Antholyza*, *Disa cornuta* and *Aloe* species.

Flight period: September to May but commonest from February to April.

Early stages: Typical of satyrines (see p. 128). Common thatch-grass (*Hyparrhenia hirta*) and *Ehrharta erecta* have been recorded as larval foodplants and I have bred them in captivity on Kikuyu-grass (*Pennisetum clandestinum*).

Bush Beauty
Bosprag
(Paralethe dendrophilus) **fig. 44**

Identification: Medium-sized to large (55–75 mm); sexes very similar, geographically very variable. Male upperside forewing dark brown (lighter at base) with scattered white spots on outer half of wing; hindwing orange-brown with narrow brown border and a row of submarginal eye-spots. Underside has a complex pattern of light to dark brown markings; white spots and eye-spots corresponding to those on upperside; additional eye-spot near tip of forewing. Female larger.

Distinguishing characters and similar species: This is a distinctive butterfly but it is variable through its range. The specimen illustrated is from the northernmost populations of the species (north-eastern Transvaal). Specimens from the southernmost populations are smaller, have a richer brown ground colour, and possess only a few small white spots on the forewing. Other populations are more or less intermediate between these extremes.

Habitat and distribution: The Bush Beauty is a common but strict inhabitant of moist temperate forest, from the eastern Cape Province northwards through Natal to the Woodbush forest in north-eastern Transvaal. Like many other satyrine species in the subregion the Bush Beauty is endemic to South Africa.

Behaviour: Flies in the semi-shaded understorey of the forest and is very fond of flying around tree trunks as well as in and out of the lower branches of forest trees. Flies in a leisurely manner, from one to five metres above the ground, perching frequently on the trunks and branches of trees but also, on occasion, on the leaves of plants in the undergrowth. Fermenting fruit and sucking-trees readily attract both sexes. They have never been recorded feeding from flowers.

Flight period: January to April.

Early stages: Typical of satyrines (see p. 128). The larvae feed on soft grasses such as *Ehrharta erecta* and broadleaved panicum (*Panicum deustum*).

WIDOWS
WEDUWEES
(Genera *Dira, Dingana, Torynesis* and *Tarsocera*)

The Widows are an interesting group of 17 species, in four genera, which are all endemic to South Africa. Within each of the four genera the species are very similar, therefore only one species of each genus is illustrated in this guide. All Widows are medium-sized, brown butterflies with rounded wings on which are well developed eye-spots. The general distribution of the Widows covers highlying grassland and grassy habitats in the Karoo and fynbos biomes. A number of species are found, in large localised colonies, in montane grassland where wire-grasses (*Merxmuellera* species) are dominant. Most species are single-brooded, flying either in spring or in autumn. Widows have a leisurely, bobbing, aimless flight pattern, about a metre above the ground. They are most active during the cooler morning hours, tending to rest in the shade of rocks during the hotter part of the day. They often fly in overcast weather and may even remain on the wing in light drizzle. The early stages are dealt with under the subfamily heading (p. 128).

Cape Autumn Widow
Kaapse herfsweduwee
(*Dira clytus*) **fig. 96**

Identification: Medium-sized (50–55 mm); sexes very similar. Male upperside dark brown with two blue-centred eye-spots near forewing tip and broken cream-yellow band across forewing; hindwing has a row of submarginal eye-spots. Underside forewing has reduced yellowish markings; hindwing has submarginal eye-spots and black zig-zag patterns. Female virtually indistinguishable in flight.

Distinguishing characters and similar species: Three other species belonging to the endemic genus *Dira* are found in South Africa. They have similar markings on the wings but are all larger than the Cape Autumn Widow. None of them is illustrated in this guide: 1) Pondoland Widow (*Dira oxylus*), 65 mm – found in the eastern Cape Province, Transkei and southern Natal (Kokstad); 2) Swanepoel's Widow (*D. swanepoeli*), 65 mm – occurs only on the Soutpansberg and Blouberg in far northern Transvaal; 3) Janse's Widow (*D. jansei*), 55–60 mm – rare; inhabits the Chuniesberg in northern Transvaal.

Habitat and distribution: The Cape Autumn Widow is a very common butterfly in grassy areas, especially around the base of mountains. It is distributed from the Cape Peninsula along the southern Cape coast, spreading out into the eastern Cape Province interior.

Behaviour: Flies relatively slowly and weakly, just above the level of the grass. The flight is often sustained, bobbing and rather aimless. Normally rests on the ground. Like many satyrines this species will often take to the wing on warm, overcast days and has even been observed flying in light drizzle.

Flight period: Only seen in the months of March to May.

Early stages: Typical of satyrines (see p. 128). The larvae feed on various species of grass.

Dingaan's Widow
Dingaan-weduwee
(*Dingana dingana*) fig. 97

Identification: Medium-sized (50–55 mm); sexes very similar. Male upperside dark brown with two conjoined eye-spots in forewing apex and uneven orange submarginal band on forewing; hindwing has five or six orange-ringed eye-spots submarginally. Underside blackish-brown with faint eye-spots and broken, orange submarginal band in forewing. Female indistinguishable in flight.

Distinguishing characters and similar species: Two other species, not illustrated, of this endemic South African genus are known: 1) Wakkerstroom Widow (*Dingana alaedeus*) – very closely related to Dingaan's Widow; appears to be restricted to the mountainous regions of south-eastern Transvaal; 2) Bowker's Widow (*D. bowkeri*) – generally smaller than the other two species and is distinguished from them by the presence of white submarginal spots in the forewing. It is found in mountainous areas in the eastern Cape Province, Transkei, Lesotho, Natal and northwards to the Lydenburg district of Transvaal.

Habitat and distribution: Dingaan's Widow occurs in high-altitude grassland, from the Natal midlands to Swaziland and the eastern Transvaal Drakensberg, as far north as the mountains south of Haenertsburg.

Behaviour: Flies on rocky, grassy mountain slopes subjected to high rainfall and periodic mist. It has a fairly fast bobbing flight which is often sustained and aimless. Most active in the morning, seeking the shade of rocks and embankments during the hottest parts of the day. One October I encountered vast numbers of this species on the Long Tom Pass between Sabie and Lydenburg. All appeared to be males, a phenomenon quite often seen in single-brooded satyrines, because the males hatch a week or so before the females. I have rarely seen this species on flowers.

Flight period: Only in October and November.

Early stages: Typical of satyrines (see p. 128). The larvae feed on various grasses.

Orange Widow
Oranje-weduwee
(Torynesis orangica) **fig. 98**

Identification: Medium-sized (50–55 mm); sexes similar. Male upperside brown with orange tinge; two eye-spots in apex of forewing and scattered, yellowish submarginal markings; hindwing has four eye-spots ringed with orange-yellow. Underside similar but eye-spots on hindwing small and veins of hindwing outlined in silvery-grey. Female with ground colour of wings paler.

Distinguishing characters and similar species: This genus is endemic to South Africa and has four other, very similar members, none of which is illustrated in this guide: 1) Mintha Widow (*Torynesis mintha*) – occurs in the south-western Cape Province and flies from March to May; 2) Hawequas Widow (*T. hawequas*) – from the inland mountains of the southern Cape Province; on the wing in late summer and autumn; 3) Magna Widow (*T. magna*) – in the north-eastern Cape Province; flies in February and March; 4) Pringle's Widow (*T. pringlei*) – in eastern Lesotho; flies in January and February.

Habitat and distribution: The Orange Widow is found in high-altitude grassland in the Golden Gate Highlands National Park and the surrounding mountains in the north-eastern Orange Free State.

Behaviour: Occurs in localised colonies in the vicinity of its presumed foodplant, a coarse tussock grass. The flight is relatively slow, random and often sustained. It flies from half a metre to a metre above the ground and is seldom seen visiting flowers. A strong colony of this insect is to be found on top of the Brandwag in Golden Gate National Park.

Flight period: Restricted to January and February.

Early stages: None of the life histories of this genus is known but since the adults are always associated with wire-grasses (*Merxmuellera* species), the larvae most probably use these as foodplants.

Cape Spring Widow
Kaapse lenteweduwee
(Tarsocera cassus) **fig. 99**

Identification: Medium-sized (45–50 mm); sexes similar. Male upperside dark brown tinged with dark reddish-brown; two confluent, white-centred eye-spots in forewing apex; three indistinct, small submarginal eye-spots on hindwing. Underside similar but hindwing has narrow, scalloped black bands. Female has more extensive reddish-brown markings on upperside and paler underside.

Distinguishing characters and similar species: This genus is yet another that is endemic to South Africa. The other six *Tarsocera* species, not illustrated, are very similar to the Cape Spring Widow and two or three species may be found flying together in the same locality. The different species can only be confidently separated by examining the genitalia of dead specimens under a microscope. In general the distribution of the species covers the south-western Cape Province, Karoo and Little Namaqualand. The adults are on the wing in spring (September and October, extending to November and even December for some species).

Habitat and distribution: The Cape Spring Widow is common in mountainous, grassy areas in the more inland portions of the south-western Cape Province, extending from Nieuwoudtville in the north to Riversdale in the south and to the Little Karoo in the east.

Behaviour: Large numbers of this butterfly may be encountered in localised colonies. It is very active and has a fairly swift and sustained flight. Frequently found feeding from flowers, especially mauve-coloured mesembryanthemums and selagos. Very dark on the wing, fresh specimens appearing to be almost black.

Flight period: September to December but most abundant in October.

Early stages: Typical of satyrines (see p. 128). The larvae feed on various species of grass.

SHADEFLIES
SKADUWEEBRUINTJIES
(Genus *Coenyra*)

A small group of three closely related species. Shadeflies are small insects that resemble the Browns and are characterised by wavy, red bands on the underside of their wings. The flight pattern is also similar to that of the Browns but their fondness for flying in the shade of large trees helps to distinguish them. The larvae are grass-feeders and the early stages are dealt with under the subfamily (p. 128).

Pondo Shadefly
Pondo-skaduweebruintjie
(*Coenyra aurantiaca*) **fig. 116**

Identification: Small (35–40 mm); sexes similar. Male upperside greyish-brown with broad, uneven orange-red bands across forewing; two well defined eye-spots on forewing and two small and two larger eye-spots on hindwing. Underside yellowish-brown with very distinct, yellow-orange-ringed eye-spots; numerous wavy, orange-red bands on both wings. Female with orange-red wavy bands present also on hindwing upperside.

Distinguishing characters and similar species: Two other species of Shadefly, neither illustrated, are found in southern Africa. Both possess the characteristic orange-red bands of the genus on their undersides: 1) Zulu Shadefly (*Coenyra hebe*) – occurs in frost-free savanna in northern Natal, Swaziland and Mozambique and is on the wing throughout the year; 2) Secucuni Shadefly (*C. rufiplaga*) – a fairly scarce species found in savanna habitats in the Transvaal Waterberg, Chuniesberg and Wolkberg; on the wing in summer.

Habitat and distribution: The Pondo Shadefly is a fairly common insect in and around certain temperate forests in the eastern Cape Province, Transkei and southern Natal.

Behaviour: The flight is weak and slow. Specimens fly close to the ground, on the outskirts of forest and along roads and paths through forest. They settle often, on the ground or on low vegetation, usually in the shade of trees. They are seldom seen on flowers.

Flight period: October to April.

Early stages: Typical of satyrines (see p. 128). The larvae feed on various soft grasses.

RINGLETS
RINGETJIES
(Genera *Physcaeneura*, *Ypthima* and others)

About a dozen species of Ringlet are found in the subcontinent. The two species of the genus *Physcaeneura* have very distinctive undersides but the other species in the group are inconspicuous, dull greyish-brown insects. As a group Ringlets occur in a variety of habitats but are found mainly in the savanna and Karoo biomes. They have the typical bobbing flight pattern of satyrines, and remain close to the ground. The early stages are discussed under the subfamily heading (p. 128).

Dark Webbed Ringlet
Gestreepte-ringetjie
(*Physcaeneura panda*) **fig. 118**

Identification: Small (30–35 mm); sexes very similar. Male upperside brown with rows of small orange-ringed eye-spots on both wings. Underside very distinctive, with interlacing pattern of black and creamy lines; rows of orange-ringed silvery eye-spots on both wings. Female slightly larger.

Distinguishing characters and similar species: There is another species belonging to this genus in southern Africa, the Light Webbed Ringlet (*Physcaeneura pione*), not illustrated, which has a similar underside but the upperside is creamy-white with blackish-brown wing margins. The Light Webbed Ringlet occurs on the eastern border of Zimbabwe and adjoining areas in Mozambique.

Habitat and distribution: The Dark Webbed Ringlet is common and widespread in savanna but occurs in more or less localised colonies. Distributed from northern Natal to Transvaal, Mozambique, Zimbabwe and Botswana.

Behaviour: Flies weakly and at random, with the typical skipping flight of the satyrines. Settles frequently, usually on the ground. Both sexes feed from small flowers growing among the grass and are also attracted to fermenting fruit. Prefers to remain close to or in the shade of trees and rarely flies more than a metre above the ground.

Flight period: October to April.

Early stages: Typical of satyrines (see p. 128). The larvae are grass-feeders.

Impure Ringlet
Onsuiwer-ringetjie
(*Ypthima impura*) **fig. 117**

Identification: Small (35–40 mm); sexes very similar. Male upperside dull greyish-brown with single eye-spot on each wing. Underside dark brown, finely irrorated with greyish-white markings; eye-spots as on upperside. Female slightly larger.

Distinguishing characters and similar species: Six other members of this genus are found in southern Africa and are very difficult to identify in the field. Their distribution, as a whole, covers most of southern Africa but excludes the western Karoo and extreme southwestern Cape Province. Most of them are on the wing all year.

Habitat and distribution: The Impure Ringlet is common and widespread in savanna, especially in arid areas. It is distributed from northern Natal to Swaziland, Transvaal, Mozambique and Zimbabwe.

Behaviour: Specimens of this butterfly are usually encountered singly in the veld. It has a leisurely, bobbing flight about half a metre above the ground, in and around bushes. Often overlooked because it is very inconspicuous. Takes fairly short flights and rests mostly on the ground.

Flight period: All year but commonest from September to March.

Early stages: These have not been described but are presumably similar to those of other satyrines (see p. 128). The larvae feed on grasses.

The danaines
(Subfamily Danainae)

This is a small subfamily with only 19 African species, seven of which occur in southern Africa. All are large, colourful, conspicuous insects found mainly in forest habitats. They are highly unpalatable to predators such as birds because of the toxins contained in their tough bodies. Not only do their warning coloration and leisurely flight deter would-be predators but they will also "play dead" when handled, a phenomenon known as thanatosis. Because of their unpalatability they serve as models for palatable butterflies such as the Mocker Swallowtail, Whitebanded Swallowtail and Diadems. Sometimes the mimicry shown by some of these edible butterflies is so accurate that the model and mimic are easily mistaken for each other: compare the African Monarch (fig. 46) with the female Common Diadem (fig. 45). The toxicity of danaines is due mainly to cardenolides present in the toxic milkweeds (Asclepiadaceae) on which the larvae feed. The larva concentrates these toxins and they are passed on to the pupa and adult. Cardenolides are "heart poisons" which, if ingested by, for example, a bird, will cause vomition at low doses and acute heart failure at higher doses. Male danaines are also known to suck fluids from certain plants containing toxins known as pyrollizidine alkaloids. Although these alkaloids may further increase the toxicity of the butterfly it is known that these compounds are used by the male to produce pheromones (volatile chemicals that are used in olfactory communication). These pheromones are secreted by the male during courtship to stimulate the female being courted.

Danaine eggs are usually laid singly and are barrel-shaped with fine longitudinal and transverse ribbing on their surfaces (fig. 329). The larvae are brightly coloured and possess a number of long, fleshy filaments on some of the body segments (fig. 330). The pupae are suspended by the tail end, have a smooth waxy surface and are often adorned with golden spots (fig. 331). In a few species the whole pupa has a metallic golden sheen, resembling a beautiful jewelled pendant.

MONARCHS
MELKBOSSKOENLAPPERS
(Genera *Danaus* and *Tirumala*)

Two species of Monarch, one of which is very common and widespread, are found in the subcontinent. The uncommon Dappled Monarch (*Tirumala petiverana*), not illustrated, is black with a dappling of pale blue spots and is found in northern Namibia. It is similar, in size and markings, to the Veined Swordtail (fig. 201), the latter being considered by some to be a mimic of the Dappled Monarch. The ubiquitous African Monarch is dealt with below.

African Monarch
Afrikaanse Melkbosskoenlapper
(*Danaus chrysippus*) **fig. 46**

Identification: Medium-sized (55–70 mm); sexes similar. Male upperside reddish-brown; forewing apex black with band of white spots on inner side; hindwing has black margin and four black spots in middle of wing. Underside like upperside but forewing apex and hindwing golden-orange. Female has only three black spots in middle of hindwing.

Distinguishing characters and similar species: This is a conspicuous and distinctive butterfly but it is widely mimicked by more palatable species of several different families. The most accurate mimic is the female of the Common Diadem (fig. 45). Other mimics include a female form of the Mocker Swallowtail, not illustrated, the Common Mimic Acraea (fig. 68) and the Monarch False Acraea, not illustrated (discussed under the Chief False Acraea, p. 93).

Habitat and distribution: The African Monarch is very common and widely distributed throughout the subcontinent.

Behaviour: Because of its unpalatability it has a leisurely, floating flight, usually from one to two metres above the ground. It often flies in a more or less straight line for long distances. Both sexes are very fond of flowers and can readily be approached when feeding from them.

Flight period: All year but commoner in summer.

Early stages: See introductory notes under danaines, above. A large number of plants belonging to the milkweed family (Asclepiadaceae) are used by the larvae as food. One of the most frequently used is milkweed (*Asclepias fruticosa*), a common roadside weed with bladder-like fruits. Other genera of plants used by the larvae include *Ceropegia* and carrion-flowers (*Stapelia* and *Huernia*). The larvae also feed on the exotic moth catcher (*Araujia sericifera*).

FRIARS
MONNIKE
(Genus *Amauris*)

The Friars are closely related to the Monarchs. There are five species in southern Africa, three of which are illustrated in this guide. They are medium-sized to large, black butterflies, boldly patterned with white or yellow markings. Friars are forest butterflies, and their size, coloration and leisurely flight make them conspicuous inhabitants of this biome. The larvae feed on highly toxic plants belonging to the family Asclepiadaceae. The early stages are discussed under the subfamily (p. 149).

Common Friar
Gewone Monnik
(Amauris niavius) **fig. 193**

Identification: Large (80–85 mm); sexes very similar. Male upperside black with large white patches in forewing apex, lower portion of forewing and on hindwing; scattered, small white spots on forewing. Underside similar to upperside but white patch on hindwing covers virtually whole of wing surface. Female slightly larger but indistinguishable in flight.

Distinguishing characters and similar species: The unpalatable Common Friar is a frequent model for mimicry. It is mimicked by, especially, form *wahlbergi* of the Variable Diadem (fig. 195) and by female form *hippocoonides* of the Mocker Swallowtail (fig. 194). The Common Friar can also be mistaken for the smaller Novice Friar (fig. 196).

Habitat and distribution: The Common Friar is a fairly plentiful inhabitant of the warmer forests of the Natal coast as far south as Umkomaas, the forests below the eastern Transvaal escarpment, Mozambique and the eastern border of Zimbabwe.

Behaviour: Has a leisurely floating flight, usually from two to five metres above the ground. It keeps to the shade of tall forest trees and also flies around in forest clearings. The large size and black and white coloration make this a very conspicuous insect.

Flight period: All year but commoner in summer.

Early stages: Not described.

Novice Friar
Outannie-monnik
(Amauris ochlea) **fig. 196**

Identification: Large (70–75 mm); sexes very similar. Male upperside black with a small white patch in forewing apex and larger white patches in middle of forewing and on hindwing. Underside similar to upperside but ground colour of forewing apex and hindwing brown. Female indistinguishable from male in flight.

Distinguishing characters and similar species: The Novice Friar is a model for the palatable but rare (in southern Africa) Deceptive Diadem (*Hypolimnas deceptor*), not illustrated. It also resembles the Common Friar (fig. 193) and its mimics, but is generally smaller than them.

Habitat and distribution: The Novice Friar is common in the coastal forests of Natal (especially the northern portions), Mozambique and the eastern border of Zimbabwe.

Behaviour: Has a slow and floating flight in the shade of forest trees and on the edges of forest. Inclined to spend much of its time resting on shrubs in the forest understorey.

Flight period: All year but scarce in midwinter.

Early stages: Typical of danaines (see p. 149). The forest climbers *Tylophora anomala* and *Cynanchum chirindense* have been recorded as larval foodplants.

Chief Friar
Hoofmonnik
(*Amauris echeria*) **fig. 228**

Identification: Medium-sized (55–75 mm); sexes very similar. Male upperside blackish-brown with scattered white to yellowish spots of variable sizes on both wings; large, block-like ochre patch on hindwing. Underside similar but ground colour is lighter brown.

Distinguishing characters and similar species: In the field the Chief Friar is impossible to distinguish from the equally common Layman Friar (*Amauris albimaculata*), not illustrated. The two species often fly together in the same forests. Both of these Friars are mimicked by a number of palatable species, including the Chief False Acraea (fig. 230), female form *cenea* of the Mocker Swallowtail (fig. 225), female of the Whitebanded Swallowtail (fig. 226) and form *mima* of the Variable Diadem (fig. 227).

Habitat and distribution: The Chief Friar is common in forests and coastal bush, from George in the southern Cape Province northeastwards to the eastern Cape Province, Transkei, Natal, Swaziland, Transvaal, Mozambique and the eastern border of Zimbabwe.

Behaviour: Has an unhurried, floating flight from one to three metres above the ground. Both sexes are very fond of flowers and on the Natal coast are sometimes seen in large numbers on the blossoms of the exotic weed *Lantana camara*. They will also feed on the tops of flowering trees in forests. The males frequently mud-puddle. Specimens of both the Chief and Layman Friar often stray long distances from forests and David Swanepoel records large numbers of specimens in Pietersburg, some 80 km from the nearest forests. On one occasion I observed a female Layman Friar laying on its foodplant, which I had planted in my garden in Pretoria, more than 300 km from the eastern Transvaal forests!

Flight period: All year but much commoner in summer.

Early stages: Typical of danaines (see p. 149). The larvae feed on the forest creepers *Tylophora anomala* and *Cynanchum chirindense*.

The libytheines
(Subfamily Libytheinae)

The libytheines are also known as Snout or Beak butterflies because of the extraordinarily long palps that project from the front of their heads, between the antennae. Some taxonomists accord libytheines full family status but as they are most closely related to the diverse nymphalid family they are treated as a subfamily of the nymphalids in this guide. Compared with the other nymphalid subfamilies the libytheine subfamily contains very few species, about a dozen being found in the tropics and subtropics of the world. They seem to represent an ancient relict group, well preserved amber fossils dating back 25 million years having been found in North America. Interestingly leaves of a plant belonging to the genus *Celtis*, species of which are still used as larval foodplants today, were embedded in the fossils in which the libytheines were found. A single widespread species is found on the African continent.

SNOUTS
SNUITSKOENLAPPERS
(Genus *Libythea*)

A single, forest-dwelling species occurs in southern Africa and is dealt with below.

African Snout
Afrikaanse Snuitskoenlapper
(*Libythea labdaca*) fig. 102

Identification: Medium-sized (45–55 mm); sexes very similar. Male upperside dark brown with three elongated white spots in forewing apex and scattered, block-like orange markings on both wings; forewing apex bluntly extended and hindwing with short, blunt tail. Underside forewing apex and hindwing pale brown, finely speckled with dark brown; forewing has scattered white spots and orange basal flush. Female larger.

Distinguishing characters and similar species: The African Snout is easily confused with the much commoner Boisduval's and Natal Tree Nymphs (figs 101 & 100). Not only are they all similar in appearance, but they also have very similar habits. If one can get close enough, the very long palps, which give the Snouts their name, may be seen. The palps project forward from the head, between the antennae. The blunt forewing apex of the African Snout also helps to distinguish it from the Tree Nymphs.

Habitat and distribution: The African Snout is a fairly common species of temperate forest, from the eastern Cape Province (East London) to Natal, eastern Transvaal, Mozambique and the eastern border of Zimbabwe.

Behaviour: Tends to keep to the shaded parts of the forest where it flies rapidly from one tree to another. Alights on the trunk or branches with the head facing down and the wings closed; then rather difficult to see. Males will occasionally mud-puddle. The males are also territorial and select perches on the tops of trees where they perch on twigs with the wings held open. In central Africa huge migrations of this species are fairly common but migrations by this butterfly have not been reported in southern Africa.

Flight period: All year but commoner in summer.

Early stages: The eggs are laid singly on leaves of the larval foodplant. The larva is cylindrical, finely hairy, and resembles a pierid larva (fig. 300). The pupa, like that of other nymphalids, is suspended, head downwards, from the tail end. The larva feeds on white stinkwood (*Celtis africana*).

THE LYCAENIDS
(Family Lycaenidae)

The lycaenids are the largest family of butterflies in both Africa (about 1 500 species) and southern Africa (418 species, more than half of which are endemic to the subcontinent). They vary in size from very small to medium-sized but most are small. Because of their diversity they have been divided into a number of subfamilies, five of which are dealt with in this guide: the liptenines (p. 158), miletines (p. 163), theclines (p. 169), lycaenines (p. 203) and polyommatines (p. 204). The uppersides of the wings are usually shades of yellow, orange, red, brown or blue while the undersides are often very different and show complex, diagnostically useful patterns. Many species possess delicate single or double tails on the hindwing which also aid in identifying them. Lycaenids are found in all biomes, and while some fly close to the ground, others dwell mainly in the treetops. The flight may be weak (as in the liptenines) or very fast (as in many theclines). Most lycaenids are very fond of flowers and many also mud-puddle. Some liptenines and miletines have a rudimentary proboscis and do not feed at all. Many lycaenids have the peculiar habit of moving their hindwings alternately up and down when perched. This has the effect of drawing attention to the tails and eye-spots at the end of the hindwing. The tails and eye-spots resemble the antennae and eyes respectively and may represent a ploy to deceive predators as to which end of the butterfly is the head end. Often lycaenids are found in the wild with a chunk of the hindwing missing and this may have the shape of a bird's beak. Although some lycaenids are continuous-brooded and are therefore on the wing year round, a number have only one brood each year and may be on the wing for only a few weeks.

Lycaenids breed on a huge variety of dicotyledonous plants, from small forbs to large trees. The larvae may feed on the flower buds, leaf shoots, leaves or seeds and fruit. The liptenines have switched from dicots to lichens growing on tree bark or on rocks. Lichens are composed of a fungus and an alga living in symbiosis. The larvae of miletines and some polyommatines (*Lepidochrysops* and *Orachrysops*), on the other hand, have become carnivorous. Miletine larvae feed on Homoptera (scale insects and their kin) while carnivorous polyommatines feed on the brood of their host ants for part of their larval stage. Lycaenid eggs are usually laid singly and are bun-shaped, often with an intricate surface tracery (fig. 332). The typical lycaenid larva is onisciform in shape (figs 339, 343 & 344) with a very thick cuticle ("skin"). The legs are hidden under the body and the head can also be retracted below the body. On the dorsum of one of the abdominal segments there is often a honey gland, from which ants obtain a sweet secretion. The larvae of liptenines and some theclines are atypical. Liptenine larvae are cylindrical in shape and the body is covered with long hairs (fig. 335). In those groups of theclines that are dependent on ants (Highfliers, Bars, Scarlets, Greys, Coppers, Opals and Arrowheads) the larvae are depressed (flattened) and possess eversible tubercles on each side of the honey gland (fig. 340). The tubercles are crowned with a rosette of tiny white spines which "flash" when erected. The function of these tubercles is not known with certainty but they are associated with communication between the larva and ant. Lycaenid pupae are usually short and broad and may lie free or be attached by the tail end (fig. 333 & 346). In some species a silken girdle is present.

The association with ants is known as myrmecophily. The degree of association of the larvae with ants varies between different lycaenid groups. Thus there are non-myrmecophiles, facultative myrmecophiles and obligate myrmecophiles. Liptenines and lycaenines are non-myrmecophiles and do not possess a honey gland. Facultative myrmecophiles, which include most of the polyommatines and a large number of theclines, have a honey gland which is "milked" by ants but they are not dependent on the ants for completion of their life cycle. Obligate myrmecophiles cannot complete their life cycles without the presence of ants. The Skollies (subfamily Miletinae) are dependent on the pugnacious ant (*Anoplolepis* species); the Bars and related groups (subfamily Theclinae) are associated with cocktail ants (*Crematogaster* species) and the polyommatine genera *Lepidochrysops* and *Orachrysops* are associated with sugar ants (*Camponotus* species). Details of these ant-larva associations are given under the respective groups.

The liptenines
(Subfamily Lipteninae)

With over 500 species in Africa the liptenines are the largest lycaenid subfamily on the continent. The subfamily is found only in Africa and is centred on the Equatorial Forest Zone. Consequently a paltry 31 species occur in southern Africa. They are small yellow, orange or brown butterflies and are weak fliers. Most are forest species that fly in the shade around the trunks of the lichen-covered trees on which they breed. The few savanna and grassland species lay their eggs mainly on lichens growing on rocks (fig. 334). Liptenines that breed on lichens on trees (Pentilas and Buffs) appear to spend much time sitting motionless among colonies of sap-sucking homopterans, sucking up the sweet excretions of these insects. On the other hand, the adults of those liptenines that breed on lichens on rocks (Zulus and Rocksitters) do not appear to feed at all. Liptenine larvae have numerous long hairs on their bodies (fig. 335) (unusual for lycaenids) which provide them with good camouflage among the lichen and possibly protect them against attack by ants. The pupae are also hairy and the skin of the final larval stage is partly retained (fig. 336).

ZULUS
ZOELOES
(Genus *Alaena*)

Zulus are very small, slow-flying butterflies found in localised colonies in rocky habitats in the grassland and savanna biomes. Four species occur in the subregion, only one of which is relatively common. The adults have a rudimentary proboscis and probably do not feed. The larvae feed on lichens growing on rocks; the early stages are dealt with under the liptenines, above.

Yellow Zulu
Geel-zoeloe
(Alaena amazoula) **fig. 42**

Identification: Very small (23–27 mm); sexes similar. Male upperside orange-yellow with blackish-brown borders; wing veins outlined in blackish-brown. Underside paler with veins clearly outlined in black. Female slightly larger, paler and with less pronounced black markings.

Distinguishing characters and similar species: Can be confused with the Namibian Zulu (*Alaena brainei*), not illustrated, which is very similar but occurs only in northern Namibia.

Habitat and distribution: The Yellow Zulu is found in grassland and in grassy areas in savanna, especially on the slopes of stony hillsides. Occurs from the eastern Cape Province to Transkei, Natal, Swaziland, Transvaal, Zimbabwe and Botswana.

Behaviour: Lives in localised colonies of about a dozen individuals, but larger colonies are sometimes encountered. Has a very slow, weak and fluttering flight, less than a metre above the ground. The flight is not sustained and it settles frequently on grass stems, or occasionally on rocks. When the insect is at rest the wings are held closed. The Yellow Zulu closely resembles a day-flying geometrid moth, which can be distinguished by the lack of clubs at the end of the antennae. Specimens are easily disturbed but will normally rest motionless for long periods.

Flight period: Mainly November to April (most numerous in December); all year in warm, wet climates.

Early stages: Typical of liptenines (see p. 158). The larvae feed on lichens growing on rocks.

PENTILAS
PENTILAS
(Genus *Pentila*)

Three species of this liptenine genus are found in forest habitats in southern Africa and are discussed below.

Spotted Pentila
Spikkelpentila
(*Pentila tropicalis*) **fig. 40**

Identification: Small (30–35 mm); sexes similar. Male upperside orange-yellow with black-tipped forewing and a few scattered, small black spots, especially on forewing. Underside orange-yellow with scattered black spots, and densely speckled with black scales. Female larger, without black forewing tip and with reduced black spotting.

Distinguishing characters and similar species: Closely related to the rare Swynnerton's Pentila (*Pentila swynnertoni*), not illustrated, and Paul's Pentila (*P. pauli*), not illustrated. The former is found in the Chirinda Forest and environs in south-eastern Zimbabwe, while the latter occurs near Victoria Falls and in the Lomagundi district in Zimbabwe. The Spotted Pentila can also be confused with the various species of Buff – see below.

Habitat and distribution: The Spotted Pentila is a common insect in subtropical forests and extends in distribution from the coasts of Transkei (Port St Johns) and Natal to Mozambique, Venda and the eastern border of Zimbabwe.

Behaviour: Has a feeble, floating flight, often many metres above the ground. Keeps strictly to the shaded subcanopy of forest. It closely resembles a common diurnal moth that occurs in the same habitat. Small colonies of Spotted Pentilas are sometimes found roosting communally on bare twigs in the understorey. Individuals rest on plants, tree trunks and twigs and have the peculiar habit of slowly opening and closing their wings while perched.

Flight period: October to May; most numerous in December and again in April.

Early stages: Typical of liptenines (see p. 158). The larvae are known to use lichens growing on tree-trunks as food.

BUFFS
GEELVLERKIES
(Genus *Baliochila* and others)

Buffs are small to very small yellow or orange-yellow insects with dark brown markings on the wings. There are 16 species, in five genera, in the subregion. Most are rare and localised butterflies that have a slow, hovering flight, in the shade of the forest canopy. The Common Buff, discussed below, is typical of the group in terms of both appearance and behaviour.

Common Buff
Natal-geelvlerkie
(*Baliochila aslanga*) **fig. 41**

Identification: Very small (23–27 mm); sexes similar. Male upperside orange-yellow with brown forewing tip and irregular brown markings on leading edge of forewing. Underside hindwing rich brown with scattered, small, orange-brown markings; forewing with brown markings similar to those on upperside. Female has reduced brown markings on leading edge of forewing.

Distinguishing characters and similar species: There are seven closely related butterflies in the subregion (four in the genus *Baliochila* and three in the genus *Cnodontes*). These species can only be identified with certainty by experts working with set specimens. In flight the Common Buff may also be confused with the larger Spotted Pentila (fig. 40).

Habitat and distribution: The Common Buff is fairly often encountered in subtropical forest and bush and is distributed along the Natal coast and in Mozambique, stretching inland to the eastern border of Zimbabwe.

Behaviour: Flies slowly and high up in the shade of the forest canopy. Like the Spotted Pentila (above) it roosts communally on bare twigs and has the same peculiar habit of opening and closing its wings while at rest. Sometimes it also sways from side to side with the wings held closed. Numbers of adults are occasionally seen clustered on a twig while feeding from the sweet excretions (honeydew) of sap-sucking homopterans such as scale insects (coccids).

Flight period: September to May.

Early stages: Typical of liptenines (see p. 158). The larvae feed on lichens growing on the bark of trees.

ROCKSITTERS
KLIPSITTERS
(Genus *Durbania* and others)

Rocksitters are extraordinary, small butterflies that not only perch on rocks, as their name implies, but actually spend their whole lives on rocks. There are only four species of Rocksitter, all of which are endemic to South Africa. One species is fully covered below and the other three are briefly discussed.

Amakosa Rocksitter
Amakosa-klipsitter
(*Durbania amakosa*) **fig. 256**

Identification: Small (25–35 mm); sexes similar; geographically variable. Male upperside blackish-brown with rows of orange spots submarginally in fore- and hindwing. Underside finely mottled with white and black; curved row of orange spots or orange band on forewing. Female larger with curved, submarginal bands on upperside sometimes very wide.

Distinguishing characters and similar species: Three other Rocksitters, not illustrated, are found in southern Africa: 1) Natal Rocksitter (*Durbania limbata*) – slightly smaller (25–30 mm); almost black, with orange-red markings on the upperside of the wings. Occurs from the Natal midlands northwards as far as the Wakkerstroom district in south-eastern Transvaal. On the wing in March and April (compare with the Amakosa Rocksitter); 2) Clark's Rocksitter (*Durbaniella clarki*) – small, with the orange markings almost covering the upperside. Found mainly on the Swartberg and Langeberg mountain ranges in the southern Cape Province. Flies from mid-September to December; 3) Boland Rocksitter (*Durbaniopsis saga*) – slightly larger than the Amakosa Rocksitter and mainly brown with rows of small orange spots on the upperside of the wings. Occurs in the fold mountains of the south-western Cape Province (Hex River

Mountains and adjoining ranges). On the wing from October to mid-January.

Habitat and distribution: The Amakosa Rocksitter occurs in colonies in rocky outcrops in grassland. Usually this is at considerable elevations, especially in the north of its range. It is found from the Port Elizabeth district in the eastern Cape Province to Transkei, Natal, Swaziland and Transvaal (as far north as Mariepskop).

Behaviour: This species literally spends its whole life on rocks, where the underside lends remarkable camouflage when it is resting among lichens on the rocks. It lives in restricted but sometimes very large colonies. The adults are reluctant to fly but when disturbed will flutter weakly, close to the ground, to the nearest rock, on which they will promptly alight. Females appear to be very sedentary as they are rarely seen. The adults have never been observed to feed and probably do not (the proboscis is rudimentary).

Flight period: From late November to mid-January; most numerous in December.

Early stages: Typical of liptenines (see p. 158). The larvae feed on lichens on rocks.

The miletines
(Subfamily Miletinae)

This is a small subfamily of some 50 African species, 31 of which are found in southern Africa. The strong representation in the subcontinent is due to the endemic Skollies (genus *Thestor*, which contains more than 25 species). Miletines are small, dull insects found in savanna (Woolly Legs) and fynbos or Karoo (Skollies). What they lack in beauty they more than make up in terms of their fascinating life histories, especially as regards the early stages. These are considered under each of the two groups, below.

WOOLLY LEGS
WOLPOOTJIES
(Genus *Lachnocnema*)

Three species of these curious, small, dull butterflies are found in the subregion. Their rapid flight and small size make them difficult to recognise as they whirl around shrubs or trees. When perching, however, they are readily identified by their fluffy legs and by the metallic spots on the underside of the wings. The adults have strange culinary habits and spend much of their time sitting among colonies of sap-sucking homopterans (for example scale insects) feeding on the honeydew. Since ants invariably tend these homopterans the woolly legs of these butterflies are thought to protect them from attacks by the ants. Not only do Woolly Legs feed on the honeydew but females also lay their eggs among the homopteran colonies. On hatching from the egg the larva feeds on the homopterans, one of the rare instances of carnivory in butterfly larvae. The ants show no aggression towards the butterfly caterpillars, indeed it has been observed that the larvae are sometimes fed by the ants. A drop of fluid appears to be passed from the mouthparts of the ant to the caterpillar during these exchanges. Pupae of Woolly Legs have been found in ants' nests at the base of the plant on which the homopterans occur and these, too, appear not to be attacked by the ants. The defence mechanisms of the early stages against ant aggression are not known.

Woolly Legs
Wolpootjie
(*Lachnocnema bibulus*) **figs 122 & 220**

Identification: Small (25–30 mm); sexes dissimilar. Male upperside dark brown. Underside brown with scattered metallic silver and gold spots; legs distinctly woolly. Female slightly larger; brown with white patches on fore- and hindwing. Underside variegated in brown and greyish-white, with metallic spots as in male.

Distinguishing characters and similar species: Easily confused with D'Urban's Woolly Legs (*Lachnocnema durbani*), not illustrated, which, in the male, is lighter brown on both the upper- and underside. The female is uniform greyish-white on the upperside. D'Urban's Woolly Legs is quite common in grassy habitats in the savanna biome and widespread in the subcontinent.

Habitat and distribution: The Woolly Legs is fairly common in savanna habitats. Widespread in the eastern half of the subregion, from the eastern Cape Province (Port Elizabeth district) to Transkei, Natal, Swaziland, Transvaal, Mozambique, Zimbabwe and Botswana.

Behaviour: Has a very rapid, whirling flight around bushes and trees – a few may occur around the same tree. Groups of individuals are also found feeding on the sweet honeydew excreted by sap-sucking coccids on the twigs of bushes and trees. Males hilltop, perching on the leaves of trees on the summit. Females are often solitary and spend much time searching for oviposition sites on low shrubs and bushes.

Flight period: All year but commonest from September to March.

Early stages: See remarks under Woolly Legs, above. The larvae are carnivorous, feeding on certain homopterans.

SKOLLIES
SKOLLIES
(Genus *Thestor*)

The Skollies derive their name from their generally scruffy appearance. The genus *Thestor* is endemic to southern Africa, by far the majority of the 27 species being found in the Cape Province. About half of the species have dull yellow or dull orange markings on the upperside (the "yellow Skollies") and the other half are dull brown and black (the "black Skollies"). Only the dedicated and observant naturalist is likely to find Skollies in the field. This is because they are inconspicuous and because they live in isolated colonies that are often not more than a hectare in extent. Skollies are closely related to Woolly Legs and, like these, their larvae are carnivorous. Unlike Woolly Legs adults, Skollies have a rudimentary proboscis and do not appear to feed as adults. Females lay their eggs (fig. 337) among or near colonies of homopterans (scale insects and others) that are tended by the very aggressive pugnacious ant (*Anoplolepis custodiens*), which is known by the Afrikaans name "malmier" (mad ant). Since the ants often attack a female Skolly as it tries to lay an egg the female oviposits very rapidly, often in mid-flight. The early stages are, however, not molested by the ants but it is not known how they prevent ant aggression. In fact the larvae (fig. 338) appear to be largely ignored by the ants. In the first three larval instars the caterpillars feed on homopterans. The later larval stages and the pupae of Skollies have been found in nests of the pugnacious ant but the diet of the later larval stages is unknown.

Boland Skolly
Bolandskollie
(*Thestor protumnus*) **fig. 79**

Identification: Small (30–40 mm); sexes similar. Male upperside orange-yellow, dusted with brown; black spots and patches on forewing. Underside forewing orange-yellow with scalloped brown margins and black spots and patches as on upperside; hindwing variegated with grey and rust-brown. Female larger, with more extensive orange-yellow coloration.

Distinguishing characters and similar species: The Boland Skolly belongs to the so-called "yellow Skolly" group. There are about a dozen predominantly yellow species of Skolly which can only be specifically identified from set, dead specimens. These species are mainly found, in various locations, in the Cape Province.

Habitat and distribution: The Boland Skolly occurs in localised colonies in the fynbos and Karoo biomes. The geographical area covered includes almost the whole of the Cape Province and the south-western Orange Free State as far north as Bloemfontein. The other yellow Skollies generally have much more restricted distributions.

Behaviour: Lives in colonies which may number from a few to dozens of individuals. The males fly very rapidly, within small territories, and regularly alight on the ground or stones where they rest with closed wings. Females have a slower, fluttering, random flight and spend most of their time resting on the ground or searching for places to lay their eggs. Colonies are usually found in sparsely vegetated, stony areas.

Flight period: Mainly September to December, but there may be a smaller second brood on the wing from February to April.

Early stages: See remarks under Skollies, above.

Knysna Skolly
Strandskollie
(Thestor brachycerus) **fig. 121**

Identification: Small (35–40 mm); sexes very similar. Male upperside dull brown with some darker markings on fore- and hindwing; cilia on wing margins chequered black and white. Underside a complex mosaic of grey, brown and black markings. Female larger.

Distinguishing characters and similar species: The Knysna Skolly belongs to the so-called "black Skollies" of which there are about 10 species. All of these species are found in various localities in the Cape Province. Like the "yellow Skollies" they are difficult to distinguish from one another in the field. Experts require set specimens to identify the various taxa and even this is not easy.

Habitat and distribution: The Knysna Skolly occurs in localised colonies in fynbos habitats along the southern Cape coast, from Still Bay in the west to Knysna in the east.

Behaviour: The colonies in which the species is found may at times be very large; they usually occupy stony ground. The males are territorial and take short, not particularly fast, flights. They perch on the ground with the wings closed, when the underside blends remarkably well with the surroundings. Females have a slow, fluttering flight and rest on the ground for long periods.

Flight period: November to January.

Early stages: See introductory remarks under Skollies, p. 165.

Basutu Skolly
Basoetoe-skollie
(Thestor basutus) **fig. 120**

Identification: Male small; female medium-sized (35–45 mm); sexes dissimilar. Male upperside dull brown with dark brown and whitish spots on forewing and, to lesser extent, on hindwing. Underside greyish-brown, irrorated with brown; some black spotting, especially in forewing. Female larger, with dark brown and whitish spots much more obvious.

Distinguishing characters and similar species: Similar to the other "black Skollies" (see Knysna Skolly, above) but the habitat and distribution of the Basutu Skolly is very different (see below).

Habitat and distribution: The Basutu Skolly is widespread, but only in localised colonies, in the eastern half of the subcontinent, in grassland and grassy habitats in savanna. Distributed from the eastern Cape Province to Transkei, Natal, the eastern Orange Free State, Lesotho, Transvaal, Zimbabwe and Botswana.

Behaviour: Within the colonies males defend territories and perch on grass stems, stones or the ground. The flight is very fast but not sustained. The females flutter around clumps of grass and are easily mistaken for moths. They spend long periods resting on the ground or grass.

Flight period: October to April.

Early stages: See remarks under Skollies, p. 165.

The theclines
(Subfamily Theclinae)

This is a large subfamily with nearly 500 species in Africa, approximately 200 of which are found in the subcontinent. The large number of species in southern Africa is accounted for by the large number of species of Coppers (genus *Aloeides*) and Opals (genus *Poecilmitis*), each with about 50 species. Most theclines are small, brightly coloured insects and generally have a rapid flight. Theclines are found in all biomes. The life histories and early stages of the various groups are diverse; more information can be found under the group headings below.

FIGTREE BUTTERFLIES
VYEBOOMVLINDERS
(Genus *Myrina*)

These small, exquisitely coloured butterflies with their prominent tails are gems of the insect world. Only two species occur in the subcontinent. The larvae feed on the leaves of a number of species of fig tree. Eggs are laid singly on young shoots or leaves of the foodplant. The larvae are slug-like and patterned with green and brown (fig. 339). The caterpillars are casually associated with ants, especially sugar ants (*Camponotus* species), which "milk" the honey gland of the larva. The short, squat, dark brown pupae are usually found among leaf debris at the base of the foodplant. Often a particular fig tree is used to breed on year after year and at times large numbers of pupae may be found at the base of such "breeding trees".

Common Figtree Butterfly
Gewone Vyeboomvlinder
(*Myrina silenus*) **fig. 160**

Identification: Small (30–35 mm); sexes similar. Male upperside bright metallic blue with brown and black forewing tip; single, long, relatively thick, twisted, brown tail on hindwing. Underside orange-brown. Female larger, with blue less extensive and not as bright as in male.

Distinguishing characters and similar species: There is a single, related species in southern Africa, the scarcer Lesser Figtree Butterfly (*Myrina dermaptera*), not illustrated. It differs from the Common Figtree Butterfly in that it has black wing tips, more delicate tails and a greyish-brown underside. The Lesser Figtree Butterfly occurs in the coastal zone, from East London north-eastwards along the Natal and Mozambique coasts, and extends inland along the Olifants River in the eastern Transvaal lowveld and to the eastern border of Zimbabwe.

Habitat and distribution: The Common Figtree Butterfly is relatively common and widespread wherever its larval foodplants (wild figs) occur, including the southern Cape Province (Mossel Bay) to Natal, Transvaal, Mozambique, Zimbabwe, Botswana, Namibia and Namaqualand.

Behaviour: Found mostly at the base and on the slopes of rocky hills, where males select territories and perch on the twigs of trees or shrubs with half-opened wings. They have a rapid flight, often in a straight line from one place to another. Females are slower, fly at random and are usually encountered in the vicinity of wild figs. Occasionally specimens are seen feeding from ripe figs that have split open. Rarely feeds from flowers but poinsettias (*Euphorbia pulcherrima*) seem to hold a special attraction.

Flight period: All year in warmer areas; September to April are the best months.

Early stages: See introduction above. A number of species of fig have been recorded as larval foodplants, including Namaqua fig (*Ficus cordata*), tickey creeper (*F. pumilia*), broom-cluster fig (*F. sur*), common wild fig (*F. natalensis*) and *F. thonningii*. Domesticated figs are also, but rarely, used.

HIGHFLIERS
SILVERROKKIES
(Genus *Aphnaeus*)

Three species of this group of beautiful insects occur in southern Africa, two of which are illustrated in this guide. They are characterised by their silver-spotted undersides and paired tails and are closely related to the Bars (p. 173). Highfliers are found in savanna habitats, in localised colonies. Females lay their eggs singly on the twigs of certain leguminous trees in spring. Only trees of the correct species that are inhabited by cocktail ants (*Crematogaster* species) are selected as oviposition sites by the female. The small, black cocktail ants live in dead branches, in which tunnels have been bored out by beetle larvae, and characteristically raise their abdomens when alarmed. Mature larvae of the Highfliers live in the tunnels with the ants and only emerge at night to feed on the foliage of the tree. The larvae are closely attended by the ants, which gain nourishment from the larval honey gland. Pupation takes place in the ants' nest. Since there is only one brood a year it is probable that the larvae or pupae diapause through winter.

Eriksson's Highflier
Eriksson-silverrokkie
(*Aphnaeus erikssoni*) fig. 119

Identification: Small (30–40 mm); sexes similar; geographically variable. Male upperside rust-brown with six orange-brown or white spots on forewing; metallic blue patches in some populations; short tail on hindwing. Underside orange-brown with faint tracery of fine, dark lines. Female larger with narrow, dark brown wing margins.

Distinguishing characters and similar species: A similar species, Marshall's Highflier (*Aphnaeus marshalli*), not illustrated, is orange-brown on the upperside with thin, black wing margins and has large, silver spots on the underside. It is restricted to the Mutare district in northern Zimbabwe.

Habitat and distribution: Eriksson's Highflier is a common insect in savanna habitats in north-eastern Zimbabwe. It also occurs, more sparingly, on the eastern border and in the Matopos in the south-west of the country.

Behaviour: Males are most likely to be found hilltopping, where they fly rapidly around the treetops. Females fly at random on the slopes of hills and ridges.

Flight period: Spring and early summer.

Early stages: See the introduction to Highfliers, above. The larvae, according to Alan Gardiner, feed on wild seringa (*Burkea africana*).

Hutchinson's Highflier
Hutchinson-silverrokkie
(*Aphnaeus hutchinsonii*) **fig. 161**

Identification: Small (30–40 mm); sexes very similar. Male upperside dark brown with extensive patches of metallic sky blue scales on both wings; several white spots in forewing apex; two tails on hindwing, upper one shorter. Underside brownish with scattered, large, black-ringed silver spots. Female larger.

Habitat and distribution: Occurs in localised colonies in savanna habitats. Distributed from the Estcourt district in Natal northwards to Swaziland, Transvaal, Mozambique, Zimbabwe and eastern Botswana.

Behaviour: Males are inveterate hilltoppers, where they perch on the twigs or leaves of bushes and small trees. They arrive on the hilltop at about 13h00 and depart by about 15h00. Females that are unmated arrive on the top between 14h00 and 15h00. Females are rarely seen but can sometimes be encountered on the slopes, flying among the branches of trees. Both sexes are occasionally seen feeding from flowers or mud-puddling.

Flight period: September to mid-November.

Early stages: See introductory notes under Highfliers, p. 171. The larvae use wild seringa (*Burkea africana*) and splendid acacia (*Acacia robusta*) but will probably also feed on other leguminous trees if the host ant is present on these.

BARS
STREEPVLERKIES
(Genus *Spindasis*)

Bars are small, brightly coloured butterflies found mainly in savanna habitats. The common name is derived from the characteristic bars on the tip of the forewing upperside and on the underside of both wings. There are 10 species in the subregion. The early stages are similar to those of the Highfliers (see p. 171) but, unlike the latter, Bars often have several broods per year and some species are continuous-brooded. The larvae (fig. 340) have an obligatory association with the host cocktail ant.

Natal Bar
Natal-streepvlerkie
(*Spindasis natalensis*) **fig. 165**

Identification: Small (30–35 mm); sexes similar. Male upperside dark brown with shiny blue patches in lower half of forewing and covering much of hindwing; distinctive brown bars, interspersed with orange at apex of forewing; two tails on hindwing. Underside creamy-yellow with gold bands and spots outlined in light brown. Female larger, with blue patches paler and suffused with white.

Distinguishing characters and similar species: Nine similar species of Bar are found in the subcontinent, one of which is dealt with below. The Bars are difficult to distinguish in the field since all of them possess the characteristic pattern of orange markings on the forewing upperside and bars on the underside.

Habitat and distribution: The Natal Bar is common in savanna throughout the eastern half of the subregion and occurs from the eastern Cape Province (Port Elizabeth district) through Natal to parts of the Orange Free State, Swaziland, Transvaal, Mozambique, Zimbabwe and Botswana.

Behaviour: Males are most often encountered on hilltops where they select perches on bushes one to two metres above ground level. They fly very rapidly but tend to remain within a small area and settle frequently, usually on the twigs or leaves of their chosen bushes. Females tend to fly at random, often on the slopes of hills. Both sexes are very fond of flowers.

Flight period: All year in frost-free habitats; September to April in colder areas.

Early stages: See introductory notes under Bars, above. Recorded larval foodplants include turkey-berry (*Canthium inerme*), white cat's whiskers (*Clerodendrum glabrum*) and cork bush (*Mundulea sericea*). I have also found them on large sour-plum (*Ximenia caffra*).

Silvery Bar
Silver-streepvlerkie
(*Spindasis phanes*) fig. 166

Identification: Small (25–30 mm); sexes somewhat dissimilar. Male upperside dull violet-blue; brown bars interspersed with orange in forewing apex; two tails on hindwing with orange spot just above them. Underside cream with irregular, orange-brown bars outlined in black. Female larger, with orange markings also on hindwing; blue scaling paler and restricted to wing bases.

Distinguishing characters and similar species: Easily confused with other species of Bar – see discussion under the Natal Bar, above.

Habitat and distribution: The Silvery Bar occurs in localised colonies in thornveld savanna in Natal, Swaziland, Transvaal, Zimbabwe, Botswana, Griqualand West and northern Namibia.

Behaviour: Both sexes are most often found on the stony slopes of ridges and hills. They have a rapid flight but remain more or less in one place and settle on low bushes frequently. Both sexes may be found feeding from flowers.

Flight period: All year but commoner in summer.

Early stages: See introductory remarks under Bars, p. 173. The larvae have only been recorded feeding on the leaves of the large sour-plum (*Ximenia caffra*).

SCARLETS
ROOIVLERKIES
(Genus *Axiocerses*)

These are small butterflies with red and black markings on the upperside of the wings and metallic spots on the underside. Characteristically they have a single, lobed tail on each hindwing. Females of the Common Scarlet lay their eggs, in batches of 10 to 50, on the shoots of small acacia bushes. The larvae are gregarious and live in shelters at the base of the foodplant, among small ants of an unknown species. Presumably the larvae spend the daylight hours in these shelters and emerge from them at night to feed on the foliage of the bush.

Common Scarlet
Ralie-rooivlerkie
(*Axiocerses tjoane*) fig. 77

Identification: Small (30–35 mm); sexes dissimilar; variable. Male upperside bright red with brown forewing tip; single, lobed tail on hindwing. Underside brown, shading to orange-brown at base of forewing; scattered, black-ringed gold spots, especially on forewing. Female larger; orange with rows of black dots on fore- and hindwing and even, brown margin on forewing. Underside as in male.

Distinguishing characters and similar species: Two other species of Scarlet, not illustrated, occur in southern Africa: 1) Bush Scarlet (*Axiocerses amanga*) – distinguished from the Common Scarlet by the presence of a few silver spots and markings at the base of the forewing underside. Fairly common in savanna habitats throughout the subcontinent; 2) Rainforest Scarlet (*A. punicea*) – has scattered, small, gold spots and a few linear silver markings on the lower edge of the forewing underside. Confined to forests on the eastern border of Zimbabwe and in Mozambique.

Habitat and distribution: The Common Scarlet is frequently encountered in savanna, in the whole of the subregion. It has been found in the eastern Cape Province, Natal, Transvaal, Mozambique, Zimbabwe and Botswana.

Behaviour: The males fly very rapidly but are territorial, keeping to a particular spot where they alight frequently on low bushes and on grass, about a metre above the ground. Males sometimes hilltop and both sexes are very fond of flowers. They are alert but can be closely approached when feeding from flowers. Females fly more slowly and are mostly found in the vicinity of small acacia bushes, on which the eggs are laid.

Flight period: Mainly September to April, but all year in warmer areas.

Early stages: See introductory remarks under Scarlets, above. The eggs are laid in batches on acacias (*Acacia* species).

ARROWHEADS
PYLKOPPIES
(Genus *Phasis*)

The four species of Arrowhead are endemic to South Africa, occurring in the fynbos and Karoo biomes. They are medium-sized insects, dark brown, with a few orange spots, and broad, paired tails on each hindwing. Eggs are laid singly on leaves or twigs of the foodplants, which are shrubs belonging to the genera *Rhus* and *Melianthus*. Female Arrowheads will only oviposit on bushes of the foodplant that are inhabited by a species of cocktail ant (*Crematogaster* species). This particular cocktail ant constructs an arboreal nest of paper-like material among the branches of the bush. These nests are more or less spherical, 100 mm to 200 mm in diameter and dark grey in colour. During the day the butterfly larvae remain within the ants' nest and at night crawl out to feed on the leaves of the foodplant. The larvae also pupate within these nests.

Common Arrowhead
Jakkalsdraf-pylkoppie
(*Phasis thero*) **fig. 255**

Identification: Medium-sized (40–45 mm); sexes similar. Male upperside dark brown with orange-red spots on forewing; two broad tails on hindwing. Underside brown with silver spots on forewing and irregular silver markings on hindwing; broad orange flush at base of forewing. Female larger, with a row of submarginal orange spots on hindwing upperside and larger orange spots on forewing.

Distinguishing characters and similar species: There are three other species of Arrowhead in southern Africa. All occur in various parts of the Cape Province and are very difficult to separate from each other in the field.

Habitat and distribution: The Common Arrowhead is found in localised colonies in fynbos and fynbos–Karoo transitions. Its distribution range includes the southwestern Cape Province, from the Clanwilliam district in the north to about Knysna in the east.

Behaviour: Has a fairly rapid, undulating flight, one to three metres above the ground. It normally keeps close to bushes, especially those of its foodplants, *Rhus* and *Melianthus* species. After their short, fast flights the males usually perch on twigs of the bushes around which they have been flying. In flight they have a very dark, almost black, colour. They are alert and wary and must be approached cautiously. Females are mostly encountered in close proximity to the foodplants. Both sexes feed at flowers such as mesembryanthemums.

Flight period: The main brood flies from August to November and a second, smaller brood is on the wing in March and April. Odd specimens are encountered from December to February.

Early stages: See introductory remarks under Arrowheads, above. The larvae feed on wild currants (*Rhus* species) and honey-flower (*Melianthus major*).

SILVERSPOTTED COPPERS
SILWERKOLKOPERVLERKIES
(Genus *Argyraspodes* and others)

There are six species, in three genera, in this group. All three genera are endemic to southern Africa. They are small butterflies with orange and black markings on the upperside and characteristic, large, irregular and numerous silver spots on the underside of the wings. The early stages are poorly known and the diet of the larvae is unknown.

Warrior Silverspotted Copper
Silwerkolkopervlerkie
(*Argyraspodes argyraspis*) **fig. 76**

Identification: Small (30–40 mm); sexes very similar. Male upperside deep orange with broad black margin on forewing and narrower black margin on hindwing; chequered white and brown cilia on wing margins; two tails on hindwing. Underside olive-brown with scattered, irregular, silver markings and very extensive basal orange flush on forewing. Female larger.

Distinguishing characters and similar species: The Warrior Silverspotted Copper is the only member of its genus (*Argyraspodes*) but there are two other, closely related, genera: *Trimenia* (four species) and *Argyrocupha* (one species). All have similarly marked, silverspotted undersides. All of these species are restricted to the fynbos and Karoo biomes and most are rare to very rare butterflies.

Habitat and distribution: The Warrior Silverspotted Copper is found in the Karoo biome and its distribution includes the Cape Province, south-western Orange Free State, southern Botswana and southern Namibia.

Behaviour: Flies fast and low down but settles frequently on the ground, stones or low bushes, with closed wings. The silver spots on the underside can often be seen while the insect is flying. It is alert and wary and is most often encountered on the slopes of stony ridges and hills. Males hilltop, where they defend territories. Both sexes are fond of flowers.

Flight period: August to April but the flight period is dependent on adequate rainfall.

Early stages: Unknown.

COPPERS
KOPERVLERKIES
(Genus *Aloeides*)

This group, which is largely southern African, is represented by more than 50 species in the subregion. The various species are mainly found in the fynbos, Karoo and grassland biomes but a few species are savanna insects. Coppers are small butterflies, usually with orange-red and black markings on the upperside but some are almost entirely orange while others are dark brown on the upperside. There is even one species that has a silvery upperside. The five species depicted in this guide illustrate this upperside variation. The undersides of the Coppers, on the other hand, have a fairly uniform and typical pattern that makes it possible to assign them to this group with reasonable certainty. Since they tend to perch on the ground with the wings closed it is the undersides that are normally visible when one is observing them in the field. Coppers are colonial butterflies and often these colonies occupy only a few hectares. The adults fly rapidly, close to the ground, and are well camouflaged when perched. The life histories of most species of Copper are unknown but a few have been studied in detail. Females spend much time walking around on the ground in search of the pheromone trails of small black ants (*Acantholepis* species). When a trail is located eggs are laid on it, sometimes on bare ground and sometimes on plant material. In some species the larvae shelter in the nest of the host ant and in others they remain on the foodplant where they are tended by the ants. The larval foodplants are always small herbaceous plants, usually of the genera *Aspalathus* and *Hermannia*. In those species where the larvae live in the ants' nest the larvae have a winter diapause in the nest, which affords them protection from veld fires during this period.

Roodepoort Copper
Roodepoort-kopervlerkie
(*Aloeides dentatis*) **fig. 80**

Identification: Small (25–30 mm); sexes very similar. Male upperside bright orange with black wing margins. Underside forewing orange, with black spots and black-ringed silver spots; hindwing brown to purplish-crimson with scattered, silvery-grey and black markings. Female has more rounded wings.

Distinguishing characters and similar species: The Roodepoort Copper belongs to the very large genus *Aloeides* which has some 50 species in southern Africa, most of which occur in the Cape Province. Many of the species are almost impossible to identify in the field (with the exception of Barkly's Copper – see below). Experts even have difficulty in identifying set specimens! It should be noted that the characteristic pattern on the underside allows for easy identification of the Coppers *per se*.

Habitat and distribution: The Roodepoort Copper is found in small, very localised colonies in the grassland biome in southern Transvaal, the north-eastern Orange Free State and western Lesotho.

Behaviour: The males have a fairly rapid, erratic flight, close to the ground, and remain within small, ill-defined territories. Females fly at random within the colonial boundaries. Both sexes alight on the ground or on stones and rest with closed wings. They are quite difficult to see because of their cryptically marked undersides. Females spend a lot of time walking on the ground searching for the pheromone trails of the host ant (see introduction to Coppers, above).

Flight period: September to March.

Early stages: See introduction to Coppers, above. The larvae feed on the small, prostrate herb "rooiopslag" (*Hermannia depressa*).

Barkly's Copper
Barkly-kopervlerkie
(*Aloeides barklyi*) **fig. 28**

Identification: Small (30–40 mm); sexes similar. Male upperside silvery-grey with narrow, black wing margins. Underside typical of Coppers. Female larger; large, orange patch in apex of forewing upperside, bordered marginally by broad, brown band.

Distinguishing characters and similar species: This is a distinctive butterfly and the only member of the Coppers that does not have an orange and/or brown upperside (compare with the other Coppers dealt with in this guide).

Habitat and distribution: Barkly's Copper is found in the higher-lying areas of the succulent Karoo, from Little Namaqualand and Bushmanland in the north to about Matjiesfontein in the south. It is thus confined to the north-western Cape Province.

Behaviour: Lives in localised colonies, especially in the vicinity of rocky outcrops and hills. The males fly very fast and erratically, in a random fashion, within the confines of the colony. They often have a sustained flight and have a silvery-white colour when on the wing. Females are much more sluggish and are found at the base of hills. Both sexes rest on the ground, or on rocks, and feed from flowers.

Flight period: August to November.

Early stages: Unknown.

Dusky Copper
Dowwekopervlerkie
(Aloeides taikosama) **fig. 127**

Identification: Small (25–35 mm); sexes similar. Male upperside brown with greyish submarginal markings on fore- and hindwing. Underside typical of Coppers. Female larger, with orange markings corresponding to greyish submarginal markings of male.

Distinguishing characters and similar species: The Dusky Copper is one of about half a dozen Coppers with predominantly brown uppersides. The undersides of all these species immediately allow them to be identified as belonging to the genus *Aloeides* (Coppers).

Habitat and distribution: The Dusky Copper is a common colonial species of grassland and savanna. Occurs in northern Natal, parts of the Orange Free State and most of Transvaal.

Behaviour: Colonies are found in open, stony areas where there is a preponderance of grass. The butterflies seem to prefer flat areas. They have a fairly rapid flight but alight frequently on the ground or on grass stems. They are rather inactive, spending long periods resting. Both sexes are occasionally seen at flowers.

Flight period: September to April.

Early stages: Unknown.

Damara Copper
Damara-kopervlerkie
(Aloeides damarensis) fig. 82

Identification: Small (30–35 mm); sexes very similar; variable. Male upperside orange with dark brown markings on leading edge of forewing, outer margin of forewing and upper, outer margin of hindwing; hindwing has toothed, black margin and clear, black submarginal spots. Underside typical of Coppers. Female larger, with rounder wings.

Distinguishing characters and similar species: Easily confused with the 45 or so other members of the genus that have orange and brown uppersides (see the Roodepoort Copper and the Aranda Copper for comparison).

Habitat and distribution: The Damara Copper is widespread, in colonies, in the savanna and Karoo biomes. Its distribution includes the western and eastern Cape Province, Natal, the Orange Free State, western and northern Transvaal, Mozambique, Zimbabwe, Botswana and Namibia.

Behaviour: Found in localised colonies, especially on stony slopes with short grass and bushes and in sandy areas. Behaves much as do other Coppers, taking short, rapid flights and settling frequently on the ground. The males are territorial.

Flight period: There are two main broods, the first on the wing from September to November and the second from February to March.

Early stages: See under Coppers, p. 179. The larvae feed on an unidentified species of *Aspalathus*.

Aranda Copper
Aranda-kopervlerkie
(Aloeides aranda) fig. 81

Identification: Small (25–30 mm); sexes very similar; variable. Male upperside bright orange with variable amount of black, of varying width, on wing margins. Underside typical of Coppers but varies from almost flat brown to reddish-brown and purplish-brown. Female larger, with rounder wings.

Distinguishing characters and similar species: Easily confused with other Coppers (see remarks under the Damara Copper, above).

Habitat and distribution: The Aranda Copper is very widespread, occurring mainly in grassland but also in parts of the Karoo. Found in all the provinces of South Africa as well as in Lesotho, Swaziland, Mozambique, Zimbabwe, Botswana and Namibia.

Behaviour: Colonies, which are sometimes very large, are found in stony, grassy habitats on the flats, sides of hills and mountains and sometimes even on the top of fairly high mountains. Like other Coppers this species flies rapidly, near the ground, settling frequently on bare ground with closed wings. It rests on the ground for long periods and if disturbed will usually fly a few metres and alight again.

Flight period: September to April.

Early stages: See under Coppers, p. 179. The larvae feed on an unidentified species of *Aspalathus*.

DAISY COPPERS
MADELIEFKOPERVLERKIES
(Genus *Chrysoritis*)

This small group of six species is closely related to the Coppers and Opals and is endemic to the subregion. They are small orange butterflies, with black markings and spots on the upperside. Daisy Coppers live in small, localised colonies and are usually found flying around their larval foodplants, which are often bushes with yellow, daisy-like flowers belonging to the genus *Chrysanthemoides*. The early stages are like those of the Opals (see below).

Karoo Daisy Copper
Karoo-madeliefkopervlerkie
(*Chrysoritis chrysantas*) **fig. 84**

Identification: Small (25–30 mm); sexes very similar. Male upperside bright orange with narrow black borders; black and white chequered cilia on wing margins; some black spots towards tip of forewing. Underside forewing largely orange, with black spotting; outer margin of fore- and hindwing variegated white, grey and brown. The female Karoo Daisy Copper is larger.

Distinguishing characters and similar species: May be confused with some members of the Coppers (*Aloeides*) but the underside pattern is very different.

Habitat and distribution: The Karoo Daisy Copper is found in the Karoo biome, occurring in the whole of the Karoo, including the Little Karoo and parts of Little Namaqualand.

Behaviour: Occurs in small colonies on flat ground or slight hillslopes. Has a fast and irregular flight, less than a metre above the ground. It is alert and wary and if disturbed it flies away to another spot. Both sexes are fond of flowers, especially mesembryanthemums. They settle on the ground or on stones.

Flight period: September to March.

Early stages: Unknown.

OPALS
OPALE
(Genus *Poecilmitis*)

The Opals comprise about 50 species in a single genus which is endemic to South Africa. They are small butterflies and the majority are orange with an opalescent basal flush. About a dozen species lack the opalescent basal flush, while a few species have extensive bluish coloration with the orange markings restricted to the lower hindwing margin. The species of Opal illustrated in this guide show this upperside variation as well as the variation that is present on the underside of the wings. Generally the underside is either dull brown or brown streaked with metallic gold markings (the majority have metallic underside markings). As a group Opals are distributed mainly in the fynbos and Karoo biomes, with some extension into montane grassland containing fynbos remnants. The various species occur in small colonies in which the males are territorial. The flight of the males is very rapid and they settle on low vegetation or on the ground. A variety of forbs are used as larval foodplants but females will only oviposit on foodplants inhabited by the correct host ant (cocktail ants of the genus *Crematogaster*). The larvae of some species live in leaf shelters on the plant, others in shelters at the base of the plant.

Lydenburg Opal
Lydenburg-opaal
(Poecilmitis aethon) **fig. 85**

Identification: Small (25–30 mm); sexes very similar. Male upperside bright metallic orange-red, with narrow, wavy, black wing margins and rows of black spots on both fore- and hindwing. Underside forewing orange with scattered black spots; hindwing more or less flat brown with small, darker spots. Female larger.

Distinguishing characters and similar species: There are about a dozen species of Opal that have a predominantly red upperside. Most are very difficult to distinguish in the field. Their distribution, taken as a whole, covers most of southern Africa.

Habitat and distribution: The Lydenburg Opal is found in rocky areas in montane grassland along parts of the Drakensberg escarpment. Its distribution is from the Vryheid district in northern Natal northwards to about Graskop in north-eastern Transvaal.

Behaviour: Occurs in localised colonies. The males have a rapid flight but are highly territorial and thus tend to remain in one small area. Within their territories they perch on bushes and bracken fern fronds, about a metre above the ground. The females are more sluggish and flutter about the rocks, searching for suitable oviposition sites. Both sexes are often seen on flowers.

Flight period: This species is double-brooded, the first brood flying in October and November and the second in February and March.

Early stages: See discussion under Opals, above. The larvae feed on a scrambling shrub, the blue karree (*Rhus zeyheri*), which grows among and over large rocks.

Water Opal
Wateropaal
(Poecilmitis palmus) **fig. 86**

Identification: Small (25–30 mm); sexes very similar. Male upperside bright orange with narrow, orange-dotted, black wing margins; single blunt tail on hindwing. Underside forewing orange with black spotting; hindwing has streaky pattern of yellowish-brown to chocolate-brown markings (typical of hindwing underside of most Opals). Female larger, with rounder wings.

Habitat and distribution: A butterfly of the fynbos biome, from the Cape Peninsula eastwards along the coast to the Port Elizabeth district.

Behaviour: Lives in localised colonies in valleys or on the slopes of hills and mountains, usually in the vicinity of streams or in marshy habitats. Males have a rapid flight, to and fro, within a restricted area. In these territories they settle on low-growing vegetation or on the ground, often with the wings held half open. Females fly at random within the colonial boundaries. Both sexes feed from flowers, especially yellow-flowered daisies (Asteraceae).

Flight period: September to April.

Early stages: See remarks under Opals, p. 184. A number of larval foodplants have been recorded, including "knopbos" (*Berzelia intermedia*) in marshy areas, bush-tick berry (*Chrysanthemoides monilifera*) in drier areas and *Osteospermum ciliatum*.

Common Opal
Pragopaal
(*Poecilmitis thysbe*) **fig. 87**

Identification: Small (25–30 mm); sexes similar. Male upperside bright orange with iridescent, pinkish-blue sheen at base of wings; narrow black margin on forewing; black spotting in orange areas on both wings. Underside typical of Opals. Female larger, with basal blue coloration much reduced and not as shiny as in male.

Distinguishing characters and similar species: There are some 30 species of Opal with this unique combination of bright orange and iridescent blue on the upperside of the wings. They are all very difficult to distinguish in the field. Taken as a whole their distribution covers most of the Cape Province (excluding the interior of the Great Karoo) and the high-lying parts of the Drakensberg escarpment of Natal and Lesotho. In all these areas colonies of these Opals are associated with fynbos or Afro-alpine vegetation.

Habitat and distribution: The Common Opal is found in low-lying coastal fynbos in the south-western Cape Province, from Lambert's Bay in the north to Port Elizabeth in the east. The colonies often occupy sandy areas close to the sea.

Behaviour: Males establish territories within the confines of the colony, which they defend against intrusion by other males. They have a rapid flight and are very alert. They perch frequently, usually on low vegetation, but sometimes also on the ground. In flight they appear almost silvery. Females fly at random and spend long periods resting on the ground. Both sexes feed from flowers.

Flight period: August to April.

Early stages: See general remarks under Opals, p. 184. A number of larval foodplants have been recorded, including "spekbroodbossie" (*Zygophyllum flexuosum*), "skilpadbossie" (*Z. morgsana*), *Z. sessilifolium*, bush-tick berry (*Chrysanthemoides monilifera*), *Lebeckia plukenetiana* and *Aspalathus* species.

Dark Opal
Bloujuweel-opaal
(Poecilmitis nigricans) **figs 88 & 268**

Identification: Small (25–30 mm); sexes dissimilar. Male upperside iridescent pearly-blue to violet, with black forewing tip; some orange spotting and markings on lower margin of hindwing, including short, blunt tail. Underside typical of Opals. Female very like that of Common Opal (fig. 87c) but with more extensive dark markings.

Distinguishing characters and similar species: This is one of only two species of Opal in which the blue on the upperside in the males almost totally replaces the orange markings.

Habitat and distribution: The Dark Opal is found in colonies in mountain fynbos in the fold mountains of the south-western Cape Province, as far east as the Swartberg range.

Behaviour: Males establish territories on the highest peaks of mountains where they perch on shrubs or on the ground. The flight is very fast and often sustained. Females fly in the same places as the males but are much more sluggish. Both sexes feed from flowers.

Flight period: September to April, but they are more numerous in

October–November and again in February–March.

Early stages: See general description under Opals, p. 184. The larvae feed on "spekbossie" (*Zygophyllum fulvum*) and *Osteospermum polygaloides*.

GREYS
VALETJIES
(Genus *Crudaria*)

Three species of these small, dull grey-brown butterflies are found in the subregion. They are insects of the savanna and Karoo biomes, especially where the sweet thorn (*Acacia karroo*) is abundant. Colonies of these butterflies sometimes contain a large number of individuals. Greys fly rapidly but settle frequently on thorn trees, bushes or the ground. Females lay their eggs singly or in small batches on the stalk of young acacia shoots. The larvae feed on the young leaves and are gregarious, keeping in small groups, during early instars. The pupa lies free in a nest-like covering of leaves.

Silverspotted Grey
Spikkelvaletjie
(*Crudaria leroma*) **fig. 133**

Identification: Small (25–30 mm); sexes similar. Male upperside dull brown with single, delicate tail on hindwing. Underside pale greyish-brown with heavy black spotting in middle of forewing and fine, black streaks on rest of underside. Female larger and slightly paler brown.

Distinguishing characters and similar species: There are two other species of Grey in southern Africa, both of which are difficult to distinguish from the Silverspotted Grey in the field.

Habitat and distribution: The Silverspotted Grey is common in thornveld savanna and the eastern Karoo, wherever acacias grow. Absent from the south-western Cape Province.

Behaviour: Found in colonies in the vicinity of acacias, flying rapidly around bushes, from one to two metres above the ground. They settle frequently, on thorn bushes or on other vegetation and even on the ground. Females are found together with males but are slightly less active. Both sexes are very fond of flowers. At times population explosions occur and large numbers may be found in a relatively small area.

Flight period: All year but commonest from September to April.

Early stages: See comments in the introduction to Greys, above. The larval foodplants are *Acacia* species, especially the sweet thorn (*Acacia karroo*).

SAPPHIRES
SAFFIERE
(Genus *Iolaus*)

Sapphires are appropriately named for the gem-like quality of the upperside markings on their wings. Many of the 21 species found in southern Africa have metallic blue uppersides and silvery-white undersides. There is a pair of tails on each hindwing, surmounted by a well developed eyespot. The majority of species are forest or savanna insects and fly mainly in summer. The larval foodplants of Sapphires are mostly semi-parasitic plants belonging to the families Loranthaceae and Viscaceae. Eggs are laid singly on the shoots or leaves, and the young larvae feed on the surface of the leaves, gouging out characteristic troughs in which they rest. The later instars feed from the edge of the leaves and resemble bird droppings or are cryptically patterned (fig. 341). Some species feed only on the candle-like flowers of the foodplant, their coloration matching that of the flowers closely. The larvae are not dependent on ants. The pupae are highly cryptic, usually resembling bits of knob-like bark (fig. 345). The pupae, when disturbed, tap their anterior end against the substrate on which they have pupated. In a number of species the pupa may diapause through winter.

Bowker's Sapphire
Bowker-saffier
(Iolaus bowkeri) **fig. 164**

Identification: Small (25–35 mm); sexes similar; geographically variable. Male upperside powder blue with brown, black and white markings; two well developed tails on hindwing. Underside mottled with greyish-white and brown.

Distinguishing characters and similar species: Very similar to the closely related Dusky Sapphire *(Iolaus subinfuscata)*, not illustrated, which is found in Little Namaqualand and Namibia.

Habitat and distribution: Bowker's Sapphire is common in the savanna and Karoo biomes in the subregion. Absent from the extreme south-western Cape Province and the grassland plateau of the interior.

Behaviour: Both sexes have the characteristic habit of perching on dead twigs inside bushes, especially thorn bushes. They have a rather slow and fluttering to hovering flight, around bushes, and settle frequently. They fly at random, one to three metres above the ground, often from one bush to the next. Both sexes occasionally feed from flowers.

Flight period: August to April. Odd specimens may be seen in the winter months.

Early stages: See introductory remarks under Sapphires, above. A number of larval foodplants have been recorded, including the large sour-plum *(Ximenia caffra)*, small sour-plum *(X. americana)*, *Moquinella rubra*, *Tapinanthus oleifolius* and *Viscum rotundifolium*.

Southern Sapphire
Kussaffier
(Iolaus silas) **fig. 159**

Identification: Small (35–40 mm); sexes dissimilar. Male upperside bright metallic blue with black wing margins; two red spots near paired hindwing tails. Underside silvery-white with thin, red line on hindwing and eye-spot near tails. Female dull blue with broad, brown forewing margin and wide, orange-red band submarginally on hindwing. Underside as in male.

Distinguishing characters and similar species: Can be confused with some of the other Sapphires, such as Trimen's Sapphire (below), the Straight-line Sapphire (*Iolaus silarus*), not illustrated, and the Lalos Sapphire (*I. lalos*), not illustrated.

Habitat and distribution: The Southern Sapphire is a fairly common species of subtropical forest and bush, from the eastern Cape Province (Port Elizabeth) to Transkei, Natal, Mozambique, Zimbabwe and northern Botswana.

Behaviour: A medium-fast insect that perches frequently on the leaves of trees. Males are territorial and rest on twigs or leaves of trees, high up, on the edges of forest or bush. When the insect is perched the wings are held closed and the silvery-white underside blends surprisingly well with the leaves on which it is resting. The females are not encountered very often and spend most of their time searching for flowers or oviposition sites in forest.

Flight period: All year but commoner in summer.

Early stages: See introductory remarks under Sapphires, p. 189. Recorded larval foodplants include *Moquinella rubra*, *Erianthemum dregei* and *Viscum obovatum*.

Trimen's Sapphire
Trimen-saffier
(Iolaus trimeni) **fig. 158**

Identification: Small (35–40 mm); sexes dissimilar. Male upperside bright metallic blue with broad black tip on forewing; two slender tails on hindwing. Underside silvery-white with very thin, discontinuous black line down hindwing. Female dull blue with broad, brown wing margins and a few red spots near tails. Underside as in male.

Habitat and distribution: A common savanna species, from northern Natal to Swaziland, Transvaal, Zimbabwe and Botswana.

Behaviour: Males are most likely to be observed hilltopping on hot, sunny days. They select perches on the leaves of trees, usually from two to four metres above the ground, and vigorously chase any intruders that pass by. Females are rarely seen, preferring to hover among the branches of mistletoe-infested trees on the slopes. Usually these trees are proteas (especially *Protea caffra*), on which a red-flowered mistletoe grows, and on which the females lay their eggs.

Flight period: All year but commonest from September to March.

Early stages: See introductory remarks under Sapphires, p. 189. The eggs are unusual in that they are coated with a sticky, yellow substance that may serve to protect them from attack by minute wasp parasitoids. In other Sapphires, where the eggs are known, these are pure white. The larval foodplant is *Tapinanthus rubromarginatus*.

Saffron Sapphire
Geelsaffier
(Iolaus pallene) **fig. 39**

Identification: Small (35–40 mm); sexes similar. Male upperside saffron yellow with orange flush near tails on hindwing; thin, black wing margins and two black tails on hindwing; dusting of brown scales on tip of forewing. Underside similar to upperside but with a few linear, black markings on both wings. Female larger and slightly paler yellow.

Distinguishing characters and similar species: From close up this is a very distinctive species but in flight it may easily be mistaken for one of the yellow pierids (p. 33).

Habitat and distribution: The Saffron Sapphire is relatively uncommon but widespread in frost-free savanna and coastal bush, from northern Natal to Swaziland, Transvaal, Mozambique and Zimbabwe.

Behaviour: Both sexes may be found singly anywhere in the veld. They fly at random, from one to three metres above the ground, and are medium-fast fliers. Males sometimes establish territories around trees in relatively flat bushveld. Females are most likely to be seen in the vicinity of the larval foodplant.

Flight period: Most months of the year but commoner in spring and summer.

Early stages: See introductory remarks under Sapphires, p. 189. The only known larval foodplant is large sour-plum (*Ximenia caffra*), an untidy shrub with dark brown bark and small, light green leaves.

Mimosa Sapphire
Doringboomsaffier
(Iolaus mimosae) **fig. 162**

Identification: Small (25–30 mm); sexes similar. Male upperside powder blue with broad, black tip on forewing; two slender tails on hindwing. Underside dove grey with fine, wavy, more or less parallel reddish-brown linear markings. Female larger and slightly paler.

Distinguishing characters and similar species: The underside pattern and coloration are similar to those of the Hairstreaks (below), but the powder blue upperside allows for fairly easy identification.

Habitat and distribution: The Mimosa Sapphire is fairly common in savanna. Distributed from the Little Karoo and the eastern Karoo in the southern Cape Province to the eastern Cape Province, Natal, Transvaal, Zimbabwe, Botswana and northern Namibia.

Behaviour: Both sexes have a fairly slow flight and are mostly seen frequenting acacias. They perch often, usually on twigs and branches within the canopy of thorn trees. Males occasionally hilltop.

Flight period: September to April.

Early stages: See introductory remarks under Sapphires, p. 189. The larvae feed on mistletoes, particularly those parasitising sweet thorn (*Acacia karroo*), including *Tapinanthus natalitius* and *Moquinella rubra*.

HAIRSTREAKS
STERTBLOUTJIES
(Genera *Hemiolaus* and *Hypolycaena*)

These small butterflies are closely related to the Sapphires and occur in forest and savanna habitats. The males have purple or blue uppersides while the females are usually brown. The undersides, in both sexes, are greyish with fine, reddish-brown, linear markings. There is a pair of delicate tails and an eye-spot on each hindwing. Five species are found in the subregion and all have a slow, hovering flight around bushes or trees. Eggs are laid singly on the leaves of various shrubs and small trees. The larvae are typical of lycaenids (see p. 156) and are not dependent on ants.

Azure Hairstreak
Venda-stertbloutjie
(Hemiolaus caeculus) **fig. 163**

Identification: Small (30–35 mm); sexes similar; slight seasonal dimorphism. Male upperside deep azure blue with wide, black margin on forewing and black transverse band on leading edge of hindwing; two tails on hindwing, above which are two black spots. Underside pinkish-grey with parallel, reddish-brown, linear markings. Female larger, with blue less extensive and duller; black markings of male replaced by dark brown in female.

Distinguishing characters and similar species: The underside coloration and patterning are similar to those of other Hairstreaks and the Mimosa Sapphire (fig. 162).

Habitat and distribution: The Azure Hairstreak is quite common in localised colonies in hot, arid savanna habitats. The distributional range includes parts of Swaziland, Transvaal, Mozambique, Zimbabwe and Botswana.

Behaviour: Both sexes are weak fliers and are found in close association with the larval foodplant, the small-fruited olax (*Olax dissitiflora*). This is a compact shrub or small tree with small, dark green leaves. Males establish territories and perch on the leaves and twigs of the foodplant. Females flutter among bushes and trees, especially those of the foodplant. Males are frequently seen sucking at damp patches when these are available.

Flight period: All year.

Early stages: Fairly characteristic of the family as a whole (see introductory remarks under lycaenids, p. 156). The only known larval foodplant is small-fruited olax (*Olax dissitiflora*).

Purple-brown Hairstreak
Persbruin-stertbloutjie
(Hypolycaena philippus) **figs 130 & 176**

Identification: Small (25–30 mm); sexes very dissimilar. Male upperside purplish-brown with two slender tails on hindwing, surmounted by two eye-spots. Underside pale grey with fine, parallel, reddish lines and orange-bordered eye-spots near tails. Female upperside brown with two rows of white markings on hindwing, just above eye-spots. Underside as in male.

Distinguishing characters and similar species: The underside is similar to that of other Hairstreaks and the Mimosa Sapphire.

Habitat and distribution: The Purple-brown Hairstreak is common and widespread in subtropical coastal bush and savanna, from the eastern Cape Province (East London) to Transkei, Natal, Transvaal, Mozambique, Zimbabwe, Botswana and Namibia.

Behaviour: Both sexes have a weak, hovering flight that is usually not sustained. They tend to settle on shrubs and low trees on the edge of thick bush. Males occasionally mud-puddle and both sexes are fond of flowers. Although the butterfly is widespread and common, specimens are generally found singly about the bush.

Flight period: All year but commoner in summer and autumn.

Early stages: Typical of the family (see introductory remarks under lycaenids, p. 156). A number of shrubs belonging to at least four different families are used by the larvae, including white cat's whiskers (*Clerodendrum glabrum*), small sour-plum (*Ximenia americana*), dune soap-berry (*Deinbollia oblongifolia*), wild medlar (*Vangueria infausta*) and ant-heap wild medlar (*V. randii*).

BLACK EYES
SWARTOGIES
(Genus *Leptomyrina*)

The four species of Black Eye in southern Africa are small insects with bronzy or grey uppersides and characteristic white-ringed black "eyes" on the margins of the wings. They are found wherever their larval foodplants occur: succulents belonging to the family Crassulaceae. They fly fairly rapidly, close to the ground, frequently settling on rocks or bare ground. The larvae bore into the succulent leaves and live inside them, but in other respects the early stages are typical of lycaenids (see p. 156). The larvae are often attended by small ants but they are not dependent on the ants for their survival.

Tailed Black Eye
Langstert-swartogie
(Leptomyrina hirundo) **fig. 134**

Identification: Small (20–25 mm); sexes similar. Male upperside charcoal grey; single, long tail on hindwing; white-ringed black spots ("eyes") on lower, outer margin of fore- and hindwing. Underside very pale grey with fine, discontinuous brown lines; small, single "black eyes" on fore- and hindwing. Female larger, with brownish upperside.

Distinguishing characters and similar species: The underside has a similar pattern to that of Hairstreaks (p. 193). The long tails and small size readily distinguish it from Hairstreaks and other Black Eyes.

Habitat and distribution: The Tailed Black Eye is found in very localised colonies in low-altitude, frost-free savanna and dry coastal bush. It occurs from the eastern Cape Province (Uitenhage) to Natal, the eastern and northern Transvaal lowveld and western Zimbabwe.

Behaviour: Although colonies of this butterfly are very localised, large numbers of individuals may be found in a particular colony. Both sexes flutter slowly, often in the shade of trees, and never rise more than a metre above the ground. They are always found in close proximity to their low-growing, succulent foodplants.

Flight period: All year but common only in summer.

Early stages: See introductory remarks under Black Eyes, above. A number of genera of plants belonging to the Crassula family (Crassulaceae) are used as food by the larvae, including *Crassula* species, *Cotyledon* species, *Kalanchoe* species and *Bryophyllum delegoense*.

Henning's Black Eye
Henning-swartogie
(Leptomyrina henningi) **fig. 131**

Identification: Small (25–30 mm); sexes very similar. Male upperside bronze-brown with white-ringed "black eyes" on margin of lower fore- and hindwing. Underside irrorated, greyish-brown, with two "black eyes" on lower, outer margin of forewing. Female larger with rounder wings.

Distinguishing characters and similar species: Two other, very similar Black Eyes, not illustrated, are found in the subcontinent and can only be distinguished from Henning's Black Eye by experts: 1) Common Black Eye (*Leptomyrina gorgias*) – widespread in the eastern and northern parts of southern Africa; 2) Cape Black Eye (*L. lara*) – an inhabitant of most of the Cape Province which also occurs in Lesotho.

Habitat and distribution: Henning's Black Eye is common and widespread in Transvaal, Griqualand West, Zimbabwe, Botswana and Namibia.

Behaviour: Both sexes have a fairly rapid flight but usually remain within a small area and settle frequently on the ground or on low vegetation. They rarely rise more than a metre above the ground. Specimens are normally encountered singly, in stony or rocky, grassy areas in which their succulent larval foodplants grow. The males are territorial and often perch on the ground with half-opened wings. The species is encountered in gardens in which the foodplant is cultivated.

Flight period: All year but much commoner in summer.

Early stages: See introductory remarks under Black Eyes, p. 195. The usual larval foodplant is pig's ears (*Cotyledon orbiculata*), but other succulent Crassulaceae are also used.

PLAYBOYS
SPELERTJIES
(Genus *Deudorix*)

The 11 species of Playboy found in southern Africa are small butterflies of the forest and savanna biomes. The males are usually red and black on the upperside (there are also blue and brown species) while the very differently marked females have a dull coloration. All the species and both sexes have similar undersides. There is a single tail, projecting from a distinct lobe, on each hindwing. An eyespot is present on the upper- and underside of this lobe. The larvae of the commoner species of Playboy feed on the fruits and seeds of a great variety of plants (fig. 342). The mouthparts of the larvae are adapted for boring into hard seed capsules and pods and they can easily chew through wood. Two species of Playboy appear to breed exclusively in a gall found on the black monkey thorn (*Acacia burkei*). Several of these gall-infested acacias may be seen in the grounds of the camp in Ndumu Game Reserve in northern Natal. The larvae are often associated with ants but are not dependent on them.

Apricot Playboy
Appelkoosspelertjie
(*Deudorix dinochares*) **figs 78 & 128**

Identification: Small (25–30 mm); sexes very different. Male upperside reddish-orange with black margin on leading and outer edge of forewing; hindwing has terminal lobe and tail. Underside brown with rows of scalloped, reddish-orange markings; two eyespots on hindwing (on lobe and above tail). Female is larger; upperside brownish with greyish-blue basal flush and flush of orange-brown towards wing margins. Underside is like that of male.

Distinguishing characters and similar species: Several other red and black Playboys are found in southern Africa, including the Orange-barred Playboy (figs 215 & 255). Three others, not illustrated, are the Coffee Playboy (*Deudorix lorisona*), the Black and Orange Playboy (*D. dariaves*) and the Orange Playboy (*D. dinomenes*), all of which are rare or localised butterflies.

Habitat and distribution: The Apricot Playboy is relatively common in savanna habitats, from the Natal south coast to Swaziland, Transvaal, Zimbabwe and Botswana.

Behaviour: Males sometimes hilltop, when they usually perch on the tops of the highest trees. They are very active in defending their territories, vigorously chasing other insects and rarely remaining on their perches for any length of time. Males also establish territories on the flats where they perch a few metres above the ground, on trees. Both sexes are fond of flowers, near the ground and on trees, and males often mudpuddle. Females are rarely seen, as they fly at random and are dispersed in the bush.

Flight period: All year, but there are two main broods: on the wing September–October and March–April.

Early stages: See introductory remarks under Playboys, above. The larvae feed on the seeds and pods of a large number of wild and cultivated plants. Wild plants include large-fruited bush-willow (*Combretum zeyheri*), boer-beans (*Schotia* species), umdoni (*Syzygium cordatum*), wild seringa (*Burkea africana*), spiny medlar (*Hyperacanthus amoenus*) and large sourplum (*Ximenia caffra*). Cultivated plants that are used include loquat (*Eriobotrya japonica*), cowpea (*Vigna unguiculata*), macadamia (*Macadamia ternifolia*), peach (*Prunus persica*) and coffee (*Coffea* species).

Orangebarred Playboy
Skaduspelertjie
(Deudorix diocles) **figs 215 & 254**

Identification: Small (30–35 mm); sexes very different. Male upperside forewing black with red patch in lower middle portion of wing; hindwing red with single, delicate tail and lobe on extremity of wing. Underside brown with fine, white, scalloped markings; eye-spots on hindwing lobe and above tail. Female larger and brown on upperside with bluish-grey basal suffusion. Underside as in male.

Distinguishing characters and similar species: The male Orangebarred Playboy can be confused with other red and black Playboys (see Apricot Playboy, above). The female is rather like the Brown Playboy female (see below).

Habitat and distribution: The

Orangebarred Playboy is a not particularly common species of forest and thick bush, from Transkei (Port St Johns) to the Natal coast, eastern and north-eastern Transvaal, Mozambique and the eastern border of Zimbabwe.

Behaviour: Males have a rapid flight and establish territories anywhere in forest and bush. Within these territories they perch on high trees, usually three to five metres above the ground. Both sexes feed from flowers, close to the ground or in trees. Females are more sluggish, fly at random and are more rarely encountered than males.

Flight period: All year; commonest from April to June.

Early stages: See introductory remarks under Playboys, p. 198. The pods and seeds of a number of trees and shrubs are used by the larvae, including umzimbeet (*Millettia grandis*), pride-of-De Kaap (*Bauhinia galpinii*), Natal camwood (*Baphia racemosa*), acacias (*Acacia* species), boer-bean (*Schotia* species), bush-willows (*Combretum* species), waterberries (*Syzygium* species), macadamia (*Macadamia ternifolia*) and peach (*Prunus persica*).

Brown Playboy
Bruinspelertjie
(Deudorix antalus) **figs 129 & 175**

Identification: Small (30–35 mm); sexes dissimilar. Male upperside brown with slight purplish sheen; single delicate tail and lobe at end of hindwing. Underside light brown with scalloped white and reddish-brown markings; eye-spot on hindwing lobe and above tail. Female brown with dove-grey suffusion, especially towards base of wings. Underside as in male.

Distinguishing characters and similar species: There are three other "dark" Playboys, not illustrated, in southern Africa: 1) Dusky Playboy (*Deudorix magda*); 2) Van Son's Playboy (*D. vansoni*); 3) Pennington's Playboy (*D. penningtoni*). All are rather rare species and unlikely to be seen unless specifically sought.

Habitat and distribution: Although never abundant, the Brown Playboy is the commonest and most widespread Playboy in the subcontinent. It is absent only from the central Karoo and from pure grassland habitats.

Behaviour: Males are mostly

observed hilltopping, where they perch mainly on the ground or on rocks, but also occasionally on low vegetation. As many as three males may occupy territories on the same hilltop. Males also establish territories on the flats, where they perch on shrubs or low trees. The flight is fast, low down and confined to a small area. Flowers attract both sexes. Females fly more slowly, at random, and may be observed anywhere about the bush or veld.

Flight period: All year in warmer areas with a peak in autumn.

Early stages: See introductory remarks under Playboys, p. 198. The larvae feed on the pods and seeds of a vast number of plants, including *Schotia, Acacia, Syzygium, Prunus, Cassia, Ximenia, Sutherlandia, Crotalaria, Dolichos, Nymania, Cardiospermum, Baphia, Bauhinia, Caesalpinia, Vigna, Pappea* and even galls growing on certain plants.

PROTEAS
SUIKERBOSSIES
(Genus *Capys*)

As their name suggests Proteas are always found in the vicinity of protea trees, which serve as larval foodplants. Four species occur in the subregion. The sexes are alike in the Orangebanded Protea but dissimilar in other species. In species showing sexual dimorphism the males are orange and black on the upperside and the females grey. All species of Protea have similar undersides. Like the related Playboys (p. 198) the larvae are able to bore through hard plant material. Eggs are laid singly at the base of protea flower buds and the larvae bore into the bud and feed on the contents. The entrance hole is enlarged by the larva just before it pupates inside the flower bud so as to make it possible for the butterfly to escape when it hatches. These holes are about 4 mm in diameter and located at the base of the bud. Ants are often present in the buds and tend the larvae but the larvae are not dependent on them.

Orangebanded Protea
Gewone Suikerbossie
(Capys alphaeus) **fig. 253**

Identification: Male small, female medium-sized (35–45 mm); sexes similar; geographically variable. Male upperside dark brown with broad, orange-red bands on both wings; short, blunt tail on hindwing extremity. Underside variegated in grey, brown and reddish-brown, with strong, orange basal flush in forewing. Female larger, with orange bands on upperside broader than in male.

Distinguishing characters and similar species: Three other Proteas, not illustrated, occur in southern Africa: 1) Russet Protea (*Capys disjunctus*) – the male is orange with narrow, brown wing margins. The female is grey with an orange submarginal line on the lower part of the hindwing. The underside is similar to that of the Orangebanded Protea. Widespread but in localised colonies in the eastern half of the subcontinent; 2) Pennington's Protea (*C. penningtoni*) – both sexes are bright orange on the upperside with narrow, brown wing margins. The underside is similar to that of the Orangebanded Protea. A rare species, confined to a few localities in the Natal midlands; 3) African Protea (*C. connexivus*) – similar to the Russet Protea but found in the subregion only in western and northern Zimbabwe.

Habitat and distribution: The Orangebanded Protea is found in mountain fynbos and montane grassland, where certain *Protea* species are dominant. Its distributional range covers the south-western, southern and eastern Cape Province, Natal, Transvaal and eastern Zimbabwe.

Behaviour: Males are avid hilltoppers and will ascend the highest peaks of mountains. They fly very fast and the flight is sustained, with only short rests on shrubs or on the ground. Females are rarely seen since they are much less active than the males and widely dispersed. The best place to look for them is in groves of proteas on the slopes of hills and mountains. Both sexes are occasionally seen feeding from flowers.

Flight period: Although specimens may be encountered in most months of the year, especially in the Cape Peninsula, there are two main broods. The spring brood (on the wing October–November) is stronger than the autumn brood (March–April).

Early stages: See introductory remarks under Proteas, above. The flower-heads of a number of species of protea are used as food by the larvae, including king protea (*Protea cynaroides*), silver protea (*P. roupelliae*), sugarbush (*P. repens*), lipped protea (*P. subvestita*), waboom (*P. nitida*) and sugar protea (*P. burchellii*).

The lycaenines
(Subfamily Lycaeninae)

Lycaenines are a relict subfamily with only three species in Africa, two of which occur in southern Africa. The subfamily is well represented in the northern hemisphere. The early stages are typical of lycaenids (see p. 156).

SORREL COPPERS
KLEINKOPERVLERKIES
(Genus *Lycaena*)

These small, copper-coloured butterflies, with black spots and markings, are not closely related to the Coppers (p. 178). The two species found in the subregion are relict species belonging to the genus *Lycaena* which is well represented in the northern hemisphere. Sorrel Coppers live in colonies in fynbos and grassland, especially in marshy habitats. The main larval foodplants are sorrels or docks (*Rumex* species). The larvae are typical of lycaenids (see p. 156), feed only on plants, and are not associated with ants.

Eastern Sorrel Copper
Oostelike-kleinkopervlerkie
(*Lycaena clarki*) **fig. 83**

Identification: Male very small, female small (20–30 mm); sexes similar. Male upperside bright orange with pinkish-violet sheen; narrow, even, brown wing margins and some black spots in apex of forewing. Underside forewing pale orange with clear black spotting; hindwing light brown with small, scattered, black spots.

Female larger, with black spots on upperside of both fore- and hindwing.

Distinguishing characters and similar species: There is another species of Sorrel Copper in the subcontinent, the Western Sorrel Copper (*Lycaena orus*), not illustrated. Very similar in appearance to the Eastern Sorrel Copper but occurs mainly near the coast from the Cape Peninsula to the Port Elizabeth district in the Cape Province.

Habitat and distribution: The Eastern Sorrel Copper is a common species of the grassland biome but is also found in grassy areas in the Karoo. Distributed from the inland districts of the western Cape Province to the Cape midlands, Orange Free State, Lesotho, Natal interior and southern Transvaal.

Behaviour: Lives in colonies of varying size, in wet, marshy areas and along stream banks. An active insect but the flight is not fast and it rarely rises more than a metre above the ground. Both sexes flit about the grass in the same places and are fond of flowers. They rest on low plants or on the ground.

Flight period: Mainly summer; most abundant from October to March.

Early stages: Typical of the lycaenid family (see introductory remarks under lycaenids, p. 156). The larvae feed on large-leaved, moisture-loving, herbaceous plants belonging to the dock or sorrel family, such as common dock (*Rumex lanceolatus*).

The polyommatines
(Subfamily Polyommatinae)

This is another large lycaenid subfamily with 420 species in Africa of which about 150 are found in southern Africa. The genus *Lepidochrysops* alone accounts for about 60 of the species in the subregion. Polyommatines are very small to medium-sized butterflies, with the upperside of the wings usually some shade of blue or brown. The underside is completely different to the upperside, having complex patterns that aid in identification of the various species and groups. They are chiefly butterflies of savanna and grassland habitats. Most are fairly weak fliers; the fast-flying Hairtails (genus *Anthene*) are exceptional. All polyommatines are very fond of flowers and often mud-puddle. The early stages are typical of lycaenids (see p. 156) with the exception of the genera *Lepidochrysops* and *Orachrysops*, which have larvae that are carnivorous on ant brood. Most other polyommatine genera are facultatively associated with ants.

HAIRTAILS
KORTSTERTJIES
(Genera *Anthene* and *Triclema*)

Hairtails are small to very small butterflies that usually have two or three hair-like tufts on each hindwing. About 25 species occur in southern Africa. The sexes are dimorphic in respect of their uppersides; males are purple, blue or brown while females are duller and often have scattered black and brown markings. Hairtails are found mainly in savanna habitats where they fly rapidly around bushes or treetops. A variety of larval foodplants have been recorded but many species use acacias. Although not closely related to the Playboys (p. 198), Hairtails have a similar pattern on the underside of the wings. The early stages are typical of lycaenids (see p. 156).

Common Hairtail
Donkerkortstertjie
(*Anthene definita*) **fig. 177**

Identification: Small (25–30 mm); sexes very different. Male upperside deep purplish-blue with three small, white-tipped tails on hindwing. Underside brown with complex pattern of scalloped, white markings and eye-spot between upper two tails. Female brown with blue basal suffusion, shading to bluish-white towards wing margins. Underside as in male but white markings more extensive.

Distinguishing characters and similar species: At least 10 similar species of Hairtail are found in southern Africa. They resemble the Common Hairtail but are all comparatively scarce. They can be identified as Hairtails by the characteristic short tails on the hindwings.

Habitat and distribution: The Common Hairtail is very common and widespread in a number of biomes. Absent from the western Karoo and from high-altitude grassland.

Behaviour: Flies very fast but settles frequently, and abruptly, on the leaves of shrubs or small trees. Both sexes are very fond of flowers (low down or in trees) and are often observed in gardens. While feeding from flowers they can easily be approached. The males are avid mud-puddlers. Males are territorial and select perches on bushes on the flats.

Flight period: All year in frost-free areas and from September to April in colder ones.

Early stages: Typical of lycaenids (see p. 156). The larvae feed on the flowers and buds of a great variety of plants belonging to some 10 different families. Examples are the African allophylus (*Allophylus africanus*), mango (*Mangifera indica*), lance-leaf waxberry (*Myrica serrata*), sweet thorn (*Acacia karroo*), boer-beans (*Schotia* species), "doppruim" (*Pappea capensis*), round-leaved crassula (*Crassula arborescens*), rose (*Rosa* species) and wild plum (*Harpephyllum caffrum*).

Blackstriped Hairtail
Swartstreep-kortstertjie
(*Anthene amarah*) **fig. 132**

Identification: Small (25–30 mm); sexes similar. Male upperside bronzy-brown with two "hairtails" and an eye-spot on hindwing. Underside light brown, chequered with white and dark brown markings; diagnostic black stripe at base of forewing; some black spots and two eye-spots on hindwing. Female deeper brown on upperside. Underside as in male.

Distinguishing characters and similar species: The bronzy coloration of the upperside, together with the black stripe on the forewing underside, is unique to this Hairtail.

Habitat and distribution: The Blackstriped Hairtail is very common in savanna habitats, wherever indigenous acacias are found. Absent from the treeless western Karoo and from the open grassland of the Orange Free State and Lesotho.

Behaviour: Flies rapidly around shrubs and trees but settles frequently, on the leaves. Males establish territories on the flats and perch on bushes or trees. Both sexes are attracted to flowers, particularly those of acacias. Males often mud-puddle.

Flight period: September to May.

Early stages: Typical of lycaenids (see p. 156). The larval foodplants are species of acacia, including the sweet thorn (*Acacia karroo*).

Pale Hairtail
Vaalkortstertjie
(*Anthene butleri*) **fig. 178**

Identification: Small (30–35 mm); sexes similar. Male upperside brown with dull pinkish-blue sheen; eye-spot and two "hairtails" on hindwing. Underside light brown with complex pattern of white and dark brown markings. Female brown with blue basal suffusion, fading to bluish-white towards wing margins. Underside as in male.

Distinguishing characters and similar species: There are several similar species of Hairtail, some of which are unnamed (undescribed), but all of them are relatively rare and are therefore unlikely to be seen by the casual observer.

Habitat and distribution: The Pale Hairtail is common and widespread in savanna habitats. Absent from the western Cape Province.

Behaviour: Males are most likely to be seen hilltopping. They select perches on bushes and trees on the summit and vigorously chase intruders from their territories, taking short rests between these fast flights. They fly from two to three metres above the ground and settle frequently. Females are rarely seen and are widely dispersed about the bush where they fly low down, searching for certain low-growing succulents on which they lay their eggs.

Flight period: Nearly all year but scarce in June and July.

Early stages: Typical of lycaenids (see p. 156). The larvae feed on the leaves of *Kalanchoe* species, including *K. crenata*, and on the flowers of *Cotyledon* species, including *C. orbiculata*.

Otacilia Hairtail
Boomkortstertjie
(*Anthene otacilia*) fig. 192

Identification: Very small (20–25 mm); sexes dissimilar. Male upperside dark brown with extensive basal flush of dark purplish-blue; "hairtails" poorly developed (vestigial); black spot on lower hindwing. Underside brown with complex pattern of scalloped, white markings; black spot at base of hindwing; two eye-spots in vicinity of tails. Female with blue paler and restricted to base of wings.

Distinguishing characters and similar species: Four other species of very small Hairtail, none illustrated, are found in the subregion, two of which are very similar to the Otacilia Hairtail: 1) Mashuna Hairtail (*Anthene contrastata*); 2) Talbot's Hairtail (*A. talboti*). The other two have pure brown uppersides in both sexes and are very small (15–18 mm): 3) Little Hairtail (*A. minima*); 4) Zimbabwe Hairtail (*A. rhodesiana*). All four of these small Hairtails are scarce to rare butterflies.

Habitat and distribution: The Otacilia Hairtail is a not particularly common inhabitant of acacia-dominated savanna, extending from the southern Cape Province (Mossel Bay), along the coast to Swaziland, Transvaal and Zimbabwe.

Behaviour: Males hilltop and tend to choose the tops of the highest trees as perches. Here they whirl around with other small lycaenids. When engaged in this behaviour they are very difficult to identify, but both sexes are often seen feeding from flowers in trees or near the ground. An active and wary little insect that should be approached with caution if the intention is not to frighten it.

Flight period: September to April but commonest in March and April.

Early stages: Typical of lycaenids (see p. 156). The larvae feed on various indigenous acacias, including sweet thorn (*Acacia karroo*).

HEARTS
HARTJIES
(Genus *Uranothauma*)

Of the four species in the subregion only one is widespread and is discussed below. The early stages are typical of lycaenids (see p. 156).

Black Heart
Swarthartjie
(*Uranothauma nubifer*) **fig. 135**

Identification: Small (25–30 mm); sexes dissimilar. Male upperside very dark brown (almost black when butterfly is flying) with faint purplish lustre; large, black, heart-shaped marking on forewing; delicate tail on hindwing. Underside brown with complex pattern of off-white markings. Female coppery-brown with blackish markings and spots on forewing. Underside as in male.

Distinguishing characters and similar species: Three species, belonging to the same genus, are found in eastern Zimbabwe and in Mozambique. In all of these the undersides are creamy-white and are overlaid with intricate patterns of brown markings. The underside markings of the Black Heart should also be compared with those of the Bush Bronze (fig. 182) and Geranium Bronze (fig. 151).

Habitat and distribution: The Black Heart is widespread but occurs in very localised populations, in thornveld savanna, in Natal, Swaziland, Transvaal, Mozambique and Zimbabwe.

Behaviour: Both sexes are fond of flowers, particularly those of acacias, and the males often mud-puddle. A shy butterfly that usually remains in the vicinity of large thorn trees, on which it breeds. Specimens are frequently seen flying rapidly around the tops of these trees.

Flight period: Mainly from October to April with peak emergence from December to February.

Early stages: Similar to other lycaenids (see p. 156). The larvae feed on the flower buds and leaves of sweet thorn (*Acacia karroo*).

BRONZES
BRONSE
(Genus *Cacyreus*)

Three of the five species in the subregion have bronzy-brown uppersides while two have blue uppersides. All Bronzes, however, have a similar, complex pattern on the underside of the wings. They are small to very small butterflies and, as a group, are found in most biomes. The early stages are typical of lycaenids (see p. 156).

Bush Bronze
Bosbrons
(*Cacyreus lingeus*) fig. 182

Identification: Small (25–30 mm); sexes dissimilar. Male upperside uniformly dull greyish-blue; single delicate tail on hindwing. Underside has complex pattern of brown and white markings; two small eye-spots on lower edge of hindwing. Female brown with powder blue basal flush on both wings and scattered white markings. Underside as in male.

Distinguishing characters and similar species: The Bush Bronze is impossible to separate in the field from the closely related Mocker Bronze (*Cacyreus virilis*), not illustrated. The latter, like the Bush Bronze, is also a common and widespread species. The underside markings of these Bronzes resemble those of the Black Heart (fig. 135).

Habitat and distribution: The Bush Bronze occurs mainly in forest and on forest margins, throughout the subregion, but is also found in savanna and fynbos habitats. Largely absent from the grassland and Karoo biomes.

Behaviour: Often seen in gardens and, in the field, on stream-banks. Flies slowly, with a hovering, erratic flight, close to low-growing vegetation. Rarely rises more than two metres above the ground and perches frequently on the forbs around which the species flies. Males often mud-puddle.

Flight period: All year but commoner in summer.

Early stages: Typical of lycaenids (see p. 156). The larvae use the flowers and buds of various members of the salvia family, such as wild sage (*Salvia africana*), wild dagga (*Leonotis leonurus*), mints, including cultivated mint (*Mentha* species), *Lavandula angustifolia* and *Plectranthus* species.

Geranium Bronze
Malvabrons
(*Cacyreus marshalli*) fig. 151

Identification: Very small (20–25 mm); sexes very similar. Male upperside bronzy-brown with chequered white and brown cilia on wing margins; single delicate tail on hindwing; black spot above tail. Underside has complex pattern of white and brown markings. Female larger than male.

Distinguishing characters and similar species: Two closely related species, both of which are scarcer than the Geranium Bronze, are found in southern Africa (neither illustrated): 1) Dickson's Bronze (*Cacyreus dicksoni*) – indistinguishable from the Geranium Bronze in the field. Found only in the western and southern Cape Province, including Little Namaqualand, and is a common butterfly; 2) Water Bronze (*C. palemon*) – similar to the Geranium Bronze but the upperside has a delicate violet sheen in certain lights. This sheen is especially noticeable in males. Widespread in the eastern half of the subcontinent; usually occurs on the banks of streams and in marshes.

Habitat and distribution: The very common Geranium Bronze occurs in a variety of habitats, wherever the foodplants are found. Absent only from the drier western Karoo.

Behaviour: Often seen in gardens, where it breeds on cultivated pelargoniums. It has a weak, slow flight, close to the ground, and settles often, on low vegetation and flowers. The larvae can damage the soft-stemmed varieties of pelargonium by boring into the stems, and cause part of the plant to die.

Flight period: All year in frost-free areas, otherwise the summer months.

Early stages: Typical of lycaenids (see p. 156). The larvae feed mainly on the buds, flowers and seeds of various species of *Pelargonium* and *Geranium*.

PIES
BONTETJIES
(Genera *Zintha* and *Tuxentius*)

Except for one species, which has a blue upperside, Pies have a chequered black and white pattern on the upperside of the wings. All four species found in the subcontinent are very small butterflies with black-spotted, white undersides. They are found mainly in savanna habitats and breed on buffalo-thorns (*Ziziphus* species). The early stages are typical of lycaenids (see p. 156).

Hintza Pie
Hintza-bontetjie
(*Zintha hintza*) **fig. 185**

Identification: Very small (25 mm); sexes dissimilar. Male upperside thinly covered with violaceous blue scales; black and white chequered cilia on wing margins. Underside white with scattered black spots and markings; single, very short tail on hindwing. Female upperside has restricted basal blue flush; rest of wing brown with scattered, rectangular white markings. Underside as in male.

Distinguishing characters and similar species: The underside of the Hintza Pie is very similar to that of the Black Pie (fig. 221; below) and also resembles the underside of the Common Dotted Blue (fig. 183).

Habitat and distribution: The Hintza Pie is fairly common and widespread in the savanna biome, from the eastern Cape Province to Natal, Transvaal, Zimbabwe, Botswana and Namibia.

Behaviour: Males fly quite fast but females are more sluggish. Both sexes fly at random and are fond of flowers. Often seen flying around the larval foodplants; is alert and wary. Males often mud-puddle.

Flight period: September to April. In warmer areas specimens are occasionally seen in the winter months.

Early stages: Typical of lycaenids (see p. 156). The larvae feed on the leaves of buffalo-thorn (*Ziziphus mucronata*) and the low-growing dwarf buffalo-thorn (*Z. zeyheriana*).

Black Pie
Swartbontetjie
(Tuxentius melaena) **fig. 221**

Identification: Very small (20–25 mm); sexes very similar; geographically variable. Male upperside black with block-like white markings on both wings; single, thin tail on hindwing. Underside white with scattered black spots and markings. Female similar but larger.

Distinguishing characters and similar species: The underside markings are similar to those of the Hintza Pie (fig. 185; above) and, to a lesser extent, the Common Dotted Blue (fig. 183). There are, in addition, two other closely related species of Pie in the subcontinent (neither illustrated): 1) White Pie (*Tuxentius calice*) – has the white patch on the forewing more extensive but is otherwise difficult to distinguish from the Black Pie, especially on the underside. The White Pie occurs in savanna in Natal, Transvaal and Zimbabwe. It thus has a more restricted distribution than the Black Pie and is decidedly rarer; 2) Western Pie (*T. hesperis*) – nearly black on the upperside and has an almost unmarked, yellow-brown underside. Known only from the Vioolsdrift area in the north-western Cape Province, near the mouth of the Orange River.

Habitat and distribution: The Black Pie is common and widespread, in savanna and on forest edges, from the eastern Cape Province to Natal, Swaziland, Transvaal, Zimbabwe, Botswana and Griqualand West.

Behaviour: This alert and wary insect appears distinctly black and white (pied) when flying around trees and bushes, from two to five metres above the ground. Frequently encountered flying around the buffalo-thorn, which is the larval foodplant. Flowers, on trees or low down, attract both sexes, and males often mud-puddle. Males also sometimes hilltop, where they select perches on the foliage of trees some two to three metres above the ground.

Flight period: All year but much commoner in midsummer and autumn.

Early stages: Typical of lycaenids (see p. 156). The main larval foodplant is buffalo-thorn (*Ziziphus mucronata*), a common and familiar tree.

BLUES
BLOUTJIES

(Genera *Tarucus, Leptotes, Lampides, Pseudonacaduba, Zizeeria, Zizula, Actizera, Freyeria, Oraidium, Lepidochrysops, Orachrysops, Euchrysops, Cupidopsis, Eicochrysops, Azanus* and others)

The Blues are a very large and diverse group with about 110 species in 20 genera in southern Africa. More than half of the species belong to a single genus (*Lepidochrysops*). Blues vary in size from very small to medium-sized and have either blue or brown uppersides. The undersides show complex patterns that help in identifying a particular species. Some species have tails while others do not. The sexes are usually dissimilar. Blues are found in every biome and are most often observed while feeding from flowers. The larval foodplants cover a wide variety of plant families but leguminous forbs are often used, indicating that this plant group was probably the one used by ancestral Blues. In most cases the larvae of Blues feed on the flower buds of their foodplants and the majority of species are associated with ants. The ant association is usually facultative (not obligatory) but in the genera *Lepidochrysops* and *Orachrysops* the larvae feed on ant-brood in some of their stages (see lycaenids, p. 156).

Common Dotted Blue
Gewone Spikkelbloutjie

(Tarucus sybaris) fig. 183

Identification: Very small (20–25 mm); sexes dissimilar. Male upperside violaceous blue with narrow, even, black wing margins; black dot in centre of forewing; single, delicate tail on hindwing. Underside white with evenly scattered, almost round, black dots. Female upperside brown with limited basal blue flush and submarginal white markings on both wings. Underside as in male.

Distinguishing characters and similar species: The underside markings are similar to those of the Black Pie (fig. 221) and the Hintza Pie (fig. 185).

Habitat and distribution: The Common Dotted Blue is very common in grassland and savanna habitats, from the eastern Cape Province to Natal, Swaziland, Transvaal, the western Orange

Free State, northern Cape Province, Mozambique, Zimbabwe, Botswana and Namibia.

Behaviour: A slow-flying butterfly that keeps close to the ground (usually under half a metre), and flies in grassy areas. When disturbed it will normally fly up, circle for a few seconds and resettle on the ground or low vegetation. Colonies of Common Dotted Blues are usually found in the vicinity of their low-growing, thorny foodplant which grows in clumps between grass. Both sexes are fond of flowers and the males, in addition, are avid mud-puddlers.

Flight period: All year in frost-free areas, otherwise from September to April.

Early stages: Typical of lycaenids (see p. 156). The main larval foodplant is dwarf buffalo-thorn (*Ziziphus zeyheriana*) but buffalo-thorn (*Z. mucronata*) is sometimes also used as food by the larvae.

Cape Dotted Blue
Fynbos-spikkelbloutjie
(Tarucus thespis) **fig. 184**

Identification: Very small (25 mm); sexes dissimilar. Male upperside bright blue with black and white chequered cilia on wing margins; no tails. Underside chequered with brown and pale yellow markings. Female upperside brown with basal blue flush and a few submarginal white spots on forewing. Underside as in male.

Distinguishing characters and similar species: Can be confused only with Bowker's Dotted Blue (*Tarucus bowkeri*), not illustrated, which has the brown and pale yellow markings on the underside much more distinct. Bowker's Dotted Blue occurs in localised colonies on the edges of montane forests, from Transkei (Port St Johns) to the Soutpansberg in northern Transvaal.

Habitat and distribution: The Cape Dotted Blue is common in fynbos and the western Karoo, from Little Namaqualand southwards along the Cape coast, as far east as the Grahamstown district in the eastern Cape Province. It is scarcer in the northern and eastern limits of its range.

Behaviour: Has a relatively slow, random flight, usually less than a metre above the ground. It flies around low bushes and rests on these or on the ground. Males select territories, in which they may remain for a number of days. Both sexes feed from flowers.

Flight period: Mainly summer; most abundant from October to March.

Early stages: Typical of lycaenids (see p. 156). The larvae feed on a small forb, *Phylica imberbis*.

Common Pea Blue
Gewone Ertjiebloutjie
(Leptotes pirithous) **fig. 179**

Identification: Small (25–30 mm); sexes dissimilar. Male upperside dull blue; delicate tail surmounted by black spot at end of hindwing. Underside marked in unevenly alternating white and brown stripes; two well developed eyespots, one on each side of tail. Female brown with basal blue suffusion and prominent brown markings, outlined in white, in middle of forewing. Underside as in male.

Distinguishing characters and similar species: Four very similar species, especially as regards the underside coloration, are found in the subcontinent. One or more of these species may fly together with the Common Pea Blue. They cannot be distinguished in the field and it is necessary to examine the genitalia of set specimens in order to identify the particular species. The exception is the rare Sesbania Pea Blue (*Leptotes pulcher*), not illustrated, which has a much lighter blue upperside than the other species.

Habitat and distribution: As its vernacular name suggests the Common Pea Blue is abundant throughout the subregion, being absent only from very arid areas.

Behaviour: Frequently encountered in gardens, where it breeds on cultivated plumbago. Usually flits around its foodplants and perches often, on leaves or flowers. If disturbed it can show a remarkable turn of speed. Males frequently mud-puddle and sometimes also hilltop. Both sexes are fond of flowers.

Flight period: All year but much commoner in summer.

Early stages: Typical of lycaenids (see p. 156). There are a large number of larval foodplants, belonging to several plant families. Recorded foodplants include plumbago

(*Plumbago auriculata*), Cape honeysuckle (*Tecomaria capensis*), wild seringa (*Burkea africana*), cork bush (*Mundulea sericea*), bastard umzimbeet (*Millettia sutherlandii*), keurboom (*Virgilia oroboides*), Judas-tree (*Cercis silquastrum*), lucerne (*Medicago* species), *Indigofera* species, *Rhynchosia* species, clovers (*Melilotus* species) and *Vigna* species.

Longtailed Pea Blue
Lusern-ertjiebloutjie
(*Lampides boeticus*) **fig. 174**

Identification: Small (30–35 mm); sexes dissimilar. Male upperside thinly covered with violet-blue scales; narrow, brown wing margins; delicate tail on hindwing, with black spot on either side of vein from which tail arises. Underside beige with intricate pattern of paler markings that form a definite whitish band across hindwing. Female upperside has blue scaling much less extensive than in male; rows of white markings marginally and submarginally on hindwing.

Habitat and distribution: An abundant species, found throughout the subcontinent in every biome.

Behaviour: A very swift butterfly, with an erratic, random flight, usually keeping about a metre above the ground. It is very difficult to identify in flight but when perched the characteristic underside allows for reasonably easy identification. Both sexes feed from flowers and males are avid mud-puddlers. The flight is often sustained and is then in a more or less straight line. The Longtailed Pea Blue is often found in gardens and in fields of cultivated lucerne.

Flight period: All year but commoner in the summer months.

Early stages: Typical of lycaenids (see p. 156). The larvae feed on the flowers and seeds of an enormous number of plant species, which explains the almost worldwide distribution of this butterfly. Most of the foodplants are indigenous or exotic legumes belonging to the family Fabaceae and include the following genera: *Crotalaria, Virgilia, Lupinus, Podalyria, Indigofera, Otholobium, Millettia, Cercis, Sutherlandia, Dolichos, Ulex, Cytisus, Colutea, Spartium, Medicago, Lathyrus* and also cultivated peas and beans.

Dusky Blue
Dowwebloutjie
(Pseudonacaduba sichela) **fig. 181**

Identification: Small (25 mm); sexes dissimilar. Male upperside uniform, dull navy blue (looks almost black when insect is flying). Underside flat greyish-brown with pattern of fine, white lines, bordered by darker brown. Female upperside brown with limited, powdery blue, basal flush on wings.

Distinguishing characters and similar species: This is a distinctive Blue, but because it is so small, one must get close enough to see the underside coloration and patterning in order to identify it.

Habitat and distribution: The Dusky Blue is a fairly common inhabitant of savanna habitats on the eastern side of the subcontinent, extending to Port Elizabeth in the eastern Cape Province.

Behaviour: Males normally fly around the tops of trees, either on top of hills (hilltopping) or on the flats. If one is lucky, numbers of specimens may be found feeding on top of a flowering tree. Males often come to damp sand or mud, when they are more readily identified.

Flight period: September to April.

Early stages: Not known in detail. The larval foodplant is thought to be a common, small, leguminous tree, the cork bush (*Mundulea sericea*).

Sooty Blue
Dubbeltjiebloutjie
(Zizeeria knysna) **fig. 189**

Identification: Very small (20–25 mm); sexes dissimilar. Male upperside dull blue with indistinct, blackish-brown wing margins. Underside light brown with scattered, minute, white-ringed black spots and submarginal brown markings. Female brown with basal dusting of bluish-grey scales. Underside as in male.

Distinguishing characters and similar species: There is a very similar, but much rarer, species in southern Africa, the Clover Blue (*Zizina antanossa*), not illustrated. Both sexes of the Clover Blue closely resemble the female of the Sooty

Blue. The Sooty Blue may also be confused with the even smaller Gaika Blue (fig. 190), which has a light grey underside, rather than a light brown one.

Habitat and distribution: The Sooty Blue is a very common and widespread species found in all biomes except forest. It is often seen in suburban gardens.

Behaviour: Flies relatively slowly and very close to the ground (less than half a metre). In gardens it flies with a zig-zag pattern, just above lawns in which the larval foodplant is growing. Settles frequently, on the ground or on grass. Flowers attract both sexes and males mud-puddle.

Flight period: All year but commonest from October to April.

Early stages: Typical of lycaenids (see p. 156). The larvae feed on a variety of plants, belonging to a number of different families, including "dubbeltjie" (*Tribulus terrestris*), pigweeds (*Amaranthus deflexus* and *A. viridis*), "ranksuring" (*Oxalis corniculata*), lucerne (*Medicago sativa*) and *Zornia* species.

Gaika Blue
Gaika-bloutjie
(Zizula hylax) **fig. 190**

Identification: Very small (18–23 mm); sexes dissimilar. Male upperside dull blue with brown wing margins. Underside light grey with minute, scattered black dots and markings. Female uniformly brown above and slightly larger than male.

Distinguishing characters and similar species: The Gaika Blue may be mistaken for the Sooty Blue (fig. 189). The differences are discussed under the latter (see above).

Habitat and distribution: The Gaika Blue is common and widespread in the subcontinent, in grassy habitats, being absent only from the Karoo and from forests.

Behaviour: Has a very weak, fluttering flight, close to the ground, and settles often, on grass stems and herbaceous plants. Both sexes feed from minute flowers among the grass. The species is quite often seen in gardens. The males sometimes mud-puddle.

Flight period: All year in warmer

areas; September to April in those subject to frost.

Early stages: Typical of lycaenids (see p. 156). The larvae feed on a number of small forbs, including *Phaulopsis imbricata, Chaetacanthus setiger, Ruellia* species, *Justicia* species, *Dyschoriste* species and "ranksuring" (*Oxalis corniculata*).

Rayed Blue
Witstreepbloutjie
(*Actizera lucida*) **fig. 191**

Identification: Very small (20–23 mm); sexes dissimilar. Male upperside dull blue, fading to dark brown on wing margins. Underside light brown with scattered, white-ringed black and brown spots; highly characteristic white "ray" running diagonally across hindwing. Female dark brown with dusting of blue scales on both wings. Underside as in male.

Distinguishing characters and similar species: The Rayed Blue can be confused with other very small Blues but, if observed at close quarters, is at once distinguished by the white stripe on the underside of the hindwing.

Habitat and distribution: The Rayed Blue is common in grassy areas in savanna and in grassland, throughout the subcontinent. Absent from the western Karoo and from the fynbos biome.

Behaviour: Flies rather slowly, half a metre, or less, above the ground. Settles frequently on grass stems or shrubs and is occasionally seen feeding from small flowers in the grass. Males are attracted to damp patches.

Flight period: All year in warmer areas; September to May in cooler ones.

Early stages: Typical of lycaenids (see p. 156). The larvae use small, herbaceous plants, including *Crotalaria lanceolata, Oxalis* species, *Argyrolobium* species, and *Rhynchosia* species for food.

Grass Jewel Blue
Grasjuweelbloutjie
(Freyeria trochylus) **fig. 153**

Identification: Very small (18–20 mm); sexes very similar. Male upperside dark brown with three orange-capped black spots on lower hindwing margin. Underside light brown with complex pattern of white-ringed black spots and white markings; three jewelled, orange-capped eye-spots corresponding to those on upperside. Female slightly larger.

Distinguishing characters and similar species: Can be confused with other very small, brown butterflies, especially the Dwarf Blue (fig. 154), which is smaller and has four eye-spots (without orange caps) on the underside of the hindwing. Compare also with the female Cupreous Small Blue (fig. 152) which has a grey underside with a single eye-spot.

Habitat and distribution: The Grass Jewel Blue is a very common inhabitant of grassland and grassy spots in savanna, throughout the subcontinent. It is absent from most of the south-western Cape Province and Karoo.

Behaviour: Both sexes fly with a weak, fluttering flight, low down among grass and forbs. Both sexes are often seen feeding from small flowers. They tend to stay within a small area and settle on low plants, grass or on the ground. Because of their small size they are not readily observed unless specifically looked for.

Flight period: All year in frost-free areas, otherwise from October to May.

Early stages: Typical of lycaenids (see p. 156). The larval foodplants include *Indigofera cryptantha* and *Heliotropium* species.

Dwarf Blue
Dwergbloutjie
(Oraidium barberae) **fig. 154**

Identification: Very small (10–15 mm); sexes similar. Male upperside dark brown with chequered cilia on wing margins. Underside light brown with scattered, darker brown, white-ringed spots; four jewelled, submarginal black spots, in a row, on hindwing. Female

Dwarf Blues are slightly larger.

Distinguishing characters and similar species: Indistinguishable in the field from the equally minute Tinktinkie Blue (*Brephidium metophis*), not illustrated, which, like the Dwarf Blue, is widespread in southern Africa, including the Karoo. Compare also with the Grass Jewel Blue (fig. 153; see above for differences).

Habitat and distribution: The Dwarf Blue occurs in localised colonies throughout the subcontinent, excluding the western Karoo (Bushmanland) and forests.

Behaviour: Has a weak, fluttering flight, close to the ground. This is one of the smallest butterflies in the world and is very difficult to see, resembling a small fly. Settles frequently, on stones or the ground. Colonies are found in stony, grassy areas, especially in dry river beds.

Flight period: September to April.

Early stages: Typical of lycaenids (see p. 156). The larval foodplant is a small forb, the "brakbossie" (*Exomis microphylla*).

Variable Blue
Verneukerbloutjie
(Lepidochrysops variabilis) **fig. 126**

Identification: Small (30–35 mm); sexes very similar. Male upperside brown with brown and white chequered cilia on wing margins. Underside has very complex and variable pattern of brown and white markings; scattered black spots on hindwing. Female slightly larger.

Distinguishing characters and similar species: At least 14 similar species of *Lepidochrysops* occur in southern Africa. The upperside coloration in these species varies from bronzy-brown to coppery-brown and dark brown, but the underside pattern and markings closely resemble those of the Variable Blue. The species, not illustrated, vary in size from the very small Wineland Blue (*L. bacchus*), 25 mm, to the large Monkey Blue (*L. methymna*), up to 45 mm. Most of these Blues are found in small, localised colonies and many are considered to be rare butterflies.

Habitat and distribution: The Variable Blue is locally common in moist, montane grassland in the mountainous regions of the African subcontinent, from the south-western Cape Province to the eastern highlands of Zimbabwe.

Behaviour: Males are inordinately fond of establishing territories on the highest peaks of mountains, as well as on low eminences and rocky knolls on the sides of mountains. Males are rapid and erratic fliers and perch on low vegetation, usually not more than half a metre above the ground. Females have a rapid, random flight, close to the ground, and are mostly encountered on the grassy slopes of mountains. They constantly search for certain low-growing forbs, on the flowers of which they feed and lay their eggs.

Flight period: October to December.

Early stages: Typical of the genus *Lepidochrysops* – see remarks under Lycaenids (p. 156). The eggs are laid on the buds and flowers of *Becium obovatum*, "bitterblombos" (*Selago corymbosa*), and *Salvia* species.

Free State Blue
Vrystaat-bloutjie
(Lepidochrysops letsea) **fig. 124**

Identification: Small (30 mm); sexes very similar. Male upperside dull brown with orange-capped black eye-spot on lower margin of hindwing. Underside light brown with white-ringed black spots and complex pattern of white markings; eye-spot corresponding to one on upperside. Female slightly larger and has larger eye-spot on hindwing.

Distinguishing characters and similar species: Easily confused with the Zulu Blue (*Lepidochrysops ignota*), not illustrated, which is smaller and darker and has a very small eye-spot on the hindwing. The Free State Blue may also be mistaken for the Common Smoky Blue (fig. 125) but the latter lacks black spots on the underside of the forewing. See also comments under the Twinspot Blue (p. 226).

Habitat and distribution: The Free State Blue occurs in localised colonies in grassland and in grassy patches in thornveld savanna. Its distribution includes the north-eastern Cape Province, western Lesotho, the eastern Orange Free State, southern Transvaal and south-western Zimbabwe.

Behaviour: Flies relatively slowly but the flight pattern is erratic and the flight is often sustained. Usually keeps about a metre above the ground and flies at random. It is found in colonies, which are associated with its low-growing, pink-flowered foodplant. Both sexes feed from the flowers of this plant and females lay their eggs on the flower buds.

Flight period: Spring or summer, some weeks after good rains have fallen.

Early stages: Not known. Females lay their eggs on the flower buds of the salvia-like plant Hemizygia pretoriae.

Potchefstroom Blue
Potchefstroom-bloutjie
(Lepidochrysops procera) **fig. 171**

Identification: Small (30–35 mm); sexes similar. Male upperside blue at base of wings, gradually fading to brown, especially on forewing margin and leading edge of hindwing; poorly developed eye-spot on hindwing. Underside brown with complex pattern of greyish-ringed, black and dark brown markings; eye-spot on hindwing margin. Female with blue less extensive on upperside.

Distinguishing characters and similar species: There are a number of species, not illustrated, of *Lepidochrysops* in southern Africa that resemble the Potchefstroom Blue: 1) Van Son's Blue (*L. vansoni*) – occurs in arid savanna; 2) Highveld Blue (*L. praeterita*) and 3) Lotana Blue (*L. lotana*) – larger (40 mm) and found in grassland in southern and central Transvaal. Three further species occur in the Inyanga Mountains in north-eastern Zimbabwe: 4) Violet Blue (*L. violetta*); 5) Nyanga Blue (*L. inyangae*); and 6) Cox's Blue (*L. coxii*). All of these species are scarce and very localised.

Habitat and distribution: The Potchefstroom Blue is a comparatively scarce butterfly that occurs in localised colonies, usually a few hectares in extent, in grassland. It is distributed from the Natal midlands to southern and south-eastern Transvaal.

Behaviour: Not very conspicuous on the wing, it flies close to the ground, with a slowish but erratic flight pattern. It flies at random and is therefore seen singly about the grassveld. The flight is often sustained but specimens may be found resting on grass stems, shrubs or the ground. Both sexes feed from flowers, especially those of the larval foodplant.

Flight period: September to November.

Early stages: Unknown. Females lay their eggs on the flower buds of *Becium obovatum*.

Koppie Blue
Koppiebloutjie
(Lepidochrysops ortygia) **fig. 169**

Identification: Medium-sized (35–45 mm); sexes dissimilar. Male upperside violaceous blue with blackish-brown wing margins; wing margins with chequered white and black cilia; eye-spot on hindwing margin. Underside brown with very complex pattern of white-ringed dark brown markings and black spots. Female upperside largely dark brown with flush of blue scaling on both wings; prominent, orange-capped black eye-spot on lower hindwing margin.

Distinguishing characters and similar species: There are more than a dozen closely related species of *Lepidochrysops* in this group, most of which occur in the fynbos biome in the south-western and southern Cape Province. The shading of blue on the upperside of the males varies from silvery-blue to deep greenish-blue but the underside pattern and markings are very similar in all of them. Expert knowledge is required to distinguish the species in this difficult group.

Habitat and distribution: The Koppie Blue is widespread but occurs only in localised colonies in hilly or mountainous grassland. It ranges from the interior of the eastern Cape Province through the eastern Orange Free State to the southern Transvaal highveld, as far north as Krugersdorp.

Behaviour: As its common name implies, males are very partial to hilltopping. They select perches and may defend the same territory for a number of days. The flight is not particularly fast but may be prolonged. Females are sluggish, fly at random and may spend long periods resting on the ground or on low vegetation.

Flight period: October to February; commonest in December and January.

Early stages: Unknown. The female lays her eggs singly on the flower buds of species of *Selago* and *Walafrida*, which are low-growing forbs.

Twinspot Blue
Dubbelkolbloutjie
(Lepidochrysops plebeia) **figs 123 & 168**

Identification: Medium-sized (35–45 mm); sexes markedly dissimilar. Male upperside greyish-brown with well developed, orange-capped black eye-spot on lower margin of hindwing; single, very short, delicate tail sometimes present on hindwing. Underside light brown with complex pattern of white-ringed, darker brown and black markings; prominent eye-spot on hindwing as on upperside. Female has extensive basal blue flush and wide, brown wing margins; well developed eye-spot on hindwing as in male. Underside and tail as in male.

Distinguishing characters and similar species: The male Twinspot Blue is superficially similar to the Free State Blue (fig. 124) and the Common Smoky Blue (fig. 125) but is much larger. The female Twinspot Blue is easily mistaken for a female of the "Patricia group" (see below) but members of the latter group have five black spots on the hindwing underside whereas the Twinspot Blue has six.

Habitat and distribution: The Twinspot Blue is common and widespread in savanna habitats, from Transkei to Natal, Swaziland, Transvaal, the western Orange Free State, Griqualand West, Zimbabwe, Botswana and Namibia.

Behaviour: Males establish territories on koppies but also on the flats and may occupy them for several days. They select shrubs or tall grass stems as perches and chase intruders from their territory. When they are flying about the veld the flight is rapid, erratic and about a metre above the ground. Females are more sluggish and spend much time resting in the shade of large thorn trees. They fly at random in search of the larval foodplant on which they feed and oviposit.

Flight period: September to April.

Early stages: Typical of the genus *Lepidochrysops* – see remarks under lycaenids (p. 156). The larval foodplant for the early instars is bird's brandy (*Lantana rugosa*). The female lays two eggs at a time, between the corolla tube and calyx of the flower, and covers the eggs with a sticky foam, which gums the two structures together. This behaviour is most unusual for a lycaenid.

Patricia Blue
Patricia-bloutjie
(Lepidochrysops patricia) fig. 167

Identification: Medium-sized (35–45 mm); sexes dissimilar. Male upperside violaceous blue with even, narrow, brown wing margins; orange-capped black eye-spot on hindwing; short tail on hindwing. Underside light brown with complex pattern of white-ringed, darker brown and black markings; eye-spot as on upperside. Female mainly brown with basal flush of scattered sky blue and whitish scales; otherwise like male.

Distinguishing characters and similar species: The underside of the Patricia Blue closely resembles that of the Twinspot Blue (see remarks above). There are eight other species, none illustrated, in the "Patricia group" in southern Africa. The upperside colour in the males of the different species varies from ice blue (Michelle's Blue, *Lepidochrysops michellae*) to royal blue (Barnes's Blue, *L. barnesi*) and even pale metallic yellowish-green (Jade Blue, *L. chloauges*) or green (Ruth's Blue, *L. ruthica*). All of these species have undersides that are very similar to that of the Patricia Blue and are savanna or grassland butterflies, with more or less restricted distributions.

Habitat and distribution: The Patricia Blue is common and widespread in grassland and, to a lesser extent, savanna. It occurs from the southern (Mossel Bay) to the eastern Cape Province, Natal, the Orange Free State, Griqualand West, Swaziland, Transvaal, eastern Botswana, north-western Zimbabwe and, according to Chris Ficq, also Namibia.

Behaviour: Males have a fast, sustained flight that is erratic and about a metre above the ground. They are not territorial and may be observed on the flats, hillslopes and the tops of koppies. Both sexes are fond of flowers. Females fly more slowly, usually in search of flowers or oviposition sites.

Flight period: September to April.

Early stages: Typical of the genus *Lepidochrysops* – see remarks under lycaenids (p. 156). Females lay their eggs singly on the flower buds of bird's brandy (*Lantana rugosa*), the exotic cherry pie (*L. camara*) and "kruipsalie" (*Salvia repens*).

Mashuna Blue
Mashuna-bloutjie
(Lepidochrysops mashuna) **fig. 170**

Identification: Small (35–40 mm); sexes similar. Male upperside sombre blue. Underside orange-brown with scattered black spots and markings; thin, even, black wing margins. Female has less extensive blue scaling on upperside; otherwise like male.

Distinguishing characters and similar species: There are two other species, not illustrated, of *Lepidochrysops* in the subcontinent with similar underside markings: 1) Peculiar Blue (*L. peculiaris*) – larger (40–45 mm) and the male is grey-brown on the upperside; 2) Giant Blue (*L. gigantea*) – very large for a Blue (50–55 mm). All three species in this group are found in Zimbabwe and Mozambique but the Mashuna Blue is the most widespread of the three.

Habitat and distribution: The Mashuna Blue is found in savanna habitats throughout Zimbabwe, in localised colonies.

Behaviour: Both sexes fly at random, close to the ground, and frequently feed from flowers.

Flight period: October to December.

Early stages: Unknown, as are the larval foodplants.

Restless Indigo Blue
Rustelose-bloutjie
(Orachrysops lacrimosa) **fig. 172**

Identification: Small (30–35 mm); sexes dissimilar. Male upperside dark, dull blue with narrow, even, blackish wing margins. Underside greyish-brown with complex pattern of black, brown and whitish markings and spots. Female dark brown with bluish basal flush.

Distinguishing characters and similar species: This endemic genus (*Orachrysops* – Indigo Blues) is taxonomically very difficult. At present it contains three described species but a further seven undescribed species have recently been identified. All Indigo Blues have the typical underside pattern as illustrated for the Restless Indigo Blue (fig. 172b) but the ground colour varies from grey to brown. The distribution of the Indigo

Blues, as a whole, extends from the southern Cape Province (Knysna) north-eastwards to the Wolkberg (Haenertsburg district) in Transvaal. Colonies are small and localised, and occur in grassland.

Habitat and distribution: The Restless Indigo Blue is fairly widespread but is found only in very localised colonies in grassland. It is distributed from the eastern Cape Province northwards to about Newcastle in northern Natal.

Behaviour: Males fly very fast and low down, with an erratic, random course. Females are slower and spend most of their time resting on the ground or on low vegetation or searching for plants on which to lay their eggs.

Flight period: October and November.

Early stages: Only partly known but the life history appears to be similar to that of the genus *Lepidochrysops* – see remarks under lycaenids (p. 156). The first two or three larval instars feed on species of *Indigofera* and the later larval stages are probably carnivorous on the host ant's brood.

Common Smoky Blue
Gewone Dowwebloutjie
(Euchrysops malathana) **fig. 125**

Identification: Small (28–33 mm); sexes dissimilar. Male upperside dull greyish-brown with prominent black spot on lower margin of hindwing, capped with an orange lunule (half-moon). Underside light brown with complex pattern of darker brown and white-ringed black markings; black spot with orange lunule as on upperside. Female dark brown with blue basal flush; orange-capped black spot on lower margin of hindwing. Underside as in male.

Distinguishing characters and similar species: The male of the Common Smoky Blue superficially resembles the Free State Blue (fig. 124) as well as the male of the much larger Twinspot Blue (fig. 123). The female Common Smoky Blue is easily confused with females of the Sabie Smoky Blue (fig. 180) and the Ashen Smoky Blue (see remarks under the Sabie Smoky Blue, below).

Habitat and distribution: The Common Smoky Blue is very common in savanna and grassland habitats in the eastern half of the subcontinent. Its distribution includes the eastern Cape Province, Natal, Transvaal, Mozambique, Zimbabwe and Botswana.

Behaviour: Flies with a slow, rather fluttering flight, usually under a metre above the ground. The flight is random and the insect tends to settle on grass stems and flowers. Males occasionally mud-puddle. The species is normally found singly, in grassy areas with forbs.

Flight period: All year but commonest in summer.

Early stages: Typical of lycaenids (see p. 156). The larval foodplants are small leguminous forbs such as wild sweet pea (*Sphenostylis angustifolia*), cow-pea (*Vigna unguiculata*), *V. tenuis* and *Canavalia* species.

Sabie Smoky Blue
Sabie-dowwebloutjie
(*Euchrysops dolorosa*) **fig. 180**

Identification: Small (25–30 mm); sexes dissimilar. Male upperside dull blue with narrow, brown wing margins; black spot capped by faint orange lunule (half-moon) on lower margin of hindwing. Underside light brown with complex pattern of darker brown and white-ringed black markings; black spot and orange lunule as on upperside. Female dark brown with bluish basal flush on both wings; orange-capped black spot on margin of hindwing. Underside as in male.

Distinguishing characters and similar species: The Sabie Smoky Blue closely resembles the Ashen Smoky Blue (*Euchrysops subpallida*), not illustrated, in both sexes. The latter occurs in northern Transvaal, Zimbabwe and northern Botswana and Namibia. Two other members, not illustrated, of the genus *Euchrysops* (Smoky Blues) with blue uppersides are found in southern Africa: 1) Osiris Smoky Blue (*E. osiris*); 2) Barker's Smoky Blue (*E. barkeri*). Both are larger than the Sabie Smoky Blue, have the blue on the upperside brighter, and have a delicate tail on the lower margin of the hindwing. The Osiris Smoky Blue and Barker's Smoky Blue are difficult to tell apart in the field and both occur in savanna and grassland habitats in the eastern and northern parts of the subregion.

Habitat and distribution: The Sabie Smoky Blue is common in the grassland biome and is also found in grassy areas in savanna, from Transkei northwards to Natal, Transvaal, Mozambique, Zimbabwe and northern Botswana and Namibia.

Behaviour: Flies slowly, randomly and erratically, close to the ground, among clumps of grass. Both sexes are fond of flowers, particularly the mauve ones of its small larval foodplants, which grow among grass. Males sometimes mud-puddle.

Flight period: September to March; commonest in October and November.

Early stages: Typical of lycaenids (see p. 156). The larval foodplants are species of *Becium* and *Salvia*.

Common Meadow Blue
Vleibloutjie
(Cupidopsis cissus) **fig. 173**

Identification: Small (30–35 mm); sexes dissimilar. Male upperside dark violaceous blue with narrow, dark brown wing margins; black spot on lower margin of hindwing, surmounted by orange spot and second orange spot at inner angle. Underside flat grey with scattered, white-ringed black spots and black and orange eye-spots, corresponding to upperside. Female has blue scaling much reduced and restricted to bases of wings; basal blue fading to bluish-white towards wide, brown wing margins.

Distinguishing characters and similar species: Easily confused with the equally common Tailed Meadow Blue (*Cupidopsis jobates*), not illustrated, which is slightly smaller and has a slender but distinct tail on the hindwing. The underside of the Common Meadow Blue should be carefully compared with that of the Common Smoky Blue (fig. 125), Sabie Smoky Blue (fig. 180), Restless Indigo Blue (fig. 172), Free State Blue (fig. 124), Potchefstroom Blue (fig. 171), Twinspot Blue (fig. 123) and Patricia Blue (fig. 167), all of which show some similarity.

Habitat and distribution: The Common Meadow Blue, as its vernacular name suggests, is found in the grassland biome, especially on mountain slopes where rainfall is high. It also occurs, less commonly, in grassy spots in savanna habitats but is absent from the Karoo and from the south-western Cape Province, not occurring west of Knysna.

Behaviour: Flies singly and at random, often stopping to visit flowers. It has a leisurely flight, usually just clearing the grass and low plants. Males sometimes mud-puddle.

Flight period: September to May.

Early stages: Typical of lycaenids (see p. 156). The larvae feed on the flowers of herbaceous, leguminous plants that grow in grassy meadows, such as *Eriosema* and *Vigna* species.

Cupreous Small Blue
Koperbloutjie
(Eicochrysops messapus) **figs 152 & 188**

Identification: Very small (18–23 mm); sexes very different; geographically variable. Male upperside blue with pinkish-orange patch covering most of forewing and part of hindwing; orange-capped black spot on lower border of hindwing. Underside greyish-brown with rows of brown spots and a few black spots on hindwing; prominent orange-capped black spot on lower margin of hindwing. Female brown with orange-capped black spot on hindwing. Underside as in male.

Distinguishing characters and similar species: In the Cape Province the males of the Cupreous Small Blue lack the pinkish-orange patches on the upperside and the females have no, or only a small, orange marking on the hindwing.

Habitat and distribution: The Cupreous Small Blue is common in grassy areas in fynbos and savanna, and in grassland. Distributed from the south-western to the southern and eastern Cape Province, south-western Orange Free State, Natal, Transvaal, Griqualand West, Mozambique, Zimbabwe and Botswana.

Behaviour: Flies slowly and weakly, less than half a metre above the ground. Perches on grass and low-growing shrubs. Both sexes are fond of flowers.

Flight period: September to May.

Early stages: Typical of lycaenids (see p. 156). The larvae feed on the buds and seeds of *Thesium* species, which are small forbs.

Velvet Spotted Blue
Fluweel-kolbloutjie
(Azanus ubaldus) **fig. 187**

Identification: Very small (20 mm); sexes dissimilar. Male upperside blue with distinct brown wing margins; large velvety-blue patch in middle of forewing. Underside light brown with darker brown markings and several white-ringed black spots on hindwing. Female plain brown with blackish wing bases. Underside as in male.

Distinguishing characters and similar species: Can be confused with other very small blues, especially the Topaz Spotted Blue (see remarks under this species, below).

Habitat and distribution: The Velvet Spotted Blue is fairly common and widespread in thornveld savanna and in the eastern and southern Karoo. Absent from the south-western Cape Province and the western Karoo.

Behaviour: Flies rapidly around the tops of thorn trees, especially sweet thorn (*Acacia karroo*), on the flowers of which the adults feed. Males are avid mud-puddlers. The Velvet Spotted Blue may be abundant in some years and scarce in others.

Flight period: September to April; commonest from December to February.

Early stages: Typical of lycaenids (see p. 156). The larvae feed on species of acacia, including sweet thorn (*Acacia karroo*).

Topaz Spotted Blue
Hemels-kolbloutjie
(Azanus jesous) **fig. 186**

Identification: Very small (20–25 mm); sexes dissimilar. Male upperside pinkish-blue with narrow, black wing margins. Underside greyish-brown with complex pattern of light brown markings and black spots. Female light brown with dusting of bluish and whitish scales on both wings. Underside as in male.

Distinguishing characters and similar species: Three other Spotted Blues (*Azanus* species), besides the Velvet Spotted Blue and Topaz Spotted Blue, occur in the subregion. They have similar dark markings on the underside but the ground colour of the underside is greyish-white, rather than greyish-brown. In addition the uppersides are dull blue, not pinkish-blue. These three species are also relatively common and the early stages and adults are closely associated with acacias.

Habitat and distribution: The Topaz Spotted Blue is very common and widespread in southern Africa and is particularly common in thornveld savanna. Absent only from the north-western Cape Province and southern Namibia.

Behaviour: Flies fairly rapidly, around the tops of trees and bushes, especially flowering sweet thorns (*Acacia karroo*) and other acacias. Both sexes feed from flowers and males often mud-puddle. Fresh males have a noticeable pinkish colour in flight. Females are usually seen in the vicinity of acacias.

Flight period: September to April; commonest in December and January.

Early stages: Typical of lycaenids (see p. 156). The larvae feed on the flowers, buds and leaves of *Acacia* species and on flowers and buds of the spiny splinter bean (*Entada spicata*).

THE HESPERIIDS
(Family Hesperiidae)

Nearly 500 species of hesperiids occur in the Afrotropical Region, 125 species being found in southern Africa. They differ somewhat from other butterflies and are placed in a superfamily separate from the other butterfly families dealt with in this guide. They are moth-like in several respects: they have drab coloration; the body is robust and hairy and the wings are relatively small; they are often crepuscular; the antennae have a terminal club that is drawn out into a hooked point. Hesperiids are small to medium-sized insects and occur mainly in the forest, savanna and grassland biomes. Many species breed on grasses and other monocotyledonous plants but a fair number use dicotyledons. The eggs are dome-shaped and often have intricate patterns on the surface (fig. 347). Eggs are usually laid singly on a leaf of the larval foodplant. The larva usually rolls or folds a leaf of the foodplant, holding it in position by means of silken threads which it spins. The larva shelters within this space and later also pupates inside it. Hesperiid larvae have a characteristic shape (fig. 348), with a large head, narrow and distinct "neck" and a cylindrical body. The head is often patterned in more than one colour. The pupa is long and cylindrical and is often covered in a waxy, white powder which may serve to waterproof it (fig. 349). The long, narrow pupa lies more or less free within the leaf shelter.

POLICEMEN
KONSTABELS
(Genus *Coeliades*)

This homogeneous group of seven species represents the largest hesperiids in southern Africa. They are robust, fast-flying insects with tapered forewings and are dull brown in colour. Like many hesperiids they are particularly active at dawn and dusk and on overcast days. They are forest or savanna butterflies and are fond of flowers. A variety of larval foodplants are used. The larvae are strikingly coloured, being banded in white, black, yellow or red, but otherwise the early stages are similar to those of other hesperiids (p. 235).

Striped Policeman
Witbroekkonstabel
(Coeliades forestan) **fig. 103**

Identification: Medium-sized (50–55 mm); sexes very similar. Male upperside dull brown with large, orange-yellow basal patch on hindwing; hindwing lobed, blackish-brown and fringed with orange. Underside dull brown with large, well demarcated white patch and small white spot on hindwing; orange fringe on hindwing lobe conspicuous. Female larger, with stouter abdomen.

Distinguishing characters and similar species: The Striped Policeman can be confused with other Policemen (genus *Coeliades*), none of which is illustrated: 1) Two-pip Policeman (*C. pisistratus*) – has two black spots and an irregular black mark in the white patch in the middle of the hindwing underside. Common in savanna habitats in Natal, Swaziland, Transvaal, Mozambique, Zimbabwe, Botswana and Namibia; 2) Red-tab Policeman (*C. keithloa*) – has two orange-red "tabs" on the hindwing underside, the larger one bisected by a black mark. Fairly common in coastal forest, from the eastern Cape Province (Port Elizabeth) to Mozambique. There are three further species of Policemen in southern Africa but they are all fairly rare and are thus unlikely to be seen by the casual observer.

Habitat and distribution: The Striped Policeman is common in wooded savanna and on the edges of forest, from the eastern Cape Province (Port Elizabeth) to Natal, the Orange Free State, Swaziland, Transvaal, Mozambique, Zimbabwe and Botswana.

Behaviour: Specimens are usually encountered singly and although they may be seen at any time of the day, they are most active at dawn and dusk (crepuscular). They also fly in overcast, cool weather. The flight is very rapid, zig-zagging and from one to three metres above the ground. They often pause to inspect clumps of bushes before moving on. Both sexes are very fond of flowers and males occasionally mud-puddle. Males will sometimes visit hilltops but rarely remain there for any length of time.

Flight period: All year but commoner in summer.

Early stages: Typical of hesperiids (see above). The larvae feed on the leaves of a variety of indigenous and exotic trees belonging to a number of different families. These include red bush-willow (*Combretum apiculatum*), hiccup nut (*C. bracteosum*), *Triaspis glaucophylla*, bug-tree (*Solanum mauritianum*), bastard umzimbeet (*Millettia sutherlandii*), *Sphedamnocarpus galphimiifolius*, locust-tree (*Robinia pseudoacacia*), Rangoon creeper (*Quisqualis indica*) and mobolaplum (*Parinari curatellifolia*).

SPRITES
BOSJAGTERTJIES
(Genus *Celaenorrhinus*)

Only one of the three species found in the subregion is common and is discussed below. Sprites are forest butterflies and, like some related groups, characteristically perch with the wings held horizontally. The early stages are discussed under hesperiids (see p. 235).

Large Sprite
Kersfeesbosjagtertjie
(*Celaenorrhinus mokeezi*) **fig. 252**

Identification: Small to medium-sized (40–45 mm); sexes very similar. Male upperside dark brown with orange-brown flush on wings; two uneven orange bars across forewing and orange spot in middle of hindwing. Underside mirrors upperside. Female indistinguishable in flight.

Distinguishing characters and similar species: Superficially the Large Sprite resembles the smaller and darker Goldspotted Sylph (fig. 257) but the latter does not perch with the wings held flat. Two other species of Sprite, not illustrated, with which the Large Sprite can be confused, are found in the subregion: 1) Orange Sprite (*Celaenorrhinus galenus*) – smaller, with the orange markings on the hindwing upperside more extensive. Much less common than the Large Sprite and found in forests in Mozambique and on the eastern border of

Zimbabwe; 2) Betton's Sprite (*C. bettoni*) – has a pale, greenish-yellow, broken band on the forewing upperside and extensive orange markings on the underside of both wings. The smallest (35 mm) and rarest of the Sprites, occurring only in forests on the Zimbabwe-Mozambique border.

Habitat and distribution: The Large Sprite is common in coastal and montane forest, from the eastern Cape Province (Port Elizabeth) to Transkei, Natal, Transvaal and Mozambique.

Behaviour: Both sexes flit about in sunny forest clearings and along the edges of forest paths and roads. They remain close to the ground, rarely rising higher than a metre, and are very fond of flowers. Characteristically they perch with flattened wings on the underside of leaves, but often also sun themselves on top of leaves, with the wings held open.

Flight period: In warm coastal forests they are double-brooded (November–December and February–March) but in temperate montane forests there is only one brood (February–March). Occasional specimens are found in the other summer months.

Early stages: Typical of hesperiids (see p. 235). The only known larval foodplant is the forest understorey herb, buckweed (*Isoglossa woodii*).

FLATS
DARTELAARTJIES
(Genera *Tagiades*, *Eagris* and *Calleagris*)

The Flats derive their name from their habit of perching with the wings held horizontally, as do many moths. They often alight on the underside of leaves. These behavioural patterns are shared by a few related groups of hesperiids, namely the Sprites, Elves, Elfins and Skippers. Flats are small to medium-sized, rather moth-like in appearance, and have dull brown coloration with some white markings. They occur mainly in forests but there are a few savanna species. Flats have a fairly rapid skipping flight and breed on various dicotyledonous plants. The early stages are discussed under hesperiids (see p. 235).

Clouded Flat
Skaduweedartelaartjie
(Tagiades flesus) **fig. 105**

Identification: Medium-sized (45–50 mm); sexes very similar; moderate seasonal dimorphism. Male wet season form upperside dark brown with scattered, blackish-brown markings on both wings; two rows of small, translucent (hyaline) spots near forewing apex. Underside forewing similar to upperside forewing; hindwing underside largely white with semicircle of irregular black spots. Female similar to male but inner row of hyaline spots on forewing upperside larger than in male. Dry season form ground colour paler brown on both upper- and underside.

Distinguishing characters and similar species: Both sexes of the Clouded Flat may be confused with the female of the Rufouswinged Flat (*Eagris nottoana*), not illustrated, which is pale brown with more distinct black spots on the upperside. The male of the Rufouswinged Flat is almost black on the upperside and uniform dark brown on the underside. The Rufouswinged Flat occurs from Knysna in the southern Cape Province northwards along the coast to Mozambique, from where it spreads out into eastern Zimbabwe.

Habitat and distribution: The Clouded Flat is common in forest and thick bush, from the eastern Cape Province to Natal, Swaziland, eastern Transvaal and Zimbabwe. Isolated populations are found in kloof vegetation in central Transvaal, such as on the northern slopes of the Magaliesberg.

Behaviour: Males select territories, often in the vicinity of streams, which they may occupy for days on end. Within these territories they fly rapidly, the white underside of the hindwing intermittently flashing in the dappled light. They have the habit of alighting abruptly on the underside of leaves, with open wings, and in so doing seem to disappear suddenly. Females fly at random in the denser parts of forest or bush. Occasionally they are seen feeding from flowers.

Flight period: All year but commoner in summer.

Early stages: Typical of hesperiids (see p. 235). The larvae feed on a forest creeper with heart-shaped leaves, the wild yam (*Dioscorea cotinifolia*).

Kroon's Flat
Kroon-dartelaartjie
(Calleagris krooni) **fig. 106**

Identification: Small to medium-sized (40–45 mm); sexes similar. Male upperside dark blackish-brown with small, scattered, hyaline spots near forewing apex. Underside similar to upperside but lighter brown, especially near trailing edge of forewing. Female slightly larger, not quite as dark as male and with hyaline spots larger.

Distinguishing characters and similar species: Very similar to the Mrs Raven Flat (*Calleagris kobela*), not illustrated, which is smaller and has a different distribution, being found in temperate forest in the eastern Cape Province and Natal.

Habitat and distribution: Kroon's Flat is fairly common in some of the temperate forests of the eastern Transvaal escarpment, from about Sabie in the south to Mariepskop in the north.

Behaviour: Both sexes keep low down in clearings and along road verges in forest. They are quite wary but settle frequently and tend to remain in one spot for long periods. Often seen feeding from the flowers of low-growing plants. Like many related species they have the habit of alighting on the underside of leaves with open wings, but also settle on the upperside of leaves with open wings to sun themselves.

Flight period: November to May but much commoner in February and March.

Early stages: Unknown, as are the larval foodplants.

ELVES
KABOUTERS
(Genus *Eretis*)

Elves are small, dark brown to blackish insects with irregularly toothed (dentate) wing margins; they perch with the wings held flat. Three species are found in southern Africa. The early stages are similar to those of other hesperiids (see p. 235).

Small Marbled Elf
Umbra-kabouter
(Eretis umbra) **fig. 140**

Identification: Small (25–30 mm); sexes very similar. Male upperside blackish-brown with uneven (dentate) wing margins, especially on hindwing; small hyaline spots in forewing. Underside brown with rust-coloured areas. Female slightly larger.

Distinguishing characters and similar species: Two similar species of Elf, not illustrated, are found in southern Africa: 1) Marbled Elf (*Eretis djaelaelae*) – slightly larger and has the underside more clearly marked with orange-brown and black. The Marbled Elf also has shiny, white forelegs but this is only easily seen in set specimens. Its distribution covers most of the eastern half of the subcontinent and it is often found flying together with the Small Marbled Elf; 2) Dusky Elf (*E. melania*) – the underside markings are dark brown, with scattered blackish markings. It is found on the edges of forest in Mozambique and eastern Zimbabwe.

Habitat and distribution: The Small Marbled Elf is common in savanna and grassland and is distributed from the southern Cape Province (Plettenberg Bay) to Transkei, Natal, Transvaal, Mozambique and Zimbabwe.

Behaviour: Flies low down in grassy areas with forbs and settles on low plants or the ground with open wings. It is a fairly active insect but the flight is not fast and specimens will often remain in a particular spot for a long time. Individuals may often be seen frequenting the shade of trees. Both sexes feed from flowers and males are sometimes found mud-puddling.

Flight period: All year but much scarcer during the winter months.

Early stages: Not known but the larvae of the very similar Marbled Elf (see 1 above) feed on *Chaetacanthus setiger*, a small herb.

ELFINS
KABOUTERTJIES
(Genus *Sarangesa*)

Seven species of these small, dull, grey to dark brown butterflies are found in the subregion. Elfins occur mainly in savanna habitats where they fly in the shade of trees, seldom venturing into areas of full sunshine. Like some related groups they settle with the wings held flat, and are often mistaken for moths. The early stages are typical of hesperiids (see p. 235).

Small Elfin
Kleinkaboutertjie
(*Sarangesa phidyle*) fig. 138

Identification: Small (30–35 mm); sexes very similar; slight seasonal dimorphism. Male wet season form upperside olive-brown with small hyaline spots and scattered, dark brown markings on forewing. Underside yellow-brown with scattered brown markings. Dry season form with dark markings on forewing upperside more pronounced. Female slightly larger.

Distinguishing characters and similar species: Six other Elfins (*Sarangesa* species), none illustrated, occur in southern Africa: 1) Lucidella Elfin (*S. lucidella*) – like the Small Elfin but with a brown underside. Found in savanna in northern Zimbabwe; 2) Dark Elfin (*S. seineri*) – the upperside of the wings is more mottled, with brown and yellowish-brown, and the hyaline spots are larger. Occurs in savanna in Natal, Transvaal, Mozambique, Zimbabwe, Botswana and Namibia; 3) Forest Elfin (*S. motozi*) – has very prominent hyaline spots and a hyaline spot is present on the hindwing. Found in densely wooded savanna and on forest edges, from the eastern Cape Province to Natal, Transvaal, Mozambique, Zimbabwe and Botswana; 4) Ruona Elfin (*S. ruona*) – very similar to the Forest Elfin but there is no hyaline spot on the hindwing. Occurs in savanna in north-eastern Transvaal and eastern Zimbabwe; 5) Whitespeckled Elfin (*S. astrigera*) – dark brown with scattered, fine, white spots on both the upper- and underside of the wings. Only found in northern Zimbabwe; 6) Namibian Elfin (*S. gaerdesi*) – small (25 mm) with two geographical variants: the one greyish-brown with a greyish-white underside and the other light brown with a yellow-orange underside. The first is found in savanna habitats in northern Namibia, the second occurs on the fringes of the Namib Desert.

Habitat and distribution: The Small Elfin is common and widespread in the warmer savanna regions of the subcontinent.

Behaviour: Like all Elfins this species spends most of its time in the shade of trees, seldom venturing out into full sunshine. Rests on low plants, or on the ground, with open wings. Both sexes are fond of flowers and males sometimes mud-puddle. On occasions I have flushed up to a dozen specimens from antbear or warthog burrows, where they were congregating in the dark interior.

Flight period: All year.

Early stages: Typical of hesperiids (see p. 235). The only known larval foodplant is a low-growing forb, *Peristrophe hensii*.

SKIPPERS
SPRINGERTJIES
(Genera *Netrobalane, Leucochitonea, Abantis* and *Caprona*)

The 10 species in this group include some of the most beautiful of the hesperiids, especially some members of the genus *Abantis*. They are small to medium-sized butterflies with a typical skipping (jerky) flight which is medium-fast to very rapid. Skippers are found mainly in savanna and males frequently hilltop. When the insect is perched the wings are held flat. A variety of foodplants are used by the larvae, species of *Grewia* and *Dombeya* predominating. The early stages are discussed under the hesperiids (see p. 235).

Bufftipped Skipper
Bruinpunt-springertjie
(Netrobalane canopus) fig. 216

Identification: Small to medium-sized (35–45 mm); sexes similar. Male upperside creamy-white with buff-coloured forewing tip and wing bases; numerous hyaline spots on both wings. Underside off-white, with forewing tip brown; black dot at inner angle of hindwing. Female significantly larger.

Habitat and distribution: Fairly common in subtropical forest and thick bush, from the eastern Cape Province (East London) to Natal, Swaziland, Transvaal, Mozambique and Zimbabwe.

Behaviour: Males establish territories on the edge of bush or in forest clearings and choose a perch, on a tree, two to four metres above the ground. They fly with a medium-fast, jerky flight within their territory and settle with open wings on, or under, a leaf or twig. They appear whitish in flight and are sometimes known to make an audible clicking sound when flying. Males are also known to hilltop.

Flight period: All year.

Early stages: Typical of hesperiids (see p. 235). The larvae feed on the leaves of a number of shrubs belonging to a few closely related plant families. Recorded foodplants include cross-berry (*Grewia occidentalis*), Natal dombeya (*Dombeya cymosa*) and *Pavonia burchellii*.

Whitecloaked Skipper
Witjas-springertjie
(Leucochitonea levubu) fig. 27

Identification: Small (35–40 mm); sexes similar. Male upperside white with black markings on forewing tip and edges, forming a reticulate pattern. Underside similar to upperside. Female larger.

Habitat and distribution: Fairly common in savanna habitats, distributed from the northernmost parts of Natal (Maputaland) to Swaziland, northern and western Transvaal, western Zimbabwe, Botswana and Griqualand West.

Behaviour: Usually the flight is fast

and skipping, one to three metres above the ground. Males establish territories on the flats or on hilltops and, within these, choose a shrub or low tree on which to perch. Both sexes are fond of flowers. Females are rarely seen and fly at random in the bush.

Flight period: November to April.

Early stages: Has been bred from larvae collected off brandy-bush (*Grewia flava*).

Spotted Velvet Skipper
Koppiespringertjie
(*Abantis tettensis*) **fig. 217**

Identification: Small (30–40 mm); sexes similar. Male upperside black with numerous, elongated white markings on forewing and large, creamy patch tinged with salmon-pink on hindwing. Underside white, tinged with salmon-pink; black markings and spots on hindwing.

Distinguishing characters and similar species: There are five other species of *Abantis* in southern Africa. All are distinctive but, since they can all be regarded as uncommon to rare, they are not illustrated or discussed in this guide.

Habitat and distribution: The Spotted Velvet Skipper is relatively uncommon but widespread in thornveld savanna in Transvaal, Griqualand West, Zimbabwe, Botswana and northern Namibia.

Behaviour: Males are most likely to be encountered while they are hilltopping, where they choose perches on low shrubs or grass stems. They normally have a medium-fast, skipping flight but fly very rapidly when chasing intruders from their territories. Their small size and whitish colour in flight allow for reasonably easy identification. Females are rarely seen; usually found while feeding from flowers.

Flight period: November to April.

Early stages: Bred from larvae found, together with those of the preceding species, on brandy-bush (*Grewia flava*).

SANDMEN
SANDMANNETJIES
(Genera *Spialia* and *Gomalia*)

There are 15 species, all confusingly similar, in this group of very small butterflies. The uppersides are brown with scattered, pale yellow markings. The undersides have yellow and brown patterns characteristic of each species. Sandmen have a buzzing flight, close to the ground, and settle frequently. They occur chiefly in grassland and in grassy spots in savanna. The larval foodplants are small forbs belonging mostly to the families Malvaceae and Sterculiaceae. The early stages are typical of hesperiids (see p. 235).

Asterodia Sandman
Asterodia-sandmannetjie
(Spialia asterodia) **fig. 218**

Identification: Very small (22–24 mm); sexes very similar. Male upperside brown with scattered, pale yellow markings; chequered cilia on wing margins. Underside variegated in pale yellow, ochre and brown, with irregular, cream band through middle of hindwing. Female slightly stouter.

Distinguishing characters and similar species: There are 14 species belonging to the genus *Spialia* in the subregion, two of which are illustrated in this guide. All of them are very similar in both appearance and behaviour and are therefore difficult to distinguish in the field. The main differences between the various species are to be found on the underside of the hindwing and this is best examined in dead, set specimens. The wingspans of the different species are between 18 mm and 27 mm, making them small to very small butterflies. Their distribution, taken as a whole, covers virtually the whole of the subcontinent.

Habitat and distribution: The Asterodia Sandman is common in grassland, from sea level to 3 000 metres. Its distributional range includes the south-western and eastern Cape Province, Natal, Lesotho, the Orange Free State and Transvaal.

Behaviour: Has a fast, skipping to buzzing flight, close to the ground. Perches, with half-opened wings, on the ground or on low vegetation. Males establish ill-defined territories on flat ground but sometimes also hilltop. Both sexes are frequently seen visiting flowers of low-growing plants.

Flight period: August to March.

Early stages: Typical of hesperiids (see p. 235). The larvae have been recorded on *Hermannia diffusa*, *H. incana* and *Hibiscus* species.

Common Sandman
Kwagga-sandmannetjie
(Spialia diomus) **fig. 219**

Identification: Small (25–27 mm); sexes very similar. Male upperside dark brown with scattered, creamy yellow spots and chequered wing margins. Underside patterned in yellow and light brown markings. Female stouter.

Distinguishing characters and similar species: See discussion under Asterodia Sandman, above.

Habitat and distribution: The Common Sandman is very common and widespread in southern Africa, predominantly in grassy habitats. It is absent from the forest and desert biomes.

Behaviour: Males are often seen hilltopping, from 10h00 to 15h00, and rest on the ground, usually with the wings half-opened. The flight is medium-fast, skipping to buzzing and not generally sustained. Rarely do they fly more than a metre above the ground. Both sexes are very fond of flowers and males, in addition, sometimes mud-puddle.

Flight period: All year in frost-free areas; August to April in colder ones.

Early stages: Typical of hesperiids (see p. 235). The larvae feed on several species of *Hermannia*, including *H. diffusa*, *H. incana*, "kapokkie" (*H. comosa*) and "geneesbossie" (*H. cuneifolia*) as well as *Hibiscus aethiopicus* and *Pavonia burchellii*.

Greenmarbled Sandman
Asjas-sandmannetjie
(Gomalia elma) **fig. 143**

Identification: Small (25–30 mm); sexes very similar. Male upperside brown with scattered, blackish-brown markings; distinct, pale yellow marking in middle of hindwing; small hyaline spots on forewing. Underside light brown with pale yellow markings; hyaline spots on forewing. Female slightly larger.

Distinguishing characters and similar species: Although this is a fairly distinctive little butterfly, its habit of perching with the wings held flat may cause it to be mistaken for one of the Flats or related groups.

Habitat and distribution: The Greenmarbled Sandman is fairly common and very widespread in a variety of biomes, ranging from savanna and grassland to Karoo. The general distribution covers the southern and eastern Cape Province, the Orange Free State, Transvaal, Mozambique, Zimbabwe, Botswana and Namibia.

Behaviour: Has a darting, zig-zag flight, less than a metre above the ground, and settles with open wings (like the Flats) on forbs or on flowers. The flight is not particularly fast or prolonged.

Flight period: All year but commoner from August to April.

Early stages: Typical of hesperiids (see p. 235). The only plant known to serve as food for the larvae is a small herb belonging to the hibiscus family, "wildemalva" (*Abutilon sonneratianum*).

DANCERS
DANSERTJIES
(Genus *Alenia*)

The two species in this group are found in dry habitats in the Karoo and are easily overlooked because of their small size. They are dark brown with fine white spotting on the upperside of the wings.

Karoo Dancer
Karoodansertjie
(Alenia sandaster) **fig. 150**

Identification: Very small (20–25 mm); sexes very similar. Male upperside dark brown with fine, white spots on forewing and chequered cilia on wing margins. Underside brown with more extensive white spotting and two irregular white bands across hindwing. Female slightly larger.

Distinguishing characters and similar species: Easily confused with its only close relative, the Namaqua Dancer (*Alenia namaqua*), not illustrated, which is darker and occurs only in Little Namaqualand and the adjoining southern portion of Namibia.

Habitat and distribution: The Karoo Dancer is fairly common in dry, stony areas in the Karoo. Its distribution is restricted to this portion of the Cape Province.

Behaviour: Lives in colonies that are always associated with stands of its larval foodplant. The flight is not fast and is skipping and very close to the ground. In flight it somewhat resembles a large, black fly. Settles, with the wings held half open, on the ground, on rocks or on its foodplant. Both sexes regularly visit flowers, particularly those of mesembryanthemums.

Flight period: August to January but influenced, to some degree, by the timing of rainfall.

Early stages: Typical of hesperiids (see p. 235). The main larval foodplant is a small forb with unpleasantly spiny leaves, *Blepharis capensis*. The larvae are also said to feed on *Barleria* species.

SYLPHS
WALSERTJIES
(Genera *Metisella*, *Tsitana* and *Astictopterus*)

Sylphs are small, dull brown butterflies with orange or white markings on the wings. The 13 species in the subregion are found mainly in forest or grassland. Most have a slow, skipping flight, just above the tops of the grass. All breed on various species of grass, the larva rolling a grass-blade into a tube, in which it shelters.

Goldspotted Sylph
Reënwoudwalsertjie
(Metisella metis) **fig. 257**

Identification: Small (27–33 mm); sexes very similar. Male upperside very dark brown with scattered, large, bright gold-orange spots on both wings. Underside similar but spots restricted to forewing. Female slightly larger, with small yellow spots on underside of hindwing (absent in male).

Distinguishing characters and similar species: The Goldspotted Sylph cannot be distinguished in flight from the Eastern Sylph *(Metisella orientalis)*, not illustrated. The latter flies in forests on the eastern border of Zimbabwe, together with the Goldspotted Sylph. The other Sylphs belonging to the genus *Metisella* are savanna or grassland insects, and are dealt with under the following species.

Habitat and distribution: The Goldspotted Sylph is common in forests, from the south-western Cape Province north-eastwards to the eastern border of Zimbabwe. In the south-western Cape Province also found in more open, damp habitats. Plantations adjoining indigenous forest are frequently inhabited, one such place being the grove of exotic cypress trees at the picnic site near the Mac-Mac Waterfall in eastern Transvaal.

Behaviour: Both sexes have a slowish, fluttering flight, just above grass or low vegetation. In forest habitats prefers to remain in dappled shade. Perches on the ground, grass or low plants, with the wings open or closed. Usually numbers of specimens are found together in the same spot. Both sexes regularly feed from flowers.

Flight period: Virtually all year, but definitely commoner in summer.

Early stages: Typical of hesperiids (see p. 235). The larval foodplants include a number of different grass species, such as broadleaved panicum *(Panicum deustum)*, coarse couch-grass *(Stenotaphrum glabrum)*, Bushman-grass *(Stipa dregeana)* and *Ehrharta erecta*.

Netted Sylph
Willem-walsertjie
(Metisella willemi) **fig. 144**

Identification: Small (30–35 mm); sexes very similar. Male upperside blackish-brown with scattered, small, cream markings in outer half of forewing. Underside forewing dark brown with small, elongate, cream markings in apex; hindwing has distinctive, reticulate pattern of cream markings on dark brown ground colour. Female slightly larger.

Distinguishing characters and similar species: The Goldspotted Sylph and Eastern Sylph (above) are forest butterflies, while the Netted Sylph is found in savanna habitats. There are four other species of Sylph belonging to the genus *Metisella* in the subregion, all of which are inhabitants of the grassland biome. As these four species are not particularly common they are not illustrated but the descriptions should allow you to identify them: 1) Mountain Sylph (*M. aegipan*) – dark brown with a single, faint, orange spot on the leading edge of the forewing. Underside orange-brown with the forewing apex orange. Occurs in marshy areas in high-altitude grassland (usually above 1 800 metres). Found from the eastern Cape Province to Natal, Lesotho, Transvaal and the Chimanimani and Inyanga mountains in eastern Zimbabwe; 2) Grassveld Sylph (*M. malgacha*) – upperside brown, dusted with orange scales and with scattered orange spots. Widespread, in grassy habitats, from the southwestern and eastern Cape Province to the Orange Free State, Lesotho, the Natal midlands and some portions of Transvaal; 3) Marsh Sylph (*M. meninx*) – very small (20–25 mm), with the upperside dark brown. The underside hindwing has diagonal white streaks and marginal orange spots. Found in scattered, small colonies in swampy areas in grassland habitats, in northern Natal and Transvaal. Flies from December to March; 4) Bamboo Sylph (*M. syrinx*) – same size as the Netted Sylph. Dark brown on the upperside with a distinctive, broad, yellow median stripe on the underside of the hindwing. A rare butterfly, closely associated with clumps of mountain bamboo (*Arundinaria tessellata*), its larval foodplant. Colonies of the butterfly are found in high-altitude grassland in the eastern Cape Province, Natal and Lesotho. Flies in January and February.

Habitat and distribution: The Netted Sylph is fairly common in savanna in Transvaal, Zimbabwe and Botswana.

Behaviour: Flies slowly, with a somewhat vibrating action, in long grass in the shade of trees. Seems to spend long periods perched on grass stems with closed wings. Local colonies are often encountered in clumps of bush on the banks of rivers and streams. In drought years it may be very scarce but may become abundant in years with successive good rains. Both sexes readily feed from flowers.

Flight period: December to May; commonest about March.

Early stages: Not known.

Dismal Sylph
Donkerwalsertjie
(Tsitana tsita) **fig. 139**

Identification: Small (30–35 mm); sexes very similar. Male upperside uniform dark brown. Underside dark brown at base of forewing, with rest of wings lighter brown; hindwing underside has variable amount of white streaking.

Distinguishing characters and similar species: Three other Sylphs belonging to the genus *Tsitana* occur in southern Africa. All are restricted to the Cape Province and, since none of them is particularly common, they are not illustrated. They are similar to the Dismal Sylph but all of them have a prominent, white, mediad radial streak on the hindwing underside: 1) Uitenhage Sylph (*T. uitenhaga*) – found in the eastern Cape Province; 2) Tulbagh Sylph (*T. tulbagha*) – occurs in the south-western Cape Province and south-western Karoo; 3) Dickson's Sylph (*T. dicksoni*) – distributed in the south-western and southern Cape Province. These three species are very difficult to distinguish in the field.

Habitat and distribution: The Dismal Sylph is common in grassland, from sea level to an altitude of about 2 500 metres. Its range includes the eastern Cape Province, Transkei, the Natal midlands, the eastern Orange Free State, Lesotho, Transvaal and Zimbabwe.

Behaviour: The flight is slow and skipping, just above the level of the grass. Often flies for relatively long distances, in a more or less straight line. Specimens rest on grass stems or on the ground. Appears to be colonial, and fair numbers may be found when the butterfly is abundant. Both sexes are occasionally seen feeding from flowers.

Early stages: Life history unknown but the larvae, like those of other Sylphs, are almost certainly grass-feeders.

Flight period: Mainly December to March.

RANGERS
WAGTERTJIES
(Genera *Kedestes* and *Ampittia*)

Fifteen of the 16 species of Ranger in the subregion belong to the genus *Kedestes*. Rangers are small, brown butterflies with white and/or orange spots on the upperside of the wings. The undersides are characteristic for each species.

Rangers are found in grassland and savanna habitats where they fly with a skipping, zig-zag flight, in places where the grass is short. They breed on grasses, cotton-wool-grass (*Imperata cylindrica*) apparently being preferred.

Fulvous Ranger
Mohozutza-wagtertjie
(Kedestes mohozutza) **fig. 145**

Identification: Small (25–30 mm); sexes slightly different. Male upperside dark brown with cilia of wing margins chequered; scattered white spots in middle of forewing and a row of small, orange markings in forewing apex. Underside forewing brown at base; orange along leading edge and apex; white spots corresponding to those on upperside. Hindwing underside reddish-brown, with orange area in middle, enclosed by black spots. Female has orange spots on forewing upperside larger; submarginal orange spots on upperside of hindwing and orange spot in centre.

Distinguishing characters and similar species: There are two very similar Rangers, not illustrated: 1) Chaca's Ranger (*Kedestes chaca*) – larger (30–35 mm), with bolder markings on the underside of the wings. Found in grassland in the eastern Cape Province and southern Natal. Flies mainly in December and January; 2) Scarce Ranger (*K. nerva*) – similar in size to the Fulvous Ranger, but with the underside hindwing paler (yellow-orange not reddish-brown). Found in localised colonies in the savanna of the Natal midlands, Transvaal and Zimbabwe. Double-brooded, flying in October–November and again from February to April.

Habitat and distribution: The Fulvous Ranger is fairly common and widespread. Found in grassland, usually at moderately high altitudes, from the eastern Cape Province to north-eastern Zimbabwe.

Behaviour: Specimens are usually encountered flying very close to the ground in short grass, with a typical, skipping, zig-zag flight. They often fly about in a particular spot, alighting frequently, on blades of grass or on the ground. Both sexes are strongly attracted to low flowers among the grass. Colonies of these butterflies are found particularly in damp areas in grassland.

Flight period: November to April.

Early stages: These are unknown.

Barber's Ranger
Barber-wagtertjie
(Kedestes barberae) **fig. 146**

Identification: Small (25–35 mm); sexes similar. Male upperside dark brown with scattered, whitish spots in centre of forewing and chequered cilia on wing margins. Underside rusty-brown with scattered, angulated, white markings on both wings and clear, white streaks in wing margins. Female larger.

Habitat and distribution: Common in montane grassland, but in the south-western Cape Province also at sea level. It has a wide distribution, including the south-western and eastern Cape Province, Transkei, Natal, Lesotho, the eastern Orange Free State, Swaziland, Transvaal and Zimbabwe.

Behaviour: Has the typical skipping and zig-zag flight of the Rangers and keeps close to the ground. Prefers areas where the grass is short and perches on low vegetation and occasionally on the ground. Both sexes are fond of flowers.

Flight period: September to April. In some areas it seems to be double-brooded (on the wing October–November and March–April).

Early stages: Typical of hesperiids (see p. 235). The larvae feed on cottonwool-grass (*Imperata cylindrica*).

Wallengren's Ranger
Wallengren-wagtertjie
(Kedestes wallengrenii) **fig. 147**

Identification: Small, (25–30 mm); sexes similar. Male upperside dark brown with scattered white markings on forewing. Underside brown with light brown area on outer forewing; prominent, white, median-radial streak on hindwing; white spots on forewing, corresponding to those on upperside. Female larger and paler brown on upperside.

Distinguishing characters and similar species: Two related species of Ranger, not illustrated, occur in southern Africa: 1) Dark Ranger (*Kedestes niveostriga*) – like Wallengren's Ranger but larger and lacking the white streak on the hindwing underside. Distributed in grassland, from Transkei northwards to the Natal midlands. Flies from September to April; 2) Unique Ranger (*K. lenis*) – the white spots on the forewing are very small and the underside is plain brown. Found mainly in high-altitude grassland (over 1 800 metres), from the south-western to the eastern Cape Province, eastern Natal and the north-eastern Orange Free State.

Habitat and distribution: Wallengren's Ranger is widespread but is found in rather localised colonies, usually near streams and damp spots, in fairly high-altitude grassland. Recorded in Natal, Transvaal, Mozambique and Zimbabwe.

Behaviour: Flies in short grassveld, often remaining in a particular spot for some time. The flight is fast and skipping but usually very close to the ground. Both sexes are frequently seen feeding from flowers. Usually rests on the ground or on a blade of grass.

Flight period: August to April.

Early stages: Unknown. The larvae of both the Dark and Unique Ranger, mentioned above, feed on cottonwool-grass (*Imperata cylindrica*).

Chequered Ranger
Lepenula-wagtertjie
(Kedestes lepenula) **fig. 260**

Identification: Small (22–28 mm); sexes similar. Male upperside brown with scattered, large, yellow-orange areas on both wings. Underside immaculate, ochre. Female larger, with orange markings on upperside less extensive.

Distinguishing characters and similar species: Three similar Rangers, none illustrated, are found in the subcontinent: 1) Blackveined Ranger (*Kedestes sublineata*) – underside also ochre but all the veins on the underside are outlined in black. Occurs only in Namibia; 2) Macomo Ranger (*K. macomo*) – underside ochre with scattered, small, black spots on both wings. The veins of the underside forewing apex are outlined in black. Found in frost-free, low-altitude savanna from the eastern Cape Province northwards to Mozambique (including the eastern Transvaal lowveld); 3) Marshall's Ranger (*K. marshalli*) – underside as in the Macomo Ranger but the ground colour is orange, not ochre. Recorded in Zimbabwe, especially the eastern half (Mashonaland).

Habitat and distribution: The Chequered Ranger is common in thornveld savanna in the eastern half of the subcontinent.

Behaviour: Flies mostly at random in grassy areas in savanna habitats. Flight rapid but it settles often, on stones, low plants or the ground. Males are known to hilltop, a behaviour that is unusual for a species of Ranger.

Flight period: September to April; commonest from February to April.

Early stages: Unrecorded. The larval foodplant is cottonwool-grass (*Imperata cylindrica*).

Pale Ranger
Bosveldwagtertjie
(Kedestes callicles) **fig. 148**

Identification: Small (25–30 mm); sexes similar. Male upperside dark brown with scattered, pale yellow markings on both wings. Underside orange-yellow with lower half of forewing blackish-grey; scattered, pale yellow markings, outlined in black, corresponding to those on upperside. Female larger and slightly paler brown on upperside.

Habitat and distribution: Common in savanna, extending from northern Natal to Swaziland, Transvaal, Mozambique, Zimbabwe, Botswana and northern Namibia.

Behaviour: Specimens are most likely to be encountered in flat bushveld, where they fly in the shade of thorn trees. The flight is skipping and quite rapid but they settle frequently, on grass blades or low vegetation, in the shade. Both sexes are occasionally seen at flowers.

Flight period: December to April.

Early stages: Unknown, as is the larval foodplant.

ORANGES
ORANJETJIES
(Genus *Parosmodes* and others)

Only the commonest member of this diverse group of six species is illustrated in this guide. The Oranges are small, brown insects with extensive orange markings on the upperside of the wings. They are found in savanna habitats, keep to shady spots, and breed on dicotyledonous plants.

Morant's Orange
Morant-oranjetjie
(Parosmodes morantii) **fig. 259**

Identification: Small (30–35 mm); sexes similar. Male upperside brown with extensive orange markings on both wings. Underside orange with brown in lower half of forewing; scattered, small, black spots on hindwing. Female has orange markings less extensive on hindwing upperside.

Distinguishing characters and similar species: Morant's Orange may be confused with the Orange-spotted Hopper (fig. 258). There are five other species of Orange in southern Africa, none illustrated in this guide. They all occur in savanna habitats in Mozambique and Zimbabwe and have the habit of settling on grass stems in the shade of trees. Three of them are: 1) Arrowhead Orange (*Teniorhinus harona*) – variable on the upperside: brown with extensive orange markings, to virtually pure orange; 2) Herilus Orange (*T. herilus*) – orange markings on the upperside less extensive than in Morant's Orange. The underside hindwing and apex of forewing are light brown, heavily irrorated with blackish-brown; 3) Axehead Orange (*Acada biseriatus*) – like Morant's Orange but the black spotting on the underside of the hindwing is much more pronounced.

Habitat and distribution: Morant's Orange is fairly common in coastal bush and in savanna, from the coastal areas of Natal to Swaziland, Transvaal, Mozambique, Zimbabwe and northern Botswana.

Behaviour: Males are regularly encountered hilltopping, where they usually settle on trees but may also select perches lower down, on shrubs or grass. Specimens are often seen on the edge of bush in the late afternoon but are also commonly observed flying around grassy spots on the flats.

Flight period: All year but commonest in April and May.

Early stages: Typical of hesperiids (see p. 235). The larvae feed on the leaves of trees such as velvet bush-willow (*Combretum molle*) and mitzeerie (*Bridelia micrantha*).

DARTS
PYLTJIES
(Genus *Acleros* and others)

Only one of the six species of Dart found in the subregion is common and is dealt with below.

Macken's Dart
Macken-pyltjie
(Acleros mackenii) **fig. 141**

Identification: Small (25–30 mm); sexes dissimilar. Male upperside black with white fringe on hindwing and abdomen with white tip. Underside forewing blackish-brown with brown apex; hindwing variegated in browns and greyish-white. Female dark brown with two whitish markings in lower middle forewing. Underside as in male.

Distinguishing characters and similar species: Ploetz's Dart (*Acleros ploetzi*), not illustrated, is very similar but is found only in northern Mozambique and north-eastern Zimbabwe.

Habitat and distribution: Macken's Dart is very common in sub-tropical and temperate forests, from Port St Johns in Transkei to Natal, Swaziland, Transvaal, southern Mozambique and the eastern border of Zimbabwe.

Behaviour: Males establish territories in the semi-shade of forest margins where they settle on the leaves of shrubs in the undergrowth. The flight is not fast and the insect is not very wary, allowing one to approach close enough to see the diagnostic, white-tipped abdomen. Usually they remain from one to two metres above the ground. Both sexes are occasionally seen feeding from flowers.

Flight period: All year.

Early stages: Typical of hesperiids (see p. 235). The larval foodplant appears not to have been recorded.

NIGHTFIGHTERS
SKEMERVEGTERS
(Genera *Moltena*, *Artitropa* and others)

The five species of Nightfighter in the subregion are medium-sized, moth-like insects and are strongly crepuscular (active at dawn and dusk). They are not often observed because they have a very rapid flight and are difficult to see as they dash about in the gloom. Nightfighters are forest butterflies and breed on several genera of large-leaved monocotyledons such as *Strelitzia*, *Dracaena* and *Phoenix*.

Strelitzia Nightfighter
Strelitzia-skemervegter
(Moltena fiara) **fig. 104**

Identification: Medium-sized (40–55 mm); sexes similar. Male upperside brown with orange-brown at base of hindwing and on leading edge of forewing; pale grey antennae. Underside light brown, finely speckled with black scales. Female much larger and with brown antennae.

Distinguishing characters and similar species: The Palm-tree Nightfighter (*Zophopetes dysmephila*), not illustrated, is smaller (35–40 mm) and darker, with some hyaline spots in the middle of the forewing and greyish wing-tips. A crepuscular hesperiid distributed along the coast, from Port Elizabeth northwards to Mozambique and spreading inland to the eastern Transvaal lowveld and eastern border of Zimbabwe. The larvae feed on leaves of the wild date-palm (*Phoenix reclinata*).

Habitat and distribution: The Strelitzia Nightfighter is common in the coastal and near-coastal zone from Port Alfred in the eastern Cape Province to Maputo in Mozambique.

Behaviour: During the day the butterflies hide in vegetation, especially inside a young, rolled-up leaf of the larval foodplant. As dusk approaches they emerge from their shelters to seek flowers or mates. The flight is exceedingly rapid and the insects are very difficult to follow as they dash about in the deepening gloom. Often they can be tracked by listening for the quite loud humming noise made by the wing-beats. Males are territorial; females fly at random in search of flowers or suitable oviposition sites.

Flight period: All year but emergences tend to be in irregular pulses and cannot be predicted accurately.

Early stages: Typical of hesperiids (see p. 235). The larvae feed on the very large-leaved Natal strelitzia (*Strelitzia nicolai*), which somewhat resembles the unrelated banana-tree.

Bush Nightfighter
Bosskemervegter
(*Artitropa erinnys*) fig. 251

Identification: Medium-sized (45–50 mm); sexes similar. Male forewing upperside brown with orange-brown at base and a few hyaline spots; hindwing black with orange markings in middle and along lower wing margin. Underside variegated in shades of brown, with whitish markings in middle of hindwing. Female larger. Specimens from northern part of the species' range have more white on undersides.

Distinguishing characters and similar species: A similar, but much rarer, Nightfighter occurs in some forests on the eastern border of Zimbabwe. This is the Scarce Nightfighter (*Artitropa comus*), not illustrated, which has a large, orange-yellow patch at the base of the hindwing upperside. Like its close relative, the Bush Nightfighter, it is also crepuscular.

Habitat and distribution: The Bush Nightfighter is not rare but, because of its habit of flying at dusk, it is seldom seen. Inhabits subtropical and temperate forests, from the eastern Cape Province (Port Elizabeth) to Natal and the eastern parts of Transvaal and Zimbabwe.

Behaviour: During the day this hesperiid rests on rocks and tree trunks among ferns and mosses on the banks of forest streams. At dusk or on warm, overcast days it emerges from its hiding place to look for flowers or mates. The flight is very rapid and the insect is difficult to follow when flying.

Flight period: All year in subtropical forests and from August to April in temperate ones.

Early stages: Typical of hesperiids (see p. 235). The larvae feed on the large-leaved dragon tree (*Dracaena* hookerana), an aloe-like shrub with a single stem and a crown of large leaves, which grows in the shady understorey of forests.

HOPPERS
HOPPERTJIES
(Genera *Platylesches*, *Zezonia* and *Fresna*)

These small hesperiids have very robust bodies and a very fast, buzzing flight. They are generally brown with white or yellow spots (*Platylesches*) but one species (*Zezonia*) has orange spots. There are 11 species in southern Africa and all are savanna insects. The main larval foodplants appear to be species of the genus *Parinari*, of the mobola-plum family (Chrysobalanaceae).

Peppered Hopper
Ayres-hoppertjie
(*Platylesches ayresii*) fig. 149

Identification: Small (25–30 mm); sexes very similar. Male upperside dark brown with small hyaline spots on forewing and dusting of yellow-brown scales in middle of hindwing. Underside brown with greyish irroration in apex of forewing and covering hindwing; hyaline spots on forewing, corresponding to those on upperside. Female slightly larger.

Distinguishing characters and similar species: There are eight other species of *Platylesches* in southern Africa. Most of them are very similar on the upperside and are not easy to distinguish in the field.

Habitat and distribution: The Peppered Hopper is common in the savanna biome, from northern Natal to Transvaal, Mozambique, Zimbabwe and Botswana.

Behaviour: Males are usually found hilltopping, where they choose perches on stones or on the ground. Both sexes are frequently found in the vicinity of their low-growing, almost stemless larval foodplant, which grows in sandy or rocky places among grass. Here they fly about rapidly, very close to the ground. They settle often, on the ground, on low vegetation or on flowers. Males occasionally mud-puddle and have been seen feeding from fresh cowpats.

Flight period: July to April.

Early stages: Typical of hesperiids (see p. 235). The larvae feed on the leaves of "grysappel" (*Parinari capensis*). Some of the other species of Hopper are known to breed on the mobola-plum (*Parinari curatellifolia*), which grows in well-wooded, frost-free savanna.

Orangespotted Hopper
Oranje-hoppertjie
(*Zezonia zeno*) **fig. 258**

Identification: Small (30–40 mm); sexes very similar. Male upperside dark brown with extensive orange markings on both wings. Underside brown, largely covered by yellow-orange markings. Female larger.

Distinguishing characters and similar species: Easily confused with Morant's Orange (fig. 259).

Habitat and distribution: The Orangespotted Hopper is fairly common in temperate forests, from Transkei to Natal, Transvaal, Mozambique and eastern Zimbabwe.

Behaviour: Both sexes are usually encountered on the outskirts of forest, where the males select and defend territories. The flight is rapid but the butterflies settle often, on grass stems or on shrubs.

Flight period: All year.

Early stages: Unknown.

SWIFTS
RATSVLIEËRS
(Genera *Pelopidas* and *Borbo*)

Swifts are small to medium-sized hesperiids with dull olive to brown coloration and hyaline spots on the forewing. The 13 species in the subregion are difficult to distinguish in the field because of their similar appearance. They occur in a variety of biomes, chiefly forest, savanna and grassland. As the common name implies they are very rapid fliers but they perch frequently and are fond of flowers.

The larvae feed on grasses and the early stages are typical of hesperiids (see p. 235).

Whitebranded Swift
Witmerk-ratsvlieër
(Pelopidas thrax) **fig. 136**

Identification: Small to medium-sized (40–45 mm); sexes similar. Male upperside brown with ochre tinge; scattered hyaline spots on forewing. Underside ochre-brown with hyaline spots on forewing, corresponding to those on upperside. Female larger, with larger hyaline spots.

Distinguishing characters and similar species: Very similar to the closely related Blackbranded Swift (*Pelopidas mathias*), not illustrated, which, like the Whitebranded Swift, is common and widespread. It can also be mistaken for any of the 11 species of Swift in the genus *Borbo* (see below).

Habitat and distribution: The Whitebranded Swift is widespread and fairly common in the whole of the subcontinent, being absent only from the drier portions of the Karoo.

Behaviour: Males establish territories on the edge of bush and on top of hills. The flight of the males is very rapid but they settle frequently. Both sexes are very fond of flowers and the males, in addition, often mud-puddle.

Flight period: All year but commoner in summer.

Early stages: Typical of hesperiids (see p. 235). The larvae feed on the leaves of cottonwool-grass (*Imperata cylindrica*).

Olivehaired Swift
Groen-ratsvlieër
(Borbo borbonica) **fig. 137**

Identification: Small (35–40 mm); sexes very similar. Male upperside dark olive-brown with conspicuous, scattered, hyaline spots on forewing. Underside olive with yellowish tinge; lower half of forewing dark brown; hyaline spots in both fore- and hindwing. Female slightly paler brown on upperside.

Distinguishing characters and similar species: There are another 10 species in the genus *Borbo* in southern Africa. All are very difficult to distinguish from one another in the field. They are also very similar to the two Swifts belonging to the genus *Pelopidas* (see above).

Habitat and distribution: The Olivehaired Swift is fairly common in both grassland and savanna. It occurs from the eastern Cape Province to Natal, the Orange Free State, Transvaal, Mozambique, Zimbabwe and northern Botswana and Namibia.

Behaviour: Both sexes are usually found flying at random about the veld and are very fond of flowers.

Flight period: All year.

Early stages: Unknown. In the three species of the genus *Borbo* in which they are known, the larvae all feed on various species of grass.

HOTTENTOTS
HOTNOTTE
(Genus *Gegenes*)

There are three species of Hottentot in southern Africa. They are small insects with yellow-brown to dark brown coloration. They are found in grassy areas in most biomes and have a rapid flight, close to the ground. Hottentots are closely related to Swifts and their larvae, like those of Swifts, feed on grasses.

Common Hottentot
Geelhotnot
(Gegenes niso) **fig. 142**

Identification: Small (25–30 mm); sexes dissimilar. Male upperside varying from dark brown, with a bronzy sheen, to yellowish-brown. Underside yellowish-brown, mixed with scattered, light brown markings. Female upperside olive-brown with scattered yellowish markings on forewing and single, pale orange mark on hindwing. Underside as in male.

Distinguishing characters and similar species: Two further species, not illustrated, of Hottentot (genus *Gegenes*) are found in the subregion, both of them common: 1) Dark Hottentot (*G. pumilio*) – very dark brown above and brown on the underside. It is widespread in southern Africa, being absent only from very dry areas; 2) Marsh Hottentot (*G. hottentota*) – the male of this species is more yellow on the upperside and has a blackish patch of scales in the middle of the forewing. The underside is like that of the Common Hottentot. The female closely resembles the Common Hottentot on both the upper- and underside. The Marsh Hottentot is rare in Transvaal but commoner in Mozambique, Zimbabwe and northern Botswana.

Habitat and distribution: The Common Hottentot, as its name indicates, is common and widespread in the subregion. Occurs in a number of different habitats, including forest margins, savanna and grassland. More abundant in habitats with relatively short grass.

Behaviour: Has a fast and erratic flight, usually less than a metre above the ground. Alights with the forewings held erect and the hindwings horizontal. Settles frequently, on the ground or on low vegetation. Both sexes often visit flowers.

Flight period: All year in warmer areas and summer in cooler ones.

Early stages: Typical of hesperiids (see p. 235). The larvae feed on various species of grass, including Kikuyu-grass (*Pennisetum clandestinum*), rooigras (*Themeda triandra*) and *Ehrharta erecta*.

PART 3

CHECKLISTS

Very common and widespread butterflies

African Clouded Yellow (*Colias electo*)
African Leopard (*Phalanta phalantha*)
African Migrant (*Catopsilia florella*)
African Monarch (*Danaus chrysippus*)
Black Pie (*Tuxentius melaena*)
Blackstriped Hairtail (*Anthene amarah*)
Blue Pansy (*Junonia oenone*)
Broadbordered Grass Yellow (*Eurema brigitta*)
Brown Playboy (*Deudorix antalus*)
Brownveined White (*Belenois aurota*)
Citrus Swallowtail (*Papilio demodocus*)
Common Diadem (*Hypolimnas misippus*)
Common Dotted Blue (*Tarucus sybaris*)
Common Dotted Border (*Mylothris agathina*)
Common Figtree Butterfly (*Myrina silenus*)
Common Hairtail (*Anthene definita*)
Common Hottentot (*Gegenes niso*)
Common Meadow Blue (*Cupidopsis cissus*)
Common Meadow White (*Pontia helice*)
Common Pea Blue (*Leptotes pirithous*)
Common Sandman (*Spialia diomus*)
Common Scarlet (*Axiocerses tjoane*)
Cupreous Small Blue (*Eicochrysops messapus*)
Foxy Charaxes (*Charaxes jasius*)
Gaika Blue (*Zizula hylax*)
Garden Acraea (*Acraea horta*)
Garden Commodore (*Precis archesia*)
Geranium Blue (*Cacyreus marshalli*)
Grass Jewel Blue (*Freyeria trochylus*)
Greenbanded Swallowtail (*Papilio nireus*)
Greenmarbled Sandman (*Gomalia elma*)
Guineafowl (*Hamanumida daedalus*)
Henning's Black Eye (*Leptomyrina henningi*)
Longtailed Pea Blue (*Lampides boeticus*)
Painted Lady (*Vanessa cardui*)
Patricia Blue (*Lepidochrysops patricia*)
Purple-brown Hairstreak (*Hypolycaena philippus*)
Sooty Blue (*Zizeeria knysna*)
Spotted Joker (*Byblia ilithyia*)
Striped Policeman (*Coeliades forestan*)
Topaz Spotted Blue (*Azanus jesous*)
Wandering Donkey Acraea (*Acraea neobule*)
Whitebranded Swift (*Pelopidas thrax*)
Yellow Pansy (*Junonia hierta*)

Butterflies commonly seen in gardens

African Clouded Yellow (*Colias electo*)
African Leopard (*Phalanta phalantha*)
African Migrant (*Catopsilia florella*)
African Monarch (*Danaus chrysippus*)
Brown Playboy (*Deudorix antalus*)
Brownveined White (*Belenois aurota*)
Citrus Swallowtail (*Papilio demodocus*)
Common Diadem (*Hypolimnas misippus*)
Common Dotted Border (*Mylothris agathina*)
Common Hairtail (*Anthene definita*)
Common Hottentot (*Gegenes niso*)
Common Pea Blue (*Leptotes pirithous*)
Common Scarlet (*Axiocerses tjoane*)
Gaika Blue (*Zizula hylax*)
Garden Acraea (*Acraea horta*)
Garden Commodore (*Precis archesia*)
Gaudy Commodore (*Precis octavia*)
Geranium Bronze (*Cacyreus marshalli*)
Greenbanded Swallowtail (*Papilio nireus*)
Longtailed Pea Blue (*Lampides boeticus*)
Painted Lady (*Vanessa cardui*)
Sooty Blue (*Zizeeria knysna*)
Striped Policeman (*Coeliades forestan*)
Yellow Pansy (*Junonia hierta*)

Forest butterflies

African Leopard (*Phalanta phalantha*)
African Migrant (*Catopsilia florella*)
African Monarch (*Danaus chrysippus*)
African Snout (*Libythea labdaca*)
African Wood White (*Leptosia alcesta*)

Battling Glider (*Cymothoe alcimeda*)
Blood-red Acraea (*Acraea petraea*)
Blotched Leopard (*Lachnoptera ayresii*)
Blue Pansy (*Junonia oenone*)
Boisduval's False Acraea (*Pseudacraea boisduvalii*)
Boisduval's Tree Nymph (*Sallya boisduvali*)
Brown Pansy (*Junonia natalica*)
Brown Playboy (*Deudorix antalus*)
Brownveined White (*Belenois aurota*)
Bufftipped Skipper (*Netrobalane canopus*)
Bush Beauty (*Paralethe dendrophilus*)
Bush Nightfighter (*Artitropa erinnys*)
Cambridge Vagrant (*Nepheronia thalassina*)
Citrus Swallowtail (*Papilio demodocus*)
Chief False Acraea (*Pseudacraea lucretia*)
Chief Friar (*Amauris echeria*)
Clouded Flat (*Tagiades flesus*)
Common Buff (*Baliochila aslanga*)
Common Bush Brown (*Bicyclus safitza*)
Common Diadem (*Hypolimnas misippus*)
Common Dotted Border (*Mylothris agathina*)
Common Figtree Butterfly (*Myrina silenus*)
Common Friar (*Amauris niavius*)
Common Hairtail (*Anthene definita*)
Common Mother-of-pearl (*Protogoniomorpha parhassus*)
Common Pea Blue (*Leptotes pirithous*)
Common Sailer (*Neptis laeta*)
Dry-leaf Commodore (*Precis tugela*)
Dusky Acraea (*Hyalites esebria*)
Duskyveined Acraea (*Hyalites igola*)
Emperor Swallowtail (*Papilio ophidicephalus*)
False Dotted Border White (*Belenois thysa*)
Flamebordered Charaxes (*Charaxes protoclea*)
Forest-king Charaxes (*Charaxes xiphares*)
Forest Queen (*Euxanthe wakefieldi*)
Forest White (*Belenois zochalia*)
Garden Acraea (*Acraea horta*)
Goldbanded Forester (*Euphaedra neophron*)
Goldspotted Sylph (*Metisella metis*)
Greenbanded Swallowtail (*Papilio nireus*)
Greenveined Charaxes (*Charaxes candiope*)
Kroon's Flat (*Calleagris krooni*)
Large Sprite (*Celaenorrhinus mokeezi*)
Large Vagrant (*Nepheronia argia*)

Longtailed Admiral (*Antanartia schaeneia*)
Longtailed Pea Blue (*Lampides boeticus*)
Macken's Dart (*Acleros mackeni*)
Mocker Swallowtail (*Papilio dardanus*)
Natal Tree Nymph (*Sallya natalensis*)
Novice Friar (*Amauris ochlea*)
Orangebarred Playboy (*Deudorix diocles*)
Orangespotted Hopper (*Zezonia zeno*)
Pearl Charaxes (*Charaxes varanes*)
Pondo Shadefly (*Coenyra aurantiaca*)
Purple-brown Hairstreak (*Hypolycaena philippus*)
Rainforest Brown (*Cassionympha cassius*)
Satyr Charaxes (*Charaxes ethalion*)
Soldier Pansy (*Junonia terea*)
Southern Sapphire (*Iolaus silas*)
Southern Wanderer (*Bematistes aganice*)
Spotted Pentila (*Pentila tropicalis*)
Spotted Sailer (*Neptis saclava*)
Strelitzia Nightfighter (*Moltena fiara*)
Trimen's Dotted Border (*Mylothris trimenia*)
Variable Diadem (*Hypolimnas anthedon*)
Whitebanded Swallowtail (*Papilio echerioides*)
Whitebarred Charaxes (*Charaxes brutus*)
Yellowbanded Acraea (*Hyalites cabira*)

Savanna butterflies

African Clouded Yellow (*Colias electo*)
African Common White (*Belenois creona*)
African Joker (*Byblia anvatara*)
African Leopard (*Phalanta phalantha*)
African Migrant (*Catopsilia florella*)
African Monarch (*Danaus chrysippus*)
African Small White (*Dixeia charina*)
African Veined White (*Belenois gidica*)
Angola White-lady Swordtail (*Graphium angolanus*)
Ant-heap Small White (*Dixeia pigea*)
Apricot Playboy (*Deudorix dinochares*)
Autumn-leaf Vagrant (*Eronia leda*)
Azure Hairstreak (*Hemiolaus caeculus*)
Banded Gold Tip (*Colotis eris*)
Black Heart (*Uranothauma nubifer*)
Black Pie (*Tuxentius melaena*)
Blackstriped Hairtail (*Anthene amarah*)
Blacktipped Acraea (*Acraea calderena*)
Blue Pansy (*Junonia oenone*)

CHECKLISTS

Bluespangled Charaxes (*Charaxes guderiana*)
Bowker's Sapphire (*Iolaus bowkeri*)
Broadbordered Acraea (*Acraea anemosa*)
Broadbordered Grass Yellow (*Eurema brigitta*)
Brown Playboy (*Deudorix antalus*)
Brownveined White (*Belenois aurota*)
Bush Bronze (*Cacyreus lingeus*)
Bushveld Charaxes (*Charaxes achaemenes*)
Chequered Ranger (*Kedestes lepenula*)
Citrus Swallowtail (*Papilio demodocus*)
Clubtailed Charaxes (*Charaxes zoolina*)
Common Diadem (*Hypolimnas misippus*)
Common Dotted Blue (*Tarucus sybaris*)
Common Dotted Border (*Mylothris agathina*)
Common Evening Brown (*Melanitis leda*)
Common Figtree Butterfly (*Myrina silenus*)
Common Hairtail (*Anthene definita*)
Common Hottentot (*Gegenes niso*)
Common Meadow Blue (*Cupidopsis cissus*)
Common Meadow White (*Pontia helice*)
Common Mimic Acraea (*Hyalites encedon*)
Common Orange Tip (*Colotis evenina*)
Common Pea Blue (*Leptotes pirithous*)
Common Sandman (*Spialia diomus*)
Common Scarlet (*Axiocerses tjoane*)
Common Smoky Blue (*Euchrysops malathana*)
Cupreous Small Blue (*Eicochrysops messapus*)
Damara Copper (*Aloeides damarensis*)
Dark Webbed Ringlet (*Physcaeneura panda*)
Diverse Rainforest White (*Appias epaphia*)
Dusky Blue (*Pseudonacaduba sichela*)
Dusky Charaxes (*Charaxes phaeus*)
Dusky Copper (*Aloeides taikosama*)
Dwarf Blue (*Oraidium barberae*)
Eriksson's Highflier (*Aphnaeus erikssoni*)
Eyed Bush Brown (*Henotesia perspicua*)
Foxy Charaxes (*Charaxes jasius*)
Free State Blue (*Lepidochrysops letsea*)
Gaika Blue (*Zizula hylax*)
Garden Acraea (*Acraea horta*)
Garden Commodore (*Precis archesia*)
Geranium Blue (*Cacyreus marshalli*)
Golden Piper (*Eurytela dryope*)
Grass Jewel Blue (*Freyeria trochylus*)
Greenbanded Swallowtail (*Papilio nireus*)

Greenmarbled Sandman (*Gomalia elma*)
Guineafowl (*Hamanumida daedalus*)
Henning's Black Eye (*Leptomyrina henningi*)
Hintza Pie (*Zintha hintza*)
Hutchinson's Highflier (*Aphnaeus hutchinsonii*)
Impure Ringlet (*Ypthima impura*)
Large Spotted Acraea (*Acraea acara*)
Large Striped Swordtail (*Graphium antheus*)
Lemon Traveller Tip (*Colotis subfasciatus*)
Little Acraea (*Acraea axina*)
Longtailed Pea Blue (*Lampides boeticus*)
Mashuna Blue (*Lepidochrysops mashuna*)
Mimosa Sapphire (*Iolaus mimosae*)
Morant's Orange (*Parosmodes morantii*)
Natal Acraea (*Acraea natalica*)
Natal Bar (*Spindasis natalensis*)
Natal Brown (*Coenyropsis natalii*)
Netted Sylph (*Metisella willemi*)
Olivehaired Swift (*Borbo borbonica*)
Otacilia Hairtail (*Anthene otacilia*)
Painted Lady (*Vanessa cardui*)
Pale Hairtail (*Anthene butleri*)
Pale Ranger (*Kedestes callicles*)
Patricia Blue (*Lepidochrysops patricia*)
Pearlspotted Charaxes (*Charaxes jahlusa*)
Peppered Hopper (*Platylesches ayresii*)
Pied Piper (*Eurytela hiarbas*)
Purple-brown Hairstreak (*Hypolycaena philippus*)
Queen Purple Tip (*Colotis regina*)
Rayed Blue (*Actizera lucida*)
Red Tip (*Colotis antevippe*)
Rooibok Acraea (*Acraea oncaea*)
Sabie Smoky Blue (*Euchrysops dolorosa*)
Saffron Sapphire (*Iolaus pallene*)
Savanna Brown (*Neita extensa*)
Scarlet Tip (*Colotis danae*)
Silverspotted Grey (*Crudaria leroma*)
Silvery Bar (*Spindasis phanes*)
Small Elfin (*Sarangesa phidyle*)
Small Marbled Elf (*Eretis umbra*)
Small Orange Tip (*Colotis evagore*)
Smoky Orange Tip (*Colotis evippe*)
Sooty Blue (*Zizeeria knysna*)
Speckled Sulphur Tip (*Colotis agoye*)
Spiller's Sulphur Small White (*Dixeia spilleri*)
Spotted Joker (*Byblia ilithyia*)

272 CHECKLISTS

Spotted Velvet Skipper (*Abantis tettensis*)
Striped Policeman (*Coeliades forestan*)
Sulphur Orange Tip (*Colotis auxo*)
Tailed Black Eye (*Leptomyrina hirundo*)
Topaz Spotted Blue (*Azanus jesous*)
Trimen's Sapphire (*Iolaus trimeni*)
Twin Dotted Border (*Mylothris rueppellii*)
Twinspot Blue (*Lepidochrysops plebeia*)
Van Son's Charaxes (*Charaxes vansoni*)
Veined Swordtail (*Graphium leonidas*)
Velvet Spotted Blue (*Azanus ubaldus*)
Vine-leaf Vagrant (*Eronia cleodora*)
Wandering Donkey Acraea (*Acraea neobule*)
Whitebranded Swift (*Pelopidas thrax*)
Whitecloaked Skipper (*Leucochitonea levubu*)
Woolly Legs (*Lachnocnema bibulus*)
Yellow Pansy (*Junonia hierta*)
Yellow Zulu (*Alaena amazoula*)
Zebra White (*Pinacopteryx eriphia*)

Grassland butterflies

African Clouded Yellow (*Colias electo*)
African Migrant (*Catopsilia florella*)
African Monarch (*Danaus chrysippus*)
Amakosa Rocksitter (*Durbania amakosa*)
Aranda Copper (*Aloeides aranda*)
Asterodia Sandman (*Spialia asterodia*)
Barber's Ranger (*Kedestes barberae*)
Basutu Skolly (*Thestor basutus*)
Blue Pansy (*Junonia oenone*)
Broadbordered Grass Yellow (*Eurema brigitta*)
Brownveined White (*Belenois aurota*)
Cape Autumn Widow (*Dira clytus*)
Cape Spring Widow (*Tarsocera cassus*)
Common Diadem (*Hypolimnas misippus*)
Common Dotted Blue (*Tarucus sybaris*)
Common Hottentot (*Gegenes niso*)
Common Meadow Blue (*Cupidopsis cissus*)
Common Meadow White (*Pontia helice*)
Common Sandman (*Spialia diomus*)
Common Smoky Blue (*Euchrysops malathana*)
Cupreous Small Blue (*Eicochrysops messapus*)
Dancing Acraea (*Hyalites eponina*)
Dingaan's Widow (*Dingana dingana*)
Dismal Sylph (*Tsitana tsita*)
Drakensberg Brown (*Pseudonympha poetula*)
Dusky Copper (*Aloeides taikosama*)

Dwarf Blue (*Oraidium barberae*)
Eastern Sorrel Copper (*Lycaena clarki*)
Eyed Pansy (*Junonia orithya*)
Free State Blue (*Lepidochrysops letsea*)
Fulvous Ranger (*Kedestes mohozutza*)
Gaika Blue (*Zizula hylax*)
Garden Commodore (*Precis archesia*)
Gaudy Commodore (*Precis octavia*)
Geranium Blue (*Cacyreus marshalli*)
Grass Jewel Blue (*Freyeria trochylus*)
Greenmarbled Sandman (*Gomalia elma*)
Greybottom Brown (*Pseudonympha magoides*)
Henning's Black Eye (*Leptomyrina henningi*)
Koppie Blue (*Lepidochrysops ortygia*)
Light-red Acraea (*Acraea nohara*)
Longtailed Pea Blue (*Lampides boeticus*)
Lydenburg Opal (*Poecilmitis aethon*)
Marsh Acraea (*Hyalites rahira*)
Marsh Commodore (*Precis ceryne*)
Mashuna Blue (*Lepidochrysops mashuna*)
Olivehaired Swift (*Borbo borbonica*)
Orange Acraea (*Hyalites anacreon*)
Orangebanded Protea (*Capys alphaeus*)
Orange Widow (*Torynesis orangica*)
Painted Lady (*Vanessa cardui*)
Patricia Blue (*Lepidochrysops patricia*)
Pirate (*Catacroptera cloanthe*)
Polka Dot (*Pardopsis punctatissima*)
Potchefstroom Blue (*Lepidochrysops procera*)
Rayed Blue (*Actizera lucida*)
Restless Indigo Blue (*Orachrysops lacrimosa*)
Roodepoort Copper (*Aloeides dentatis*)
Sabie Smoky Blue (*Euchrysops dolorosa*)
Sooty Blue (*Zizeeria knysna*)
Spotted-eye Brown (*Pseudonympha narycia*)
Table Mountain Beauty (*Aeropetes tulbaghia*)
Variable Blue (*Lepidochrysops variabilis*)
Wallengren's Ranger (*Kedestes wallengrenii*)
Western Hillside Brown (*Stygionympha vigilans*)
Yellow Pansy (*Junonia hierta*)
Yellow Zulu (*Alaena amazoula*)

Karoo butterflies

African Clouded Yellow (*Colias electo*)
African Monarch (*Danaus chrysippus*)

Aranda Copper (*Aloeides aranda*)
Barkly's Copper (*Aloeides barklyi*)
Blackstriped Hairtail (*Anthene amarah*)
Boland Skolly (*Thestor protumnus*)
Bowker's Sapphire (*Iolaus bowkeri*)
Brownveined White (*Belenois aurota*)
Cape Dotted Blue (*Tarucus thespis*)
Citrus Swallowtail (*Papilio demodocus*)
Common Dotted Border (*Mylothris agathina*)
Common Figtree Butterfly (*Myrina silenus*)
Common Hairtail (*Anthene definita*)
Common Sandman (*Spialia diomus*)
Damara Copper (*Aloeides damarensis*)
Dwarf Blue (*Oraidium barberae*)
Geranium Blue (*Cacyreus marshalli*)
Karoo Daisy Copper (*Chrysoritis chrysantas*)
Karoo Dancer (*Alenia sandaster*)
Longtailed Pea Blue (*Lampides boeticus*)
Mimosa Sapphire (*Iolaus mimosae*)
Painted Lady (*Vanessa cardui*)
Sooty Blue (*Zizeeria knysna*)
Warrior Silverspotted Copper (*Argyraspodes argyraspis*)

Fynbos butterflies

African Clouded Yellow (*Colias electo*)
African Monarch (*Danaus chrysippus*)
Boland Skolly (*Thestor protumnus*)
Cape Dotted Blue (*Tarucus thespis*)
Citrus Swallowtail (*Papilio demodocus*)
Common Arrowhead (*Phasis thero*)
Common Dotted Border (*Mylothris agathina*)
Common Hairtail (*Anthene definita*)
Common Meadow White (*Pontia helice*)
Common Opal (*Poecilmitis thysbe*)
Common Sandman (*Spialia diomus*)
Cupreous Small Blue (*Eicochrysops messapus*)
Dark Opal (*Poecilmitis nigricans*)
Gaika Blue (*Zizula hylax*)
Garden Acraea (*Acraea horta*)
Geranium Blue (*Cacyreus marshalli*)
Knysna Skolly (*Thestor brachycerus*)
Longtailed Pea Blue (*Lampides boeticus*)
Orangebanded Protea (*Capys alphaeus*)
Painted Lady (*Vanessa cardui*)
Sooty Blue (*Zizeeria knysna*)
Water Opal (*Poecilmitis palmus*)
Yellow Pansy (*Junonia hierta*)

GENERA AND FAMILIES OF LARVAL FOODPLANTS

Abutilon – Acanthaceae (Greenmarbled Sandman)
Acacia – Fabaceae (Clubtailed Charaxes, Satyr Charaxes, Dusky Charaxes, Hutchinson's Highflier, Common Scarlet, Silverspotted Grey, Orangebarred Playboy, Brown Playboy, Common Hairtail, Blackstriped Hairtail, Otacilia Hairtail, Black Heart, Velvet Spotted Blue, Topaz Spotted Blue)
Acalypha – Euphorbiaceae (Spotted Sailer, Common Sailer)
Adenia – Passifloraceae (Southern Wanderer, Wandering Donkey Acraea, Orange Acraea, Natal Acraea, Rooibok Acraea, Large Spotted Acraea, Broadbordered Acraea)
Adhatoda – Acanthaceae (Yellow Pansy, Blue Pansy)
Aeschynomene – Fabaceae (Orange Acraea)
Afzelia – Fabaceae (Flamebordered Charaxes, Foxy Charaxes)
Albizia – Fabaceae (Satyr Charaxes)
Allophylus – Sapindaceae (Pearl Charaxes, Common Hairtail)
Alyssum – Brassicaceae (Common Meadow White)
Amaranthus – Amaranthaceae (Sooty Blue)
Amblygonocarpus – Fabaceae (Bluespangled Charaxes)
Annona – Annonaceae (Angola White-lady Swordtail, Large Striped Swordtail)
Araujia – Asclepiadaceae (African Monarch)
Arctotis – Asteraceae (Painted Lady)
Argyrolobium – Fabaceae (Rayed Blue)
Artabotrys – Annonaceae (Large Striped Swordtail)
Asclepias – Asclepiadaceae (African Monarch)
Aspalathus – Fabaceae (Damara Copper, Aranda Copper, Common Opal)
Asystasia – Acanthaceae (Yellow Pansy, Blue Pansy, Soldier Pansy, Brown Pansy, Common Mother-of-pearl, Common Diadem)

Baphia – Fabaceae (Orangebarred Playboy, Brown Playboy)
Barleria – Acanthaceae (Yellow Pansy, Karoo Dancer)
Basananthe – Passifloraceae (Light-red Acraea)
Bauhinia – Fabaceae (Foxy Charaxes, Bushveld Charaxes, Orangebarred Playboy, Brown Playboy)
Becium – Lamiaceae (Sabie Smoky Blue, Variable Blue, Potchefstroom Blue)
Bequaertiodendron – Sapotaceae (Boisduval's False Acraea, Chief False Acraea)
Berkheya – Asteraceae (Painted Lady)
Berzelia – Bruniaceae (Water Opal)
Blepharis – Acanthaceae (Karoo Dancer)
Boscia – Capparaceae (Zebra White, Brownveined White, African Common White, Queen Purple Tip, Red Tip, Speckled Sulphur Tip, Smoky Orange Tip, Small Orange Tip, Banded Gold Tip, Lemon Traveller Tip)
Brachystegia – Fabaceae (Flamebordered Charaxes, Foxy Charaxes, Bushveld Charaxes,

Bluespangled Charaxes)
Bridelia – Euphorbiaceae (Morant's Orange)
Bryophyllum – Crassulaceae (Tailed Black Eye)
Burkea – Fabaceae (Foxy Charaxes, Eriksson's Highflier, Hutchinson's Highflier, Apricot Playboy, Common Pea Blue)

Cadaba – Capparaceae (Scarlet Tip, Sulphur Orange Tip, Speckled Sulphur Tip, Smoky Orange Tip, Small Orange Tip)
Caesalpinia – Fabaceae (Brown Playboy)
Calodendrum – Rutaceae (Citrus Swallowtail, Greenbanded Swallowtail)
Canavalia – Fabaceae (Common Smoky Blue)
Canthium – Rubiaceae (Natal Bar)
Capparis – Capparaceae (False Dotted Border White, African Common White, African Veined White, African Small White, Ant-heap Small White, Spiller's Sulphur Small White, Diverse Rainforest White, African Wood White, Vine-leaf Vagrant, Autumn-leaf Vagrant, Queen Purple Tip, Red Tip, Common Orange Tip, Smoky Orange Tip, Small Orange Tip)
Cardiospermum – Sapindaceae (Pearl Charaxes, Brown Playboy)
Carduus – Asteraceae (Painted Lady)
Cassia – Fabaceae (African Migrant, Broadbordered Grass Yellow, Brown Playboy)
Cassipourea – Rhizophoraceae (Large Vagrant)
Celtis – Ulmaceae (African Snout)
Cercis – Fabaceae (Longtailed Pea Blue, Common Pea Blue)
Ceropegia – Asclepiadaceae (African Monarch)
Chaetacanthus – Acanthaceae (Yellow Pansy, Gaika Blue, Small Marbled Elf)
Chaetacme – Ulmaceae (Forest-king Charaxes)
Chrysanthemoides – Asteraceae (Water Opal, Common Opal)
Chrysophyllum – Sapotaceae (Boisduval's False Acraea, Chief False Acraea)
Citrus – Rutaceae (Mocker Swallowtail, Citrus Swallowtail, Greenbanded Swallowtail)
Clausena – Rutaceae (Whitebanded Swallowtail, Greenbanded Swallowtail, Emperor Swallowtail)
Clerodendrum – Verbenaceae (Natal Bar, Purple-brown Hairstreak)
Cliffortia – Rosaceae (Orange Acraea)
Coffea – Rubiaceae (Apricot Playboy)
Colpoon – Santalaceae (Common Dotted Border)
Colutea – Fabaceae (Longtailed Pea Blue)
Combretum – Combretaceae (Spotted Sailer, Guineafowl, Apricot Playboy, Orangebarred Playboy, Striped Policeman, Morant's Orange)
Commelina – Commelinaceae (Common Mimic Acraea)
Conyza – Asteraceae (Marsh Acraea)
Cotyledon – Crassulaceae (Tailed Black Eye, Henning's Black Eye, Pale Hairtail)
Crassula – Crassulaceae (Tailed Black Eye, Common Hairtail)
Crotalaria – Fabaceae (Brown Playboy, Longtailed Pea Blue, Rayed Blue)
Croton – Euphorbiaceae (Greenveined Charaxes)
Cryptocarya – Lauraceae (Forest-king Charaxes)
Cycnium – Scrophulariaceae (Eyed Pansy)
Cynanchum – Asclepiadaceae (Novice Friar, Chief Friar)
Cynodon – Poaceae (Common Evening Brown)

Cytisus – Fabaceae (Longtailed Pea Blue)

Dalbergia – Fabaceae (Common Sailer, Bushveld Charaxes)
Dalechampia – Euphorbiaceae (Pied Piper, Spotted Joker, African Joker)
Deinbollia – Sapindaceae (Goldbanded Forester, Forest Queen, Purple-brown Hairstreak)
Dioscorea – Dioscoraceae (Clouded Flat)
Dolichos – Fabaceae (Brown Playboy, Longtailed Pea Blue)
Dombeya – Sterculiaceae (Bufftipped Skipper)
Dovyalis – Flacourtiaceae (African Leopard)
Dracaena – Agavaceae (Bush Nightfighter)
Drypetes – Euphorbiaceae (Forest-king Charaxes)
Dyschoriste – Acanthaceae (Gaika Blue)

Ehrharta – Poaceae (Common Bush Brown, Eyed Bush Brown, Table Mountain Beauty, Bush Beauty, Goldspotted Sylph, Common Hottentot)
Ekebergia – Meliaceae (Whitebarred Charaxes)
Entada – Fabaceae (Clubtailed Charaxes, Topaz Spotted Blue)
Erianthemum – Loranthaceae (Common Dotted Border, Southern Sapphire)
Eriobotrya – Rosaceae (Apricot Playboy)
Eriosema – Fabaceae (Common Meadow Blue)
Exomis – Chenopodiaceae (Dwarf Blue)

Ficus – Moraceae (Common Figtree Butterfly)
Foeniculum – Apiaceae (Citrus Swallowtail)

Gazania – Asteraceae (Painted Lady)
Geranium – Geraniaceae (Geranium Bronze)
Gnaphalium – Asteraceae (Painted Lady)
Graderia – Scrophulariaceae (Eyed Pansy)
Grewia – Tiliaceae (Bufftipped Skipper, Whitecloaked Skipper, Spotted Velvet Skipper)

Harpephyllum – Anacardiaceae (Common Hairtail)
Heliophila – Brassicaceae (Common Meadow White)
Heliotropium – Boraginaceae (Grass Jewel Blue)
Hemizygia – Lamiaceae (Free State Blue)
Hermannia – Sterculiaceae (Dancing Acraea, Yellowbanded Acraea, Roodepoort Copper, Asterodia Sandman, Common Sandman)
Hexalobus – Annonaceae (Large Striped Swordtail)
Hibiscus – Malvaceae (Asterodia Sandman, Common Sandman)
Hippocratea – Celastraceae (Cambridge Vagrant)
Huernia – Asclepiadaceae (African Monarch)
Hybanthus – Violaceae (Polka Dot)
Hygrophila – Acanthaceae (Eyed Pansy)
Hyparrhenia – Poaceae (Table Mountain Beauty)

Hyperacanthus – Rubiaceae (Apricot Playboy)
Hypericum – Clusiaceae (Broadbordered Grass Yellow)

Imperata – Poaceae (Barber's Ranger, Wallengren's Ranger, Chequered Ranger, White-branded Swift)
Indigofera – Fabaceae (Longtailed Pea Blue, Common Pea Blue, Restless Indigo Blue, Grass Jewel Blue)
Isoglossa – Acanthaceae (Common Mother-of-pearl, Large Sprite)

Julbernardia – Fabaceae (Bluespangled Charaxes)
Juncus – Juncaceae (Rainforest Brown)
Justicia – Acanthaceae (Pirate, Gaika Blue)

Kalanchoe – Crassulaceae (Tailed Black Eye, Pale Hairtail)
Kiggelaria – Flacourtiaceae (Battling Glider, Garden Acraea)

Lantana – Verbenaceae (Twinspot Blue, Patricia Blue)
Laportea – Urticaceae (Longtailed Admiral, Variable Diadem, Dusky Acraea)
Lathyrus – Fabaceae (Longtailed Pea Blue)
Lavandula – Lamiaceae (Bush Bronze)
Lebeckia – Fabaceae (Common Opal)
Leonotis – Lamiaceae (Bush Bronze)
Lepidium – Brassicaceae (Common Meadow White)
Lupinus – Fabaceae (Longtailed Pea Blue)

Macadamia – Proteaceae (Apricot Playboy, Orangebarred Playboy)
Maerua – Capparaceae (Zebra White, False Dotted Border White, Forest White, Brownveined White, African Common White, Diverse Rainforest White, Veined Tip, Scarlet Tip, Red Tip, Smoky Orange Tip, Small Orange Tip)
Malva – Malvaceae (Painted Lady)
Mangifera – Anacardiaceae (Common Hairtail)
Manilkara – Sapotaceae (Boisduval's False Acraea)
Maytenus – Celastraceae (African Leopard)
Medicago – Fabaceae (African Clouded Yellow, Longtailed Pea Blue, Common Pea Blue, Sooty Blue)
Melianthus – Melianthaceae (Common Arrowhead)
Melilotus – Fabaceae (Common Pea Blue)
Mentha – Lamiaceae (Bush Bronze)
Merxmuellera – Poaceae (Orange Widow)
Millettia – Fabaceae (Orangebarred Playboy, Longtailed Pea Blue, Common Pea Blue, Striped Policeman)
Mimusops – Sapotaceae (Boisduval's False Acraea, Chief False Acraea)
Monanthotaxis – Annonaceae (Veined Swordtail)
Moquinella – Loranthaceae (Bowker's Sapphire, Southern Sapphire, Mimosa Sapphire)

Mundulea – Fabaceae (Natal Bar, Dusky Blue, Common Pea Blue)
Myrica – Myricaceae (Common Hairtail)

Nymania – Meliaceae (Brown Playboy)

Obetia – Urticaceae (Dusky Acraea)
Olax – Olacaceae (Azure Hairstreak)
Oricia – Rutaceae (Mocker Swallowtail)
Osteospermum – Asteraceae (Water Opal, Dark Opal)
Osyris – Santalaceae (Common Dotted Border)
Otholobium – Fabaceae (Longtailed Pea Blue)
Oxalis – Oxalidaceae (Sooty Blue, Rayed Blue, Gaika Blue)

Panicum – Poaceae (Bush Beauty, Goldspotted Sylph)
Pappea – Sapindaceae (Pearlspotted Charaxes, Brown Playboy, Common Hairtail)
Parinari – Chrysobalanaceae (Striped Policeman, Peppered Hopper)
Passiflora – Passifloraceae (Southern Wanderer, Garden Acraea, Wandering Donkey Acraea, Natal Acraea, Large Spotted Acraea)
Pavonia – Malvaceae (Bufftipped Skipper, Common Sandman)
Pelargonium – Geraniaceae (Geranium Bronze)
Peltophorum – Fabaceae (Van Son's Charaxes)
Pennisetum – Poaceae (Common Evening Brown, Eyed Bush Brown, Table Mountain Beauty, Common Hottentot)
Pentaschistis – Poaceae (Rainforest Brown)
Peristrophe – Acanthaceae (Small Elfin)
Phaulopsis – Acanthaceae (Soldier Pansy, Brown Pansy, Gaika Blue)
Phylica – Rhamnaceae (Cape Dotted Blue)
Plectranthus – Lamiaceae (Garden Commodore, Dry-leaf Commodore, Gaudy Commodore, Eyed Pansy, Bush Bronze)
Plumbago – Plumbaginaceae (Common Pea Blue)
Podalyria – Fabaceae (Longtailed Pea Blue)
Polygonum – Polygonaceae (Marsh Acraea)
Populus – Salicaceae (African Leopard)
Portulaca – Portulacaceae (Common Diadem)
Pouzolzia – Urticaceae (Longtailed Admiral, Dusky Acraea)
Protea – Proteaceae (Orangebanded Protea)
Prunus – Rosaceae (Apricot Playboy, Orangebarred Playboy, Brown Playboy)
Ptaeroxylon – Ptaeroxylaceae (Citrus Swallowtail)
Pterocarpus – Fabaceae (Bushveld Charaxes)
Pycnostachys – Lamiaceae (Marsh Commodore, Gaudy Commodore)

Quisqualis – Combretaceae (Spotted Sailer, Striped Policeman)

Rabdosiella – Lamiaceae (Gaudy Commodore)

Rapistrum – Brassicaceae (Common Meadow White)
Rawsonia – Flacourtiaceae (Blotched Leopard)
Reseda – Resedaceae (Common Meadow White)
Restio – Restionaceae (Western Hillside Brown)
Rhamnus – Rhamnaceae (Forest-king Charaxes)
Rhus – Anacardiaceae (Common Arrowhead, Lydenburg Opal)
Rhynchosia – Fabaceae (Common Pea Blue, Rayed Blue)
Ricinus – Euphorbiaceae (Pied Piper, Golden Piper, Spotted Sailer)
Robinia – Fabaceae (African Clouded Yellow, Striped Policeman)
Rosa – Rosaceae (Common Hairtial)
Ruellia – Acanthaceae (Yellow Pansy, Soldier Pansy, Brown Pansy, Pirate, Gaika Blue)
Rumex – Polygonaceae (Eastern Sorrel Copper)

Salix – Salicaceae (African Leopard)
Salvia – Lamiaceae (Bush Bronze, Sabie Smoky Blue, Variable Blue, Patricia Blue)
Sapium – Euphorbiaceae (Boisduval's Tree Nymph, Natal Tree Nymph)
Schotia – Fabaceae (Foxy Charaxes, Apricot Playboy, Orangebarred Playboy, Brown Playboy, Common Hairtail)
Scutia – Rhamnaceae (Forest-king Charaxes)
Selago – Selaginaceae (Variable Blue, Koppie Blue)
Setaria – Poaceae (Common Evening Brown)
Sisymbrium – Brassicaceae (Common Meadow White)
Solanum – Solanaceae (Striped Policeman)
Spartium – Fabaceae (Longtailed Pea Blue)
Sphedamnocarpus – Malpighiaceae (Angola White-lady Swordtail, Striped Policeman)
Sphenostylis – Fabaceae (Common Smoky Blue)
Stapelia – Asclepiadaceae (African Monarch)
Stenotaphrum – Poaceae (Goldspotted Sylph)
Stipa – Poaceae (Goldspotted Sylph)
Strelitzia – Strelitziaceae (Strelitzia Nightfighter)
Sutherlandia – Fabaceae (Brown Playboy, Longtailed Pea Blue)
Syzygium – Myrtaceae (Flamebordered Charaxes, Apricot Playboy, Orangebarred Playboy, Brown playboy)

Talinum – Portulacaceae (Common Diadem)
Tamarindus – Fabaceae (Satyr Charaxes, Dusky Charaxes)
Tapinanthus – Loranthaceae (Common Dotted Border, Twin Dotted Border, Trimen's Dotted Border, Bowker's Sapphire, Trimen's Sapphire, Mimosa Sapphire)
Teclea – Rutaceae (Mocker Swallowtail, Greenbanded Swallowtail)
Tecomaria – Bignoniaceae (Common Pea Blue)
Terminalia – Combretaceae (Guineafowl)
Themeda – Poaceae (Common Hottentot)
Thesium – Santalaceae (Cupreous Small Blue)
Tieghemia – Loranthaceae (Common Dotted Border, Trimen's Dotted Border)
Tragia – Euphorbiaceae (Pied Piper, Golden Piper, Spotted Joker, African Joker)
Triaspis – Malpighiaceae (Striped Policeman)
Tribulus – Zygophyllaceae (Sooty Blue)

Trichilia – Meliaceae (Whitebarred Charaxes)
Tricliceras – Turneraceae (Natal Acraea, Blacktipped Acraea, Rooibok Acraea, Light-red Acraea)
Trifolium – Fabaceae (African Clouded Yellow)
Trimeria – Flacourtiaceae (African Leopard)
Triumfetta – Tiliaceae (Dancing Acraea, Yellowbanded Acraea)
Turraea – Meliaceae (Whitebarred Charaxes)
Tylophora – Asclepiadaceae (Novice Friar, Chief Friar)

Ulex – Fabaceae (Longtailed Pea Blue)
Urera – Urticaceae (Duskyveined Acraea)
Uvaria – Annonaceae (Veined Swordtail, Large Striped Swordtail)

Vangueria – Rubiaceae (Purple-brown Hairstreak)
Vepris – Rutaceae (Mocker Swallowtail, Greenbanded Swallowtail)
Vicia – Fabaceae (African Clouded Yellow)
Vigna – Fabaceae (Apricot Playboy, Brown Playboy, Common Meadow Blue, Common Pea Blue, Common Smoky Blue)
Virgilia – Fabaceae (Longtailed Pea Blue, Common Pea Blue)
Viscum – Viscaceae (Bowker's Sapphire, Southern Sapphire)

Walafrida – Selaginaceae (Koppie Blue)

Xanthocercis – Fabaceae (Bushveld Charaxes)
Ximenia – Olacaceae (Natal Bar, Silvery Bar, Bowker's Sapphire, Saffron Sapphire, Purple-brown Hairstreak, Apricot Playboy, Brown Playboy)
Xylotheca – Flacourtiaceae (Rooibok Acraea, Blood-red Acraea)

Zanthoxylum – Rutaceae (Citrus Swallowtail, Emperor Swallowtail)
Ziziphus – Rhamnaceae (Black Pie, Common Dotted Blue, Hintza Pie)
Zornia – Fabaceae (Sooty Blue)
Zygophyllum – Zygophyllaceae (Common Opal, Dark Opal)

BIBLIOGRAPHY

CLAASSENS, A.J.M. 1976. Observations on the myrmecophilous relationships and the parasites of *Lepidochrysops methymna* (Trimen) and *L. trimeni* (Bethune-Baker) (Lepidoptera: Lycaenidae). *Journal of the Entomological Society of Southern Africa* **39**:279–289.

A detailed account of experimental work on the relationships between Blues belonging to the genus *Lepidochrysops* and their host ants.

CLAASSENS, A.J.M. & DICKSON, C.G.C. 1977. A study of the myrmecophilous behaviour of the immature stages of *Aloeides thyra* (L.) (Lep. Lycaenidae) with special reference to the function of the retractile tubercles and with additional notes on the general biology of the species. *Entomologist's Record and Journal of Variation* **89**:225–231.

Detailed laboratory studies on the fascinating relationship of Coppers (genus *Aloeides*) and their host ants.

CLAASSENS, A.J.M. & DICKSON, C.G.C. 1980. *The Butterflies of the Table Mountain Range.* C. Struik, Cape Town.

An in-depth, well illustrated book that is essential reading for anyone living in the Cape Peninsula. All of the species occurring on the Table Mountain Range are dealt with.

CLARK, G.C. & DICKSON, C.G.C. 1971. *Life Histories of the South African Lycaenid Butterflies.* Purnell & Sons, Cape Town.

A seminal work on the very interesting early stages of the lycaenid species. Brings together all the information on those species for which the life histories were partly or completely known at the time. Clark's colour paintings of the early stages rival anything ever produced in this field.

COTTRELL, C.B. 1965. A study of the *methymna* group of the genus *Lepidochrysops* Hedicke (Lepidoptera: Lycaenidae). *Memoirs of the Entomological Society of Southern Africa* **9**: 1–110.

A highly technical and thorough work recommended only for those with a fair amount of basic knowledge of lepidopterology.

COTTRELL, C.B. 1978. Aspects of the biogeography of southern African butterflies. Supplement to *Zambezia*, the Journal of the University of Rhodesia, **1978**:i–viii, 1–100.

Well researched and considered overview of the zoogeography of southern African butterflies.

COTTRELL, C.B. 1984. Aphytophagy in butterflies: its relationship to myrmecophily. *Zoological Journal of the Linnean Society* **79**:1–57.

A detailed review of current worldwide knowledge concerning non-herbivorous feeding habits of butterfly larvae and the relationship this has to larval-ant associations.

DICKSON, C.G.C. & KROON, D.M. (Eds) 1978. *Pennington's Butterflies of Southern Africa.* Ad Donker, Johannesburg.

The most up to date definitive work on southern African butterflies. Lavishly illustrated and concerned mainly with the adults. An essential laboratory manual for identification and study. Unfortunately out of print but a second edition is in press (1994).

HENNING, S.F. 1983. Chemical communication between lycaenid larvae (Lepidoptera: Lycaenidae) and ants (Hymenoptera: Formicidae). *Journal of the Entomological Society of Southern Africa* **46**:341–366.

A technical paper for those interested in this field of lepidopterology.

HENNING, S.F. 1987. Myrmecophilous Lycaenidae (or how ants help butterflies). *South African Journal of Science* **83**:8–9.

An easy to understand and brief review of associations between butterfly larvae and ants.

HENNING, S.F. 1989. *The Charaxinae Butterflies of Africa.* Aloe Books, Johannesburg.

A massive, comprehensive and beautifully illustrated book that is an essential reference work for anyone interested in the spectacular butterflies belonging to this subfamily.

HENNING, S.F. & HENNING, G.A. 1989. *South African Red Data Book – Butterflies.* South African National Scientific Programmes Report no. 158, Foundation for Research Development, CSIR, Pretoria.

The only work dealing with all the South African butterfly species that are under some kind of threat. General aspects of butterfly conservation are also dealt with.

MIGDOLL, I. 1987. *Field Guide to the Butterflies of Southern Africa.* C. Struik, Cape Town.

A popular but nevertheless scientific book, with a large number of beautiful photographs. Although titled as a field guide it is more suitable as a reference work for the novice collector.

MURRAY, D.P. 1935. *South African Butterflies. A Monograph of the Family Lycaenidae.* John Bale, Sons and Danielsson, London.

An out of date work that is nevertheless obligatory reading for anyone primarily interested in lycaenids.

PINHEY, E. 1965. *Butterflies of Southern Africa.* Nelson, Cape Town.

A good introductory text for the subregion. Largely unobtainable except in large libraries.

SCHOLTZ, C.H. & HOLM, E. (Eds) 1985. *Insects of Southern Africa.* Butterworths, Durban.

A fairly technical but readable book that places butterflies within the perspective of other insect orders and groups in southern Africa.

SCOBLE, M.J. 1986. The structure and affinities of the Hedyloidea: a new concept of the butterflies. *Bulletin of the British Museum (Natural History), Entomology Series* **53**:251–286.

A very technical publication recommended only for those interested in the higher taxonomy (classification) of butterflies.

SWANEPOEL, D.A. 1953. *Butterflies of South Africa: Where, When and How They Fly.* Maskew Miller, Cape Town.

A highly readable book written in a very informal and passionate style. Unfortunately long since out of print and badly out of date with respect to the scientific names of the various species.

TRIMEN, R. 1862–66. *Rhopalocera Africae Australis* **1**:1–183; **2**:184–352. W.F. Matthew, Cape Town.

This work and the one below are included because they are the first comprehensive works written about the butterflies of the subcontinent. Only available in some reference libraries and in private book collections.

TRIMEN, R. & BOWKER, J.H. 1887–89. *South African Butterflies: A Monograph of the Extra-Tropical Species,* 3 Vols, Trübner, London.

See remarks above.

VAN SON, G. 1949. The Butterflies of Southern Africa. Part 1. Papilionidae and Pieridae. *Transvaal Museum Memoirs* **3**:1–237.

This work and the three given below are detailed monographs of some of the butterfly families in southern Africa. They are indispensable reference sources for the serious lepidopterist. Numerous life histories, together with plates by Gowan Clark, are included.

VAN SON, G. 1955. The Butterflies of Southern Africa. Part 2. Nymphalidae: Danainae and Satyrinae. *Transvaal Museum Memoirs* **8**:1–166.

VAN SON, G. 1963. The Butterflies of Southern Africa. Part 3. Nymphalidae: Acraeinae. *Transvaal Museum Memoirs* **14**:1–130.

VAN SON, G. (Ed. Vári, L.) 1979. The Butterflies of Southern Africa. Part 4. Nymphalidae: Nymphalinae. *Transvaal Museum Memoirs* **22**:1–186.

VÁRI, L. & KROON, D.M. 1986. *Southern African Lepidoptera – A Series of Cross Referenced Indices.* The Lepidopterists' Society of Southern Africa and the Transvaal Museum, Pretoria.

A checklist of the scientific names of all the moths and butterflies of southern Africa.

WOODHALL, S.E. (Ed.) 1992. *A Practical Guide to Butterflies and Moths in Southern Africa.* The Lepidopterists' Society of Southern Africa, Florida Hills.

A comprehensive laboratory manual covering all aspects of lepidopterology, including collecting, preserving, breeding and photographing butterflies.

The **Lepidopterists' Society of Southern Africa** was established in 1983 and caters for both amateurs and professionals with an interest in butterflies and moths. The address is:

The Hon. Secretary
Lepidopterists' Society of Southern Africa
P O Box 470
FLORIDA HILLS
1716

GLOSSARY

basal – the portion of the fore- and hindwing closest to the body of the butterfly (see figure p. 16).
biome – the largest land community region recognised by ecologists, e.g. savanna, grassland and desert.
cilia – fine hair-like protrusions forming a fringe on the outer margins of the wings of some species of butterfly. The cilia are modified scales.
continuous-brooded – butterflies that do not have a break in their life cycle because of diapause in one or more of the stages. When favourable environmental conditions exist the stages are shortened, while under unfavourable conditions they are prolonged. There are a number of generations of adult butterflies each year.
crepuscular – active at twilight or in the hours preceding dawn.
diapause – a state that may arise at any stage of the life cycle, in which development is suspended and cannot be resumed, even in the presence of apparently favourable conditions, unless the diapause is first "broken" by an appropriate environmental change.
dicotyledons (= dicots) – flowering plants of which the embryo has two seed leaves (cotyledons), the parts of the flowers are in twos, fives or multiples of these numbers, and the leaves commonly net-veined.
dimorphic – existing in two distinct forms.
dimorphism – the condition of having two distinct forms.
distal – pertaining to or situated at the outer end; farthest from the point of attachment (cf. proximal).
double-brooded – having two generations of adults each year, one in spring and one in autumn.
eversible – able to be protruded outwards.
fly at random – not strictly bound to a particular territory; not staying in a particular place for any length of time.
foodplant – see larval foodplant.
genetically variable – the variation between individuals of a population due to differences in their genotype (chromosomal make-up).
hyaline – glass-like; the translucent or transparent parts on the wings of some butterflies, consisting of unpigmented scales.
imago – the form assumed by an insect after its last moult (ecdysis), when it has become fully mature; pl. imagines.
instars – the form assumed by an insect during a particular stage in its life cycle between two consecutive moults (ecdyses).
irrorations – the finely speckled pattern on the wings of some butterflies made up of scattered patches of differently coloured scales.
larva – the young stage of an animal if it differs appreciably in form from the adult.
larval foodplant – the particular plant or plants on which the larvae of a specific butterfly feed.
lunule – a crescent-shaped mark.
mediad – situated near, or tending towards, the median axis; refers to the wing of a butterfly (see figure p. 16).
mimetic – adj. of mimicry (see below).

286 GLOSSARY

mimic – verb of mimicry; noun denoting something that mimics.

mimicry – the adoption by one species of the colour, habits, sounds or structure of another species. In butterflies colour and to a lesser extent habits are involved.

monocotyledons (= monocots) – flowering plants of which the embryo characteristically has one seed leaf (cotyledon), the parts of the flowers are in threes or sixes and the leaves often have the main veins parallel.

mud-puddling – a behaviour shown especially by the males of some species of butterfly whereby salts and micronutrients are filtered from water sucked up by means of the proboscis from mud and damp sandbanks.

ocellated – having a series of ocelli (eye-spots) in a row; often on the outer margin of the hindwing in species of Acraea.

onisciform – curved in an arc; refers to the typical shape of lycaenid larvae (see figs 339, 343 & 344).

osmeterium – in the larvae of certain papilionids, a forked sac that can be protruded through a slitlike aperture in the first thoracic segment. Gives off a disagreeable citrus-like odour.

oviposit – to lay eggs.

oviposition – the act of laying eggs.

oviposition site – the particular place selected by a female butterfly in which to lay her eggs.

polymorphism – having many different forms; refers to the colour patterns on the wings of butterflies.

processes – extensions or projections, as in danaine larvae (see fig. 330).

proximal – pertaining to or situated at the inner end, nearest to the point of attachment (cf. distal).

pupa – an inactive stage in the life cycle of an insect during which it does not feed and re-organisation is taking place to transform the larval body into that of the imago (adult). Adj. pupal.

random (see fly at random) – completely unorganised flight patterns.

relict – a species which occurs at the present time in environmental circumstances different from those in which it originated.

reticulate – resembling a net.

scaling – the arrangement of scales on the surface of the butterfly wing; the scales contain various coloured pigments or refract light to give the wings their characteristic colours.

single-brooded – butterflies that have only one generation of adults a year. The larval or pupal stages of the life cycle are prolonged by means of diapause.

species – a group of individuals of which the members 1) actually or potentially interbreed with each other but not with members of other such groups, 2) show continuous morphological variation within the group but are distinct from members of other such groups. Other definitions for species exist and some authorities maintain that the concept cannot be defined.

sucking-holes – holes bored by beetles and other insects into the trunk or branches of trees from which fermenting sap exudes which in turn attracts various insects, including butterflies. The butterflies gain nourishment by sucking up the exudations.

sucking-trees – specific trees which have sucking-holes in their trunk or branches (see sucking-holes above).

taxonomic – the use of taxonomy, the science of classification as applied to living organisms, including study of the means of formation of species.

INDEX TO SCIENTIFIC NAMES

Abantis
  tettensis fig. 217; 245
Acada
  biseriatus 258
Acleros
  mackenii fig. 141; 259
  ploetzi 259
Acraea
  acara fig. 48; 124
  aglaonice fig. 50; 123
  anemosa fig. 52; 125
  axina fig. 71; 122
  barberi 124
  boopis 114
  calderena fig. 63; 121
  horta fig. 64; 114
  machequena 114
  natalica fig. 49; 120
  neobule fig. 65; 115
  nohara fig. 70; 125
  oncaea fig. 62; 122
  petraea fig. 66; 126
  trimeni 124
  zetes 124
ACRAEINAE (subfamily) 112–27
Actizera
  lucida fig. 191; 220
Aeropetes
  tulbaghia fig. 239; 139
Alaena
  amazoula fig. 42; 159
  brainei 159
Alenia
  namaqua 249
  sandaster fig. 150; 249
Aloeides
  aranda fig. 81; 182
  barklyi fig. 28; 180
  damarensis fig. 82; 182
  dentatis fig. 80; 179
  taikosama fig. 127; 181
Amauris
  albimaculata 152

  echeria fig. 228; 152
  niavius fig. 193; 151
  ochlea fig. 196; 151
Antanartia
  dimorphica 68
  hippomene 68
  schaeneia fig. 248; 68
Anthene
  amarah fig. 132; 206
  butleri fig. 178; 207
  contrastata 208
  definita fig. 177; 205
  minima 208
  otacilia fig. 192; 208
  rhodesiana 208
  talboti 208
Aphnaeus
  erikssoni fig. 119; 171
  hutchinsonii fig. 161; 172
  marshalli 171
Appias
  epaphia figs 15, 213; 42
  sabina 42
Argyraspodes
  argyraspis fig. 76; 178
Artitropa
  comus 261
  erinnys fig. 251; 261
Axiocerses
  amanga 175
  punicea 175
  tjoane fig. 77; 175
Azanus
  jesous fig. 186; 233
  ubaldus fig. 187; 233

Baliochila
  aslanga fig. 41; 161
Belenois
  aurota fig. 14; 37
  creona figs 13, 235; 37
  gidica figs 11, 233; 38
  thysa figs 7, 32; 35

zochalia fig. 12; 36
Bematistes
  aganice figs 203, 231; 113
Bicyclus
  safitza fig. 107; 131
Borbo
  borbonica fig. 137; 265
Brephidium
  metophis 222
Byblia
  anvatara fig. 61; 87
  ilithyia fig. 60; 86

Cacyreus
  dicksoni 211
  lingeus fig. 182; 210
  marshalli fig. 151; 211
  palemon 211
  virilis 210
Calleagris
  kobela 240
  krooni fig. 106; 240
Capys
  alphaeus fig. 253; 202
  connexivus 202
  disjunctus 202
  penningtoni 202
Cassionympha
  cassius fig. 113; 133
Catacroptera
  cloanthe fig. 57; 79
Catopsilia
  florella figs 4, 29; 62
Celaenorrhinus
  bettoni 238
  galenus 237
  mokeezi fig. 252; 237
Charaxes
  achaemenes figs 205, 243; 106
  acuminatus 99
  alpinus 107
  bohemani 104
  brainei 109
  brutus fig. 198; 102
  candiope fig. 240; 100
  castor 102
  chittyi 108
  cithaeron 103
  druceanus 102
  etesipe 106
  ethalion figs 91, 206; 107
  fulgurata 108
  gallagheri 110
  guderiana figs 90, 244; 110
  jahlusa fig. 54; 105
  jasius fig. 242; 101
  karkloof 107
  manica 108
  marieps 107
  pelias 101
  penricei 106
  phaeus figs 93, 265; 108
  pollux 102
  pondoensis 107
  protoclea fig. 241; 100
  pseudophaeus 108
  vansoni figs 92, 207; 109
  varanes fig. 43; 99
  violetta 103
  xiphares figs 199, 229, 264; 103
  zoolina figs 53, 208; 104
CHARAXINAE (subfamily) 98–111
Chrysoritis
  chrysantas fig. 84; 183
Coeliades
  forestan fig. 103; 236
  keithloa 236
  pisistratus 236
Coenyra
  aurantiaca fig. 116; 145
  hebe 146
  rufiplaga 146
Coenyropsis
  bera 135
  natalii fig. 114; 135
Colias
  electo figs 75, 214; 61
Colotis
  agoye fig. 24; 53
  amata 49
  antevippe fig. 20; 52
  auxo fig. 36; 51
  celimene 50
  danae fig. 19; 50
  doubledayi 49
  eris fig. 18; 56
  erone 50
  eunoma 50

SCIENTIFIC NAMES 289

evagore fig. 23; 55
evenina fig. 21; 53
evippe fig. 22; 54
ione 50
lais 53
pallene 54
regina fig. 6; 49
subfasciatus fig. 34; 56
vesta fig. 236; 49
Crudaria
   leroma fig. 133; 188
Cupidopsis
   cissus fig. 173; 231
   jobates 231
Cymothoe
   alcimeda figs 35, 209; 95
   coranus 95
   vumbui 95

DANAINAE (subfamily) 148–53
Danaus
   chrysippus fig. 46; 149
Deudorix
   antalus figs 129, 175; 200
   dariaves 198
   dinochares figs 78, 128; 198
   dinomenes 198
   diocles figs 215, 254; 199
   lorisona 198
   magda 200
   penningtoni 200
   vansoni 200
Dingana
   alaedeus 142
   bowkeri 142
   dingana fig. 97; 142
Dira
   clytus fig. 96; 141
   jansei 142
   oxylus 142
   swanepoeli 142
Dixeia
   charina fig. 17; 39
   doxo 39
   leucophanes 39
   pigea figs 16, 33; 40
   spilleri fig. 37; 41
Durbania
   amakosa fig. 256; 162

   limbata 162
Durbaniella
   clarki 162
Durbaniopsis
   saga 163

Eagris
   nottoana 239
Eicochrysops
   messapus figs 152, 188; 232
Eretis
   djaelaelae 241
   melania 241
   umbra fig. 140; 241
Eronia
   cleodora fig. 5; 45
   leda fig. 30; 45
Euchrysops
   barkeri 230
   dolorosa fig. 180; 230
   malathana fig. 125; 229
   osiris 230
   subpallida 230
Euphaedra
   neophron fig. 156; 96
Eurema
   brigitta fig. 38; 63
   desjardinsii 64
   hapale 64
   hecabe 64
   regularis 64
Eurytela
   dryope fig. 250; 85
   hiarbas fig. 210; 84
Euxanthe
   wakefieldi fig. 263; 111

Freyeria
   trochylus fig. 153; 221

Gegenes
   hottentota 266
   niso fig. 142; 266
   pumilio 266
Gomalia
   elma fig. 143; 248
Graphium
   angolanus fig. 202; 30
   antheus fig. 262; 31

colonna 32
junodi 32
leonidas fig. 201; 31
morania 30
policenes 32
polistratus 32
porthaon 32
schaffgotschi 30

Hamanumida
  daedalus fig. 95; 97
HEDYLOIDEA (superfamily) 19
Hemiolaus
  caeculus fig. 163; 194
Henotesia
  perspicua fig. 108; 132
  simonsii 132
HESPERIIDAE (family) 235–66
HESPERIOIDEA (superfamily) 19
Hyalites
  acerata 118
  anacreon fig. 67; 117
  cabira fig. 238; 118
  cerasa 114
  encedon fig. 68; 120
  eponina fig. 72; 117
  esebria figs 51, 204, 232; 119
  igola fig. 69; 115
  induna 117
  obeira 114
  rahira fig. 73; 116
Hypolimnas
  anthedon figs 195, 227; 83
  deceptor 83, 152
  misippus figs 45, 200; 82
Hypolycaena
  philippus figs 130, 176; 194

Iolaus
  bowkeri fig. 164; 190
  lalos 191
  mimosae fig. 162; 193
  pallene fig. 39; 192
  silarus 191
  silas fig. 159; 190
  subinfuscata 190
  trimeni fig. 158; 191

Junonia
  hierta fig. 237; 75
  natalica fig. 94; 78
  oenone fig. 266; 76
  orithya fig. 267; 77
  terea fig. 246; 77

Kedestes
  barberae fig. 146; 254
  callicles fig. 148; 257
  chaca 253
  lenis 255
  lepenula fig. 260; 256
  macomo 256
  marshalli 256
  mohozutza fig. 145; 253
  nerva 254
  niveostriga 255
  sublineata 256
  wallengrenii fig. 147; 255

Lachnocnema
  bibulus figs 122, 220; 164
  durbani 164
Lachnoptera
  ayresii fig. 59; 67
Lampides
  boeticus fig. 174; 217
Lepidochrysops
  bacchus 222
  barnesi 227
  chloauges 227
  coxii 224
  gigantea 228
  ignota 223
  inyangae 224
  letsea fig. 124; 223
  lotana 224
  mashuna fig. 170; 228
  methymna 222
  michellae 227
  ortygia fig. 169; 225
  patricia fig. 167; 227
  peculiaris 228
  plebeia figs 123, 168; 226
  praeterita 224
  procera fig. 171; 224
  ruthica 227

SCIENTIFIC NAMES

vansoni 224
variabilis fig. 126; 222
violetta 224
Leptomyrina
　gorgias 197
　henningi fig. 131; 197
　hirundo fig. 134; 196
　lara 197
Leptosia
　alcesta fig. 26; 43
Leptotes
　pirithous fig. 179; 216
　pulcher 216
Leucochitonea
　levubu fig. 27; 244
Libythea
　labdaca fig. 102; 154
LIBYTHEINAE (subfamily) 153–5
LIPTENINAE (subfamily) 158–63
Lycaena
　clarki fig. 83; 203
　orus 204
LYCAENIDAE (family) 156–234
LYCAENINAE (subfamily) 203–4

Melanitis
　leda fig. 89; 129
　libya 129
Metisella
　aegipan 251
　malgacha 251
　meninx 251
　metis fig. 257; 250
　orientalis 250
　syrinx 251
　willemi fig. 144; 251
MILETINAE (subfamily) 163–8
Moltena
　fiara fig. 104; 260
Mylothris
　agathina figs 8, 31; 58
　carcassoni 60
　rubricosta 59
　rueppellii fig. 9; 59
　sagala 60
　trimenia fig. 10; 60
　yulei 59
Myrina
　dermaptera 170

silenus fig. 160; 170

Neita
　extensa fig. 109; 134
Nepheronia
　argia fig. 2; 46
　buquetii 44, 62
　thalassina figs 3, 155; 47
Neptis
　alta 90
　goochi 90
　laeta fig. 211; 91
　saclava fig. 212; 90
Netrobalane
　canopus fig. 216; 244
NYMPHALIDAE (family) 65–155
NYMPHALINAE (subfamily) 65–97

Orachrysops
　lacrimosa fig. 172; 228
Oraidium
　barberae fig. 154; 221

Papilio
　constantinus 27
　dardanus figs 194, 224, 225; 25
　demodocus fig. 223; 27
　echerioides figs 197, 226; 26
　euphranor 27
　nireus fig. 261; 28
　ophidicephalus fig. 222; 28
PAPILIONIDAE (family) 23–32
PAPILIONOIDEA (superfamily) 19
Paralethe
　dendrophilus fig. 44; 140
Pardopsis
　punctatissima fig. 74; 127
Parosmodes
　morantii fig. 259; 258
Pelopidas
　mathias 264
　thrax fig. 136; 264
Pentila
　pauli 160
　swynnertoni 160
　tropicalis fig. 40; 160
Phalanta
　eurytis 66
　phalantha fig. 58; 66

Phasis
  thero fig. 255; 176
Physcaeneura
  panda fig. 118; 147
  pione 147
PIERIDAE (family) 33–64
Pinacopteryx
  eriphia fig. 234; 34
Platylesches
  ayresii fig. 149; 262
Poecilmitis
  aethon fig. 85; 185
  nigricans figs 88, 268; 187
  palmus fig. 86; 185
  thysbe fig. 87; 186
POLYOMMATINAE (subfamily) 204–34
Pontia
  helice fig. 25; 43
Precis
  actia 71
  antilope 73
  archesia fig. 247; 71
  ceryne fig. 249; 73
  cuama 73
  octavia figs 56, 157; 74
  tugela fig. 245; 72
Protogoniomorpha
  anacardii 80
  parhassus fig. 1; 80
Pseudacraea
  boisduvalii fig. 47; 92
  eurytus 93
  lucretia fig. 230; 93
  poggei 93
Pseudonacaduba
  sichela fig. 181; 218
Pseudonympha
  gaika 136
  machacha 136
  magoides fig. 111; 136
  narycia fig. 115; 137
  paragaika 136
  poetula fig. 112; 135
  trimenii 136

Salamis
  cacta 80
Sallya
  amulia 89
  boisduvali fig. 101; 88
  morantii 89
  natalensis fig. 100; 89
  rosa 89
  trimeni 89
Sarangesa
  astrigera 242
  gaerdesi 242
  lucidella 242
  motozi 242
  phidyle fig. 138; 242
  ruona 242
  seineri 242
SATYRINAE (subfamily) 128–48
Spialia
  asterodia fig. 218; 246
  diomus fig. 219; 247
Spindasis
  natalensis fig. 165; 173
  phanes fig. 166; 174
Stygionympha
  scotina 138
  vigilans fig. 110; 138
  wichgrafi 138

Tagiades
  flesus fig. 105; 239
Tarsocera
  cassus fig. 99; 144
Tarucus
  bowkeri 215
  sybaris fig. 183; 214
  thespis fig. 184; 215
Teniorhinus
  harona 258
  herilus 258
THECLINAE (subfamily) 169–203
Thestor
  basutus fig. 120; 168
  brachycerus fig. 121; 167
  protumnus fig. 79; 166
Tirumala
  petiverana 149
Torynesis
  hawequas 143
  magna 143
  mintha 143
  orangica fig. 98; 143
  pringlei 144

Tsitana
  dicksoni 252
  tsita fig. 139; 252
  tulbagha 252
  uitenhaga 252
Tuxentius
  calice 213
  hesperis 213
  melaena fig. 221; 213

Uranothauma
  nubifer fig. 135; 209

Vanessa
  cardui fig. 55; 69

Ypthima
  impura fig. 117; 147

Zezonia
  zeno fig. 258; 263
Zintha
  hintza fig. 185; 212
Zizeeria
  knysna fig. 189; 218
Zizina
  antanossa 218
Zizula
  hylax fig. 190; 219
Zophopetes
  dysmephila 260

INDEX TO AFRIKAANS COMMON NAMES

Afrikaanse Gewone Witjie fig. 13, 235; 37
Afrikaanse Luiperd fig. 58; 66
Afrikaanse Melkbosskoenlapper fig. 46; 149
Afrikaanse Migreerder fig. 4, 29; 62
Afrikaanse Snuitskoenlapper fig. 102; 154
Alsie-witkoppie fig. 35, 209; 95
Amakosa-klipsitter fig. 256; 162
Angola-witnooientjie fig. 202; 30
Appelkoosspelertjie fig. 78, 128; 198
Aranda-kopervlerkie fig. 81; 182
Asjas-sandmannetjie fig. 143; 248
Asterodia-sandmannetjie fig. 218; 246
Ayres-hoppertjie fig. 149; 262

Barber-wagtertjie fig. 146; 254
Barkly-kopervlerkie fig. 28; 180
Basoetoe-skollie fig. 120; 168
Bergbruintjie fig. 111; 136
Bergprag fig. 239; 139
Bergrooitjie fig. 70; 125
BLAARVLERKE (groep) 70-4
Bloedrooitjie fig. 66; 126
Blougesiggie fig. 266; 76
Blougevlekte-dubbelstert fig. 90, 244; 110
Bloujuweel-opaal fig. 88, 268; 187
Blouswerwer fig. 3, 155; 47
BLOUTJIES (groep) 214-34
Boisduval-boombruintjie fig. 101; 88
Boisduval-valsrooitjie fig. 47; 92
Bolandskollie fig. 79; 166
BONTETJIES (groep) 212-13
Bontpuntjie fig. 236; 49
Bontrokkie fig. 25; 43
Bont-swaardstert fig. 201; 31
Bont-valsrooitjie fig. 230; 93
BOOMBRUINTJIES (groep) 87-9
Boomkortstertjie fig. 192; 208
Bosbrons fig. 182; 210
BOSBRUINTJIES (groep) 130-2
Bosgesiggie fig. 246; 77

BOSJAGTERTJIES (groep) 237-8
Boskoning-dubbelstert fig. 199, 229, 264; 103
BOSNOOIENTJIES (groep) 68-9
Bosprag fig. 44; 140
Bosskemervegter fig. 251; 261
Bosveldbruintjie fig. 109; 134
Bosveld-dubbelstert fig. 205, 243; 106
Bosveldwagtertjie fig. 148; 257
BOSVLIEËRS (groep) 84-5
Boswitjie fig. 12; 36
Bowker-saffier fig. 164; 190
BRONSE (groep) 210-11
Bruingesiggie fig. 94; 78
Bruinpunt-springertjie fig. 216; 244
Bruinspelertjie fig. 129, 175; 200
BRUINTJIES (groep) 133-8

Damara-kopervlerkie fig. 82; 182
DANSERTJIES (groep) 248-9
DARTELAARTJIES (groep) 238-40
Dingaan-weduwee fig. 97; 142
Donkerkortstertjie fig. 177; 205
Donker-oranjepuntjie fig. 22; 54
Donkerwalsertjie fig. 139; 252
Doringboomsaffier fig. 162; 193
Dowwebloutjie fig. 181; 218
Dowwe-dubbelstert fig. 93, 265; 108
Dowwekopervlerkie fig. 127; 181
Dowwerooitjie fig. 51, 204, 232; 119
Drakensberg-bruintjie fig. 112; 135
Druiweblaarswerwer fig. 5; 45
Dubbelkolbloutjie fig. 123, 168; 226
DUBBELSTERTE (groep) 98-110
Dubbeltjiebloutjie fig. 189; 218
Dwaalesel-rooitjie fig. 65; 115
Dwergbloutjie fig. 154; 221

Eriksson-silverrokkie fig. 119; 171

Fladderpapiertjie fig. 26; 43
Fluweel-kolbloutjie fig. 187; 233
Fynbos-spikkelbloutjie fig. 184; 215

AFRIKAANS COMMON NAMES 295

Gaika-bloutjie fig. 190; 219
Geel-gesiggie fig. 237; 75
Geelhotnot fig. 142; 266
Geelsaffier fig. 39; 192
Geelstreeprooitjie fig. 238; 118
GEELVLERKIES (groep) 161–2
Geel-zoeloe fig. 42; 159
GESIGGIES (groep) 75–9
Gestreepte-ringetjie fig. 118; 147
Gewone Dowwebloutjie fig. 125; 229
Gewone Ertjiebloutjie fig. 179; 216
Gewone Grasveldgeletjie fig. 38; 63
Gewone Monnik fig. 193; 151
Gewone Na-aper fig. 45, 200; 82
Gewone Oranjepuntjie fig. 21; 53
Gewone Perlemoenskoenlapper fig. 1; 80
Gewone Skemerbruintjie fig. 89; 129
Gewone Spikkelbloutjie fig. 183; 214
Gewone Spikkelrandjie fig. 8, 31; 58
Gewone Suikerbossie fig. 253; 202
Gewone Vyeboomvlinder fig. 160; 170
Goudpuntjie fig. 18; 56
Grasjuweelbloutjie fig. 153; 221
GRASVELDGELETJIES (groep) 63–4
Grasveld-geelpuntjie fig. 24; 53
Grasveldwitjie fig. 14; 37
GRASVEGTERS (groep) 85–7
Groenlint-swaelstert fig. 261; 28
Groen-ratsvlieër fig. 137; 265
Grootswerwer fig. 2; 46

HARTJIES (groep) 209
Hemels-kolbloutjie fig. 186; 233
Henning-swartogie fig. 131; 197
Herfsblaarswerwer fig. 30; 45
Hintza-bontetjie fig. 185; 212
Hoofmonnik fig. 228; 152
HOPPERTJIES (groep) 262–3
HOTNOTTE (groep) 265–6
Hutchinson-silverrokkie fig. 161; 172

Jag-swaardstert fig. 262; 31
Jakkalsdraf-pylkoppie fig. 255; 176

Kaapse herfsweduwee fig. 96; 141
Kaapse lenteweduwee fig. 99; 144
KABOUTERS (groep) 240–1
KABOUTERTJIES (groep) 242–3
Karoodansertjie fig. 150; 249

Karoo-madeliefkopervlerkie fig. 84; 183
Kersboomrooitjie fig. 52; 125
Kersfeesbosjagtertjie fig. 252; 237
Kleinkaboutertjie fig. 138; 242
KLEINKOPERVLERKIES (groep) 203–4
Klein-oranjepuntjie fig. 23; 55
Klein-oranjerooitjie fig. 72; 117
KLIPSITTERS (groep) 162–3
Koloogbruintjie fig. 115; 137
KONINGINNE (groep) 111
Koningin-perspuntjie fig. 6; 49
Koning-swaelstert fig. 222; 28
KONSTABELS (groep) 235–7
Koperbloutjie fig. 152, 188; 232
KOPERVLERKIES (groep) 178–83
Koppiebloutjie fig. 169; 225
Koppiedubbelstert fig. 242; 101
Koppiespringertjie fig. 217; 245
KORTSTERTJIES (groep) 205–8
Kroon-dartelaartjie fig. 106; 240
Kuikenrooitjie fig. 71; 122
Kusdubbelstert fig. 91, 206; 107
Kussaffier fig. 159; 190
Kusstreek-witjie fig. 17; 39
Kwagga fig. 234; 34
Kwagga-sandmannetjie fig. 219; 247

Laeveldwitjie fig. 11, 233; 38
Langstert-bosnooientjie fig. 248; 68
Langstert-swartogie fig. 134; 196
Lelie-grasvegter fig. 60; 86
Lemoen-swaelstert fig. 223; 27
Lepenula-wagtertjie fig. 260; 256
LUIPERDS (groep) 66–7
Lusern-ertjiebloutjie fig. 174; 217
Lusernvlinder fig. 75, 214; 61
LUSERNVLINDERS (groep) 61
Lydenburg-opaal fig. 85; 185

Macken-pyltjie fig. 141; 259
MADELIEFKOPERVLERKIES (groep) 183–4
Malvabrons fig. 151; 211
Mashuna-bloutjie fig. 170; 228
MELKBOSSKOENLAPPERS (groep) 149–50
Miershoopwitjie fig. 16, 33; 40
MIGREERDERS (groep) 62–3
Moeras-blaarvlerk fig. 249; 73

296 AFRIKAANS COMMON NAMES

Moeras-bosbruintjie fig. 108; 132
Moerasrooitjie fig. 73; 116
Mohozutza-wagtertjie fig. 145; 253
MONNIKE (groep) 150–3
Morant-oranjetjie fig. 259; 258

NA-APERS (groep) 81–3
Na-aper-swaelstert fig. 194, 224, 225; 25
Natal-boombruintjie fig. 100; 89
Natal-bruintjie fig. 114; 135
Natal-geelvlerkie fig. 41; 161
Natal-rooitjie fig. 49; 120
Natal-streepvlerkie fig. 165; 173

Onsuiwer-ringetjie fig. 117; 147
Oostelike-kleinkopervlerkie fig. 83; 203
OPALE (groep) 184–8
Oranje-hoppertjie fig. 258; 263
Oranjelint- bosvlieër fig. 250; 85
Oranjerooitjie fig. 67; 117
ORANJETJIES (groep) 257–8
Oranjevlerk-spikkelrandjie fig. 9; 59
Oranje-weduwee fig. 98; 143
Outannie-monnik fig. 196; 151

Padwagtertjie fig. 267; 77
Patricia-bloutjie fig. 167; 227
PENTILAS (groep) 160–1
Pêreldubbelstert fig. 43; 99
PERLEMOENSKOENLAPPERS (groep) 80–1
Persbruin-stertbloutjie fig. 130, 176; 194
POLKASTIPPEL (groep) 127
Polkastippel fig. 74; 127
Pondo-skaduweebruintjie fig. 116; 145
Potchefstroom-bloutjie fig. 171; 224
Pragopaal fig. 87; 186
PRAGS (groep) 139–41
PUNTJIES (groep) 48–57
PYLKOPPIES (groep) 176–7
PYLTJIES (groep) 259

Ralie-rooivlerkie fig. 77; 175
Rantbruintjie fig. 110; 138
RATSVLIEËRS (groep) 263–5
Reënwoudbruintjie fig. 113; 133
Reënwoudswewer fig. 211; 91
Reënwoudwalsertjie fig. 257; 250
Ridderrooitjie fig. 48; 124

RINGETJIES (groep) 146–8
RONDDWALERS (groep) 112–13
Roodepoort-kopervlerkie fig. 80; 179
Rooibokkie fig. 62; 122
Rooi-en-blou-blaarvlerk fig. 56, 157; 74
Rooipuntjie fig. 20; 52
ROOITJIES (groep) 113–27
ROOIVLERKIES (groep) 175–6
Rots-blaarvlerk fig. 247; 71
Rustelose-bloutjie fig. 172; 228

Sabie-dowwebloutjie 230
SAFFIERE (groep) 189–93
SANDMANNETJIES (groep) 246–8
SEEROWER (groep) 79–80
Seerower fig. 57; 79
Silverkol-dubbelstert fig. 54; 105
Silverkolkopervlerkie fig. 76; 178
SILVERKOLKOPERVLERKIES (groep) 177–8
SILVERROKKIES (groep) 171–2
Silver-streepvlerkie fig. 166; 174
Skaduspelertjie fig. 215, 254; 199
SKADUWEEBRUINTJIES (groep) 145–6
Skaduweedansertjie fig. 156; 96
SKADUWEEDANSERTJIES (groep) 96
Skaduweedartelaartjie fig. 105; 239
Skarlakenpuntjie fig.19; 50
Skelmdubbelstert fig. 240; 100
SKEMERBRUINTJIES (groep) 129–30
SKEMERVEGTERS (groep) 260–2
SKOLLIES (groep) 165–8
SNUITSKOENLAPPERS (groep) 154–5
SONDAGSROKKIE (groep) 69–70
Sondagsrokkie fig. 55; 69
SPELERTJIES (groep) 198–201
Spikkelpentila fig. 40; 160
SPIKKELRANDJIES (groep) 57–60
Spikkelswewer fig. 212; 90
Spikkelvaletjie fig. 133; 188
Spiller-geletjie fig. 37; 41
SPRINGERTJIES (groep) 243–5
STERTBLOUTJIES (groep) 193–5
Strandskollie fig. 121; 167
STREEPVLERKIES (groep) 173–4
Strelitzia-skemervegter fig. 104; 260
SUIKERBOSSIES (groep) 201–3
Suurlemoensmous fig. 34; 56
SWAARDSTERTE (groep) 29–32

AFRIKAANS COMMON NAMES 297

Swael-oranjepuntjie fig. 36; 51
SWAELSTERTE (groep) 24–9
Swartbontetjie fig. 221; 213
Swartbont-ronddwaler fig. 203, 231; 113
Swart-bosbruintjie fig. 107; 131
Swarthartjie fig. 135; 209
SWARTOGIES (groep) 195–7
Swartpuntrooitjie fig. 63; 121
Swartstreep-kortstertjie fig. 132; 206
SWERWERS (groep) 44–8
SWEWERS (groep) 90–1

TARENTAALTJIE (groep) 97
Tarentaaltjie fig. 95; 97
Tollie-grasvegter fig. 61; 87
Trimen-saffier fig. 158; 191
Trimen-spikkelrandjie fig. 10; 60
Tugela-blaarvlerk fig. 245; 72
Tuinrooitjie fig. 64; 114

Umbra-kabouter fig. 140; 241

Vaalkol-luiperd fig. 59; 67
Vaalkortstertjie fig. 178; 207
VALETJIES (groep) 188–9
VALSROOITJIES (groep) 92–4
Valsvoëlent-witjie fig. 7, 32; 35
Van Son-dubbelstert fig. 92, 207; 109
Venda-stertbloutjie fig. 163; 194
Vensterrooitjie fig. 50; 123
Verneukerbloutjie fig. 126; 222

Verneukertjie fig. 195, 227; 83
Vlamdubbelstert fig. 241; 100
Vleibloutjie fig. 173; 231
Vrystaat-bloutjie fig. 124; 223
Vuilvenster-rooitjie fig. 69; 115
VYEBOOMVLINDERS (groep) 169–70

WAGTERTJIES (groep) 253–7
Wallengren-wagtertjie fig. 147; 255
WALSERTJIES (groep) 249–53
Wateropaal fig. 86; 185
WEDUWEES (groep) 141–5
Willawitjie fig. 15, 213; 42
Willem-walsertjie fig. 144; 251
Witbroekkonstabel fig. 103; 236
Wit-en-bruin-dubbelstert fig. 53, 208; 104
WITKOPPIES (groep) 94–5
Witjas-springertjie fig. 27; 244
WITJIES (groep) 33–44
Witlint-bosvlieër fig. 210; 84
Witlint-swaelstert fig. 197, 226; 26
Witmerk-ratsvlieër fig. 136; 264
Witstreepbloutjie fig. 191; 220
Witstreepdubbelstert fig. 198; 102
Witstreeprooitjie fig. 68; 120
Wolpootjie fig. 122, 220; 164
WOLPOOTJIES (groep) 164–5
Woudkoningin fig. 263; 111

ZOELOES (groep) 158–9

INDEX TO ENGLISH COMMON NAMES

ACRAEAS (group) 113–27
ACRAEINES (subfamily) 112–27
ADMIRALS (group) 68–9
African Clouded Yellow fig. 75; 61
African Common White figs 13, 235; 37
African Joker fig. 61; 87
African Leopard fig. 58; 66
African Migrant figs 4, 29; 62
African Monarch fig. 46; 149
African Protea 202
African Small White fig. 17; 39
African Snout fig. 102; 154
African Veined White figs 11, 233; 38
African Wood White fig. 26; 43
Air Commodore 71
Albatross Rainforest White 42
Amakosa Rocksitter fig. 256; 162
Angled Grass Yellow 64
Angola White-lady Swordtail fig. 202; 30
Ant-heap Small White figs 16, 33; 40
Apricot Playboy figs 78, 128; 198
Aranda Copper fig. 81; 182
Arrowhead Orange 258
ARROWHEADS (group) 176–7
Ashen Smoky Blue 230
Asterodia Sandman fig. 218; 246
Autumn-leaf Vagrant fig. 30; 45
Axehead Orange 258
Azure Hairstreak fig. 163; 194

Bamboo Sylph 251
Banded Gold Tip fig. 18; 56
Barber's Acraea 124
Barber's Ranger fig. 146; 254
Barker's Smoky Blue 230
Barkly's Copper fig. 28; 180
Barnes's Blue 227
BARS (group) 173–4
Basutu Skolly fig. 120; 168
Battling Glider figs 35, 209; 95
BEAUTIES (group) 139–41
Bera Brown 135

Betton's Sprite 238
Black and Orange Playboy 198
Blackbordered Charaxes 102
Blackbranded Swift 264
BLACK EYES (group) 195–7
Black Heart fig. 135; 209
Black Pie fig. 221; 213
Blackstriped Hairtail fig. 132; 206
Blacktipped Acraea fig. 63; 121
Blackveined Ranger 256
Blackveined Small White 39
Blonde Glider 95
Blood-red Acraea fig. 66; 126
Blotched Leopard fig. 59; 67
Bluemarked Charaxes 106
Blue Pansy fig. 266; 76
BLUES (group) 214–34
Bluespangled Charaxes figs 90, 244; 110
Bluespotted Charaxes 103
Boisduval's False Acraea fig. 47; 92
Boisduval's Tree Nymph fig. 101; 88
Boland Rocksitter 163
Boland Skolly fig. 79; 166
Bowker's Dotted Blue 214
Bowker's Sapphire fig. 164; 190
Bowker's Widow 142
Braine's Charaxes 109
Broadbordered Acraea fig. 52; 125
Broadbordered Grass Yellow fig. 38; 63
BRONZES (group) 210–11
Brown Pansy fig. 94; 78
Brown Playboy figs 129, 175; 200
BROWNS (group) 133–8
Brownveined White fig. 14; 37
BUFFS (group) 161–2
Bufftipped Skipper fig. 216; 244
Buquet's Vagrant 44, 62
Bush Beauty fig. 44; 140
Bush Bronze fig. 182; 210
BUSH BROWNS (group) 130–2
Bush-kite Swallowtail 27
Bush Nightfighter fig. 251; 261

ENGLISH COMMON NAMES 299

Bush Scarlet 175
Bushveld Charaxes figs 205, 243; 106
Bushveld Orange Tip 54
Bushveld Purple Tip 50

Cambridge Vagrant figs 3, 155; 47
Cape Autumn Widow fig. 96; 141
Cape Black Eye 197
Cape Dotted Blue fig. 184; 215
Cape Spring Widow fig. 99; 144
Carcasson's Dotted Border 60
Chaca's Ranger 253
CHARAXES (group) 98–110
CHARAXINES (subfamily) 98–111
Chequered Ranger fig. 260; 256
Chief False Acraea fig. 230; 93
Chief Friar fig. 228; 152
Citrus Swallowtail fig. 223; 27
Clark's Rocksitter 162
Clouded Flat fig. 105; 239
CLOUDED YELLOWS (group) 61
Clouded Mother-of-pearl 80
Clover Blue 218
Clubtailed Charaxes figs 53, 208; 104
Coast Purple Tip 50
Coffee Playboy 198
COMMODORES (group) 70–4
Common Arrowhead fig. 255; 176
Common Black Eye 197
Common Buff fig. 41; 161
Common Bush Brown fig. 107; 131
Common Diadem figs 45, 200; 82
Common Dotted Blue fig. 183; 214
Common Dotted Border figs 8, 31; 58
Common Evening Brown fig. 89; 129
Common Figtree Butterfly fig. 160; 170
Common Friar fig. 193; 151
Common Grass Yellow 64
Common Hairtail fig. 177; 205
Common Hottentot fig. 142; 266
Common Meadow Blue fig. 173; 231
Common Meadow White fig. 25; 43
Common Mimic Acraea fig. 68; 120
Common Mother-of-pearl fig. 1; 80
Common Opal fig. 87; 186
Common Orange Tip fig. 21; 53
Common Pea Blue fig. 179; 216
Common Sailer fig. 211; 91
Common Sandman fig. 219; 247

Common Scarlet fig. 77; 175
Common Smoky Blue fig. 125; 229
Constantine's Swallowtail 27
COPPERS (group) 178–83
Cox's Blue 224
Cupreous Small Blue figs 152, 188; 232

DAISY COPPERS (group) 183–4
Damara Copper fig. 82; 182
DANAINES (subfamily) 148–53
DANCERS (group) 248–9
Dancing Acraea fig. 72; 117
Dancing Swordtail 32
Dappled Monarch 149
Dark Elfin 242
Darker Commodore 73
Dark Hottentot 266
Dark Opal figs 88, 268; 187
Dark Ranger 255
Dark Swordtail 32
Dark Webbed Ringlet fig. 118; 147
DARTS (group) 259
DIADEMS (group) 81–3
Deceptive Diadem 83, 152
Dickson's Bronze 211
Dickson's Sylph 252
Dingaan's Widow fig. 97; 142
Dismal Sylph fig. 139; 252
Diverse Rainforest White figs 15, 213; 42
DOTTED BORDERS (group) 57–60
Doubleday's Tip 49
Drakensberg Brown fig. 112; 135
Dry-leaf Commodore fig. 245; 72
Dune Purple Tip 50
D'Urbans Woolly Legs 164
Dusky Acraea figs 51, 204, 232; 119
Dusky Blue fig. 181; 218
Dusky Charaxes figs 93, 265; 108
Dusky Copper fig. 127; 181
Dusky Elf 241
Dusky Playboy 200
Dusky Sapphire 190
Duskyveined Acraea fig. 69; 115
Dwarf Blue fig. 154; 221

Eastern Hillside Brown 138
Eastern Sorrel Copper fig. 83; 203
Eastern Sylph 250
ELFINS (group) 242–3

300 ENGLISH COMMON NAMES

ELVES (group) 240–1
Emperor Swallowtail fig. 222; 28
Eriksson's Highflier fig. 119; 171
Evenbordered Grass Yellow 64
EVENING BROWNS (group) 129–30
Eyed Bush Brown fig. 108; 132
Eyed Pansy fig. 267; 77

FALSE ACRAEAS (group) 92–4
False Dotted Border White figs 7, 32; 35
FIGTREE BUTTERFLIES (group) 169–70
Flamebordered Charaxes fig. 241; 100
FLATS (group) 238–40
Forest Elfin 242
FORESTERS (group) 96
Forest-king Charaxes figs 199, 229, 264; 103
Forest Leopard 66
Forest Queen fig. 263; 111
Forest White fig. 12; 36
Foxy Charaxes fig. 242; 101
Free State Blue fig. 124; 223
FRIARS (group) 150–3
Fulvous Ranger fig. 145; 253

Gaika Blue fig. 190; 219
Gaika Brown 136
Gallagher's Charaxes 110
Garden Acraea fig. 64; 114
Garden Commodore fig. 247; 71
Gaudy Commodore figs 56, 157; 74
Geranium Bronze fig. 151; 211
Giant Blue 228
Giant Charaxes 102
GLIDERS (group) 94–5
Goldbanded Forester fig. 156; 96
Golden Gate Brown 136
Golden Piper fig. 250; 85
Goldspotted Sylph fig. 257; 250
Grass Jewel Blue fig. 153; 221
Grassveld Sylph 251
GRASS YELLOWS (group) 63–4
Greenbanded Swallowtail fig. 261; 28
Greenmarbled Sandman fig. 143; 248
Greenveined Charaxes fig. 240; 100
Greybottom Brown fig. 111; 136
GREYS (group) 188–9
GUINEAFOWL (group) 97
Guineafowl fig. 95; 97

HAIRSTREAKS (group) 193–5
HAIRTAILS (group) 205–8
Hawequas Widow 143
HEARTS (group) 209
HEDYLOIDS (superfamily) 19
Henning's Black Eye fig. 131; 197
Herilus Orange 258
HESPERIIDS (family) 235–66
HESPEROIDS (superfamily) 19
HIGHFLIERS (group) 171–2
Highveld Blue 224
Hintza Pie fig. 185; 212
HOPPERS (group) 262–3
HOTTENTOTS (group) 265–6
Hutchinson's Highflier fig. 161; 172

Impure Ringlet fig. 117; 147

Jade Blue 227
Janse's Widow 142
JOKERS (group) 85–7
Junod's Swordtail 32

Kalahari Orange Tip 53
Karkloof Charaxes 107
Karoo Daisy Copper fig. 84; 183
Karoo Dancer fig. 150; 249
Knysna Skolly fig. 121; 167
Koppie Blue fig. 169; 225
Kroon's Flat fig. 106; 240

Lalos Sapphire 191
Large Blue Charaxes 104
Large Spotted Acraea fig. 48; 124
Large Sprite fig. 252; 237
Large Striped Swordtail fig. 262; 31
Large Vagrant fig. 2; 46
Layman Friar 152
Lemon Dotted Border 60
Lemon Traveller Tip fig. 34; 56
LEOPARDS (group) 66–7
Lesser figtree Butterfly 170
LIBYTHEINES (subfamily) 153–5
Light-red Acraea fig. 70; 125
Light Webbed Ringlet 147
Lilac Mother-of-pearl 80
Lilac Tip 50
Lilac Tree Nymph 89
LIPTENINES (subfamily) 158–63

ENGLISH COMMON NAMES 301

Little Acraea fig. 71; 122
Little Hairtail 208
Longtailed Admiral fig. 248; 68
Longtailed Pea blue fig. 179; 217
Lotana Blue 224
Lucidella Elfin 242
LYCAENIDS (family) 156–234
LYCAENINES (subfamily) 203–4
Lydenburg Opal fig. 85; 185

Machacha Brown 136
Machequena Acraea 114
Macken's Dart fig. 141; 259
Macomo Ranger 256
Magna Widow 143
Mamba Swordtail 32
Marbled Elf 241
Marieps Charaxes 107
Marsh Acraea fig. 73; 116
Marshall's Highflier 171
Marshall's Ranger 256
Marsh Commodore fig. 249; 73
Marsh Hottentot 266
Marsh Sylph 251
Mashuna Blue fig. 170; 228
Mashuna Hairtail 208
Michelle's Blue 227
MIGRANTS (group) 62–3
MILETINES (subfamily) 163–8
Mimosa Sapphire fig. 162; 193
Mintha Widow 143
Mocker Bronze 210
Mocker Swallowtail figs 194, 224, 225; 25
Monarch False Acraea 93
MONARCHS (group) 149–50
Monkey Blue 222
Montane Charaxes 107
Morant's Orange fig. 259; 258
Morant's Tree Nymph 89
MOTHER-OF-PEARLS (group) 80–1
Mountain Sylph 251
Mrs Raven Flat 240

Namaqua Dancer 249
Namibian Elfin 242
Namibian Zulu 159
Natal Acraea fig. 49; 120
Natal Bar fig. 165; 173
Natal Brown fig. 114; 135

Natal Rocksitter 162
Natal Tree Nymph fig. 100; 89
Netted Sylph fig. 144; 251
NIGHT FIGHTERS (group) 260–2
Northern Short-tailed Admiral 68
Novice Friar fig. 196; 151
Nyanga Blue 224
NYMPHALIDS (family) 65–155
NYMPHALINES (subfamily) 65–97

Old Sailer 90
Olivehaired Swift fig. 137; 265
OPALS (group) 184–8
Orange Acraea fig. 67; 117
Orangebanded Protea fig. 253; 202
Orangebarred Playboy figs 215, 254; 199
Orange Playboy 198
ORANGES (group) 257–8
Orangespotted Hopper fig. 258; 263
Orange Sprite 237
Orange Widow fig. 98; 143
Osiris Smoky Blue 230
Otacilia Hairtail fig. 192; 208

PAINTED LADY (group) 69–70
Painted Lady fig. 55; 69
Pale Bush Brown 132
Pale Grass Yellow 64
Pale Hairtail fig. 178; 207
Pale Ranger fig. 148; 257
Paler Commodore 73
Pale-yellow Acraea 114
Palm-tree Night fighter 260
PANSIES (group) 75–9
PAPILIONIDS (family) 23–32
PAPILIONOIDS (superfamily) 19
Patricia Blue fig. 167; 227
Paul's Pentila 160
Pearl Charaxes fig. 43; 99
Pearlspotted Charaxes fig. 54; 105
Peculiar Blue 228
Pennington's Playboy 200
Pennington's Protea 202
PENTILAS (group) 160–1
Peppered Hopper fig. 149; 262
Pied Piper fig. 210; 84
PIERIDS (family) 33–64
PIES (group) 212–13
PIPERS (group) 84–5

302 ENGLISH COMMON NAMES

Pirate fig. 57; 79
PIRATE (group) 79–80
PLAYBOYS (group) 198–201
Ploetz's Dart 259
Pointed Pearl Charaxes 99
POLICEMEN (group) 235–7
Polka Dot fig. 74; 127
POLKA DOT (group) 127
POLYOMMATINES (subfamily) 204–34
Pondo Charaxes 107
Pondoland Widow 142
Pondo Shadefly fig. 116; 145
Potchefstroom Blue fig. 171; 224
Pringle's Widow 144
Protea Charaxes 101
PROTEAS (group) 201–3
Purple-brown Hairstreak figs 130, 176; 194

Queen Purple Tip fig. 6; 49
QUEENS (group) 111

Rainforest Acraea 114
Rainforest Brown fig. 113; 133
Rainforest Scarlet 175
RANGERS (group) 253–7
Rayed Blue fig. 191; 220
Red-tab Policeman 236
Red Tip fig. 20; 52
Restless Indigo Blue fig. 172; 228
RINGLETS (group) 146–8
ROCKSITTERS (group) 162–3
Roodepoort Copper fig. 80; 179
Rooibok Acraea fig. 62; 122
Rose's Tree Nymph 89
Rufouswinged Flat 239
Ruona Elfin 242
Russet Protea 202
Ruth's Blue 227

Sabie Smoky Blue fig. 180; 230
Saffron Sapphire fig. 39; 192
SAILERS (group) 90–1
SANDMEN (group) 246–8
SAPPHIRES (group) 189–93
Satyr Charaxes figs 91, 206; 107
SATYRINES (subfamily) 128–48
Savanna Brown fig. 109; 134
Scarce Night fighter 261
Scarce Ranger 254

Scarce Savanna Charaxes 106
SCARLETS (group) 175–6
Scarlet Tip fig. 19; 50
Schaffgotsch's White-lady Swordtail 30
Secucuni Shadefly 146
Sesbania Pea Blue 216
SHADEFLIES (group) 145–6
Silverbarred Charaxes 102
SILVERSPOTTED COPPERS (group) 177–8
Silverspotted Grey fig. 133; 188
Silvery Bar fig. 166; 174
SKIPPERS (group) 243–5
SKOLLIES (group) 165–8
Small Elfin fig. 138; 242
Small Marbled Elf fig. 140; 241
Small Orange Tip fig. 23; 55
Small Striped Swordtail 32
Small White-lady Swordtail 30
Small Yellowbanded Acraea 118
Smoky Orange Tip fig. 22; 54
SNOUTS (group) 154–5
Soldier Pansy fig. 246; 77
Sooty Blue fig. 189; 218
SORREL COPPERS (group) 203–4
Southern Sapphire fig. 159; 190
Southern Short-tailed Admiral 68
Southern Wanderer figs 203, 231; 113
Speckled Sulphur Tip fig. 24; 53
Spiller's Sulphur Small White fig. 37; 41
Spotless Small White 39
Spotted-eye Brown fig. 115; 137
Spotted Joker fig. 60; 86
Spotted Pentila fig. 40; 160
Spotted Sailer fig. 212; 90
Spotted Velvet Skipper fig. 217; 245
SPRITES (group) 237–8
Straight-line Sapphire 191
Streaked Dotted Border 59
Streaked Sailer 90
Strelitzia Night fighter fig. 104; 260
Striped Policeman fig. 103; 236
Sulphur Orange Tip fig. 36; 51
SWALLOWTAILS (group) 24–9
Swanepoel's Widow 142
SWIFTS (group) 263–5
SWORDTAILS (group) 29–32
Swynnerton's Pentila 160
SYLPHS (group) 249–53

ENGLISH COMMON NAMES 303

Table Mountain Beauty fig. 239; 139
Tailed Black Eye fig. 134; 196
Tailed Meadow Blue 231
Talbot's Hairtail 208
THECLINES (subfamily) 169–203
Tinktinkie Blue 222
TIPS (group) 48–57
Topaz Spotted Blue fig. 186; 233
Topaz Tip 49
TREE NYMPHS (group) 87–9
Treetop Acraea 114
Trimen's Acraea 124
Trimen's Brown 136
Trimen's Dotted Border fig. 10; 60
Trimen's Sapphire fig. 158; 191
Trimen's Tree Nymph 89
Tulbagh Sylph 252
Twin Dotted Border fig. 9; 59
Twinspot Blue figs 123, 168; 226
Two-pip Policeman 236

Uitenhage Sylph 252
Unique Ranger 255

VAGRANTS (group) 44–8
Van Son's Blue 224
Van Son's Charaxes figs 92, 207; 109
Van Son's Playboy 200
Variable Blue fig. 126; 222
Variable Diadem figs 195, 227; 83
Veined Swordtail fig. 201; 31
Veined Tip fig. 236; 49
Velvet Spotted Blue fig. 187; 233
Vine-leaf Vagrant fig. 5; 45
Violet Blue 224
Violeteyed Evening Brown 129
Violetspotted Charaxes 103
Vumba Glider 95

Wakkerstroom Widow 142
Wallengren's Ranger fig. 147; 255
Wanderer False Acraea 93
WANDERERS (group) 112–13
Wandering Donkey Acraea fig. 65; 115
Warrior Silverspotted Copper fig. 76; 178
Water Bronze 211
Water Opal fig. 86; 185
Western Hillside Brown fig. 110; 138
Western Pie 213
Western Sorrel Copper 204
Whitebanded Swallowtail figs 197, 226; 26
Whitebarred Charaxes fig. 198; 102
Whitebranded Swift fig. 136; 264
Whitecloaked Skipper fig. 27; 244
White Pie 213
WHITES (group) 33–44
Whitespeckled Elfin 242
Wichgraf's Brown 138
WIDOWS (group) 141–5
Window Acraea fig. 50; 123
Wineland Blue 222
WOOLLY LEGS (group) 164–5
Woolly Legs figs 122, 220; 164

Yellowbanded Acraea fig. 238; 118
Yellow Pansy fig. 237; 75
Yellow Zulu fig. 42; 159
Yule's Dotted Border 59

Zebra White fig. 234; 34
Zetes Acraea 124
Zimbabwe Hairtail 208
Zulu Blue 223
ZULUS (group) 158–9
Zulu Shadefly 146

Set in 10 on 12 pt Palatino
by Unifoto (Pty) Ltd.
Printed and bound by National Book Printers, Cape